The Moxie Encyclopedia

**Volume I
The History**

The
Moxie
Encyclopedia

by
Q. David Bowers

The Vestal Press

Library of Congress Cataloging in Publication Data
Main entry under title:

The Moxie encyclopedia.

    Includes index.
    Contents: v. 1. The history.
    1. New England Moxie Company—History.
I. Bowers, Q. David.
HD9349.S634N485   1985   338.7′66362′0974   85-5325
ISBN 0-911572-43-0 (v. 1)

THE VESTAL PRESS, LTD.
Box 97
Vestal, NY 13850
Write for catalogue of other Vestal Press publications.

The Moxie trademark has been reproduced with the permission
of Moxie Industries, Inc.

"A Moxie Girl" was the caption used on this portrait when it appeared as part of a large framed sign. The same Moxie Girl was used in many other advertising forms, including tip or change trays (from which the above photographic enlargement was made), round hanging plaques, and in brochures. She wears a white dress trimmed in purple and was used during the first several years of the twentieth century.

Augustin Thompson, M.D. (1835-1903)

Contents

Dave Bowers

About the Author

Q. David Bowers, a 1960 graduate of the Pennsylvania State University, received in 1976 the Alumni Achievement Award from that institution's College of Business Administration. His collecting interests are many, and over the years he has done research in many fields. He is the author or co-author of over two dozen books, including *Put Another Nickel In, Guidebook of Automatic Musical Instruments, Vol. I, Guidebook of Automatic Musical Instruments, Vol. II, Encyclopedia of Automatic Musical Instruments, Treasures of Mechanical Music, Robert Robinson: American Illustrator, The Postcards of Alphonse Mucha, Harrison Fisher, The History of United States Coinage* (for The Johns Hopkins University), and many others.

He has contributed to the *Encyclopedia Americana*, articles by him have appeared in such diverse publications as *American Heritage, Reader's Digest,* and *Barron's,* and he has appeared on ABC, CBS, NBC, Metromedia, and other television networks.

The author continues his research and study of Moxie history and memorabilia. Readers with information are invited to contact him at the following address: Q. David Bowers, Box 1224, Wolfeboro, NH 03894. Telephone (603) 569-5095 weekdays.

where it can be found), and the countless Moxie souvenirs and novelties of an earlier age are sought after as collectibles.

Years ago, people fell in love with Moxie. Proud parents would send The Moxie Company snapshots of their children posed with Moxie bottles and toys. College girls would bring the Moxie Boy's image into their dormitory rooms. Large cardboard cut-outs of the Moxie Boy were photographed with pretty girls, shopkeepers, and others standing next to him—as if he were real. Perhaps he was real. Accounts show that on several occasions policemen "arrested" him, that he "stood guard" in stores, and that otherwise he kept an eye on things, including the activities of youngsters.

It is not my function to predict the future. My assignment is, or was, to report the history of the past—the annals of Moxie. But, as research ended for the present volume, I cound not help but reflect that in a way Moxie is "all dressed up but has nowhere to go"—that is, Moxie has lots of past tradition and, possibly, future potential, but is today the right time and place for such a sentimental product? Try as they might, various American corporations have spent untold millions of dollars for publicity and have not had the public fall in love with their product. Moxie is different—it engenders and inspires *affection*. Perhaps today's world of computers, instant communications, space exploration, and the omnipresent spectre of nuclear annihilation is not the right forum for Moxie.

Perhaps Moxie is an anachronism, a relic of the horse and buggy days or, more properly, the Horsemobile Age. And yet, just perhaps, a coming generation will capture the quintessential spirit of Moxie and carry it forward to new accomplishments. (Frank Armstrong, are you listening?)

As a student of American history and, in particular, American business history, I know that the Moxie story is absolutely unique. There is no other like it. At the same time, like an artist who falls in love with his model, I have fallen in love with Moxie. With affection, the Moxie story is presented to you...

—Q. David Bowers
  Wolfeboro, New Hampshire
  February 14, 1985

The Moxie Encyclopedia

Chapter 1

The Legend
of
Lieutenant Moxie

"Anything goes" was the guide used by many advertisers in the mid 1880s. Imagination flourished, and products ranging from pills on the family medicine shelf to stocks and bonds were trumpeted in unblushing prose. No claim was seemingly too wild or preposterous to reach print.

At the same time, things were peaceful on the American scene. The most recent United States census, that of 1880, showed the population at slightly over 50 million. Another five million immigrants were to arrive during the ensuing decade. American domestic life was for the most part tranquil. A worker normally spent six days in the factory or in the field, resting on the seventh, perhaps enjoying a picnic or outing. A typical evening was apt to be spent reading by the light of the kerosene lamp. *Ben-Hur*, by Gen. Lew Wallace, was a favorite book of the period. So absorbed were Americans with the story that numerous products adopted Ben Hur as a trade name. *Five Little Peppers and How They Grew*, published in 1880, the same year as *Ben-Hur*, went on to sell a half million copies during the next 10 years. In 1884 *The Adventures of Huckleberry Finn*, by Mark Twain, was published. In the same year the erection of the Statue of Liberty was commenced on Bedloe's Island in the bay a short distance from the lower tip of Manhattan. In the hotly-contested presidential election of 1884, Grover Cleveland narrowly edged James G. Blaine. The latter candidate, from the state of Maine, faced accusations of bribery and allegiance to special interests.

In Lowell, Massachusetts, an industrial city primarily known for its huge textile factories, several manufacturers of patent medicines turned out their wares. Actually, such products were never patented in the usual sense of the word. Rather, the specific names or trademarks were registered with the United States Patent Office. The ingredients were usually kept secret, which made them all the more interesting. The makers of such nostrums often referred to them as *proprietary* rather than *patent* medicines. Although articles in *Collier's, The Ladies' Home Journal,* and elsewhere, plus Upton Sinclair's expose of conditions in meat packing factories, were to result in the Pure Food and Drugs Act years later in 1906, in the mid 1880s few voices were raised against medical claims. Indeed, part of this was due to the advertising clout wielded by the patent medicine manufacturers themselves. Such firms were the largest national users of newspaper advertising space. Often a typical contract would state that advertising would be run only if the publication carried no unfavorable editorial material on the subject of patent medicines or their advertising claims. So, while millions of citizens consumed products that were essentially worthless for the cures designated, and while they suffered the consequences of not seeking proper medical attention in the meantime, the vast majority of newspapers and magazines remained silent on the subject.

In Lowell two firms were dominant: the J.C. Ayer Co. and C.I. Hood & Co. Each employed approximately 300 people and each distributed products all over the world. Ayer, one of the nation's largest manufacturers of patent medicines, offered Ayer's Sarsaparilla, Cherry Pectoral, Ague Cure, Hair Vigor, and, in particular, Ayer's Pills. Advertising was by virtually every medium imaginable, including billboards along railroad rights of way, colorfully lithographed trade cards, almanacs (issued continuously from the 1850s onward), newspapers, magazines, and posters. The Ayer enterprise was so successful that the owners branched out into the textile, real estate, and railroad businesses, became involved in politics, and were prominent on the American financial scene. James Cook Ayer donated a town hall to a Massachusetts village, which promptly changed its name to Ayer.

C.I. Hood & Co., which ranked with the enterprise of Dr. J. C. Ayer, did business from a four-story factory, styled as a "laboratory," on Thorndike Street and claimed to produce 75 million pieces of advertising per year, including four million calendars! The factory workers numbered 275, plus 50 clerks and a dozen or so incidental helpers. Hood's Sarsaparilla was the best-known product, but Hood's Vegetable Pills, Tooth Powder, and Olive Ointment all found a market. From their earliest years, children were educated in the merits of Hood's products, with Hood's Rainy Day Puzzles being especially popular with the younger set.

In addition to Ayer and Hood, several other Lowell patent medicine makers were active during the 1880s. C.E. Carter produced Allen's Root Beer Extract, Blood Syrup, Toothache Drops, and the curiously-named Electric Nerve Pencil, while A.W. Dows & Co. made Dows' Cough Cure, Diarrhea Syrup, and Soothing Cordial. So-called soothing cordials were a popular product and often consisted of an extract of opium. Their primary use was to quiet cranky, crying, or temperamental babies, often with addictive or fatal results.

In the same city, A.L. Field turned out Dr. Leroy's Wild Cherry Balsam and Tar, Field's Kidney and Liver Remedy, Field's Magnetic Liniment, and Field's Cholera Mixture.

George S. Hull & Co., another Lowell medicine enterprise, made Lyford's Magic Pain Cure, Harvard Bronchial Syrup, and Hull's Veterinary Liniment, doing business from what must have been modest quarters in the basement of the Five-Cent Savings Bank building. The Ingalls Medical Co. made Ingalls' Mandrake Compound (for liver and kidneys) and Ingalls' Throat and Lung Specific.

Dr. J.A. Masta, who lived at 38 Varney Street, not far from another doctor who was to far outstrip him in fame, turned out Dr. Masta's Celebrated Cough Balsam and claimed to have established his business in 1854. Dr. George S. Mowe turned out Dr. Mowe's Cough Balsam, with the claim that it had been in use since the 1840s.

A.C. Stevens stated he was the originator of Stevens' Sarsaparilla and Stevens' Dandelion Pills, a claim which probably no one cared to dispute. He also turned out various types of plasters which were individually described as strengthening, porous, porous belladonna, and rheumatic. His modest enterprise, which employed just three workers, also turned out a cough mixture and a tooth powder. Not much larger was the S.E. Tweed Co., located at 218 Middlesex Street in Lowell, which employed four men to turn out Tweed's Liniment, "Good For Man or Beast."

Other Lowell entrepreneurs jumped on the bandwagon. McAlvin's Dyspepsia Pills were sent by mail to all parts of the world, according to claims of the proprietor, while the prolific Dr. G.W. Hilton made 14 remedies but was especially proud of Dr. Hilton's Specific No. 3 which claimed to cure colds. Magee's Emulsion Co., under the management of A.J. Lynch, turned out Magee's Emulsion of Cod Liver Oil.

Into the vigorous Lowell patent medicine activity in 1885—or was it 1884?—jumped Dr. Augustin Thompson with his entry, Moxie Nerve Food. At a time in which secret ingredients were the rule and in which the more mysterious a product appeared to be, the better chances it had for capturing the fancy of the public, Thompson either fabricated or reported the story of the "discovery" of Moxie Nerve Food. Put up in bottles, and billed as a healthful beverage and

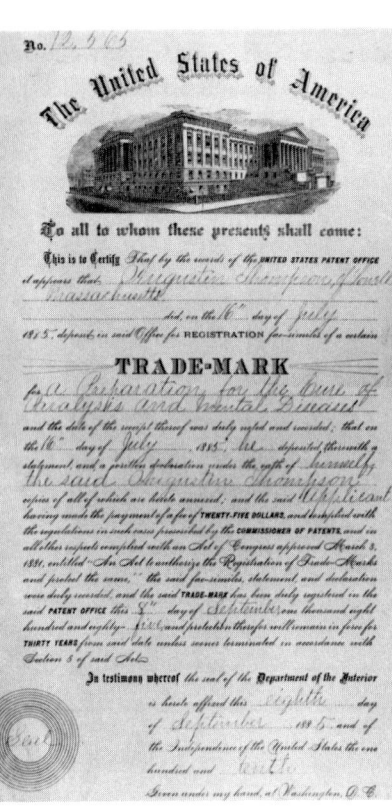

Cover of the trademark notice sent to Dr. Augustin Thompson by the United States Patent Office.

An early notice from the Moxie Nerve Food Company lists the officials connected with it and various branches.

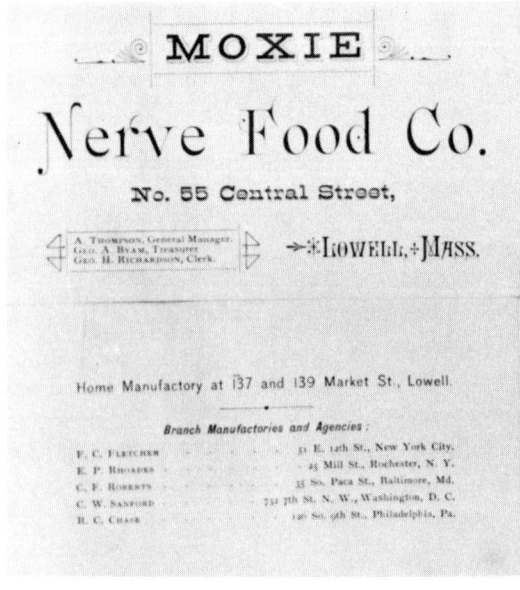

medicine combination, Moxie antedated Coca-Cola (1886), Hires Root Beer (which was available in extract form at the time but which was not bottled until years later), and other popular carbonated beverages. It is not that there wasn't competition in 1885, for many bottlers were in the act. By 1890, Lowell alone had five soda water manufacturers. However, the products of most of the others soon were forgotten, while Moxie went on to achieve great fame.

Whether Moxie Nerve Food was first made in 1884 or whether it saw the light of day for the first time in 1885 has been a matter of conjecture among collectors and historians. Advertisements printed years later, beginning in the 1920s, often placed 1884 as the inception date. From the 1940s onward, a "Since 1884" notice became a prominent part of Moxie publicity. However, it was not so in earlier times, and one has but to scan Moxie advertisements and other printed material of the 19th and early 20th centuries to find the date 1885 used nearly exclusively.

In the declaration made by Dr. Augustin Thompson for trademark registration No. 12,565, filed on July 16, 1885 (registered on September 8, 1885), he noted:

"Be it known that I, Augustin Thompson, citizen of the United States, residing at Lowell, in the County of Middlesex and State of Massachusetts, and doing business at No. 139 Market Street in said city, have adopted for my use a trademark for Nerve Food, of which the following is a clear and exact specification.

"My trademark consists of the word 'Moxie.' This has generally been arranged as shown in the accompanying facsimile, which represents a picture of a woman clad in loose clothing, bearing a sheaf of grain on her left shoulder, held there by her right hand, while in her left hand she carries a cycle [sic]. To the left of this representation is the word 'Moxie,' below which are the words 'Nerve Food; Has not a drop of Medicine, Poison, Stimulant, or Alcohol in its composition.' Following these words is descriptive and advertising matter, applicant's name and place of business, etc.; but these latter words are unimportant, and the entire picture may be omitted or changed at pleasure without materially affecting the character of my trademark, the essential feature of which is the arbitrary word 'Moxie.'

"This trademark I have used continuously in my business since April 1, 1885, and a particular description of goods is a liquid preparation charged with soda for the cure of paralysis, softening of the brain, and mental imbecility and called the 'Moxie Nerve Food.' It is comprised in the class of medical compounds.

A. THOMPSON.

A PREPARATION FOR THE CURE OF PARALYSIS AND MENTAL DISEASES.

No. 12,565.   Registered Sept. 8, 1885.

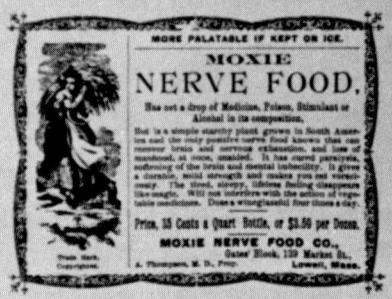

The issued trademark for Moxie registered by the United States Patent Office on September 8, 1885 as No. 12565. The initial application was filed on July 16, 1885.

UNITED STATES PATENT OFFICE.

AUGUSTIN THOMPSON, OF LOWELL, MASSACHUSETTS.

TRADE-MARK FOR A PREPARATION FOR THE CURE OF PARALYSIS AND MENTAL DISEASES.

STATEMENT and DECLARATION of Trade-Mark No. 12,565, registered September 8, 1885.

Application filed July 16, 1885.

STATEMENT.

To all whom it may concern:

Be it known that I, AUGUSTIN THOMPSON, a citizen of the United States, residing at Lowell, in the county of Middlesex and State of Massachusetts, and doing business at No. 139 Market street, in said city, have adopted for my use a Trade-Mark for Nerve Food, of which the following is a clear and exact specification.

My trade-mark consists of the word "Moxie." This has generally been arranged as shown in the accompanying fac-simile, which represents the picture of a woman clad in loose clothing, bearing a sheaf of grain on her left shoulder, held there by her right hand, while in her left hand she carries a cycle. To the left of this representation is the word "Moxie," below which are the words "Nerve Food; Has not a drop of Medicine, Poison, Stimulant, or Alcohol in its composition." Following these words is descriptive and advertising matter, applicant's name and place of business, &c.; but these latter words are unimportant, and the entire picture may be omitted or changed at pleasure without materially affecting the character of my trade-mark, the essential feature of which is the arbitrary word "MOXIE."

This trade-mark I have used continuously in my business since April 1, 1885, and the particular description of goods is a liquid preparation charged with soda for the cure of paralysis, softening of the brain, and mental imbecility, and called the "Moxie Nerve Food." It is comprised in the class of medical compounds.

It is my practice to apply my trade-mark to the bottles containing the nerve food by means of suitable labels, of which the fac simile inclosed is an exact copy, on which this word "Moxie" and its associate words "Nerve Food" are printed, as above described. These words are sometimes blown into the bottles.

AUGUSTIN THOMPSON.

Witnesses:
J. W. HUNTOON,
A. W. HILL.

DECLARATION.

State of Massachusetts, county of Middlesex, ss:

AUGUSTIN THOMPSON, being duly sworn, deposes and says that he is the applicant named in the foregoing statement; that he verily believes that the foregoing statement is true; that he has at this time a right to the use of the trade-mark therein described; that no other person, firm, or corporation has the right to such use, either in the identical form or in any such near resemblance thereto as might be calculated to deceive; that it is used by him in commerce between the United States and foreign nations or Indian tribes, and particularly with England, France, and the Choctaw and Penobscot tribes of Indians, and that the description and fac-similes presented for record truly represent the trade mark sought to be registered.

AUGUSTIN THOMPSON.

Sworn and subscribed before me, a justice of the peace, at Lowell, Massachusetts, this twenty fourth day of July, 1885.

J. N. MARSHALL,
Justice of the Peace.

In the trademark application Augustin Thompson stated that Moxie was an arbitrary word and it had been "used continuously in my business since April 1, 1885." Significantly, the patent description notes that it was "charged with soda" (carbonated) from the very beginning. At the outset it was not billed as a refreshing beverage as such. Rather, it was a patent medicine for "the cure of paralysis, softening of the brain, and mental imbecility."

"It is my practice to apply my trademark to the bottles containing the nerve food by means of suitable labels, of which the facsimile enclosed is an exact copy, on which this word 'Moxie' and its associate words 'Nerve Food' are printed, as above described. These words are sometimes blown into the bottles. —Augustin Thompson."

The same declaration noted that the trademark Moxie was used "in commerce between the United States and foreign nations or Indian tribes, and particularly with England, France, and the Choctaw and Penobscot tribes of Indians."

The Moxie Nerve Food label accompanying the July 16, 1885 trademark filing noted, in part:

"MOXIE NERVE FOOD, Has not a drop of Medicine, Poison, Stimulant or Alcohol in its composition, but is a simple starchy plant grown in South America and the only positive nerve food known that can recover brain and nervous exhaustion, and loss of manhood, at once, unaided. It has cured paralysis, softening of the brain and mental imbecility. It gives a durable, solid strength and makes you eat voraciously. The tired, sleepy, lifeless feeling disappears like magic. Will not interfere with the action of vegetable medicines. Dose a wineglassful four times a day. Price 35 Cents a Quart Bottle, or $3.50 per Dozen.

"MOXIE NERVE FOOD CO., Gates' Block, 139 Market St., Lowell, Mass. A. Thompson, M.D., Prop."

The trademark application and label text indicate several things. Thompson stated that the word "Moxie" was arbitrary. No mention was made of any specific origin of the term. Later labels were to recite the tale of Lieut. Moxie, but the early label did not, nor did the trademark application mention him. It was noted that Moxie was "charged with soda," or carbonated. This and numerous other early references to carbonation refute certain statements published decades later that carbonation was first added to Moxie after the Pure Food and Drugs Act was passed in 1906.

The trademark application makes clear the intent of Moxie: it was intended to cure paralysis, softening of the brain, and mental imbecility and to have other healthful benefits. In other words, it was designated as a proprietary medicine or "food."

Shortly after filing his trademark application, it occurred to Dr. Thompson that what later became known as "the Lieut. Moxie legend" would add to the mystery and perhaps to the sale of the product. Soon the label was revised in part to state:

"It is prepared from a simple sugar cane-like plant grown near the equator. It was lately discovered by Lieut. Moxie, who placed the discovery in the hands of Dr. Augustin Thompson, who has demonstrated its value as a food for the nervous system."

The medical claims were expanded slightly, and the new text noted beneficial effects when used for "locomotor ataxia, and insanity when caused by nervous exhaustion." It was also stated that Moxie "removes fatigue from mental and physical overwork and brings refreshing sleep at night."

Dr. Thompson prepared several versions of the Lieut. Moxie story, at one time placing his fortuitous discovery near the equator, and another time locating the wandering lieutenant many thousands of miles to the south "near the Strait of Magellan." The historian can piece together the biography of the elusive Lieut. Moxie from Dr. Thompson's own words. An early statement related:

"While exploring near the Strait of Magellan in South America, Lieut. Moxie observed that the natives, when about to undergo any exhausting effort, drank freely of the decoction of a starchy plant much like our asparagus. As it seemed to have no disturbing effect, but rather to give a durable, vigorous feeling to the nervous system, he learned to believe that it was as much a special food for the nervous system as beef steak and carbonate and phosphate of lime are for the muscles and bones. This constrained him to introduce it into the United States as an essential to this great nerve-wearing people, and because it would have no competition worthy of note. It has been found to digest and assimilate best in combination with soda and sugar. There is not a drop of alcohol in its composition. Its first introduction was in Lowell, where its sale...has been unprecedented... One bottle will not cure you, any more than one meal will make you fat. It should be taken freely. It is a great thing for the languor from hot weather, and when kept on ice is the finest beverage in America. One bottle used sells a dozen more... 30 Cents a quart bottle, or $3 per dozen, or 40 Cents per siphon, siphon returned. Moxie Nerve Food Company, Gates' Block, 139 Market St., Lowell."

The preceding notes that Lieut. Moxie himself played an active part in the promotion of the product bearing his name, for he is named as the one who introduced it in the United States as being essential for the population and because there was little competition. Note also that the price is given as 30c a quart, a slight change from that on the trademark application label.

More information on the subject appeared in a brochure issued toward the end of 1885, here quoted in part:

"Lieut. Moxie was a dear old friend. Through speculations in oil lands he amassed a great fortune. He inherited tubercular consumption from his mother, from which he died last May in Lower California. Last year [this identifies the discovery date as 1884], while hunting for health in the mountain regions of South America, he found the people using what they called the Food Plant, as we do greens. Surprised at its effect on his own nervous system, he shipped a bale and its history to me, asking me to determine its character. Prepared in decoction, wherever I have used it, the patient said, 'It gives me a solid, durable strength and a very large appetite.'

"I found it cured anything caused by nervous exhaustion. It restored nervous people who were tired out mentally or physically; stopped the appetite for intoxicants in old drunkards, insanity, blindness from overtaxing the sight, paralysis, all but hereditary sick-headache, loss of manhood from excesses, made people able to stand twice their usual amount of labor, mentally or physically, with less fatigue. It cured two cases of softening of the brain, and recovered helpless limbs. I found it to be neither medicine nor stimulant, but a nerve food, and harmless as milk.

"It has taken me 20 years, with an enormous practice, to learn that nine-tenths of the prevailing illness comes from nervous exhaustion... I do not like to advertise like a quack, but my friends say that I must give it to the world. With flavoring extracts used to make it palatable, the people say it is the best beverage made. In honor of its discoverer, I have called it Moxie Nerve Food. The rush for it is so large I have put in facilities to make 27,000 bottles per week. When I first received it, the immense cost for transportation so far caused me to think I should never see my money again. In fact, I felt chagrined to think I had become the victim of such circumstances. The decoction gave me a wonderful appetite and strength all winter [indicating it may have been formulated before the spring of 1885; possibly in 1884]. After settling its uncertainties on myself, I resolved to test it on others.

"My first opportunity was a case of apparent progressive paralysis. The lady was about 65, and helpless, she had been given up by her physician and friends. I first tried medicine without effect, her mind was nearly as bad as her body. The Moxie brought about a complete recovery in 13 days. To say that her friends and myself were astonished is drawing it mild.

"The next case was a prominent Lowell lady with paralysis of the right arm and the utmost nervous exhaustion. The Moxie recovered her in 15 days. A case of complete, dead paralysis of the right side, seven weeks standing, was first tried with medicine and electricity without avail. The Moxie, after five days, produced an intense activity of the nerves in the paralyzed parts, and a very sensitive condition. There is now a slow progress toward the restoration of motion.

"Another case is of a prominent journalist, who had been overworked mentally and had neglected proper exercise. He had loss of memory, tendency to mix ideas, and an inability to walk without support; mental labor was impossible. The Moxie completely recovered this case in 10 days. The man is now editing his paper, with mind and body vigorous and active. But he says Moxie will be his drink in the future, for he can stand twice the mental labor with less fatigue, when using it...

"The soda fountains supply it all over the country. Its introduction into the city of Lowell last July was the most remarkable ever known. The rush for it overwhelmed me. At the end of five months I was compelled to establish four large factories in New England and New York and over 500,000 quart bottles were sold inside that time. Now the wholesale dealers tell me the demand next year will require from 12 million to 15 million bottles. The liquor saloons say two-thirds of their customers drink it exclusively, saying it makes them feel better than stimulants, stops the hankering for rum, and gives them great power of endurance, leaving no reaction, but solid, vigorous strength, big appetite and sweet good sleep. The women say it is just what they want. Nervousness and nervous exhaustion disappear like magic. But the greatest hope is that it will supersede intoxicants. This is a large story and will be treated as another patent medicine swindle at first, but the next year will disabuse the public mind of that. Write to any part of New England and you will learn that the excitement over it is intense. Come to Lowell and we can convince you in two hours that the story is larger than we have told. I refer you to the whole city of Lowell, Massachusetts to substantiate my statement... Price 35 Cents a quart bottle, $3.50 a dozen. Moxie Nerve Food Company, 139 Market Street, Lowell, Mass."

By the end of 1885 Thompson had several other Moxie agents, including E.P. Rhoades at 23, 25 and 27 Mill Street, Rochester, New York; C.F. Roberts, 35 South Paca Street, Baltimore; F.C. Fletcher, 51 East 12th Street, New York City; and George P. Walker, 33 North State Street, Chicago. Walker was to prove to be a headache when a scandal involving him erupted several years later.

The production figures Thompson gave at the end of 1885 for Moxie are to be taken with a large grain of salt, for the firm's financial ledgers in the author's possession do not substantiate his advertising claims.

A few months later Thompson was to make the immodest claim that Moxie was "a discovery that will shake this country more than telephones and telegraphs; a harmless, simple food that will supersede the use of stimulants and nervines, that will and is destroying the rum trade, and recovers nervousness, insomnia, nervous and mental exhaustion at once, leaves no reaction."

A few years later, in 1892, Augustin Thompson again told of the beginnings of the Moxie beverage, slightly confusing the recovery times and sequence of his initial patients (when compared to the preceding text):

"THE FAMOUS MOXIE. An episode in South American history. To the public: While exploring in the South American mountains, Lieut. Moxie (not of the United States Army) found the natives using a decoction from a sugar cane-like plant as a common drink when they were exhausted from overexertion. Upon trial he found it much superior to 'cocoa,' and believing it to be a valuable medicine, he shipped a large bale to me for trial. I found it to be one of the best nerve foods yet found, and that large quantities do not disturb the system, as medicines can, but upon microscopic examination it was found to be a rich, vegetable albumenoid. Its first trial came upon an old lady of 65, who, acquiring a dyspeptic habit, became a hopeless case of mental imbecility and progressive paralysis, caused by malnutrition of the nervous system. Patient fully recovered in 63 days. The second trial was on an overworked eminent journalist. His case was much like the other but not so far advanced, or as bad. He recovered after 35 days and went to his office to work... But the sale is now [1892] over 300,000 cases per year, and is doubling every 16 months, and this is the famous Moxie, which after six years is the best gigantic trade of its kind the world ever saw. —A. Thompson, M.D."

As years went on, numerous other versions of the Moxie legend were recited. *Printers Ink*, the advertising industry trade publication, noted as part of a May 26th, 1921 article:

"There was, for example, the story of Lieut. Moxie and the Bolivian beans. It was a peach of a story, full of thrills, and entirely harmless. It told how the bold lieutenant, pushing his way through the pathless Bolivian wilderness, discovered a plant of marvelous medicinal qualities and brought the seeds to civilization at great personal risk from the enraged savages. Perhaps I am wrong; it may not have been a bean, and I'm not sure about the savages. But that

The famous Moxie.

An episode in South American History.

To the public:— While exploring in the South American mountains, Lieut. Moxie (not of the U.S. Army) found the natives using a decoction from a sugar cane like plant, as a common drink, when they were exhausted from over exertion. Upon trial, he found it much superior to "cocoa", and believing it to be a valuable medicine, he shipped a large bale to me for trial. I found it to be one of the best nerve foods yet found, and that large quantities did not disturb the system, as medicines can, but upon microscopic examination, it was found to be a rich, vegetable albuminoid. Its first trial was upon an old lady of 65, who, acquiring a dyspeptic habit, became a hopeless case of mental imbecility and progressive paralysis caused by malnutrition of the nervous system. Patient fully recovered in 63 days. The second was upon an overworked, eminent journalist. His case was much like the other, but not so far advanced, as as bad. He recovered after 35 days & went to his office to work. From taking small quantities, continually, he remained well. These cases were followed by the recovery of a young girl who was speechless and helpless for years. Another, a naval officer, who was a helpless imbecile for three and a half years. Two other cases, partially blind and unable to stand mental labor, caused by a fall and concussion of the head, all these recovered. There was an intense excitement, other physicians tried it and confirmed my impressions. It was a nerve food & non-reactive. Insomnia from frights, nervous overwork, or excitement, yielded to it at once. Very soon old drunkards began to tell me that it took away that terrible thirst for liquors & made them feel better than stimulants, and the heavy mental & physical workers said it seemed to give them a remarkable sweet, natural feeling of rest, when tired. They said they could stand more labor with less fatigue, while using it, that it left no reaction; bad effects, or abnormal appetites, but acted, or had the same effect as food. Thinking it over to get it into general use, I knew it must be a luxury and be sold cheaply. I then flavored it into a luscious beverage and put it up in 26 oz. bottles, in 1 doz. bottle cases; to be retailed for 20 cts a bottle or $2.50 for 12 bottles. I then conceived the idea of putting delivery teams into the large cities, and buying back the empty cases & bottles, in which case it would cost the consumer but 16 cts per bottle. It left but 3 cts a bottle, profit, but the sale is now over 300,000 cases per year, and doubling every 16 months, and this is the famous Moxie, which after six years, is the most gigantic trade in its kind, the world ever saw. A. Thompson M.D. Lowell Mass.

Most Moxie publicity and advertising was personally written by Dr. Augustin Thompson. Above in his hand is one of several slightly divergent histories telling of Lieut. Moxie and the beginning of Moxie Nerve Food.

really doesn't matter, for neither Lieut. Moxie nor the miraculous plant were ever shown to exist outside of the copy writer's imagination. But the drink which was named for the fictitious lieutenant which was alleged to contain the juice of the fabulous plant grew strong in the public favor, and attracted the attention of an unregenerate spirit who promptly countered with 'Modox.'

"There was a lawsuit, in which the lieutenant and the medicinal properties of the plant were prominent topics of discussion. And, as neither could be shown to exist, the hard-hearted court indicated the exit sign to both parties and asked them to close the door gently when they went out.

"Later on, the Moxie Company, having abandoned the lieutenant and the medicinal herbs (without seriously interfering with the sale of the beverage), reappeared and secured an injunction restraining further sales of Modox. But the time and money spent in prosecuting the first suit was entirely lost, together with a large number of sales which were illegitimately acquired by the infringer. There was also the chagrin and embarrassment of having one's pet idea called opprobrious names by the court. And the probabilities are that the company had no intention of swindling anybody. Extravagant claims were far more common in those days than they are now, and the intention was doubtless merely that of getting a talking point which was sensational enough to attract attention."

An article in the November 17, 1926 edition of the *Evening Gazette*, Worcester, Massachusetts, told of an interview with David MacKay, then specialty advertising manager of The Moxie Company:

"Moxie received its name, Mr. MacKay said, after Lieut. Moxie, a classmate at West Point of Dr. Thompson, the inventor of the beverage. Lieut. Moxie, he said, was stricken with a fever while on duty in the tropics. A beverage concocted of herbs by a native restored him to health. A sample of these herbs he sent to Dr. Thompson, who at the time was studying medicine, and after several years the doctor blended them into a beverage."

Although the Lieut. Moxie legend dominated advertising of the firm from soon after its inception through the early 20th century, in later years certain historians, competitors, and others suggested that the name was simply swiped from Maine geography. It could be that Augustin Thompson was influenced by Moxie as a place name in his native state, for the Moxie term on Maine maps antedated the advent of his nerve food in the mid-1880s. The "Map of the District of Maine," then a portion of Massachusetts, by Moses

M|O|X|E!

A GOLDEN OPPORTUNITY FOR GROCERS.

A food plant extract that is creating more interest and excitement in the United States than the discovery of the Telegraph and Telephone, and taken by everybody.

Removes the effects of dissipation, alcoholism, the liquor appetite, nervousness, nervous exhaustion, and all their results, even to paralysis and insanity, while it is as harmless as milk, and the finest beverage in America.

Thousands of women in the East order it regularly from their grocer. The leading wholesale houses will tell you the size of its sale has never been equalled in the history of the country. 5,000,000 bottles sold during the first fourteen months, and the demand is doubling every three months; because thousands of old inebriates, and hundreds of thousands of moderate drinkers find it does better and satisfies the thirst for liquors better than stimulants, without reaction, leaving only the best results—a sweet sleep, large appetite, and double powers of endurance.

It is the only remedy known that will cure nervousness, exhaustion, the terrible tired feeling in women, or the always present mental and physical tired out within a few hours, leaving no reaction more than food. The women swarm after it like mad. It is fast substituting liquors in the saloons, bars and hotels. Is pronounced by one of the most eminent Boston physicians the best discovery ever made, and who says it has come to stay, because its place can never be filled.

It is fast rendering prohibitory laws unnecessary, because the drinkers prefer it, and the dealer makes most money on it. We have three great agencies in the United States :

REED, MURDOCK & FISCHER, State Street, Chicago, Ill.
THOMAS DANA & CO., 9 & 11 Commercial Street, Boston,
THUBBER, WHYLAND & CO., New York City,

Who also have control of our export trade.

PRICES:

Moxie XX, $4.00 per case, twelve 26 ounce bottles, or $3.80 in gross lots.
Moxie Syrup, for Soda fountains, $7.00 per case, same size, or $6.50 in gross lots.

Order through these or the wholesale trade. Agencies and Manufactories at :

137 Market Street, Lowell, Mass.	25 Mill Street, Rochester, N. Y.
33 North State Street, Chicago, Ill.	35 So. Paca Street, Baltimore, Md.

51 East 12th Street, New York City.

A. THOMPSON, M. D.,

GENERAL MANAGER MOXIE NERVE FOOD Co.

This early Moxie advertisement is from a personal scrapbook kept by Dr. Augustin Thompson and dates from the earliest years of the beverage.

Greenleaf, October 1815, depicts Moxy's Pond and Moxy Mountain. By 1884 the *Atlas of the State of Maine*, published by George N. Colby & Co., designated the same features as Moxie Pond and, in a slightly different geographical location (in East Moxie Township), Moxie Mountain. Moxie Stream was also noted. Other sources named Moxie Cove (in Round Pond near Friendship, Maine), Moxie Falls, Moxie Trail, Moxie Camp (on Moxie Lake or Pond), and Moxie Woods. The aspect of Maine geography is important, for later lawsuits were to claim that the beverage was named after one or more of these locations and, as such, the Moxie name was available to anyone caring to use it.

By 1886, the subject of nerve foods in general and Moxie Nerve Food in particular attracted the attention of the editor of *The Druggists Circular and Chemical Gazette,* a journal published in New York, which was about as close as any periodical of the time to objective reporting (without bias induced by advertisers). The November 1886 issue contained an article, "Nerve Foods," which called Thompson on the carpet and requested an explanation of the Moxie legend:

"When the great Dr. Johnson said, 'I like to dine, sir; I like to dine,' he awakened a sympathetic response in many a stomach. Most of us like to dine; there is something very agreeable about the ingestive process by which we tickle our palates and repair our systems. Food is the great panacea for exhaustion, and no one objects to the remedy.

"When it comes to medicine the case is quite different, however. When the repairing needed is of a character beyond the reach of food, the customary means of repair are looked on with more or less suspicion. Medicine is a somewhat forbidden word. It is no wonder, then, that the idea of a 'food cure' is welcomed.

"This idea has been utilized in connection with various parts of the human system—most recently the nerves have been provided with 'nutrients' in confusing numbers.

"The most prominent of these, perhaps, is the 'Moxie,' a preparation which has lately been much talked of. This 'food' is said to be prepared from a certain plant not hitherto recognized as a remedial agent, and with a view to enlightening its readers as to the new remedy, the Circular asked from the manufacturers of 'Moxie' the favor of a specimen of this plant.

"In reply to the request Dr. Thompson sends a letter, from which we take the following:

Chapter 2

Dr. Augustin Thompson

Augustin Thompson, born in Union, Maine, in 1835, numbered among his ancestors John Thompson, a Welshman born in 1616, who came to America at the age of 6, in May 1622, and landed at Plymouth. The *Illustrated History of Lowell, Massachusetts*, 1897, relates that this forebear purchased in March 1645 land from Samuel Eddy, near Spring Hill, and on December 6, 1645, married Mary Cook, the daughter of Francis Cook, a *Mayflower* passenger. John Thompson later purchased land from the Indians in the district which became Halifax.

Augustin Thompson's grandfather, also named John Thompson, was born in New Hampshire but moved at an early time to Union, in the eastern district of Massachusetts which later (1820) became the separate state of Maine. He served as a captain in the Revolutionary War and died in battle near Saratoga, according to the account. Augustin Thompson's grandmother was Mehitable Richards, who was born in England. His father, James Thompson, a farmer, was born in 1805. His mother, Harriet Maxfield, was born in Union in 1812 and died there in 1878, to be followed three years later by his father's death in Union in 1881.

Augustin Thompson studied in the public schools in Union. He was fascinated by the world around him and sought to gain additional knowledge by reading. He assembled a modest library on various subjects, with history and science being favorites. At the same time he became acquainted with the plays of Shakespeare and others, which led him to develop a flair for the melodramatic, an ability that was to become valuable in later years.

At the age of 16 he became apprenticed to a blacksmith. After following the trade for a short time, he found it too confining. Blacksmithing, masonry, and draying were engaged in, but his heart was not in it, and he spent most of his available time studying books. He learned Latin and German. His library grew, and added to his

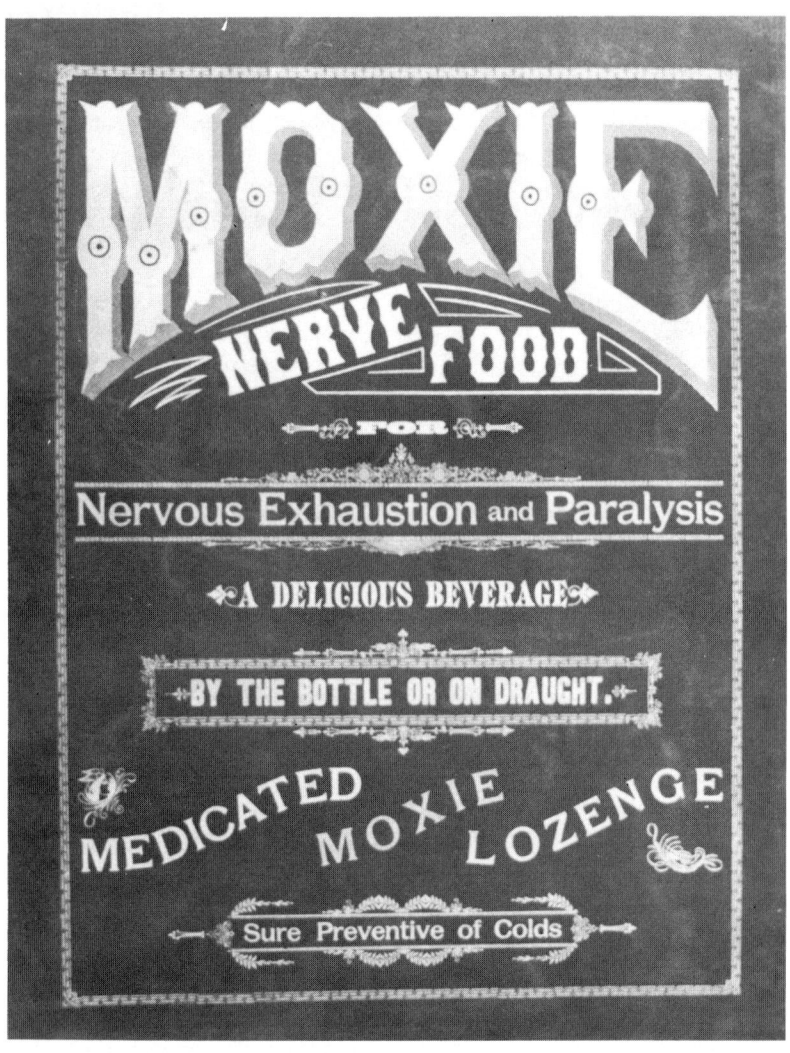

The above advertisement, a reproduction of a poster featuring gold and silver lettering on a black background, dates from the 19th century and features Moxie Nerve Food as a beverage and also the Medicated Moxie Lozenge, which was described as "Sure Preventive of Colds."

own volumes were numerous texts borrowed from others. As an adult, Thompson stood five feet, ten inches tall, had light brown hair and eyes that were variously described as gray or blue. By the advent of the Civil War, Augustin Thompson was what would be known in later years as an intellectual.

On September 10, 1862, Augustin Thompson enlisted in the Union forces with Company G of the 28th Infantry, Maine Volunteers. On September 20th he received the rank of captain and was placed in charge of a company of men he helped recruit from his home area in Maine. He subsequently served in numerous engagements and was recommended twice for gallant work in battle. He was among the defenders of the federal works at Fort Butler, Donaldsonville, Louisiana, and served under Gen. Nathaniel Banks.

Struck in the chest by a rifle butt, he developed complications, including the diagnosis of tuberculosis. He left the scenes of battle and went north to Maine, where he was honorably discharged from the service in Augusta on August 31, 1863. Later, Col. Woodman was to issue the following report:

"I hereby certify that Captain Augustin Thompson of Co. G, 28th Maine Infantry Volunteers, served under my command eleven months, that he with his company took prominent part in repulsing the desperate assault of the rebels upon Fort Butler, Donaldsonville, La., on the 28th of June, 1863, in which the rebels were overwhelmingly defeated with a loss in, killed, equal to the whole number of men opposed to them, in wounded twice as many, in taken prisoners as many enlisted men as there were in the Fort, and twice as many commissioned officers.

"I also certify that Captain Thompson, together with the officers engaged in the repulse, each by name was recommended for promotion by Brig. Genl. Chas. C. Stone in his official report of the battle to Genl. Banks."

A lengthy commendation, quoted here in part, was penned on February 1, 1869, by a friend who submitted a report to the governor of Maine. Apparently, Thompson was considering returning to the Army:

"Gov. Corry—I desire to address you in behalf of a worthy and deserving officer, Capt. Augustin Thompson, who, I understand, will soon make an application for a position and enter the Army again. I have conversed with his second lieutenant and many of his men from whom I gathered the following facts.

Augustin Thompson (front row center) and several of his Civil War compatriots. This photograph was taken shortly after he suffered a lung injury from being struck by the butt of a rifle. Note that his uniform jacket is partially unbuttoned.

Augustin Thompson (front row center with ceremonial sword) and his Civil War company.

"First, his moral character is without a stain. Secondly, he is well informed and of good address. Thirdly, he has been a hard working man in his business and is imbued with great energy and tenacity of purpose. Fourthly, his courage is good.

"His knowledge of the laws of health and his great and earnest care of his men saved them from disease, though exposed much and in hard service. (But three of his men died of disease while in the service, while the other companies lost from 10 to 30, as I have been informed.) His men seem to be devoted to him and speak of him with respect and admiration, which is seldom the case among returned soldiers. Men of other regiments speak well of him. The order from Gen. Stone recommending him to Gen. Banks for immediate promotion, you undoubtedly have. The occasion for this, as I have learned from a number of sources, is as follows—

"June 1st, from scouting in Iberville Parish, Louisiana, to keep communications open with New Orleans, he was ordered to the latter place for the defense of the city against the Texans who were threatening positions below to compel the raising of the siege of Port Hudson, Donaldsonville, at the head of Bayou Sara—force had but a hospital for a defense and he was sent there with 46 of his men to defend it. The small earthwork there mounted six 24-pounders. This was the key to communications with New Orleans. Convalescents and all the garrison numbered 130 men fit to do duty under Major G.D. Bullen, 28th Maine. It was attacked at midnight, June 28, by seven regiments of Texans, with artillery. A desperate assault and the front was beaten back with heavy loss to the enemy.

"An assault on the right flank out of reach of the guns, where Capt. Thompson commanded with 31 men, was then made with 600 men. A desperate fight at the outer works, and he was driven from the stockade (which was forced) to the corner of the earthwork where he poured such a hot fire of musketry into them that more than 300 ran. The others assaulted. A volley and the bayonet drove them under cover. Again and again they rushed on him until more than one-third of his men were killed and wounded... For two hours the fight raged with only a bank between the combatants. A reinforcement of four men was sent to him. Posting them so as to cut off the enemy's retreat, they surrendered. The prisoners numbered 128, including 10 commissioned officers. 34 lay dead on and under the bank and 12 mortally wounded including four commissioned officers.

"They confessed to have carried off enough wounded to make 75 or more. They acknowledged their assaulting force to be in all seven regiments numbering 3,100 men. Their whole loss, killed and wounded and prisoners, 600 men. This was obtained from their pickets, captured two days after. From the front they carried off five flatboats full of wounded. Reinforcement arrived the next day from Port Hudson. The order first named was then issued.

"In corroboration of these statements I refer you to any Maine officer who served in the Department of the Gulf. Your excellency, does not such call for the attention of all good citizens in asking that such men shall be remembered? And when I ask your attention to these facts, I repeat what every man in this section would say. I have sent this to Capt. Thompson upon such consideration."

After recuperating more than a year from his chest injury, he re-entered the service with the 7th Company, Maine, on October 27, 1864, serving until he was honorably discharged on July 6th, 1865. During his second tenure he played an important part in the fortification of Fort Popham, on the Maine coast. After the close of the Civil War, Thompson was given the lieutenant colonel rank by an act of Congress.

The name Augustin was an unfamiliar one, and many of his military records were spelled "Augustine." Such misspellings as Augustine and Augustus were to occur throughout his life.

Shortly thereafter he went to the Hahnemann Homeopathic College in Philadelphia, where he studied medicine. The institution derived its name from Samuel Christian Friedrich Hahnemann (April 10, 1755-July 2, 1843), a German physician who devised the so-called "law of similars," which was to influence Thompson for the rest of his life. *The American Cyclopaedia*, 1874, told of Hahnemann's work:

"In 1790, while engaged upon a translation of Cullen's *Materia Medica*, he was struck with the contradictory properties ascribed to Peruvian bark, and the various explanations given of its operation in intermittent fever. He resolved to try upon himself the effects of the medicine, and, after several powerful doses, discovered symptoms analogous to those of intermittent fever. The fact that a drug had produced upon a man in health the very symptoms which were required to cure a sick man immediately suggested to him the law, *Similia similibus curantur* ("Like cures like"), which is the ground work of the homeopathic system..."

Homeopathy was introduced into the United States in 1825 by Hans B. Gram, a native of Boston who was educated in Denmark. "His success attracted the attention of several physicians, among whom were Gray, Channing, Willson, Hall, and Hering. A careful study of the principles of the new theory [the law of similars] secured their adherence; and its success, not only in ordinary diseases, but in usually fatal epidemics, soon won for the system a large support," the same 1874 account noted. By a half century after its American introduction, about 6,000 doctors specialized in homeopathy, and there were nine homeopathic colleges, dozens of hospitals and dispensaries, and 13 periodicals devoted to the discipline.

Augustin Thompson's earlier studies provided him with an excellent background, and at the Hahnemann Homeopathic College he learned rapidly. Graduating at the head of his class, he decided to establish a medical practice in New England. At the time Lowell was a busy industrial city. He envisioned the possibility for rewarding activity there. He also may have been inspired by the tremendous success of Dr. J.C. Ayer, whose patent medicines, made in Lowell, were advertised intensely in virtually every American newspaper. He settled in Lowell sometime before June 1867, and from then until 1885 developed a large practice, a medical business which was stated to be not only the largest among the nearly 150 other physicians in the town but, remarkably, the largest in all of New England.

In 1869 he had second thoughts about his career, and he considered re-enlisting in the Army, but nothing came of the idea. A later (1903) writer was to note that "he gave much of his service to the poor people of the city, for which he received little pecuniary return, therefore did not amass much wealth from his practice." This may have been the case, for a tally sheet in Thompson's own hand reveals that from June 1, 1867 to March 31, 1884 his "medical business" amounted to $241,132.83 total work, but payment was received for only $91,680.16 of this amount. On a cash basis this amounted to about $5,000 per year, but undoubtedly some work was done in trade for other goods and services, as was the practice of the time. From the standpoint of total billings, the figure was slightly over $13,000 per year, which correlates with his statement, "I left a $15,000 business to put [Moxie] on the market," given to *The Druggists Circular and Chemical Gazette* in 1886. He worked six hours per day and advertised that in emergencies he could be reached at any time. He once stated he worked an average of nearly 18 hours per day. An 1897 biography noted:

"[He conducted his practice] without a day of vacation, or an hour for church in all that time. So assiduously did he devote himself to the safety of his families, though extremely vigorous, he broke down and was obliged to build himself to vigor again, when he invented

Augustin and Sarah Thompson.

the famous Moxie, which became so popular among his families he was obliged to set up a large manufactory...

"Dr. Thompson has never used liquors or tobacco and is extremely abstemious and simple in his habits, which accounts for his extreme vigor and intellectual strength. So closely has he applied himself to a scientific work, he has never seen a game of baseball or a boat race. He still assists his sons in the organization and the management of the largest individual business in New England, though up in the sixties, and presents in his person the finest picture of health and vigor your eyes ever looked upon."

The statement that Thompson never used liquor is idealistic, for Thompson himself related his enjoyment for beer. It is doubtful that he never saw a baseball game, for his younger son, Harry, was a member of a Lowell amateur baseball team for several years, and a later business associate, Freeman N. Young, was intensely interested in the sport.

On July 4, 1861, he married Sarah Stewart, of Union, Maine. Two sons resulted: Francis Edward, born in Union, Maine, July 1, 1864 (in the same house in which Augustin Thompson was born in 1835), and Harry Augustin, born in Lowell, February 7, 1872.

Following the establishment of his practice in Lowell in 1867, Thompson engaged in many other activities. Doubtless, his 18-hour working day also contained a measure of enjoyment, for he became a recognized playwright. Several dramas were produced, with *True to the Heart* (published in 1874), subtitled *The Conflict and Reconciliation*, a drama in six acts, gaining favorable recognition. A half dozen or so other plays were written, including *The Siege of Atlanta, or The Guerrilla Chief* (1878), *Yankee Corporal* (1879), *Exiled* (1880), and *Zina: The Slave Girl* (1882). Several of his plays had the same characters, including such names as Sally Rideout, Hezekiah Goferum, and Zina Brightly (or Zina Morgan). During summers he frequently attended Grand Army of the Republic reunions and encampments, where he fraternized with his Civil War buddies. Other activities included being a Mason and membership in the Odd Fellows and the Royal Arcanum. In religion he was a Spiritualist, and although his political leanings changed from time to time, he considered himself to be a Republican.

From the earliest times in his medical practice he prepared various remedies and so-called "cures." Alcoholism became a particular interest, and in 1876 he announced a solution to the addiction. Later, the New England Cure for Alcoholism achieved a limited popularity and apparently was used by other professionals as well. A printed notice stated: "Present systems [of the New England Cure for Alcoholism] distance by treatment upon the same principle as the application of the very useful anti-toxine. Proposition to all regularly educated physicians who may apply it in their practice." The term "regularly educated" with regard to physicians is important, for at the time many so-called "doctors" were physicians in name only and had little or no formal medical training.

The New England Cure for Alcoholism was not without its problems, for an article printed years later in the Lowell *Daily News*, February 8, 1895, related that "many of our people remember that Dr. Thompson was curing inebriates in 1876, but unlike the systems now in vogue, his did not prevent relapse."

The 1880 United States census gave Thompson's address in Lowell at 16 (number later changed to 36) Varney Street. Living with him was his wife Sarah, who kept house, assisted by Nellie L. Holt, a servant, age 21, from New Hampshire. His two sons lived at home and attended local schools. His practice as a homeopathic physician was conducted at No. 4 Wyman's Exchange, although contemporary notices revealed that he could be reached at his home at night.

Thompson kept careful journals, noting the illness of various patients, the recommended treatment, and the result for each. Eventually he developed a theory, which he later expanded into book form, that illness should be treated gradually. He believed that as diseases developed from small beginnings, it was logical to administer medicine in the same way—with small doses at first, progressing to larger doses. Much of this theory was derived from the published works of Hahnemann and his successors. Later, he was to investigate that marvelous medium, electricity, and its supposed curative powers, as well as the beneficial effects of various gases and vapors.

By the mid 1880s the genre of so-called "nerve foods" had become well established. By the time Moxie arrived on the scene the nerve food term was well known to readers of newspaper advertisements. Commenting on the popularity of the field, *The Druggists Circular and Chemical Gazette* published an article, "Nerve Foods as Dispensed at the Soda Fountain," in November 1886, the same issue that contained the previously-quoted explanation of Lieut. Macksey:

"Whether the popular notion demands it, or the popular demand proceeds from a notion based upon advertised and placarded results, certain it is that there has been a marvelous increase in the use of "phosphate" beverages at the soda fountain, and of other beverages claiming the same results, but with the most indeterminate and mystifying names. They all assert the same positive properties, and all

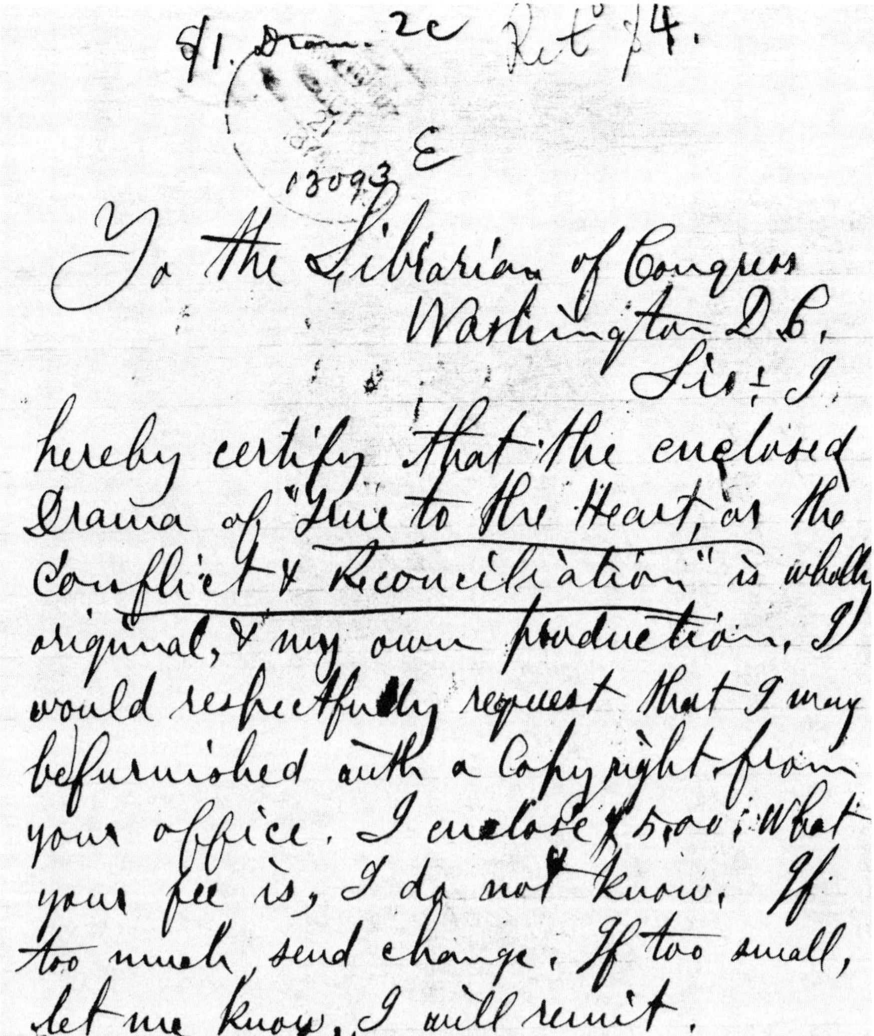

$1. Dram. 2c Rec'd 74.

13093 E

To the Librarian of Congress
Washington D.C.

Sir: I

hereby certify that the enclosed
Drama of "True to the Heart, or the
Conflict & Reconciliation" is wholly
original, & my own production. I
would respectfully request that I may
be furnished with a Copyright from
your office. I enclose $5.00; What
your fee is, I do not know. If
too much, send change. If too small,
let me know, I will remit.
    Very Resp. yours truly
            A. Thompson M.D.
    a.   14 Central St,
            Lowell Mass.

Lowell Mass, Oct. 1, 1874.

Dr. Augustin Thompson's copyright application for a drama he wrote, "True to the Heart, or The Conflict and Reconciliation," October 1874.

On April 28, 1880, Dr. Augustin Thompson applied for a copyright on his play, "Exiled!" or "Which the Traitor."

Facing is the title page of the play, which lists the characters, with humorous descriptions of their activities.

George Goodale (Lowell) 10
Mary C. Langley (Lowell) 100
George A. Byam (Lowell).........................100
Francis E. Thompson (Lowell).....................100
Augustin Thompson (Lowell).....................4,170

Five directors were elected: George A. Byam, Augustin Thompson, John L. Hunt, Israel Hungerford, and Charles Langley, with Hunt named as president and Byam as treasurer. The incorporation papers were received by the State of Maine on July 14, 1885, and the corporation became a reality on July 22nd.

The incorporators had bigger things in mind, and on January 29, 1886, J.F. Chute, clerk of The Moxie Nerve Food Company (Chute was publisher of *The Pythian Herald* in Portland and simply served a legal function; he was not active in the company), submitted the following petition to the Secretary of State of Maine:

"This is to give notice as required by the laws of Maine that The Moxie Nerve Food Company...finds that the amount of its capital stock ($500,000) is insufficient for the purpose for which said corporation was organized, and in a meeting of said corporation held in Portland this day...the stockholders, by a vote representing 4,415 shares of the 5,000 shares issued, increased the amount of its capital stock to the amount of $2,000,000, the same to be divided into 20,000 shares of $100 each."

The business prospered, and Thompson appointed distributors in several other eastern cities. Typically, such distributors were sent Moxie syrup, from which they bottled their own product. At the home office in Lowell other beverages were sold as well. The records show, for example, that on July 19th one case of ginger ale was sent to Thomas Stot for $1, a half barrel of N.F. Beer was shipped to Colby W. Bean, and a case of the same beer at $1.25 was shipped to another customer. Beer and ginger ale were sold to many others as well, as were cases of soda water.

In the summer of 1885 a new Moxie product appeared: Moxie XX. On July 30th, Charles Langley, a Moxie stockholder, was shipped 15 bottles of this. In August occasional orders for Moxie XX at $3.50 per dozen were booked, in comparison to $2.60 per dozen for the regular Moxie (although some customers were charged $3 per dozen for the regular). Sometimes customers would buy both regular and Moxie XX. For example, on August 13, a Boston client purchased 12 dozen regular Moxie at $2.40 per dozen and two dozen Moxie XX at $3.50 per dozen. Other customers were regularly charged $4 per dozen Moxie XX. The prices of both regular Moxie and Moxie

More Palatable if kept on Ice.   Will keep anywhere.

Double XX Moxie Nerve Food,

Contains not a drop of Medicine, Poison, Stimulant or Alcohol.

But is a simple sugar-cane-like plant, grown near the Equator and farther south, was lately accidentally discovered by Lieut. Moxie, and has proved itself to be the only harmless and effective nerve food known that can recover brain and nervous exhaustion; loss of manhood, imbecility and helplessness. It has recovered paralysis, softening of the brain, locomotor ataxia, and insanity when caused by nervous exhaustion. It gives a durable, solid strength, and makes you eat voraciously, takes away the tired, sleepy, lifeless feeling like magic, removes the fatigue from mental and physical overwork, at once, will not interfere with the action of vegetable medicines.

Dose, One Ounce Each Four Hours.

The loss of gas from the bottle does not weaken or injure the Moxie.

Price, 50 Cents a Quart Bottle, or $5.00 per Dozen.

For sale by principal druggists and apothecaries.

MOXIE NERVE FOOD CO.,

A. Thompson, M. D., Gen. Manager.   Lowell, Mass.

TRADE MARK.
Copyrighted.

More Palatable if kept on Ice.   Will keep anywhere.

Extract of Moxie Nerve Food,

Contains not a drop of Medicine, Poison, Stimulant or Alcohol.

But is a simple sugar-cane-like plant grown near the Equator and farther south, was lately accidentally discovered by Lieut. Moxie, and has proved itself to be the only harmless and effective nerve food known that can recover brain and nervous exhaustion; loss of manhood, imbecility and helplessness. It has recovered paralysis, softening of the brain, locomotor ataxia, and insanity when caused by nervous exhaustion. It gives a durable, solid strength, and makes you eat voraciously, takes away the tired, sleepy, lifeless feeling like magic, removes the fatigue from mental and physical overwork, at once, will not interfere with the action of vegetable medicines.

Dose, a Wineglassful Four Times a Day.

The loss of gas from the bottle does not weaken or injure the Moxie. Look out for counterfeits.

Price, 35 Cents a Quart Bottle, or $3.50 per Dozen.

For sale by principal druggists and apothecaries.

MOXIE NERVE FOOD CO.,

Gates' Block, 139 Market St.,
A. Thompson, M. D., Gen. Manager.   Lowell, Mass.

SAWYER, KINGSBURY & COPELAND,

BANGOR, MAINE.

AGENTS FOR

MOXI

NERV

FOO

A montage of various Moxie labels from the 19th century. Double XX Moxie Nerve Food was a short-lived product.

More Palatable if kept on Ice.   Will keep anywhere.

Beverage Moxie Nerve Food

Contains not a drop of Medicine, Poison, Stimulant or Alcohol.

Dose, a Wineglass Full Four Times a Day.

The loss of gas from the bottle does not weaken or injure the Moxie.

Price 25 Cents a Quart Bottle, or $2.50 per Dozen,

Sawyer, Kingsbury & Copeland,

(Successors to J. A. Wallis.)

110 Exchange Street,   Bangor, Maine.

XX seemed to have varied, possibly because of delivery differences or deposits refunded on returned bottles. On August 18th, George C. Goodwin & Co., a Boston wholesaler of patent medicines, purchased 36 dozen regular Moxie at $2.40 per dozen and 12 dozen Moxie XX at $3.50 per dozen, an unusually large order for the time. Occasional shipments of N.F. Beer continued to be registered.

The records also show deliveries of Moxie XXXX at the same price as Moxie XX. Among the larger orders registered for the 1885 year was that of E.P. Rhoades, of Troy, New York, (Rhoades, a traveling agent, had several other addresses as well) who bought 100 dozen Moxie for $290 on October 5th. The company's financial records reveal that in general a credit of 5c per bottle was given for empty returns. F.A. Winchester, of Los Angeles, purchased 12 gallons of Moxie extract or syrup for $96 on October 3, 1885 and "one ream of paper," presumably printed with an advertising message, for $1.08. Moxie distribution was truly nationwide! Sales increased, and on November 12th of the same year 687 dozen bottles of Moxie XX were shipped to Savannah, Georgia, amidst many other large orders.

The Moxie Nerve Food Company supplied advertising to its distributors. For example, C.F. Dearborn on September 3, 1885 was charged $1.32 for three showcards; on December 21, 1885, E.P. Rhoades was sent 100 five-sheet outdoor billboard posters for $18 and 200 other posters for $320; and on December 31, 1885, Charles Langley, at an address in Syracuse, was sent 24 reams of advertising circulars for $18.

By the end of 1885, Moxie was a household word throughout New England, with scattered recognition in other parts of America as well. A visitor to Lowell was apt to see Moxie posters plastered on the sides of buildings, on fences, and on separate billboards. Moxie in one year was rapidly overtaking the fame of its Lowell contemporaries, Ayer and Hood. Success begat success, and as the word spread, more and more druggists, grocery stores, beverage wholesalers, and others sent their orders to Lowell, where the Standard Bottling Company was kept busy turning out countless thousands of bottles of the compound. In 1886 Thompson wrote:

"The leading wholesale houses will tell you that the size of [the sale of Moxie] has never been equalled in the history of the country. Five million bottles sold during the first 14 months, the demand is doubling every three months, because thousands of old inebriates, and hundreds of thousands of moderate drinkers find that it does better and satisfies the thirst for liquors better than stimulants, without reaction, leaving only the best results—a sweet sleep, large appetite, and double powers of endurance..."

The main agencies at the time were listed as Reed, Murdock & Fisher, State Street, Chicago; Thomas Dana & Co., 9 and 11 Commercial Street, Boston; and Thubber, Whyland & Co., New York City, with additional outlets in Rochester and Baltimore. Thompson oversaw every aspect of the business and was general manager.

On May 28, 1886 the Western Moxie Nerve Food Company was incorporated in Maine, with Augustin Thompson as treasurer. Offices were given at Thompson's home address, 36 Varney Street, Lowell. (This corporation became defunct in 1901, according to State of Maine records.) Activities were primarily conducted at 33 North State Street, Chicago, under the management of George P. Walker. The arrangement was to end in scandal. In January 1889 the business was assigned to the Chicago Moxie Nerve Food Company. The Western Moxie Nerve Food Company name was later used in St. Louis.

A milestone in Moxie history occurred in July 1886, when Francis E. Thompson (the elder son of Augustin) and Freeman N. Young completed the first Moxie Bottle Wagon. The device consisted of a four-wheel cart on which a large replica of a Moxie bottle was built toward the back. Horse-drawn, the Bottle Wagon was a frequent sight in Lowell streets during the first summer. During the next three decades many variations of the Moxie Bottle Wagon were made, including smaller pony-drawn versions, a hand-pulled type, and a cycle-mounted style. However, most were large in format and had a space inside the bottle for a uniformed attendant to dispense the beverage for a nickel a glass.

A view of the early days of Moxie is found in a turn of the century article, "Moxie and Its Advertising," by John S. Grey:

"One of the little schoolmaster's pupils recently saw a Moxie advertisement in a drugstore and took a drink of it to assuage both his thrist and his curiosity. It had a particular taste—first like sarsaparilla, then somewhat bitter like gentian, and finally a very pleasant flavor. The next day he saw Moxie advertised in a big double-column space in the New York papers, and later saw the pretty advertising wagons in the street of the metropolis. So he called at 469 West Broadway to find out what he could about the advertising of Moxie, past, present, and to come.

"He was received by Mr. F.N. Young, one of the members of The Moxie Nerve Food Company, who told him that Moxie was first produced at Lowell, Massachusetts in 1885. At that time Mr. Young used to buy Moxie to retail again, and it was not advertised except by means of decorative wagons, shaped like a bottle, from which

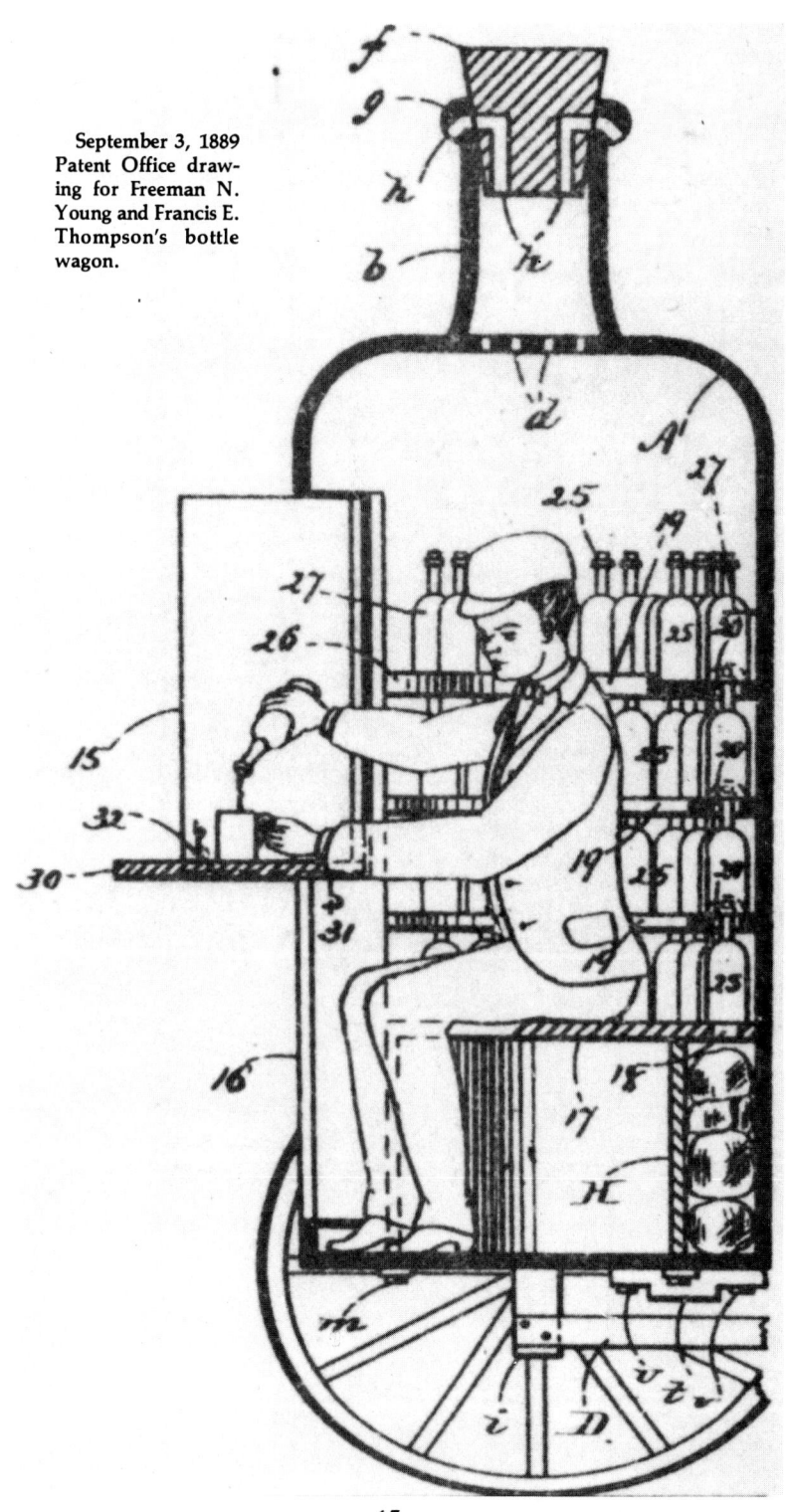

September 3, 1889 Patent Office drawing for Freeman N. Young and Francis E. Thompson's bottle wagon.

The Moxie Bottle Wagon as shown in an early photograph, possibly taken in the summer of 1886. The young lad shown to the left in front of the wagon wheel is Harry A. Thompson, while his brother Francis Edward Thompson is seated on the right on the Bottle Wagon itself.

The Moxie Bottle Wagon made its first appearance in the streets of Lowell in the summer of 1886. It caught on, and before long many duplicates were to be seen in other Massachusetts towns. Bottle Wagons were used until about 1920, although their popularity faded after the introduction of the Horsemobile in 1916.

An enlargement from the preceding photograph shows Francis E. Thompson seated on the Moxie Bottle Wagon with a dog in his lap. The maiden with the sickle or scythe was derived from the label used on Moxie bottles.

Above: This petite Moxie Bottle Wagon could be drawn by hand or by a pony. Only a few such small units were made.

Left: An 1898 advertisement for Moxie Nerve Food as it appeared in the "Cycling Courier," of Waltham, Massachusetts.

Below: The original Moxie Nerve Food bottle label in use in the summer of 1885. The Lieut. Moxie legend had not yet been used.

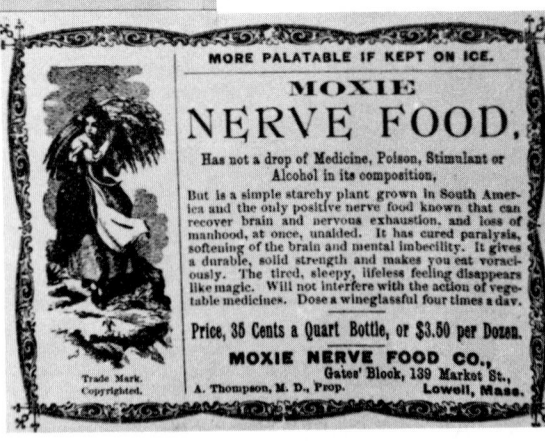

the beverage was sold at 5c per glass. Mr. Young went into partnership with another young man [Francis E. Thompson], and before long they were selling two-thirds of the total output of Moxie. They were then taken into partnership and decided to push Moxie for all it was worth.

" 'We first advertised it in Boston,' said Mr. Young in reply to a question, 'and it was not long before we got Moxie into every drugstore, hotel and saloon in the city. Moxie is a nerve food and invigorator as well as a wholesome summer drink. It became popular in saloons as a 'chaser' to be taken after liquor, much the same as soda and ginger ale are generally used. But it was found that the appetite for Moxie decreased the appetite for whiskey, and except as a separate temperance drink, its saloon sale as a 'chaser' was soon stopped by the saloon keepers themselves.'

" 'When you advertised, you used large spaces?'

" 'I don't believe in anything else. There is no use in doing a thing in halves. When we went to Albany I spent $2,000 in less than a week in advertising, first the words 'Moxie is Coming' and, afterwards, 'Moxie has Arrived.' We took Albany by storm...'

" '[What will you be spending] in New York for advertising purposes?'

" 'About $20,000 and we propose to lay it out in various ways. We want all the stores handling our goods to serve Moxie as it should be served, and then we are sure it will become popular.'

" 'What do you mean by the insinuation?'

" 'Moxie is sold in 26-ounce bottles at 25c retail. Some unscrupulous druggists have been selling a little Moxie and a lot of their own cheap syrup at 5c a glass. This has done us considerable harm, as it is not the nerve food we advertise. We cannot afford to have our goods monkeyed with by anybody. The genuine Moxie is poured from a Moxie bottle and is not adulterated or diluted in any way. We advertise straight goods that must be sold straight. We refuse to supply new dealers caught tampering with them.'

" 'Do you suffer from substitution?'

" 'Only in the way I have just mentioned. Some druggists have laughingly told me that they could make their own Moxie. The following of this assertion can be best understood when I tell you that some time ago we gave an expert analyst $100 to analyze Moxie thoroughly and report on the ingredients. After a few days he told us four out of the 18 ingredients, and that was near as he could come

Of all the two dozen or so versions made of the Moxie Bottle Wagon, the example shown on this page was one of the most rustic. Note that there is a "cork" in the top of the bottle.

to it! You may guess what chance there is for a passable substitute for Moxie.'

" 'The formula is a secret then?'

" 'Certainly. Even I do not know it. It is the prescription of Dr. Augustin Thompson, of Lowell, and as these testimonials will tell you, it has been wonderfully successful as a medicine in case of nervous disorders and partial paralysis, and yet it is a palatable, popular and wholesome drink for the hot weather. Its most remarkable property is that, unlike other so-called summer drinks, it really slakes the thirst instead of inducing it.'

" 'Besides newspaper advertising, what do you intend doing in New York?'

" 'I do not know as yet, but we shall try everything or anything that commends itself as good advertising. We have here seven cases of fancy 'outline' lithographs, just arrived from Germany, which we intend putting in stores where our goods are handled. Then we have six of our bottle-shaped wagons scattered throughout the city, and besides selling goods, they are splendid advertisements for us. We have one wagon for night use which is all lighted by electricity and has a very pretty and startling effect.' "

Freeman N. Young's later recollections notwithstanding, Moxie was advertised many different ways by mid 1886. The company records show numerous shipments of advertising materials, including lithographs in color, five-sheet posters, showcards and the like. Some of these were produced in formidable quantities. For example, on March 15, 1886, G.W. Rines was shipped 30,000 circulars, and on the same date F.W. Sargent, Jr. was shipped 30 lithographs and posters and 34,500 circulars.

Moxie was bottled at many different locations. Ledgers show that labels were shipped to distributors to be affixed to bottles. For example, on March 8, 1886, J. McLeue, the Denver Moxie agent, was shipped 10 gallons of XX extract for $120, 10,000 labels for $2.50, 20 posters for $1.50, and 50 showcards for $1.50. The Denver enterprise had its own distinctive glass bottles, perhaps blown at Lyndeboro, New Hampshire (for most were of a clear, bright aqua glass similar to that used on Lowell bottles attributed to Lyndeboro for the 1885-1886 years). The Western Moxie Nerve Food Company, Chicago, also had its own bottles, and it may be that other distributors did as well. However, most distributors apparently affixed official Moxie labels to plain bottles (without raised lettering in the glass).

The Moxie Bottle Wagon at a fairground, late 19th century, as shown in a faded photograph. To the right on the ground are many wooden Moxie crates. Several people wait in line for the attendant within the bottle to dispense Moxie for a nickel a glass.

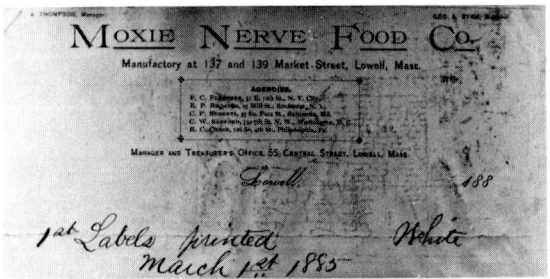

The billhead and first two lines of a record sheet from the 1880s. It is noted that the first Moxie Nerve Food labels were printed on white stock on March 1, 1885. The billhead, printed at a later date, notes that the Moxie Nerve Food Company manufactory was at 137 and 139 Market Street, Lowell, while the Manager and Treasurer's Office was at 55 Central Street in the same city. Agencies were listed as follows: F.C. Fletcher, 51 East 12th Street, New York, New York; E.P. Rhoades, 25 Mill Street, Rochester, New York; C.F. Roberts, 35 South Paca Street, Baltimore; C.W. Sanford, 732 7th Street N.W., Washington, D.C.; and R.C. Chase, 126 South 9th Street, Philadelphia.

The dramatic scope of the Moxie business is evidenced by transactions recorded in the company ledgers. On March 16, 1886, William Taylor, then traveling in Upstate New York (later to relocate to Lowell and to play a prominent part in Moxie history), was shipped 50 five-sheet posters, 35,000 "50 Circulars," and 100 dozen bottles of Moxie XX (at $3.60 per dozen). On March 19, C.W. Sanford was sent 25,000 circulars, while on March 29th John A. Wallis, Bangor, Maine, was sent 10,000 labels at 25c per thousand, 5,000 bottle wrappers (at $1.85 per thousand), 5,000 circulars, 200 posters, 200 window cards, and 100 large advertising sheets. On April 3rd, J. McLeue, the Denver agent, was sent 30 gallons of extract at $12 per gallon, five lithographs, and 200 streamers—all shipped via Chicago and Kansas City. On April 10th, Dr. H. Baer, Charleston, South Carolina, was shipped 775 dozen bottles of Moxie plus seven extra bottles for an invoice totaling $2,598.20. On April 12th F.C. Fletcher was sent 15,000 circulars and 100 streamers. On April 18th E.P. Rhoades was sent 50,000 Moxie XX labels at 25c per thousand and 50,000 Moxie XXX labels at 25c per thousand.

On June 12, 1886 the Western Moxie Nerve Food Company, Chicago, was shipped $6,000 worth of extract. On the same day James A. Hart, 1780 Notre Dame Street, Montreal, Quebec, was also sent the same amount of the substance. On June 14th G.F. Groskrantz, who was associated with J.B. McLeue (he of Denver distributorship fame), was sent 25,000 labels in Houston, Texas. On the same day the Elliott Temperance Society bought one dozen gallons of syrup.

By the summer of 1886, most sales were of regular Moxie, sometimes called Moxie X in the company ledgers, with frequent sales of Moxie XX and Moxie XXXX, punctuated by scattered sales of Moxie XXX.

Francis E. Thompson and Freeman N. Young, trading under the name of Thompson & Young, opened outlets in New York and Boston and bottled Moxie using extract shipped from Lowell. At the time their address was 184 Portland Street, Boston. Later, the addresses were 8 New Washington Street and 112 Union Street. Soon, most sales in Boston and New York were under control of that partnership. William Taylor continued his activities in Upstate New York, with shipments addressed to him in Rochester, Utica, Poughkeepsie, and Syracuse. By autumn 1886, bottled Moxie and Moxie extract was shipped to all areas of the United States as well as much of eastern Canada.

On September 21st a ledger entry recorded as "10 gallon bitter" was posted at $5 per gallon for shipment to William Taylor. Whether this refers to a product in the "bitters" category—a popular type of flavored alcohol—is conjectural. *For Bitters Only*, a book on the subject of bitters, by Carlyn Ring, lists a "Moxie Bitters" product, but no other information has been seen by the author.

The same day, September 21st, saw what was probably the first shipment of another Augustin Thompson brainchild: Moxie Lozenges. Backed by advertising, Moxie Lozenges quickly became popular. Shipments increased, and, as an example, on October 18th, 30 gross of Moxie Lozenges were shipped to F.C. Fletcher, New York City.

A brief commentary concerning Moxie activities of the period appears in *A History of the Soft Drink Industry*, by John J. Riley, 1958:

"During that same time period (1885) the well-known 'Moxie' was originated in bottles by the Moxie Nerve Food Company in the Boston area. Others among Boston's bottling plants getting started in those years were such firms as Fairbanks-Snyder Co., and Clark & Roberts. Then there were individuals, too, with their own shops, including Otis T. Neal, Jacob Worth, George W. Brigham, all of whom became prominently identified with the trade. S.T. Driscoll & Co. were active too, bottling 'Grape Nectar' and another item they called 'Boston Bitter Brown Beer.' A ginger ale named 'Cold Blast' was being produced by F.L. Hazelton. In 1890 there were five bottling plants in each of the cities of Lynn, Springfield, Worcester, Lowell... By 1900 there were 129 soda water bottlers in Massachusetts. Moxie in the northeast was another example of a popular innovation."

The same text noted that Coca-Cola, first produced by Dr. John S. Pemberton in Atlanta in 1886, was first bottled in 1894, "but bottling generally started under a franchise-contract with Benjamin F. Thomas and Joseph P. Whitehead, Chattanooga, in 1899... By 1904 there were 123 plants authorized to bottle Coca-Cola." It was further noted that Hires Root Beer, sold for a long time in extract form for home use, was first bottled in Philadelphia about 1897, and the Pepsi-Cola Company was organized in North Carolina in 1903.

The activities of the Coca-Cola Company were viewed as competitive, and in later years the principals of Moxie carefully clipped newspaper and magazine articles that indicated the growth of Coca-Cola sales or, particularly, pointed to the deleterious effects of cocaine, once a Coca-Cola ingredient. One article related that each morning in Atlanta large crowds assembled at the drugstores so that

Several dozen Moxie Bottle Wagons were built over the years. This view from the 1890s shows a uniformed attendant dispensing the beverage for a nickel per glass in front of the Boston Post Office.

This early tintype shows a reversed image of a Moxie Tricycle
Bottle Wagon, a very rare type of conveyance. The text on the
"bottle" reads: "MOXIE— The Best Drink for Bicyclists and Every
Body Else." The photograph probably dates from the 1890s.

each person could get his daily "fix" of Coca-Cola to give him energy for the day. Another article observed that the caffeine in Coca-Cola was known to cause insanity, particularly among those in the South who drank vast amounts of the beverage. Moxie never contained coca or cocaine, and in the early years caffeine was not an ingredient either.

In January 1888 the Circuit Court of the United States, District of Massachusetts, held hearings on an action filed by The Moxie Nerve Food Company against eight defendants who were selling Moxie imitations or other preparations bearing the name "nerve food." The decision was rendered that Moxie had the right to use the words "nerve food" in connection with a beverage. Although other products had used the nerve food term earlier, they were not beverages. Moxie exploited this extensively in later advertising.

In 1926 Moxie put out a brochure titled *1884 Moxie 1926*, which, curiously, mentioned in the text that *1885* was the date of inception of the beverage. However, by 1926 the 1884 date had crept into scattered advertising as well. An interview with Frank M. Archer, then vice-president of the firm, was quoted:

"Our Moxie trademark is, I think, the oldest soft drink trademark in use today. It was registered in 1885, when we were a new concern with a new product. It took only two years for the pirates to discover us. We brought the very first suit on a soft drink registered trademark in 1887 against a gentleman in Texas, who flattered us by imitating our goods and putting his concoction out under our mark and in a bottle like ours."

Counterfeiting reared its ugly head in several ways. Druggists would compound their own syrup, perhaps using a formula published in *The Druggists Circular and Chemical Gazette* or another trade publication, then when Moxie was called for, something else would be served. Others were more creative and counterfeited Moxie labels to put on a falsely bottled product. Still others contrived names (such as Noxie) that were imitative of Moxie.

On August 8, 1887, The Moxie Nerve Food Company printed an announcement that official Moxie dealers would be provided with a framed certificate stating that they were offering Moxie Nerve Food directly from the Lowell factory. On April 1, 1888, the following was published:

"NOTICE TO THE TRADE—To protect ourselves and the public against imitations and counterfeits, 'genuine Moxie Nerve Food' in the future will have a label over the cork of each bottle printed in red and black ink, with the signature of Augustin Thompson, M.D.,

MOXIE

PRICE LIST FOR 1887.

To Our Patrons:

Gentlemen:—Constantly appearing imitations of our goods, sold at the soda fountains, has caused us to substitute our XXXX and Syrup with a much stronger article called Triple Extract Moxie Syrup. This is three times as strong as the old syrup. While it gives us a very small margin, we hope dealers will use it instead of pushing us to the law for protection. They can make $46.50 above all, on a case of this at 5 cents a glass, which is better than can be done on a counterfeit.

PRICES.

X Moxie, $2.90 per case, $2.75 in gross lots.

XX Moxie, $4.00 per case, $3.80 in gross lots.

Triple Extract Moxie Syrup, $8.00 per case, ~~or $3.50 per gallon~~.

Ten per cent. off to jobbers, freight free, who take five gross lots, two per cent. additional for cash. All goods sold on the rebate plan.

MOXIE NERVE FOOD CO.,

21 Branch Street,

Lowell, Mass.

This 1887 price list, issued two years after the initial introduction of Moxie Nerve Food, reflects the changing nature of the Moxie product. In following years, many different sizes, strengths, and title variations were tried. Counterfeiting was a continuing problem, and the above advertisement appeals to the soda fountain owner's sense of profit, rather than to his honesty.

and his vignette thereon. All genuine Moxie has this label. It is forgery and imprisonment to counterfeit. And goods which are represented the same as ours are frauds unless they bear the name Moxie and have this label over the cork bearing the name of Augustin Thompson, M.D."

Around the same time, regular Moxie retailed at 35c a bottle or $2.95 per dozen, while Moxie XX sold for 50c a bottle or $4 a dozen. Small bottles of Moxie syrup were available at 75c each, or $6 a dozen.

A strange lawsuit involving Dr. Thompson occurred in 1888, was tried in the courts, appealed, and was subsequently reported in the December 1888 issue of *The Druggists Circular and Chemical Gazette:*

"NERVE FOOD PROFITS. Dr. Augustin Thompson, of Lowell, Massachusetts, was recently a defendant in a lawsuit brought by Mrs. Myra Beals for $30,000 damages. Dr. Thompson was accused of alienating Mrs. Beals' husband's affections. The trial was quite interesting, and resulted in a verdict against the doctor for the full amount, $30,000. Dr. Thompson immediately appealed to the Superior Court, which promptly refused to set aside the verdict.

"Dr. Thompson was formerly a homeopathic physician in Lowell, but since his romantic meeting with the late Lieut. Macksey or Moxie, which was reported some time ago in the Circular, he has been largely engaged in the manufacture of the Moxie Nerve Food. The value of the great discovery of the now-celebrated Macksey or Moxie is best shown by the fact that Dr. Thompson testified in the above trial that his yearly income was over one hundred thousand dollars."

The case eventually reached the Massachusetts Supreme Judicial Court, where it was argued in early 1889. Court testimony revealed that when Mira (*sic*) was a single girl in the early 1880s, Augustin Thompson "had lent [to her], and expended on her behalf, various sums of money for the purpose of educating her for the stage, and in supporting her while fitting her for that profession, in taking care of her when ill and in sending her to the South for the benefit of her health."

Mira subsequently married James H. Beals, who was described as "a man of wealth and social position." Upon learning of this, Thompson sought to recover $2,882 from Mira, stating that this was only a part of the approximately $4,000 he had "loaned" to her. Mira refused to pay.

Subsequently, Thompson sent a series of letters to her husband, one of which stated:

The Great Remedy for Nervous and Mental Exhaustion !

OFFICE OF

MOXIE NERVE FOOD COMPANY,

137 & 139 MARKET ST., LOWELL, MASS.

AGENCIES: F. C. Fletcher, 51 East 12th Streets, New York; C. F. Roberts, 35 So. Paca Street, Baltimore, Md.; E. P. Rhoades, Rochester, N. Y.; Wm. Taylor, Poughkeepsie, N. Y.; G. W. Rines, Jacksonville, Fla.; Dr. H. Baer, 133 Meeting Street, Charleston, S. C.; R. C. Chase, 126 South 9th Street, Philadelphia, Penn.

All Bills Payable at the Lowell Office.

——◄•►——

Rules for Jobbers.

RULE 1.   The price of Moxie Nerve Food in 25 dozen lots, freight paid, will be as follows: X Moxie, $2.60 per doz.; XX Moxie, $3.60 per doz.; XXXX Moxie, for soda fountains and bar-rooms, $4.00 per doz.; Moxie Syrup, $6.00 per doz.   2 per cent. off for cash.

RULE 2.   Jobbers will wholesale X Moxie for $2.90 per doz.; XX Moxie for $4.00 per doz.; XXXX Moxie for $5.00 per doz.; and Moxie Syrup for $7.00 per doz.

RULE 3.   Jobbers who sell a retailer one gross at one sale, may make a discount of 15 cents per dozen on X Moxie, 20 cts. per doz. on XX Moxie, 50 cts. per doz. on XXXX Moxie, and 50 cts. per doz. on Moxie Syrup

RULE 4.   Jobbers will be required not to break or cut these prices, except under the conditions of rule 3.

RULE 5.   Orders will be declined when it is known that a dealer refuses to abide by the above regulations.

AUGUSTIN THOMPSON, M. D.,

Gen. Manager Moxie Nerve Food Co.,

LOWELL, MASS.

Various types of Moxie are featured in this early price list distributed to jobbers and agents.

"Rumors came to me from Boston of her intended marriage to someone... The object all around seemed to be to have the intended marriage concealed until it should transpire. I did not interfere, as I had no disposition to do so, after I learned that she would marry great wealth, as I saw a chance to recover my loans. I sent Mira a bill of all she has borrowed, and of bills paid by her direction. I also sent a note covering the amount, saying that she could sign and return the note, and have time enough to pay gradually from her allowances from you. She replied with the most unreasonable, insulting letter a woman could write, refusing to pay a cent. This after she had written me over and over again of her intention to pay it when able. I have her private letters asking for the largest portion of the money, and acknowledging its date of receipt. I can prove the account easy enough, but I do not wish to drag her private business and letters in to a court of law, where evidence and her letters would tend to show her an adventuress, swindler, and obtaining money under false pretenses... It would take very much provocation to make me do anything to injure her, but I shall have my debt. If she was poor I would never ask it. Under the circumstances, I can see but one way for me, i.e., to go to the courts, prove the account and agreement by her private letters in my possession, get an execution, and wait until she comes in possession of property that can be levied upon. Aside from the insulting violation of my rights in this manner, Mira, seemingly as an excuse for her treatment of me, has lately accused me to her friends of a dishonorable act, which I can disprove by her letters. I have written to undo the wrong, or I should communicate the matter to you. I shall certainly exact reparation. It will be better for her reputation in Boston to do right by me.. I do not ask you pay her debts, but to use your influence to have her do right, and not provoke me to take measures that will scandalize her in Boston and in Lowell... I have drawn this as mildly as the circumstances will allow, for I do not want you to think I am threatening to obtain money. I have plenty, and an income of $9,000 (sic) a year. Mira has insulted and betrayed my confidence shamefully...

"I must leave Mira as partially insane, for I believe from my heart she is one of the purest girls I ever knew. She is a gem of the first water when she is herself. Her brother here believes as I do, that she may be. I have loved Mira as if she was my own child, and I would strike down any man who would defame her. In this matter I can hardly believe the evidence of my own senses. I do not understand it. She talks rational enough. I have not presented her with a bill of two-thirds I have paid out for her... You may show

Above: In 1907 a wooden watering trough with a Moxie sign on its side was a fixture along East Boothbay Road in Boothbay Harbor, Maine.

Below: One of the earliest public displays of Moxie outdoor advertising is shown in the multiple "MOXIE" signs in this photograph taken on August 29, 1889 on Kennebec Street, Portland, Maine, "near the old stove foundry." The Pettengill Pickle Factory is in the background.

and vicinity will have 150,000 posters and lithographs, and other cities in like proportions. Our own teams will deliver to the retail trade in all the large cities and pick up the empty bottles and cases and pay you for them.

"Beverage Moxie, per case of 12 26-ounce bottles, wholesale $2.10. We return to you for the empty bottles and case 60c, a net cost of contents of a case to the trade $1.50.

"It is the only known article that will restore loss of sexual strength without reaction. We challenge the world at this point. If made a common use of it, it will prevent injury from excesses.

"We can produce a statement signed by over 50,000 people, that they consider it the most luscious and useful beverage ever put on the market. The genuine has Dr. Thompson's vignette and picture on the label pasted across the cork. Headquarters: Lowell, Mass., 21 Branch Street (General Office); Boston, Mass., 8 New Washington Street; New York City, Merritt's Hotel, 60 East 10th Street."

Around this time, Thompson resumed his private medical practice. In 1889 he advertised as a surgeon and homeopathic physician with offices at 14 Central Street, Lowell, stating that he normally was at his office from 7 to 9 a.m. and again from 1 to 3 p.m. and 7 to 9 p.m. "I can be called by telephone at any time in the night by waking the boy at the Central Office, Shattuck's Block, 36 Central Street."

Living as a boarder at Thompson's residence at 16 Varney Street was William A. Taylor, who for the preceding several years had been an active Moxie agent in Upstate New York. On January 29, 1889, Augustin Thompson entered into an arrangement with Taylor, trading as William Taylor & Company, to become lessees of The Moxie Nerve Food Company for the business within Massachusetts, with a special arrangement providing for the continuation of Thompson & Young as Boston agents. A licensing fee of $5,000 per year was paid to Thompson, while a lump-sum payment was given to George A. Byam, treasurer of the earlier company.

William Taylor, 68 years of age (he was born in New Hampshire in April 1820), became president of the company bearing his name. George A. Byam was named as treasurer, while Augustin Thompson occupied the office of general manager. An 1889 Lowell directory noted that the firm employed 50 people and owned five horses. To meet increased demands, the Highland Skating Rink property, with 19,060 square feet, was purchased, providing the capacity of filling 30,000 bottles per day. In addition to the beverage, Moxie Lozenges, also called Moxie Medicated Lozenges, were manufactured "from the nerve food." During the first year Taylor paid himself a salary of $1,200.

Various Lowell addresses were occupied during the late 1880s, including 21 Branch Street (office and manufactory), 137 and 139 Market Street (factory), 55 Central Street (offices of manager and treasurer), and the main seat of activity for William Taylor & Co., 398 Middlesex Street.

The reason for the transfer of certain Moxie business to William Taylor & Co. can only be surmised. Perhaps Thompson wanted to devote himself to other interests. At the time he was engaged in writing a lengthy book manuscript and, ever the entrepreneur, he was set to formulate several new proprietary medical products and to engage in expansion of Moxie beyond Massachusetts. A new venture was announced early in 1890:

"MOXIE, now the great money maker of the United States. No part of the eastern company can be bought for twice the face value of its stock.

"On the first day of January 1890, all the territory of the United States west of the Alleghanies was sold to the Western Moxie Nerve Food Company. Dr. Augustin Thompson will manage it and leave the eastern company to his sons. It requires all the loose capital of the eastern company to handle it, so fast does its business grow, and none can be shared with the West. The eastern company has put $12,000 into the western company and has started 40 cities, with headquarters at 1002 North Broadway, St. Louis.

"The goodwill of the company is now worth $50,000 because it is earning 8% on that. It is believed by western men that its stock will be at par in three years. It is stocked at $500,000, and owes nothing, all that is in it belongs to the stockholders or company. Dr. Thompson as immediate manager and treasurer will take no salary until the stock is at par. Money paid for stock will be loaned to the company without interest until the stock is at par and will then be drawn out as the property of The Moxie Nerve Food Company of New England that will retain a controlling interest. $200,000 of the western stock will be sold for half its face to do business. Buyers of stock will be asked to furnish an assistant manager. When at par the company will be organized in each state and sold out. The most promising scheme in legitimate business known.

"A. Thompson, M.D., treasurer and manager, 36 Varney Street [street number changed from 16 to 36 Varney Street], Lowell, Massachusetts."

MOXIE.

Now the great money maker of the United States.

No part of the Eastern Co, can be bought for twice the face value of its stock.

On the first day of Jan. 1890, all the territory of the U. S. west of the Alleghanies was sold to the Western Moxie Nerve Food Co. Dr. A. Thompson will manage it and leave the Eastern Co. to his sons. It requires all the loose capital of the Eastern Co. to handle it, so fast does its business grow, and none can be shared with the west. The Eastern Co. has put $12,000.00 into the Western Co. and have started 40 cities, with headquarteas at 1002 N. Broadway, St. Louis.

The good will of the Co. is now worth $50,000.00 because it is earning 8 per cent. on that. It is beleived by western men that its stock will be at par in three years. It is stocked at $500,000.00, it owes nothing, all that is in it belongs to the stockholders or Co. Dr. Thompson as immediate manager and treasurer will take no salary until the stock is at par. Money paid for stock will be loaned to the Co. without interest until the stock is at par and will then be drawn out as the property of the Moxie Nerve Food Co. of New England, that will retain a controlling interest. $200,000.00 of the Western stock will be sold for half its face to do its business.

Buyers of stock will be asked to furnish an asst. manager. When at par a company will be organized in each state and sold out. The most promising scheme in legitimate business known.

A. THOMPSON M, D.

Treasurer and Manager,

36 Varney St. Lowell, Mass.

Ever the entrepreneur, Dr. Augustin Thompson solicits prospective investors to participate in the establishment of the Western Moxie Nerve Food Company, 1002 North Broadway, St. Louis, noting that Thompson will personally manage it, leaving the eastern activities to his sons.

Thompson was never one to be modest, and his statement that the proposed investment was "the most promising scheme in legitimate business known" is reflective of this.

MOXIE LOZENGES
or Nervousness, Nervous
and mental exhaustion.

epared by Lowell Lozenge Co.,
79 Central Street,
Lowell, Mass.

or insanity, while it is neither medicine, stimulant nor tonic.
Prof. Jones of Kansas City Medical College, the finest chemist in America, after a careful examination, says it is harmless, and a very fine nerve remedy. It is generally believed it has saved 225,000 drunkards, and 389,000 nervous
wrecks during the last year. It is on sale everywhere for
35 and 50 cents a quart bottle. Any druggist or grocer in
America can obtain it for you. We make the above esti-
         on the size of sale and reports in Lowell. We warn
         blic against the thousands of unprincipled liquor
         and druggists who are selling a bogus thing fla-
         tle like ours, when a drinking customer asks for
         ne are putting their vile stuff into our old bot-
         d suspicion. Don't buy of such men: go to a
         ler. We are hunting such vermin with de-
         See that Moxie is on you

Moxie Lozenges, also
called Medicated Moxie
Lozenges, were a popular
product of the Moxie Nerve
Food Company in Lowell
during the 1880s and early
1890s. On this page are
shown two different box
styles, the lower with an
advertisement for the Moxie beverage pasted on the
long sides and back (the
panel from the back is shown
above).

William Taylor & Co. continued to advertise Moxie aggressively, stating its medicinal properties. To Moxie were added several other products, including one with an unspecified name advertised as follows:

"A REVOLUTION IN THE TREATMENT OF GONORRHEA AND SYPHILIS—NO MORE BONE ROTTING MERCURY OR NASTY COPAIVA. A harmless and much more effective remedy discovered in France, that will not foul your breath, destroy your teeth, nor leave a constitutional taint of these diseases to undermine your constitution and make your old age miserable.

"During the last French Imperial Regime the court physician gave a citizen a prescription for a very painful dyspepsia. It not only cured this, but it completely removed an old case of gleet and constitutional syphilis of many years standing. He was so much impressed with the result, that he at once placed the prescription on the market as a patent medicine, when he soon learned that it was equally as good for catarrh, burns, cuts, bruises, humors, old ulcers, erysipelas, rheumatism, sprains and kidney diseases. It soon became a household remedy throughout France, and has obtained a large sale in other parts of Europe... It has secured three cases of Bright's disease advanced to the stage of albumenurian epithetial casts, but will not cure a full-fledged case.

"For use in the treatment of syphilitic ulcers, take a teaspoonful and 10 parts of cold soft water three times a day... For treatment of gonorrhea, take a teaspoonful and 10 parts of water four times a day... For sale by all druggists. Price $1 per bottle, or six bottles for $5. William Taylor & Co., 398 Middlesex Street, Lowell, Mass. Sole Proprietors in North America."

William Taylor continued the sale of Moxie Lozenges, also called Moxie Nerve Food Lozenges and Moxie Medicated Lozenges. An early advertisement for these noted:

"There is an old physician in The Moxie Nerve Food Company [presumably Thompson] who has long been in the habit of giving his patrons a little harmless remedy that has been found to prevent colds after a severe exposure. He has persuaded the company to make a cheap lozenge from the nerve food and medicate it with this. They are to sell a package of 36 for 10c, which will be a popular price... When coming from an overheated hall into the cold air, or after exposure to drafts, or getting wet, one on the tongue prevents a cold, and, what is better, does not render you more liable to a cold after taking it. This will prevent a multitude of pneumonias, rheumatisms, fevers, etc. and save the loss of much time and expenditure of money.

All the jobbers, druggists, and confectioners have them. For nervous prostration the bottled food is best. Keep a few Lozenges in your vest pocket for use, and you are safe under any severe exposure."

A 1892 advertisement gave additional information:

"MOXIE NERVE FOOD LOZENGES. These are the famous Moxie, condensed in sugar. They are held to be more easily taken along, while on a journey, or we have the same in bottles. Price, Lozenges 10c per two-ounce package. Bottles 16 ounces 50c, three pounds $1. For sale everywhere, or by mail or express. Most people prefer the beverage Moxie, because it is such a luxury. Priced the same in relative quantities. William Taylor & Co., Lowell, Mass., Proprietors."

Testimonials were a popular way of promoting patent medicines in the early 1890s. Indeed, the yearly almanacs of J.C. Ayer and a host of other proprietors were largely filled with statements from satisfied patrons. Never mind that most patients would have recovered anyway with the normal passage of time. Success was attributed to The Cure, whatever it may have been—Drake's Plantation Bitters, Ayer's Sarsaparilla, or one of a thousand others. The mysterious asparagus-like, or turnip-tasting, or sugar cane-like plant used in Moxie, still not identified, was mentioned in passing in a circa 1892 reference to competitors:

"[Moxie] does not contain any more alcohol than bread or ice cream, and is the richest nerve nutrition ever put upon the market. We offer any chemist or other person $5,000 if they can find it contains any opium, laudanum, morphine, cocoa [coca], cocaine, arsenic, strychnine, iron, nux-vomica, quinine, or any other element more deleterious than common bitterroot and wintergreen, used in the flavoring; and when other dealers say their bogus nerve foods are the same thing, it is false in every particular, except an imitation of its flavoring. We hereby agree to give any person $10,000 if they can show their preparations contain any Moxie, or if they can produce any of the plant, or its beneficial results."

So far as is known, "the plant" remained mysterious, and the $10,000 was never claimed. It seems, at least to the present author, that if the miraculous plant indeed existed, and was common in South America (as Lieut. Macksey is stated to have said), and considering the various agents employed in importing the plant, not to overlook those handling it in the Moxie factory, that someone would have secured a specimen and claimed the reward had such a plant not been fictitious. After all, $10,000 was quite an incentive in 1892, for

We
Just Love

MOXIE

Many varieties of colorfully lithographed cardboard cut-outs were imported from Germany by The Moxie Nerve Food Company of New England during the 1890s. Typically, these measure about 10 inches high and are fitted with a folding cardboard easel appendage on the back, such stand-up mechanism bearing the patent date 1892. A representative example is shown here. These found their ideal use on soda fountain and restaurant counters.

it was equal to more than 10 years' salary for a typical executive and nearly 20 years' wages for a factory worker!

Winfield S. Tucker, of the Navy, was stricken with progressive paralysis and insanity on board ship in the China seas, according to a Moxie advertisement of this period. He was brought home and sent to the Massachusetts General Hospital. After four and one-half months he was sent home, a helpless imbecile, to die. After being helpless three and one-half years, failing meantime, Moxie finally recovered him in mind and body in two months, a testimonial proclaimed. Other reports were as glowing:

"My daughter was a long time speechless from complete paralysis of the left side. Moxie completely restored her. —Louis Berger, 953 Folsom Street, San Francisco. Sworn to before Justice of the Peace.

"Miss May Fletcher, 254 Merrimack Street, Lowell, Mass., was for years nearly blind from a severe concussion of the brain. Moxie recovered her sight and removed all the bad effects from the injury in two weeks.

"Angus Bell, of 110 Cross Street, Lowell, Mass., was a helpless, emaciated paralytic, given up by the doctors, and had to be attended to like a baby for 22 months. The Moxie Nerve Food recovered him in two and a half months, and he has been at hard muscular labor for over three years.

"A 12-year old daughter of John Nicholson, rear of No. 103 Madison Street, Malden, Mass., was a long time utterly helpless and speechless from general paralysis, old case. The Moxie Nerve Food fed her helpless limbs rapidly to life, and she is now a healthy, romping schoolgirl, with a glib tongue in her head. Her recovery, by using the Moxie, caused the wildest excitement, and for two weeks after their house was thronged with crowds from far and near, who came to see the case [obviously, for some, Moxie was equal to the Second Coming!].

"Col. W.H. Sinclair, president of the Great Railway, says he believes a man can do an almost incredible amount of overwork while taking Moxie, and not break down.

" 'I use Moxie in my family and practice. I find all that is claimed for it to be true. I believe it to be harmless, and am surprised at the remarkable results obtained.' —W.G. Hawkes, M.D. Note—Dr. Hawkes is a leading professor in one of the great colleges in the Northwest and a leading physician in Chicago. He resides at 241 Dearborn Avenue, Chicago, Illinois. His statement is voluntary."

"I Just Love Moxie," a popular advertising theme of
the period, is shown on this lithographed cardboard cut-
out produced in Germany in the mid-1890s.

THE FAMOUS BEVERAGE

MOXIE
NERVE FOOD.

A Little Insignificant Weed Revolutionizing the Habits of the World. The Wild Period of Dissipation, Overwork, Mental Exhaustion and Broken Constitutions finds a Recovering, Mending Support. Weakly Nervous Women do Double Work with Less Fatigue on 3 cent's worth per Day. To Sustain Nervous, Weakly Women, it is Incomparable.

It takes the place of stimulants without harm or reaction. Feeds the nerves to a remarkable, durable vigor, and never loses its effect, more than other food, has recovered a host of helpless cases of paralysis; takes the tired, nervous feeling from weakly women, and the overworked in an hour, without stimulation or reaction; stops the after effect from liquors and tobacco at once, removing their odor from the breath in a few seconds; makes the terrible thirst from summer heat quicker and for a longer time than anything ever before discovered. It does not contain any more alcohol than bread or ice cream, and is the richest nerve nutrition ever put upon the market. We offer any chemist or other person five thousand dollars if they can find it contains any opium, laudanum, morphine, cocoa, cocaine, arsenic, strychnine, iron, nux-vomica, quinine or any other element more deleterious than common bitter root and wintergreen, used in the flavoring; and when other dealers say their bogus nerve foods are the same thing, it is false in every particular, except an imitation of its flavoring. We hereby agree to give any person $10,000 if they can show their preparations contains any Moxie, or if they can produce any of the plant, or its beneficial results.

Winfield S. Tucker, of the navy, was stricken with progressive paralysis and insanity on board ship in the China seas. He was brought home and sent to the Mass. Gen. Hospital. After four and one-half months he was sent home, a helpless imbecile, to die. After being helpless three and one-half years, failing meantime, Moxie fully recovered him in mind and body in two months.

My daughter was a long time speechless from complete paralysis of the left side. Moxie completely restored her. —Louis Berger, 80 Folsom street, San Francisco. Sworn to before Justice of the Peace.

Miss May Fletcher, 254 Merrimack street, Lowell, Mass., was for years partly blind from a severe concussion of the brain. Moxie recovered her eyesight and removed all the bad effects from the injury in two weeks.

WE CHALLENGE THE WORLD TO SHOW RESULTS LIKE THIS

Angus Bell, of 110 Cross street, Lowell, Mass., was a helpless, emaciated paralytic given up by the doctors, and had to be attended to like a baby for 22 months. The Moxie Nerve Food recovered him in 2½ months, and he has been at hard, muscular labor over 3 years.

THE HISTORY OF THE WORLD CANNOT MATCH IT.

A 12-year-old daughter of John Nicholson, rear of No. 103 Madison street, Malden, Mass., was a long time utterly helpless and speechless from general paralysis, old case. The Moxie Nerve Food fed her helpless limbs rapidly to life, and she is now a healthy, romping school girl, with a glib tongue in her head. Her recovery, by using the Moxie, caused the wildest excitement, and for two weeks after their house was thronged with crowds from far and near, who came to see the case.

Col. W. H. Sinclair, president of a great railway, says he believes a man can do an almost incredible amount of overwork while taking Moxie, and not break down. Mrs. A. Carnahan says the same, and Mrs. D. H. Bryan says, it makes me feel so rested after a hard day, when I take a dose late in the afternoon. Mrs. D. H. Villas says, I was so nervous I could not sleep at night for years, or think well. Now after a wine-glass full of Moxie in the evening, it steadies my nerves, and I sleep so sweet, and feel so rested and strong in the morning it surprises me.

I use Moxie regularly in my family and practice, I find all that is claimed for it to be true. I believe it to be harmless, and am surprised at the remarkable results obtained.—W. G. Hawkes, M. D. Note—Dr. Hawkes is a leading professor in one of the great colleges in the Northwest, and a leading physician in Chicago. He resides at 201 Dearborn Ave., Chicago, Ill. His statement is voluntary.

Moxie is now used by the young city bloods to remove the effects from liquors and a night of dissipation. A tumbler full will break a recent intoxication in an hour.

Old men use Moxie the year round to keep their nervous systems strong enough to support the functions of the body, and mend up the break-down of a long business life.

Prof. Babcock, of Boston, and Prof. Wm. Jones, of Kansas City, both chemists of national reputation, as experts, made oath before the United States Courts, that they had examined the Moxie Nerve Food by analysis, and found it contained about the same proportion of alcohol as ice cream. Prof. Jones said he believed it to be a nerve food, and a remarkable and useful discovery.

A noted inventor in New York became insane from excessive study. Moxie recovered him at once.

Col. Bennett, the famous Philadelphia eight millionaire, says the Moxie saved my life from a hopeless condition. I intend to build a monument to it in Fairmount Park. To recover a broken constitution from a hard business life, I do not believe the world ever saw its equal. As a nerve nutrition, it is marvelous.

Judge Brewster, of the Supreme Court, speaks very highly of it, and says he uses it the year round, to support the hard wear of his judicial work.

Moxie is the best thing for tired, nervous, overworked people I ever saw. It makes you feel like a new person in half an hour.—Mrs. A. H. Stevens, Georgia.

FROM ELEANOR CARY, THE FAMOUS ACTRESS.

I was absolutely prostrated from acting the very heavy role of Isolene. The Moxie, my husband obtained from you, seemed to be just what I wanted. It has been of the greatest material benefit and fully sustains me. Sincerely, ELEANOR CARY.

If it can cure paralysis, what can it do for the overworked? Moxie is compounded from well-known flavors, and the richest, predigested nerve food ever discovered, by one of the most successful old physicians in New England. No one dissents from the opinion that it is the most valuable nerve food beverage ever invented. It is harmless as common food, and capable of sustaining the most intense brain and nerve wear. Neither a medicine or stimulant, it is taken by sick and well alike for nervous exhaustion. It will not cure paralysis caused by effusion, but will from malnutrition or overwear of the nervous system.

It requires sixteen manufactories to supply the gigantic call for it in the United States alone. It is a dollar article sold for 35 cents to get a large sale. Though it costs twice as much as dollar patent medicines, we sell it for 25 cents a bottle, or $2.00 per case of 12, twenty-six ounce bottles. Look out for imitations. The genuine has the vignette and signature of Augustin Thompson, M. D., on a black, red and white strip over the cork, and is turned directly into your glass by dealers and nothing added. Soda fountain syrup is withdrawn because of counterfeiting. For sale at Druggists, Confectioners, Grocers, Saloons, Hotels, and Fruit stands. Grocers will deliver it.

WM. TAYLOR & CO., Lessees Moxie Company.	**MOXIE NERVE FOOD CO.,** No. 21 Branch Street, Lowell, Mass.

Printed circa 1891-1892 by William Taylor & Company, makers of the Moxie product at the time, this small advertising piece reproduces many testimonials. It is related that Col. Bennett, a famous Philadelphia millionaire, said that "Moxie saved my life from a hopeless condition. I intend to build a monument to it in Fairmount Park." It is further told that Winfield S. Tucker, a Navy man, "was stricken with progressive paralysis and insanity on board ship in the China seas. He was brought home and sent to the Massachusetts General Hospital. After four and one-half months he was sent home, a helpless imbecile, to die. After being helpless three and one-half years, failing meantime, Moxie fully recovered him in mind and body in two months."

In later years the patent medicine angle was dropped from Moxie advertising, and Moxie Nerve Food became simply Moxie, a refreshing beverage.

During the early 1890s, Augustin Thompson spent much time in St. Louis at the Western Moxie Nerve Food Company offices at 1002 North Broadway. His 36 Varney Street, Lowell address appeared in many advertisements and served as a shipping depot for a variety of remedies, including Family Safeguard or Moxie Catarrh Cure, Sunbeam (a remedy for alcohol consumption), Moxie Lozenges, and J.S.Q. Nerve Food.

Advertising for the Family Safeguard noted:

"25c will keep a doctor out of the house most of the year. Carry it in your vest pocket, always ready. During exposures in drafts, wet or sudden changes, dissolve a little harmless pellet on the tongue and you are safe from a cold, pneumonia, or rheumatism. One trial will settle it... Its popularity in the East is unbounded. Positive proof with each package of high-class scientific origin, harmless character, that it did not lose a single case of pneumonia in 20 years of the largest medical practice in New England.

"25c prevents 525 colds after exposure. 25c cures eight well-settled colds. 25c cures 20 hard, painful cold coughs. 25c breaks up 26 threatened pneumonias. 25c treats eight cases of pneumonia successfully. 25c breaks 52 threatened fevers. 25c breaks 10 attacks of acute rheumatism. 25c will treat a rheumatic fever successfully. 25c gives much comfort to incurable cases.

"One of the most noted physicians in the United States used this in his practice 20 years and gave it to the public on his retiring... To avoid the counterfeiters this will be sold only by mail. Wrap a quarter in paper, seal it before the postmaster, and we will be responsible for its safety. FAMILY SAFEGUARD, 1002 North Broadway, St. Louis, Mo."

The Family Safeguard or Moxie Catarrh Cure was sold by many agents. It could be ordered from William Taylor & Co. in Lowell as well as from Thompson at his Varney Street address, Thompson & Young supplied it from their depot at 8 New Washington Street, Boston, and agencies in other cities were sources as well. Instructions for use were signed by Francis E. Thompson:

"INSTRUCTIONS FOR THE CATARRH CURE AND SAFEGUARD: Use the Catarrh Cure freely as you would a smelling bottle. And old catarrh, catarrhal and pervious headaches, deafness, cold in the head, and weak lungs go like magic.

"Melt five pellets from the Safeguard on your tongue before retiring and it will do away with the effects from exposure to colds and epidemic diseases during the day. If attacked with aching and fever

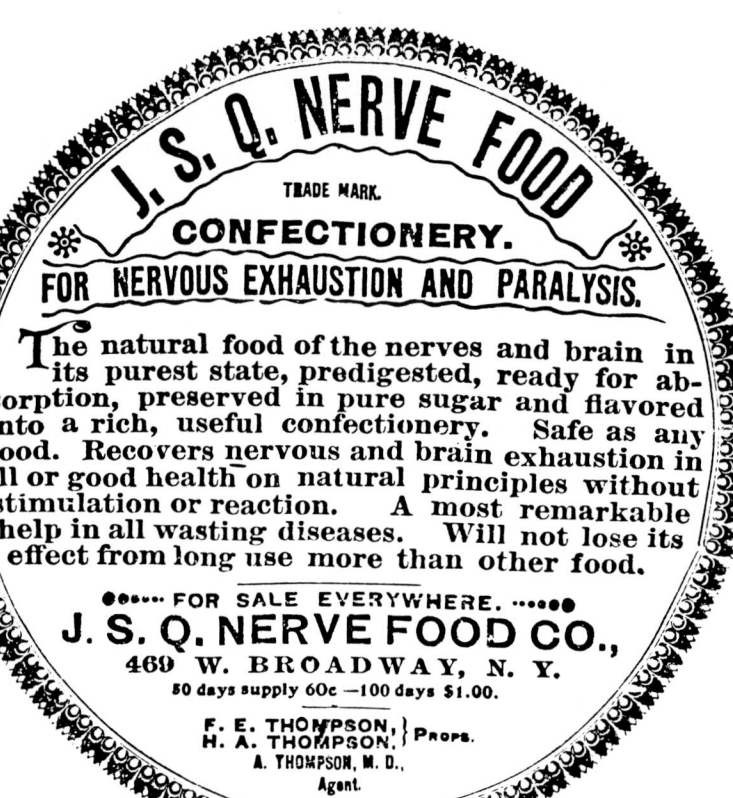

J.S.Q. Nerve Food, marketed during the 1890s, was an ephemeral Moxie derivative. In candy form, the essence of Moxie was offered as a cure for "nervous and brain exhaustion in ill or good health" and for "help in all wasting diseases." In an era in which claims were neither regulated nor checked by government agencies or anyone else, various patent medicine firms, those operated by the Thompsons included, vied to outdo each other in claims which a later generation would view as preposterous.

from a cold, or threatened with grippe, pneumonia, typhoid fever, or rheumatism, dissolve 30 pellets in half a tumbler of cold water. Dose, tablespoonful each half hour. It will break them at once. Both are harmless. F.E. THOMPSON, Proprietor, 8 New Washington Street, Boston, Mass."

Another advertisement noted:

"NEW NATURAL LAW DISCOVERED. A noted Massachusetts physician has discovered that certain combinations of non-poison medicines, when their odors are inhaled as a cologne, will prevent the effects of contagious disease miasmas floating in the air. His theory is, if disease miasmas attack that way, they ought to be cured that way. He prevents smallpox, scarlet fever, measles, diptheria, etc. by the inhaling of harmless odors of simples, capable of destroying the microbe of each individual contagion. Examination of the secretion of catarrh indicates that the irritation and inflammation originates from a microbe. He has made a rich, harmless cologne that obliterates them. The effects of smelling the odors clears the head and lungs of excretion and strengthens them wonderfully without any irritation or sneezing. A drop on your handkerchief will furnish effective odors for three days, taking the place of cologne, removes nervous headaches by clearing the membranes and stopping the cause of the irritation. The fluid is so simple it can be taken into the stomach without harm.

"The Moxie Company at Lowell, Massachusetts have bought this and call it the Moxie Catarrh Cure and Safeguard and sell it through the druggist or prepaid by mail. Price 25c, 50c, and $1. A little watch-shape bottle for your vest pocket."

Apparently, the Family Safeguard or Moxie Catarrh Cure was labeled in at least two locations, for surviving examples have been seen with imprints of William Taylor & Co., Lowell, as well as A. Thompson, St. Louis.

It may have been that the Moxie Catarrh Cure was inspired by Hahnemann's success a century earlier with administering tiny pellets of camphor to ward off or cure cholera, as widely cited in the annals of homeopathic medicine.

Although the good doctor occasionally enjoyed a glass of beer or a sip of champagne, he spent much time in efforts to cure alcoholism and to mitigate the effects of hard liquor. In St. Louis he created another brainchild, Sunbeam, also called Liberty's Sunbeam, which was advertised to the trade by the Sunbeam Company, Broadway and Washington Streets, St. Louis, such notices bearing the signature of A. Thompson, M.D., treasurer of the Western Moxie Nerve Food

This exhibit of F.A. Wheeler, a Moxie agent, probably dates from the 1890s. On the counter in front of the attendants are rows of Moxie bottles, an early style without the crown and seal. Handled glass mugs await customers. In the back are several tiers of Moxie bottles, some wrapped in protective paper.

Company. Apparently, Sunbeam was a medicated, concentrated Moxie syrup in one-ounce (available for $1.20 per dozen) and 32-ounce bottles, the latter priced at $1 and intended for use by soda fountains and saloons. The compound was intended to be added to soda water. Great plans were envisioned, for Thompson noted that "We shall establish agencies in all the large cities to deliver to you, to prevent counterfeiters from imposing upon you."

Advertisements were directed primarily to the saloon trade, with the novel proposition that by selling their customers Sunbeam, they could sell more liquor as well! A sample notice:

"You get from it all the effects of the Moxie. You may load up with the richest food, strong coffee and liquors, play the rounder, drink to your fill—following with a half ounce of the Sunbeam and a wineglass of ice or soda water you will never hear from them. You will awake in the morning and never feel that you had a night out. An ounce phial of it procured from a saloon will surprise you, while it as safe as sarsaparilla. The club men of the large eastern cities always buy the large bottle and take a phial of it in their vest pocket when they go out. With the assurance that Sunbeam will stop the ill effects after your customers are done drinking, they will drink much more and thereby increase your business..."

In the mid 1890s a similar message aimed at saloon keepers featured regular Moxie. A circular for the liquor trade was prepared, hinting at confidentiality and noting that the message furnished "some things we can't print in the papers." The text stated:

"The secret of our immense success came 10 years ago. Then a large number who had been physically ruined by a fast life told us that by the use of Moxie they had recovered the use of helpless limbs, and their sexual power came back within a few days; and their half-destroyed intellect returned to power; and from taking a glass of Moxie before starting out on a round of the saloons, they could drink twice the usual amount of liquor and not get intoxicated. After a big drunk it would remove the ill effect in from one to six hours; that after a night out, a glass before retiring and they would awake in the morning and never know from their feelings they had a night of it, but its greatest point was its ability to restore sexual power and hold it, even under abuse, because it is a nerve food and not a stimulant.

"The St. Louis saloon men discredited this claim, and we asked them to appoint a committee to examine St. Louis cases. They did; here's the report:

LIBERTY'S SUNBEAM.

I Bring Peace, Protection and Prosperity to Everyone

—AND—

Render the Saloons Unobjectionable.

The richest beverage ever made. Twice as profitable as soda drinks or beef, and conceded to be the most useful ever invented.

None genuine without this signature.

Augustin Thompson M.D.

$1.00 per Bottle. Six Bottles for $5.00

General Office, ST. LOUIS, MO.

Grand Complimentary Picnic

GIVEN BY THE

M·O·X·I·E

NERVE FOOD CO.

SUNDAY, AUGUST 14th, '98,

at HOEHN'S GROVE.

MOXIE gives double powers of endurance without stimulation or reaction, harmless as gruel; rich in useful results, yet does not contain any alcohol, medicine or poison. Its sales east of the Alleghanies during the last 12 years have doubled every 22 months. For sale everywhere by case, bottle or glass. 16c a bottle if bought by the case.

MOXIE CO.,

1002 NORTH BROADWAY.

Moxie Nerve Food Co., N. E.

A. THOMPSON, M. D., General Manager.

FACTORIES AND OFFICES AT

513 WASH STREET, St. Louis, Mo.

14 Charles Place, CHICAGO, ILL.
126 Plymouth Avenue, MINNEAPOLIS, MINN.
209 Market Street, PITTSBURG, PA.
21 Branch Street, LOWELL, MASS.
GENERAL OFFICE .... 68 Beverly St. .... BOSTON, MASS.

Telephone 2724.   CHAS. J. DONNELLY, St. Louis Agent.

Augustin Thompson's activities in St. Louis included promoting Sunbeam, a substance that was said to mitigate the effects of alcohol. A separate firm, the Sunbeam Company, was set up at the address of the Moxie Company.

Sunbeam Company,
St. Louis, Mo.

Address: SUNBEAM COMPANY, NO. 513 WASH STREET, ST. LOUIS, MISSOURI.

Or, General Delivery—New York, Philadelphia and Chicago.
Manchester, London and Glasgow, Great Britain.
Melbourne, Australia.

Sunbeam——

The richest, safest, and most useful Beverage ever invented.
Removes the secondary effects of Alcohol.
Prevents injury from excesses in Drinking.

For the terrible nerve weary from overwork ; nervous exhaustion from excesses ; and the terrible blue depression of the mind and want of appetite, and insomnia, it has no equal.

Some late 19th-century items from Augustin Thompson's scrapbook show various imprints of the St. Louis, Cleveland, and Chicago Moxie enterprises. Thompson took particular interest in the St. Louis entity and for a period of time personally managed it.

" 'We, the undersigned, declare that we were appointed a committee to examine the record of the Moxie Nerve Food beverage, and we find as fact that Moxie alone recovered Samuel Corey, 3130 Sheridan Avenue, who was helpless and hopelessly wrecked from the abuse of liquors for many years, though still drinking we now know he is a clerk in a large dry goods store, as well as ever.

" 'James H. Logan, 2703 Lafayette Avenue, was for three years helpless and mind wrecked, treated meantime by the most famous specialist in the world who said that no earthly thing could help him. Moxie recovered him within four weeks. Many other cases were proved before us, both men and women. We were surprised and now do not doubt their general claims. We ourselves have tried it with surprising results. It is harmless. It will break an intoxication in an hour—Bart Ready, 212 North Sixth Street, leading saloon proprietor of St. Louis; Albert A. Aal, 515 Olive Street, merchant known all over the world; W.A. Hobbs, 408 Commercial Building, a leading city officer for many years; Alphonso Lefko, 310 Union Trust Building, leading lawyer; S.M. Burke, northwest corner of Levee and Washington Street, saloon proprietor and great steamship man.'

"In its rebuilding the sexual power it does not act as a stimulant that leaves you worse than before, but is a food and holds you there if constantly used, until extreme old age. For nervousness and nervous exhaustion it is unexcelled. It pays a larger profit than beer. $10 worth under continuous use will last you a year and save your health from being wrecked while following a dissipated life... We will deliver it at your saloon with the finest team in the city for $2.10 per case of 12 26-ounce bottles... Moxie Nerve Food Company, 469 West Broadway, F.E. Thompson, treasurer and manager. General office, 68 Beverly, Boston."

Another advertisement directed toward saloon keepers followed a similar theme:

"HOW TO INCREASE THE PATRONAGE OF YOUR BAR AND SEND YOUR CUSTOMERS HOME PERFECTLY SOBER. When a customer begins to show signs of intoxication, give him a glass of Moxie. In a half hour he will be sober enough to take as much more liquor. One more glass as he leaves for home, and he will be sober before he has traveled six blocks, and awake in the morning with no feeling that he has had a night out. Moxie will not cure the liquor habit, but will stop the ill effect of liquors at once. It will mend the results of any kind of dissipation and restore lost sexual power and keep it. The best saloon men in the United States admit it to be the most useful thing for their business that has ever been invented.

CASTALLIAN
PRICE LIST.

TO THE RETAIL DRUG TRADE.

The last great discovery in the Rocky Mountains, that promises to find a sale next to the Moxie, is now ready for distribution from the General Agency—Geo. C. Goodwin & Co., 36 and 38 Hanover Street, Boston. This "Castallian" is now creating the most intense excitement in New York and the large western cities, from its ability to cure the hitherto incurable Bright's disease. It is to be advertised largely. Lay in a stock, for you will have calls for it at once.

Price to retail trade, $8.00 per dozen, 10 per cent. off to jobbers. Price to consumers, $1.00 per bottle, or six bottles for five dollars. 100 doses in each bottle.

GEO. C. GOODWIN & CO.,
38 Hanover Street, Boston,

GENERAL DISTRIBUTING AGENTS FOR NEW ENGLAND.

George C. Goodwin & Co., a leading drug and patent medicine wholesaler, introduced a "discovery" from the Rocky Mountains which it noted "promises to find a sale next to the Moxie," a product called Castallian. This was brought to the notice of the Moxie entrepreneurs, and after this date advertisements featuring Castallian were watchfully kept in a scrapbook at Moxie headquarters.

The sales are already over 500,000 cases per year after only eight years on the market."

What appears to have been a more serious attempt to work on the alcohol problem is related by an article in the Lowell *Daily News*, February 8th, 1895:

"DR. THOMPSON SHUNS SOCIETY AND POLITICS TO DISCOVER PERMANENT HELP FOR THE INEBRIATES AND INSANE. His discovery is startling, and to be scattered broadcast—every physician to be told how to use them—a system like no other.

"Many of our people remember that Dr. Thompson was curing inebriates in 1876, but unlike systems now in vogue, his did not prevent relapse. The Doctor learned from experience that the mind needed curing as much as the appetite, that inebriism was a species of insanity. Four years ago, while trying to perfect a system for the cure of insanity, he believed he struck a conclusive point for the inebriate, whose mind is the most difficult matter for successful treatment.

"During the last three years, 26 of the worse hereditary cases that could be found in New England have been treated as tests. Some of these so low, morally, that no indignity could insult them, if a nickel was forthcoming for a drink. All of these cases have been cured over two years and not one has relapsed. The doctor believes the discovery is reliable and will save at least 95% of the worse cases. The same of incipient insanity, which system is not yet fully perfected. The doctor proposes to teach every physician in the world how to use it, and if they will agree to help themselves after they get out—will cure every helpless inebriate in the Massachusetts penal institutions, free of charge.

"The doctor is already receiving letters of inquiry from some of the most noted men in New York and Boston. During treatments, patients do not need to leave home or business or pay extortionate prices. Every physician will be held to the latter. Every case will be concealed from the public."

In the 1890s, Cleveland was an active Moxie distribution center, but not without its problems from imitators and counterfeiters. The Moxie Nerve Food Company, Cleveland, listed Augustin Thompson, M.D. as general manager, F.E. Thompson as treasurer, and Harry A. Thompson as president. Premises were maintained at 70 Frankfort Street. An early advertisement noted:

"CHEAPER AND BETTER THAN YOUR FOODS... MOXIE... SCIENCE IS SPOILING THE FRAUDS. THE WORLD IS MOVING INTENSELY.

"We come to you with something new to this section, but intensely known in Europe and in this country east of the Alleghanies. In Boston and New York it has become a veritable craze. Every store carries a large stock. It is in the windows and on the street stands everywhere.

"While it does not contain a drop of poison, medicine or alcohol, or anything deleterious, the lucky find of the manner of its preparation by a scientist, that makes it so effective as a nerve builder, has made it the king of them all... Except when caused by effusion, it has even recovered hundreds of old cases of paralysis. To make a rich popular luxury, it has been richly flavored and charged with soda into a beverage. Everybody in the East drinks it cold from the ice... It is cheaper than your food. Only 17c for a 26-ounce bottle if bought by the case and empty bottles and the case returned. Your grocer will deliver it and take empties away."

Another advertisement noted that the product "will soon be sold every place of business in Cleveland handling such drinks. You can buy Moxie at druggists and soda fountains or have it delivered in dozen-bottle cases by your grocer."

Moxie sales were growing apace in other cities. For example, in Kansas City, Missouri, The Moxie Nerve Food Company was located at 1701 Charlotte Street and had as its manager W.D. Duncan, with G.W. Chandler serving as secretary. The Kansas City area was blanketed with Moxie advertisements.

Chapter 4

Dr. Thompson's Final Decade

At the end of 1892 a reorganization took place. The activities of William Taylor & Co. were curtailed (although unsold inventory bearing the Taylor label was to be distributed over the next few years), and a new firm was organized. A meeting was held at Saco, Maine at the office of attorney Hampden Fairfield on Monday, December 26, 1892, to establish The Moxie Nerve Food Company of New England. The purposes and stock distribution were stated as follows:

"To engage in the general business of manufacturing and selling proprietary articles, beverages, and medicines, particular reference being had to the beverage known as Moxie or Moxie Nerve Food, heretofore originated and manufactured by Dr. Augustin Thompson of Lowell, Mass., and to the various medicines and remedies also heretofore prepared and sold by said Thompson; to acquire and hold any patent rights, inventions, letters patent, trademarks, copyrights or formulas necessary to said business or desirable to be acquired by said corporation; to acquire and hold such machinery, tools and appliances...

"The amount of capital stock is $500,000. The amount of capital stock already paid in is $500. The par value of the shares is $100. The following people each own one share: William Taylor, Lowell, Mass.; Augustin Thompson, Lowell, Mass.; Francis E. Thompson, Somerville, Mass.; Arthur M. Evans, Worcester, Mass.; and Frank A. Dearborn, Newburyport, Mass. The balance of the stock remains in the treasury unissued."

Frank A. Dearborn was named as president, while Francis E. Thompson was tapped to serve as treasurer. The other stockholders became members of the board of directors. On December 27, 1892 the attorney general's office of the State of Maine confirmed the validity of the incorporation agreement. In this basic corporate form, the Moxie enterprise was conducted for a period of many years, until dissolved decades later by an action of the board of directors on November 10, 1927.

Through the 1890s, The Moxie Nerve Food Company of New England maintained two primary addresses: 68 Beverly Street, Boston, and the facilities established earlier at 21 Branch Street, Lowell. Factories were operated at these two locations as well as 469 West Broadway, New York City. For part of the 1890s, William A. Taylor, then in his seventies, was president of the firm. Freeman N. Young and Francis E. Thompson managed most of the business activities. Augustin Thompson lent his name to the enterprise but was rarely involved in day to day operations. William Taylor continued to reside in Thompson's Lowell residence at 36 Varney Street for the balance of the decade. Augustin Thompson relocated to 567 Tremont Street, Boston, but his home and office at Varney Street, Lowell was maintained and the family of his son Harry lived there. In advertisements and printed messages Thompson alternated between his Lowell and Boston addresses toward the end of the decade. His wife, the former Sarah Stewart, passed away. Dr. Thompson soon married Miss Flora Forbes of Providence, Rhode Island, who eventually survived him.

On March 10, 1893, another corporation, The Moxie Nerve Food Company of Illinois, was established following a meeting at attorney Fairfield's office in Saco, Maine. The purposes were stated to be similar to those of the earlier Moxie Nerve Food Company of New England charter. The amount of capital stock was likewise set at $500,000 consisting of shares of $100 par value each. Just $500 was paid in, with one share assigned to each of the following: Frank A. Dearborn, Newburyport, Mass.; Edward W. Cate, Boston; Francis E. Thompson, Somerville, Mass.; Augustin Thompson, Lowell, Mass.; and Freeman N. Young, Somerville, Mass. Dearborn was named as president, while Cate served as treasurer. The intent was to pick up the pieces from the Chicago Moxie Nerve Food Company fiasco. For a time, an agency was maintained at 14 Charles Place, Chicago in connection with the Consolidated Bottling Company at that address. The Moxie Nerve Food Company of Illinois remained active for the balance of the decade. On June 13, 1901, notice was received by the State of Maine that the firm had ceased doing business.

After the publication of *A Waif in the Conflict of Two Civilizations* in 1892, Thompson concentrated his writing energies on Moxie-related advertisements, and, in particular, on continuing a volumin-

Harry Augustin Thompson (standing at the center with a flower on his lapel), a youth of 16 years of age, with some baseball playing buddies. Photograph taken at Willow Dale, Lowell, Massachusetts, June 30, 1888.

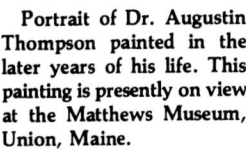

Portrait of Dr. Augustin Thompson painted in the later years of his life. This painting is presently on view at the Matthews Museum, Union, Maine.

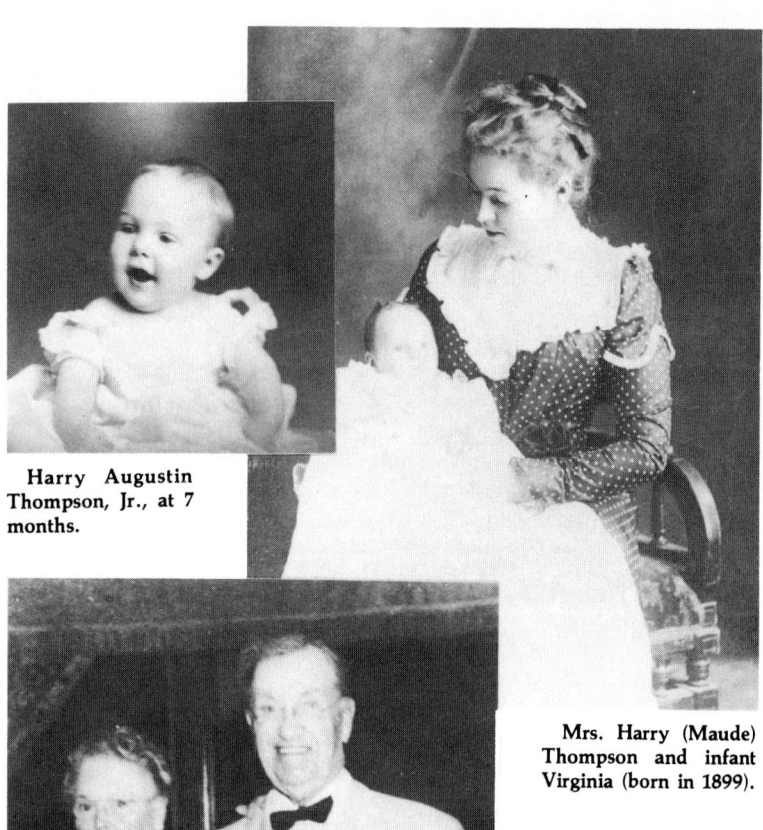

Harry Augustin Thompson, Jr., at 7 months.

Mrs. Harry (Maude) Thompson and infant Virginia (born in 1899).

Above: Mr. and Mrs. Harry A. Thompson on his 80th birthday. Photograph taken in Clearwater, Florida. Right: Harry A. Thompson and daughter Virginia on her 16th birthday.

ous series of letters to newspaper editors. The weather, geography, economics, politics, and the law were favorite subjects, but virtually no topic escaped his observation.

On July 15, 1893 he penned a comment concerning Pittsburgh, Pennsylvania:

"Here we are in the smoky city again. When I say smoky, I mean all it implies. Mother Earth has told them that even her enormous resources are limited in the land of waste. For 30 years they pumped oil from her caverns. Exhaustion soon gave place to gas. On the hillside they lit and made useless bonfires, until that was gone, winning for nature's favor basic ingratitude for thieving speculators, for there was no more to prop their shiftless indulgence with profits..."

Thompson then went on to give a general statement that the nation's economic problems were caused by an overinflated stock market, about a million swindlers taking advantage of people, and various government excesses. This was the year of the Panic of '93, and Thompson was a prime observer. From New York City on August 4, 1893 he wrote that he had learned the cause of all the financial problems, as given to him by one of the best minds in New York. He stated that many stocks were inflated, and that the recent correction was normal and overdue. He then observed that England and other countries with investments in the United States became disgusted with the shrewd stock operations on Wall Street and withdrew their capital, after which New York banks became frightened and refused to make loans. He went on to state that there were many rays of hope and that with the great assets of America things would soon be better than ever.

Thompson was always on the lookout for business opportunities. The next year, during a visit to Ontario in Canada, he wrote that he saw the richest lands ever outside of Louisiana, but there was scarcely a fruit tree in sight. He noted that all the land needed was a "live Yankee" to start exploiting the many resources. "This country, the doctor says, is rubbing its muscles and getting ready to knock the stuffing out of free trade and prohibitory protection," noted a newspaper which received Thompson's message.

Proud of his many published letters to editors, Thompson carefully pasted them in two large ledgers.

On May 28, 1896, Dr. Thompson, then in St. Louis, wrote to the Lowell *Daily News*:

"St. Louis could not have been more completely wrecked in 24 hours by half a dozen first class battleships than it was last night

Mrs. Augustin (Sarah) Thompson and her two sons, Harry A. (born 1872) and Francis E. (born 1864).

Francis Edward Thompson

in 20 minutes by a cyclone sent to us from the tropics. It came up the river and met an electric storm from the west. For two weeks there had been an almost uninterrupted series of violent thunderstorms. Fifty-eight in 13 days, mostly in the afternoons and at night. At five o'clock last night it grew suddenly dark. I was writing at my desk. For a half an hour there had been many sharp flashes of lightning and heavy peals of thunder in the distance, which had grown to be so common we had learned to treat it with no concern. This time the darkness became so intense, so suddenly, it alarmed me. I sprang to the door and then out on the sidewalk.

"The city was enveloped in a dense black cloud filled with intermittent flashes of lightning every two or three seconds. The peals of thunder were deafening. Already I could hear the crash of falling buildings on the riverfront, six blocks away. From previous descriptions, I knew what was coming. I called to the men to get between the heavy brick walls intended for an iron safe covering, that a cyclone was coming and close by. We were nearby heavy brick blocks, four stories in height, old and rotten. I watched at the door to see if I could avoid their debris, if they should succumb. The first of the wind storm struck us. Wagons were torn from horses in an instant and went kiting up the streets like empty baskets. The horses were prostrated, trembling with terror. Fortunately the wind blew by our door, not into it. It struck a big four story brick block not 100 feet away. In 10 seconds it was a wreck. The air was full of debris—bricks, wagons, tin roofs, window blinds, glass, dry goods, groceries, whiskey bottles, jugs, plate glass, and delivered nothing to anybody. It was a general distribution. Lightning was apparently striking in all parts of the city every two or three seconds. It was an indescribable scene of terror. Soon the red glare of burning buildings on both sides of the river were building their dreaded columns of flame and light in the black darkness of the clouds, too numerous to count. Not a fire laddie dared to enter the streets with his team...

"[After the storm I realized that] I had a heavy invoice of Moxie on one of the boats on the Anchor line of steamers, bound for New Orleans. It was at the bottom of the river. Heavens, what a nerve the Mississippi fish will have! Of more than 50 steamboats at the levee two hours before the storm, some were at the bottom of the river or driven onto the Illinois shore; only one remained at its moorings...

"St. Louis is a scene of indescribable ruin. It will require months of repair for it. I hope to escape with a loss of $500 or $600. Give me New England for all of any other dod blasted country that ever

Above: Harry A. Thompson (standing far out front to the right) and his friends at the 30th Triennial Conclave of the Knights Templar of the United States, Saratoga Springs, New York, July 7-14, 1907.

Freeman

Hildreth Building
LOWELL, MASS.

Left: Harry A. Thompson in full uniform as a member of the Massachusetts ambulance corps in the Spanish-American War, 1898.

Portrait of Harry Augustin Thompson as a middle aged man.

grew. That is how I feel now. I came away with a picture impressed on my memory that will never be effaced."

On May 30th, Thompson sent a follow-up letter, noting that 7,000 homes had been wrecked and 45,000 people were killed, wounded, or driven into the streets at night in a deluge of wind and rain. "$50 million will not repair the city and pay for the ruined personal property."

The Free Silver question, the hallmark of the Bryan-McKinley presidential campaign of 1896, was prominent in Thompson's mind, and he voiced many opinions concerning it. When William Jennings Bryan gave his famous "Cross of Gold" speech, Thompson dutifully pasted a transcript of it in his scrapbook. On June 8, 1896, he wrote a newspaper editorial:

"I had a chance to address a labor organization the other night. They wanted to hear the gold argument as I looked at it. They knew I had no selfish interest at stake. I began by asking them a question— when wheat is worth sixty cents, what man among you would give a dollar for it? A dozen responded. But if the world will use silver, the price will appreciate to gold. But, gentlemen, every nation on the face of the earth has more silver in circulation than gold. They circulate all of it that they can, yet silver is worth only fifty-seven cents. Why? The law of supply and demand compels it. Is it what a man wants that coaxes his efforts? With both silver and gold in your fingers, which would you hoard? Your wants govern the world...

"Suppose the government declared for the free coinage of silver. The world would bring its silver here for coinage. The government stamp on it would make it responsible to back every 57-cent dollar with a gold one. How long can you stand it? You are the government... That lodge wore sober faces and began to think."

A September 20, 1896 clipping from the *Lowell News* reveals that Thompson, who had railed against the legal profession for many years, apparently decided to join a system he could not effectively fight:

"I am just in from the northern cities of Missouri and those of the river border below Dubuque. I am surprised at the educated intelligence I have met everywhere, which in no instance is below that of Massachusetts, which is only superior to these states in age and its schools. Iowa and Missouri will pronounce for an honest dollar [a commentary on the Free Silver political campaign of 1896]; nevertheless, the blustering demigodry of the cheap newspapers that have to yell constantly to keep the breath of life within their cause. Let me give you samples: Friday night I came into contact with the big reunion of the blue and gray at Lagrange, Missouri. When they saw my G.A.R. button and the hotel register told them I was from Massachusetts, they captured me—pinned their decorations on my coat, and I must respond from Massachusetts at the next meeting and bonfire in the park. I am not much on a speech, but *since I have become a lawyer* [italics added] I have accumulated enough impudence and cheek to be able to impose upon people frightfully. With an air of respectability I face the 10,000 people in the park with a stump speech on the 'Red Schoolhouse of New England'—the colporteur of civil liberty that has made Missouri the equal of Massachusetts... The country farmers we are so wont to ridicule are infinitely more intelligent and reliable than the city populations, because they are more reasonably educated and more conservative in their judgment. I met the farmers at the hotels everywhere. Don't you mistake, there is a better business sense here than you think. It is all tariff talk now. Home soon for a few days. Respectfully, A. Thompson."

Writing from St. Louis on April 15, 1898, Thompson sent a letter to a newspaper editor stating he had just arrived from canvassing the cities of the river valleys and Lake Erie. He told of an innovative hotel he had seen in New York City earlier. A man of great personal wealth, Thompson apparently enjoyed spending just 50c for a full day of what he referred to as "high living":

"The West is boisterous for war—especially those people that carry no bullet holes and never have laid on the ground on cold rainy nights and fed on dry, hard salt junk and hard bread. Those who are least liable to go yell the loudest. I contemplate another possible army of wrecks—orphaned children and helpless mothers—with a pittance from an overtaxed people to live on. Times rise good when the government is wasting its money for an avalanche of useless expenses.

"Some wars are justifiable. This is not. Spain could have been compelled to humanity long ago. Now when 400,000 have been starved by our negligence, we have to send $100,000,000 and thousands of brave men after them—for what? Nothing but for revenge for what might have been avoided. We are where we must fight, now, and PDQ, too. The quicker the better. It can be rushed to a quick conclusion if there is no more cowardice. I have believed we shall have no war, for there was a good business chance to avoid it once.

"While war is already straining vivid imaginations, shrewd men in New York are planning for the bitter poverty of the large cities that will come with the reaction. Going down Bleecker Street, I noticed an enormous new 10-story building near 6th Avenue. I was told it was a hotel of the future, that men could live there in luxury for 50c per day. I said to myself: the Lord is good, I will go in and see. On the first floor were over 1,000 men, reading, playing checkers, whist. There is a big library and 1,500 bedrooms, fine beds, sitting, reading, smoking rooms, baths, lavatories, elevators, steam heat, and electric lights. Fine meals, 10c; real coffee, and 20c for a room to sleep in. The floors and stairway are Italian marble, everything grand and imposing. There is a big marble and iron washroom and dryer. If a dirty man comes, he is told he can stop if he will take a bath, and he can wash and iron his clothes in the free room that is for such a purpose. A man can go in and be provided with a wrapper, tub and soap, dry and iron every rag on him in an hour, and it doesn't cost him a cent. I said, I want to board here. I did. Fifty cents expense at high living for 24 hours. Two more hotels of the same kind are building. This is making money. George Francis Train lives here.

"Respectfully, A. Thompson."

More on the Spanish-American War appeared in a letter datelined St. Louis, April 28, 1898:

"St. Louis declared war today. The city is full of bunting and wind. Every man I have met wants to volunteer if he can have a commission cut. So far there are not enough privates to go around. I put out a Cuban flag and Old Glory at high noon, at the risk of being licked by some Spaniard. The theatres are bursting with patriotism. The South wants to fight the whole thing alone. A fair chance for them would knit us together. Their old generals should be recognized—especially Lee, who has betrayed as much business sense as the president. I have more confidence in McKinley and Reed than I used to have. I have no choice between them and Lee for the next president.

"There is too much party in this country. The Lee family has shown itself to be a strong one; party jealously will prevent it this time. It needs an experienced sound business naval man in Long's place. How can a lawyer know anything but his own business? The same is true of any other profession.

"When war was imminent, he ought to have had some good sense to retire in favor of some of the old admirals. A man is good for nothing but the profession he is educated for. Think of a man being elected from the mill hands to be a city physician or a city solicitor? Roosevelt is egotistic and foolhardy, if he is truthfully reported. The

This faded photograph shows a Moxie booth from the turn of the century. Affixed to the stand are dozens of colorfully lithographed Moxie cut-outs from Germany. "A Pretty Moxie Girl, Free to Every Customer" notes the banner across the top.

"GOOD FOR YOUR NERVES"—THE MOXIE MAN AND HIS BOTTLE.

This newspaper photograph, date and location unknown, is probably from the turn of the century. Shown is the familiar Moxie Bottle Wagon, a conveyance first built in 1886 and duplicated many times after then. The original company ledgers reveal that a typical Bottle Wagon, including advertisements and fittings, was apt to cost close to $500.

The Moxie Bottle Wagon was a familiar sight on the streets in the northeastern section of the United States. Many duplicate rigs were made so that the Bottle Wagon could be in many places at the same time—just like a department store Santa Claus. The outfit shown above is in a particularly ornate carriage.

fountains and restaurants. Pressed-steel, commonly called "tin," signs were made in large quantities by several New York firms and often featured a pretty girl with an advertising message for the beverage.

Various novelties were tried. Frank S. Ober, a solicitor of patents in New York City, prepared a sketch of a device shaped like an upright Moxie bottle, made of clear glass, apparently designed so that a coin could be dropped through the neck at the top, to be deflected by a small pyramid below, and then to fall into any one of several recesses marked with different fortunes such as "Your Lucky Day," "You Drink Too Much," "Letter Coming," "Bad Luck," or "Money Coming." A small door at the bottom permitted the extraction of a prize or the collecting of money. In Philadelphia in 1900 a new novelty was introduced: an aluminum advertising token which could be redeemed for a 5c glass of Moxie at the Bottle Wagon. It is believed that between 15,000 and 20,000 of these were made. Their use continued until about 1904.

The public was wearying of patent medicine claims, and various cures and nostrums came in for an increasing share of criticism, often in print in newspapers and magazines which would not have dared to print a word on the subject a few years earlier. The proprietors of Moxie recognized the shift, and *Beverage* Moxie Nerve Food labels were used with increasing frequency. Advertisements in New England (in particular) magazines and newspapers told of Moxie's healthful and beneficial character but also emphasized the enjoyment Moxie provided as a refreshing drink for the entire family. Still, the patent medicine scenario lingered, especially in advertising copy penned by Augustin Thompson. An 1897 notice for Moxie Lozenges, written by Thompson, is in this vein:

"NEW IDEAS FROM THE SCIENTIFIC WORLD: The nerves are the seat of animal life, they generate force from certain foods to control the functions of the body. A Massachusetts scientist [Thompson himself] has discovered how to extract and pre-digest these elements, ready for absorption, which the necessary amount of crude foods cannot furnish without disastrously overloading the stomach. Thus science substitutes for injurious medicines and stimulants a safe, natural agent. For 12 years this discovery has excited the whole country. Hundreds of nervous wrecks, even paralytics, have been restored to health by its use. It relieves the terrible nerve-weariness—that nervousness from worry and the effects of overstudy and overwork, and the abuses of the nerves and brains. It gives the weak double powers of endurance without stimulation or reaction. Testimonials from all parts of New England and the West mailed free. We court scientific investigation. This wonderful preparation is the Moxie

Nerve Food, put into solid form [as Moxie Lozenges] so that it can be sent by mail. A 30 day supply $1, a five month supply $5. To prevent counterfeiting it can be secured by mail only. A. Thompson, M.D. agent. 469 West Broadway, New York."

Thompson was designated as "general manager" or "agent" in many different locations throughout the 1890s, although in practice he was primarily in St. Louis during the early part of the decade and in Lowell and Boston toward the end.

Early Moxie bottles were sealed with a number of closures, including the Hutchinson style with an inner seal and external metal loop, a standard cork covered with a paper seal, a wire closure with a ceramic top, and other formats. Beginning in the early 1890s, the cork-lined metal caps made by the Crown Cork and Seal Company, Baltimore, Maryland were adopted. By July 1, 1898, use of this format on new bottles was exclusive, and The Moxie Nerve Food Company of New England noted that after that date no refunds would be given on empty bottles of any other style.

Around the same time, Moxie mugs with handles were made available to soda fountain operators, druggists, and restaurant owners. Priced at 75c per dozen, these bore the Moxie imprint on the side. Five full glasses of Moxie could be obtained from each bottle of the product, thereby yielding a profit of nearly 100% at the rate of $2.10 per dozen full Moxie bottles, less a rebate of 42c per dozen when the empties were returned—according to an advertisement.

The various Moxie branches were kind to their employees and offered many benefits unusual for the era. On August 14, 1898, the St. Louis division hosted a "grand complimentary picnic" which feted Moxie employees and which the public was invited to attend, to enjoy themselves and also to get acquainted with the product. An invitational advertisement noted: "Moxie gives double the powers of endurance without stimulation or reaction, harmless as gruel; rich and useful results... Its sales east of the Alleghanies during the past 12 years have doubled every 22 months... 16c a bottle if bought by the case."

In Boston, Freeman N. Young often hosted gatherings for Moxie employees at his suburban home, treating them to magic lantern shows, a sumptuous variety of food, and outdoor recreation. Moxie employees became intensely loyal, a feeling that was to characterize the organization for decades to come.

In Lowell, Moxie was made in at least two locations. On September 25, 1899, the factory at 21 Branch Street burned. Pic-

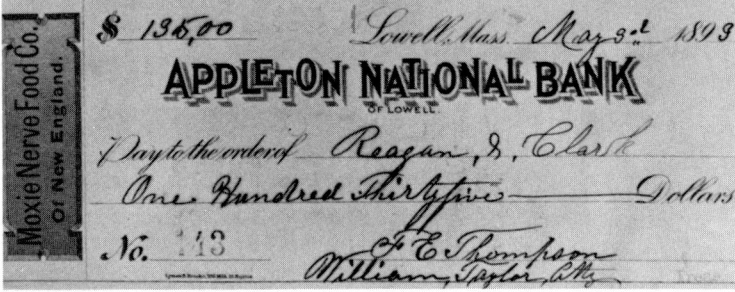

Above: A Moxie Nerve Food Company of New England check drawn in 1899 on the Appleton National Bank of Lowell, signed by F.E. Thompson and William Taylor.

Left: A Moxie advertisement, circa 1898-1899, enticing people to part with nickels in exchange for "that great thirst alleviating, refreshment-bringing, health-promoting summer tonic."

Below: On May 13, 1898, Dr. Augustin Thompson wrote to Hon. Roger Wolcott, governor of Massachusetts, offering to help in the Spanish-American War.

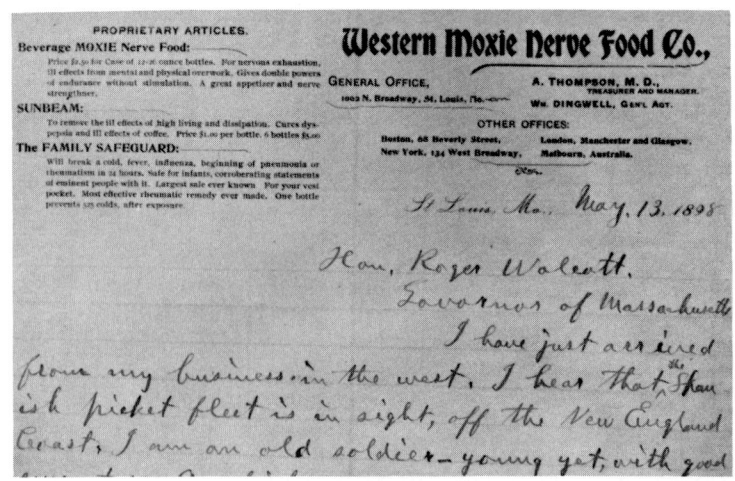

tures of the wreckage show racks of bottles amidst charred remains. Little was salvageable. The Standard Bottling Company, in which Augustin Thompson had purchased an interest years earlier, came to the forefront. Located at 848 Middlesex Street, the Standard Bottling Company, Inc., billed itself as "manufacturers of high-class carbonated beverages and flavoring extracts. Local agents for the celebrated Moxie Nerve Food." Francis E. Thompson was treasurer, Freeman N. Young served as secretary, J.L. Beauchain was vice-president, and William L. Hills was president.

A notice dated June 12, 1900 observed that due to the increased demand for goods, and undoubtedly also prompted by the burning of the other Moxie production facility a year earlier, the Standard Bottling Company had been incorporated under the laws of New Jersey with a capital stock of $50,000 divided into $25,000 in 7% cumulative preferred stock and $25,000 in common stock. William L. Hills was in charge of operations. Standard's 848 Middlesex Street address in Lowell also served as an address for the Moxie Nerve Food Company of New England in various advertisements.

Young's Champagne Cider, popular during the 1890s, was supplanted by a new product, Ureka Aerated Champagne Cider, whose name was derived as a result of a public contest advertised in Lowell newspapers. Nellie McDonald furnished the winning name and received a prize of $50 for her effort. Ureka was featured in advertisements for much of the following decade.

In 1900 the census-taker for the United States government visited 36 Varney Street, Lowell, and learned that Augustin Thompson, although he had relocated his office to Boston, still claimed Lowell as his home address. Primary occupants of the home were Harry A. Thompson, age 28, his wife Maude (born in Massachusetts in March 1875), and an infant daughter, Virginia, born in Lowell in September 1899. Later, another child, Harry A. Thompson, Jr., was born to the couple. While a teenager, Harry, Jr. suffered severe mental problems, diagnosed as dementia praecox, and was institutionalized for the rest of his life, although he lived to the age of 74. Virginia McElwee (nee Thompson), interviewed by the author in 1984, was the only living blood relative of Augustin Thompson at the time, for neither she nor her uncle, Francis E. Thompson, ever had children.

In the 1984 interview, Mrs. McElwee noted that she had few recollections of Dr. Thompson, for she was not quite four years of age when he died in 1903. She remembered seeing him in his casket and remembered visiting a studio featuring the Thompson Vitalizer

This ornate business card issued by Thompson & Young shows the Moxie Bottle Wagon and notes that it is available for picnics, fairs, and other gatherings.

In 1899 the main Moxie bottling facility in Lowell was gutted by fire. The photograph shown here, taken shortly after the event, shows several people standing amidst smoke-blackened bottles and debris.

felt that the Moxie Cooler would promote sales by permitting the beverage to be dispensed from bottles kept on ice within the device. About once each year, the Moxie Coolers were returned to the nearest Moxie depot for cleaning, reconditioning, and repainting.

Francis E. Thompson and Freeman N. Young, as partners or individually, patented numerous other devices, including a registering faucet for syrup bottles (January 28, 1902), a bottle washing machine (January 17, 1905), a bottle rinsing machine (October 27, 1905), other bottle washing machines (October 31, 1905, January 15, 1907, February 5, 1907), a bottle labeling machine (February 15, 1910), and a headlight controller for automobiles, whereby turning the steering wheel also directed the headlamps (March 26, 1912).

In 1900, Moxie imitators and counterfeiters continued to be a problem. The *Dramatic Review*, issue of November 10th of that year, carried a cartoon of a shabbily dressed gentleman approaching a prosperous actor. The following caption was given:

"PROSPEROUS ACTOR: Why should you need help? I thought you were a popular druggist's clerk.

"BEGGAR: So I was, but I substituted an imitation nerve food for Moxie. The Moxie Company found it out and now I can't get a job anywhere. Once a substitutor, always a substitutor, you know.

"PROSPEROUS ACTOR: I'll help you a bit, but you don't deserve it. True Moxie is the popular cure for brain-fag in the theatrical profession, and we will not stand for substitutes."

One would-be imitator placed a classified ad in the *Boston Globe*, December 9, 1900, noting: "Wanted: a party with $10,000 to manufacture a drink equal to Moxie. N.5. Globe Office."

Whether the advertisement bore fruit may never be known, but enough other imitators arose that Moxie filled many scrapbook pages with articles and transcripts of legal actions concerning them.

Although in 1900 a few stray examples of the Moxie Catarrh Cure were shipped, most of Augustin Thompson's pet proprietary "discoveries" were abandoned. Moxie alone became the primary product. In 1900 a list showed pint-size Moxie available in quantities of three dozen bottles per case, at $3.60 per case. According to Moxie's definition, the "pint" size contained 12 ounces. The "quart" size, which according to Moxie contained 26 ounces, was priced at $2.10 per dozen bottles. Actually, such terms as "pint" and "quart" were very loosely defined in the beverage industry at the time, and bot-

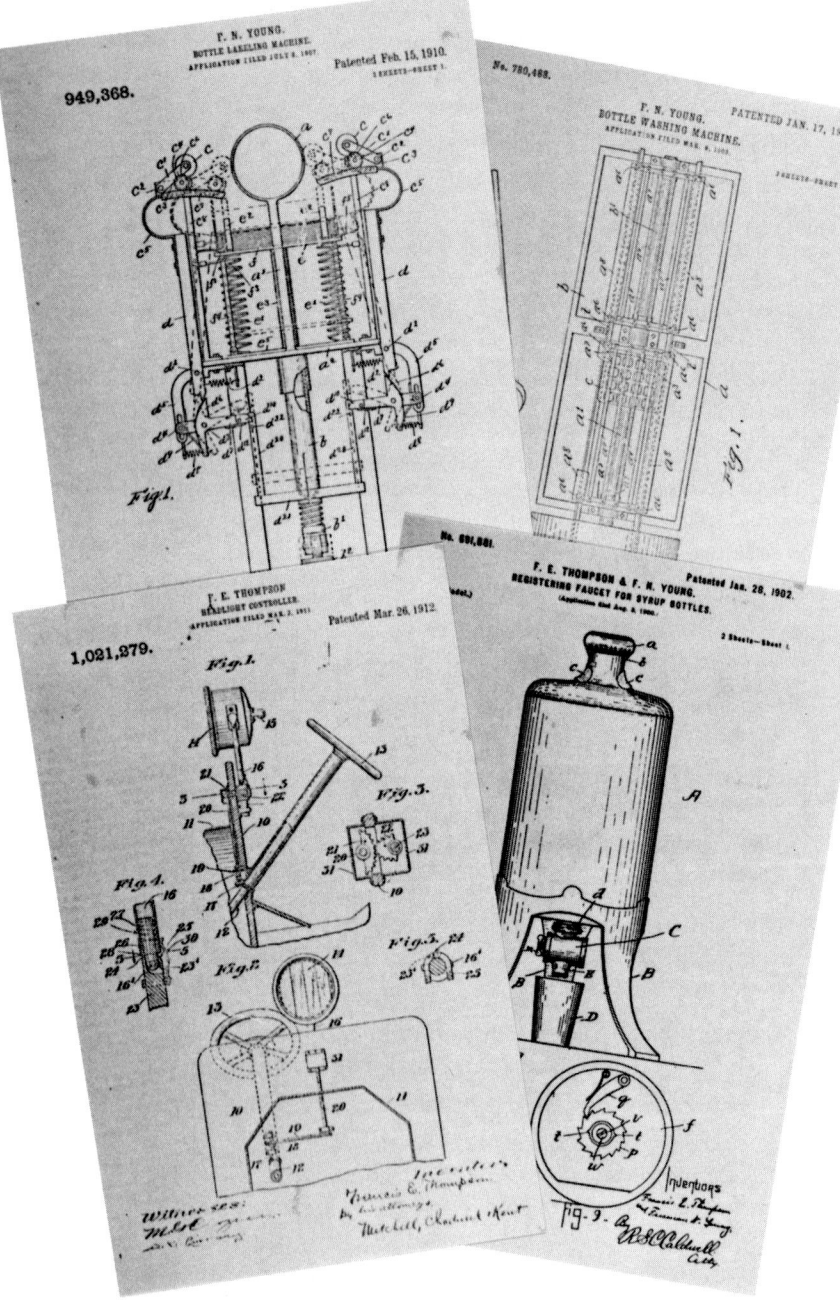

Freeman N. Young and Francis E. Thompson were prolific inventors, with Young producing several devices relating to bottle filling and handling. Patents on this page include those for a bottle labeling machine, bottle washing machine, headlight controller, and registering faucet for syrup bottles.

tles bearing the labels of various proprietors were apt to vary widely in actual contents. The day of truth in advertising had not yet come.

The highlight of Moxie advertising in the year 1900 was the Bottle Wagon. These varied in format from simple to plain. Fancier versions were decorated with flags and bunting, often with the horse draped in patriotic regalia as well. The coachwork was functionally simple on others and rococo on the more expensive versions, with gradations in between. In addition to their use on city streets in the northeastern part of the United States, bottle wagons followed the fair circuit, which usually ran from July through October. One bottle wagon reported an itinerary in the year 1900 which included Lewiston, Maine, Rochester and Portsmouth, New Hampshire, Taunton and Reading, Massachusetts, back to Maine to Bangor and Old Orchard, then to Worcester and Brockton, Massachusetts.

In September 1900 a Moxie Bottle Wagon in Worcester sold an average of $50 worth of the product per day at 5c per glass. Salesman Pitts at the Lewiston, Maine Fair in 1900 used 592 bottles of Moxie to fill glasses over a period of several days. Seven bottles were broken, and the contents of 14 bottles were given away free. Each Bottle Wagon turned in its performance report to the Boston office, where the results were carefully entered in a large ledger.

At the Rochester, New Hampshire Fair, Pitts sold the contents of 176 bottles, had nine bottles stolen, and dispensed the contents of six bottles free of charge. At the same event, salesman Tucker, in another Bottle Wagon, sold the contents of 224 bottles, reported 14 bottles broken, had two dozen bottles stolen, and dispensed the contents of eight bottles free. It was customary to give Moxie without charge to local policemen and fair officials.

Typical Moxie Bottle Wagons cost $450 to $550 when new. Each required extra fittings, advertising signs, and equipment, which usually cost about $100 more. Each year the conveyances were subject to repairs and renovations. For example, to hand-letter a typical Moxie Bottle Wagon in 1900 cost $15. Often electric signs and advertising posters were taken to display near the Bottle Wagon to attract customers.

While the public enjoyed the Bottle Wagon, some indoor purveyors of the product were less than satisfied. A letter to the editor of *Practical Druggist*, September 1900, noted:

"Complaints are being made that Moxie is being sold at retail from wagons in the street to the detriment of the trade, after druggists had been drummed and persuaded to keep it for sale."

This casual snapshot, taken at a fair in Maine, shows two Moxie signs (and an enlargement for detail). Presumably, the Moxie Bottle Wagon was somewhere in the offing.

Another advertising novelty of the year 1900 was the Moxie puzzle. Costing a fraction over 1c each, these were copyrighted in 1899 and were housed in a pink box. A typical puzzle measured 11 inches wide by 7 inches deep and was arranged in triangular and trapezoidal pieces. Of simple design, the puzzle bore the inscription LEARN TO DRINK MOXIE, IT'S HEALTHFUL, with a picture of a Moxie glass in the background.

In January 1900, 1,300 Moxie puzzles were ordered for the Philadelphia Food Fair, followed by an order for 2,500 more on March 1st, 3,000 more on March 9th, and 2,500 additional on December 1st. Moxie puzzles were short-lived, and within a year or two they were discontinued. Years later, in the late 1920s, a related form of Moxie puzzle was made as part of a bottle carrying carton.

The height of Moxie activity at the turn of the century was in Boston, where the facility at 65-71 Haverhill Street was superintended by J.L. Beauchain. The advertising was largely under the direction of Frank M. Archer, assisted by two professional agencies and several printing firms. Archer drew a yearly salary of $4,000, an immense sum at the time, while Beauchain earned $3,500 per year. During the same time, a factory worker in a Lowell textile mill was apt to earn on the order of $400 to $600 per year. Augustin Thompson, in the twilight years of his life, received a yearly royalty of $5,000 but was not active in daily Moxie affairs.

Francis E. Thompson and Freeman N. Young were paid on a royalty basis at the rate of 10c per dozen for quart Moxie and 5c per dozen for pint Moxie, an arrangement which was soon discontinued. Production for the year consisted of 204,938 dozen large Moxie in Boston and 45,304 large Moxie in New York, plus 700 dozen large Moxie shipped to New York from Boston and counted as part of the Boston inventory. 2,810 dozen small Moxies were credited to Boston, 2,431 to New York. The royalty amounted to $25,216.25, which split equally amounted to $12,608.12 each for these two men. Company records reveal that in the year 1900 The Moxie Nerve Food Company of New England and its branches made $56,824.84 profit.

On December 31, 1900, the interest of George A. Byam, who had been prominent in the Moxie enterprise since 1885, was purchased by Francis E. Thompson for $2,250. Included were 999 shares of the Chicago Moxie Nerve Food Company, 1,422 shares of The Moxie Nerve Food Company of New England, and a mortgage from The Moxie Nerve Food Company dated January 28, 1889. A waiver was given assigning to Thompson "all of the right, title and interest of George A. Byam in and to an agreement between the said Byam and Augustin Thompson dated August 7, 1885."

The Standard Bottling Company, Lowell, Massachusetts, was owned by Augustin Thompson and his associates and produced products for The Moxie Nerve Food Company of New England. The firm was also New England agent for Kentora Hop Bitter Ale, a non-alcoholic beverage. To the left is shown a "Learn to Drink Moxie" sign on one of the factory buildings, while below is a scene of the bottling process within the plant.

Advertising took many forms, including large billboards which were plastered over surfaces in Boston, Providence, New York, Philadelphia, and elsewhere. Large cardboard signs emblazoned "Don't Forget to Order Moxie" were popular, as were muslin banners, small and large glass signs, advertising boards affixed to the sides of wagons, railroad and street car signs, and window displays.

Moxie had a very ingenious arrangement involving window displays, a procedure that was to last for many years and which was to prove very effective. What were called "compensation cases" of Moxie were given free of charge to retailers who agreed to devote one window of their establishment to an exclusive Moxie display. Typically such a display consisted of various bottles of Moxie, often a few wooden crates, and a variety of posters and signs. Proud of these displays, various druggists, confectioners, and others took photographs of them and submitted the results to Moxie headquarters, where a growing file of them was kept.

Over the years Moxie ordered bottles from many sources. In 1900 the Olean Glass Co. (located in Olean, New York, affiliated with the United States Glass Co.), the Cumberland Glass Manufacturing Co., and the Modes-Turner Glass Co. were suppliers of bottles. For example, on April 11, 1900, Modes-Turner submitted a bill for 179 gross of Moxie bottles.

Losses of bottles were extensive due to handling in the factories, chipping, exposure to weather, and other hazards. For the year 1900 the firm's ledgers reveal that the seemingly large quantity of 2,857 dozen empty bottles were broken in the factory during the year and that 3,919 dozen full bottles were broken in the factory, on teams, and in the shipping room during the same period. During the winter, freezing was a hazard. Moxie orders often specified shipment by "warm car" on the railroad, but this request was often overlooked, and much breakage resulted from transit and also from storage on shipping docks. Explosions were another problem, and many were the instances of filled bottles bursting in crates when exposed to sun or heat, or when handled roughly. Retrieving bottles from distributors and customers was a continual task, and Moxie constantly urged the return of empties. Broken bottles and pieces were gathered and sold periodically for use as cullet in the glass manufacturing process. Tons of cullet were shipped over the years.

Relations with branch offices were primarily conducted from the Boston facility. Advertising material printed in the Boston area was shipped to various agencies. For example, on May 11, 1900, 2,313 tin signs were sent to Cleveland and invoiced at 10c each, 20 Moxie

Enlarged from a color postcard, this view shows the Moxie Bottle Wagon at the Brockton (Massachusetts) Fair, shortly before 1910. The Moxie Bottle Wagon, of which there were many examples and varieties, was a familiar fixture at fairs, parades, and other public gatherings. From within the bottle, an attendant dispensed glasses of Moxie.

Actual-size and enlarged illustrations of the 32mm (1¼-inch) aluminum token "Good for One Drink of MOXIE at the Moxie Bottle Wagon." In the foreground the young boy and girl are in front of the Moxie Bottle Wagon counter at which a uniformed attendant offers a glass of Moxie. Although such tokens were issued by the thousands, they are fairly elusive today.

Coolers were sent at $1 each, 1,900 fountain signs at 1½c each, 400 one-sheet posters were billed at the rate of $7.86 per thousand, 9 white coats and one cap were sent ($4 for the lot), and 316 8-sheet posters were billed at the rate of $140 per thousand.

The Moxie Nerve Food Company of Philadelphia was especially active during the first few years of the 20th century. The year 1900 saw 11,060 dozen crates of Moxie shipped to Philadelphia from Boston, invoiced at $1.15 each (after a rebate). On the other hand, the Moxie Company of Atlanta, Georgia, seemed to be more autonomous and prepared its own ornate labels and bottle wrappers which differed from the designs used by the northeastern outlets.

Among the Moxie sales representatives submitting expense accounts for the year 1900 were F.C. Drake, W.H. Irish, J. Adams, H.F. Winn, W.W. Tucker, C.C. Ryder, and W.H. Wolffe. Most of these salesmen operated Moxie Bottle Wagons at various times throughout the year.

The Standard Bottling Company, Lowell, continued its activity and produced Ureka Champagne Cider in quart bottles and Fleur De Lis Ginger Ale in pints and half pints. Many free cases of ginger ale were shipped to hotels, resorts, and other places as samples to solicit business. Not all shipments had a commercial intent, however, and on July 1, 1901, six cases of the ginger ale were sent aboard Francis E. Thompson's yacht *Gertrude* and billed to Thompson at the rate of 85c per case. Interestingly, there were few free samples or other considerations given to owners and officers affiliated with the various Moxie enterprises. The company ledgers reveal that even the slightest incidental expenses were billed to the Thompson brothers, Archer, and others at regular intervals.

The year 1901 saw a net profit after wages, salaries, and bonuses of $57,766.14 for The Moxie Nerve Food Company of New England and its various branches. The Philadelphia branch in particular was active. In addition, Moxie was introduced to Norfolk, Virginia, during which time 98 dozen bottles were given away free to help open up the territory. Some shipments were made to Pittsburgh, but there was little activity with other outlets. Apparently the Cleveland agency was closed, following the step taken earlier with the St. Louis outlet.

In 1901 the Moxie Bottle Wagons continued their great activity. W.H. Wolffe took a unit to Washington, D.C. in July 1901 to introduce Moxie to the populace, giving away the contents of 48 dozen bottles in the process. New bottles were ordered from several earlier sources as well as the Manufacturers Bottle Co. and the related Flac-

Moxie in action around the turn of the century. The top illustration shows the Moxie Bottle Wagon at a seaside pavilion, while below it is the Moxie Bottle Wagon at a revival meeting. Then comes a horse-drawn delivery truck filled with wooden crates of Moxie, standing in front of a drugstore with a Moxie awning and a large Moxie window display. Below, the Moxie Bottle Wagon is shown on a city street in the financial district.

Turn of the century sketches showing Moxie at the soda fountain and
in the home. The soda fountain scene, above, shows a Moxie Cooler with
an attendant in the background opening the rear doors to it.

Vignettes of the Moxie Nerve Food Company facilities, inside and out, at 68 Beverly Street, Boston, around the turn of the century. A magnifying glass used on the original illustrations reproduced below shows a common sign in both of the rooms: "TIME IS MONEY—BE BRIEF." In the illustration immediately below a uniformed office boy proudly displays the word "MOXIE" across the front of his jacket.

cus Glass Co. Bottles remained in short supply, and the usual efforts to reclaim empties were intensified. In the following year, 1902, the Queen City Glass Co., the Moore Brothers Glass Co. and the Cohansey Glass Co. were among the suppliers.

Advertising took many forms, and to catalogue the specific items used for the year 1901 alone would require many pages. Company literature and ledger entries give a picture of the activity. A prospective Moxie client could order Moxie Girl pictures, sidewalk signs, dummy cases, fountain signs, display cards, Moxie change trays (an innovation), cloth signs, Bottle Wagon cut-outs, stickers, and fire-gilt signs. Pictures of the Moxie Girl were particularly popular and were distributed in many ways, including by issuing tickets, 25 of which could be redeemed for a picture in a "neat frame." Sample ledger entries concerning advertising material included:

May 22, 1901—300 "red tin signs on frames" 22c each were shipped; and May 31, 1901—483 "bicycle tin signs with frames" at 25c each were shipped.

June 14, 1901, the following were shipped from Boston to the Philadelphia office: 1,300 fountain signs at 3¾c each, 2,000 stickers, large size $1.50 per thousand, 200 panels at $19 per thousand, 500 Moxie 5c at $2.05 per thousand, 100 paraffin cloths at 4.76c each and 20 awning cloths at 3.3c each.

On July 27, 1901, "500 Moxie Girl signs, varnished, at 25c each" were entered in the ledger as were "100 glass fountain signs measuring 4½ x 7 inches at 18c each."

On July 31, 1901 the following advertising items were noted: 25 Moxie ice boxes at 65c each; 200 openers at $1.25 per gross; five 8-sheet posters at 14c each; 100 awning signs at 3.3c each; 200 small fountain signs at 3¾c each, 100 cloth signs at 4.76c each; 100 large signs at 15½c each; 25 varnished Moxie Girl signs at 25c each; 200 tin signs at 26c each; 50 small glass fountain signs at 18c each; 2,000 stickers at $1.50 per thousand; 100 old streetcar signs at 3.1c each; 200 Moxie 5c signs at $2.05 per thousand; 50 "Take Home Bottle Moxie" signs at 4¾c each; 200 panels at $19 per thousand; and 200 girl metal trays at $8 per thousand.

From time to time when Moxie won court decisions against competitors or imitators, the victory was trumpeted in advertising circulars which were sent by the thousands to distributors. The year 1901 saw notices of the "Provost" and "Bow" injunctions printed in quantity.

Salaries for the year 1901 included the following: Francis E. Thompson $8,500, Freeman N. Young $4,000, Harry A. Thompson $2,500, J.L. Beauchain $4,000, Frank M. Archer $3,500, W.H. Wolffe and E.E. Wildes $1,500 each, and W.L. Hills $1,800. In addition, bonuses to certain individuals were paid.

Chapter 6

The Automobile Age

In 1902 Moxie entered the automobile age. Following a trial of the new gadgets, several Stanley Steamers were bought from the Stanley Dry Plate Company from April through June at prices in the $600 to $700 range per vehicle. In the company's account ledgers, the heading "Horses, Wagons and Harnesses" was crossed out, and a new account, "Automobile," was created. However, horses and wagons remained an important part of Moxie equipage for many years thereafter, finally being phased out around 1920. By the end of 1902, The Moxie Nerve Food Company of New England had six motorized vehicles in its garage.

Although automobiles created a lot of attention, and Francis E. Thompson in particular enjoyed telling newspaper reporters about their use, Moxie Bottle Wagons were more important to the company's sales. Nearly a dozen different units were kept busy in New England as well as in several Virginia locations.

The patent medicine aspect of Moxie was fading, although hundreds of Moxie samples, nearly all of pint size, were delivered to physicians each month in the hope that they would recommend the product to their patients. Moxie was an acquired taste. The transition from medicine to refreshing popular beverage was not particularly smooth. The unique and somewhat bitter taste, derived in part from gentian root, was not appealing to everyone. Frank Archer later noted: "Many have said 'when I first tasted Moxie I didn't like it. When I had taken one or two glasses, served ice cold, I found it to be delicious and satisfying and it made me eat, sleep, and feel better.'" The "eat, sleep, and feel better" phrase became an advertising theme, and during the next quarter century it was used in many forms. Success often furnishes the opportunity for satire, and soon a cartoon was published with the caption: "DRINK FOXIE—Sleep Less, Feel Worse, Eat Nothing"! Indeed, there was a Moxie imitator named Foxie, but it is doubtful that the cartoonist knew of it.

In the advertising department framed metal signs became increasingly popular. Typically these were ordered from New York manufacturers and then shipped to Milford, New Hampshire, where the Milford Sign Frame Company added frames for indoor display or legs and braces for those intended for sidewalk use. "Yes! We sell MOXIE. Very Healthful—Feeds the Nerves" was the inscription on a popular oval metal sign of the period. The manufacturing cost of such signs, not including the frames, ranged from 21c to 25c each, depending on the design. Another popular variety featured "A Moxie Girl," a winsome lass wearing a white dress with purple trimmings, leaning over a chair, holding a bottle of Moxie in her right hand and a glass in her left.

Theodore Roosevelt entered Moxie advertising around this time. From the Rotograph Company a standing portrait of Roosevelt, taken in 1898, was obtained. Billed as "The Leading Exponent of the Strenuous Life," Roosevelt made an ideal Moxie salesman. The "strenuous life" term was derived from one of Roosevelt's own statements: "I wish to preach not the doctrine of ignoble ease, but the doctrine of the strenuous life, the life of toil and effort, of labor and strife; to preach that highest form of success which comes, not to the man who desires mere easy peace, but to the man who does not shrink from danger, from hardship, or from bitter toil, and who out of these wins the splendid ultimate triumph."

It is doubtful if the President of the United States ever personally endorsed Moxie, but the use of his image and the "strenuous life" phrase was so widespread during the early years of his administration that undoubtedly he took notice of it. Cardboard cut-outs were made in a variety of sizes from table-top format to examples measuring several feet high. In an era in when most metal advertising signs cost 25c each or less, the company's ledgers show several "large Roosevelt pictures" shipped at $25 plus $5.75 framing each. These must have been immense versions of the popular theme. At a later time, Frank Archer told Moxie distributors that earlier Moxie advertising signs were selling for up to $25 each for "use in the dens of wealthy people." Perhaps he was referring to some of these early Roosevelt items. Roosevelt was to remain a fixture in Moxie advertising for several years, after which he was almost forgotten. Almost, but not quite. During the 1920s, The Moxie Company ran numerous advertisements in Boston newspapers stating that America should celebrate Roosevelt's birthday in addition to those of Lincoln and Washington.

Advertising was the key to Moxie success, and there is no doubt the comeback in fortunes experienced by the firm after 1900 was

Theodore Roosevelt, one of the most prominent public figures at the turn of the century, was an unwitting and unpaid salesman for Moxie. Using an 1898 photograph, the Moxie Nerve Food Company of New England prepared cardboard cut-outs of various sizes to show Roosevelt standing in a suit, with the inscription "The Leading Exponent of the Strenuous Life" below. The implication was that drinking Moxie would permit one to lead a strenuous life, just like Roosevelt. The theme was forgotten for a decade, then in 1919 the word "strenuous" became one of the most used adjectives in Frank Archer's book, "The TNT Cowboy." Fred, the hero of that piece of fiction, also enjoyed the strenuous life and, like Roosevelt, was an easterner who moved West and then back again.

Theodore Roosevelt, born to a wealthy New York family in 1858, was ill during much of his youth. By rigorous exercise, including horseback riding, shooting, and boxing, he overcame his condition. Graduating from Harvard with a law degree in 1880, he spurned his chosen profession to become an author. Then for a while he took up ranching in the West, returning to engage in heroic service with the Rough Riders in Cuba during the Spanish American War. Nominated as McKinley's vice-president on the 1900 Republican ticket, he was subsequently elected. Following McKinley's death in September 1901, Roosevelt became president. In 1904 he was re-elected to the same office. During his administration in 1906 the Pure Food and Drugs Act was passed, eventually leading to the "Nerve Food" description being dropped from the Moxie corporate title and bottle label. It is not known if Roosevelt personally drank Moxie, but he certainly lead "the strenuous life."

"The Leading Exponent of the Strenuous Life"

fueled by an intensive advertising campaign that saw dozens of different signs, posters, banners, and other aids available to dealers at low cost. In many instances such items were given away free. Lists show the availability in 1902 of such items as "dummy" Moxie bottles for display at 9c each, metal as well as leatherette soda fountain syrup lists (surmounted by the Moxie logotype) at 20c each, "double bottle lithographs" at $5.40 per thousand (10,000 of these printed items were shipped on June 16, 1902 alone!), "single bottle lithographs" at $2.70 per thousand, outdoor advertising posters of many types and varieties, oval and rectangular metal signs, tip or change trays, all sorts of printed material featuring President Theodore Roosevelt, Moxie Coolers, cloth banners, advertising fountain pens, posters and cut-outs featuring the Moxie Bottle Wagon, adhesive stickers, and other novelties in mind-boggling variety.

1902, the year of the advent of the automobile, the flowering of Theodore Roosevelt, and an increased advertising emphasis, saw a profit of $38,301.65 plus a separate profit of $5,497.35 for the Philadelphia office. It was the last full year of Augustin Thompson's participation. The aging doctor, who was preoccupied with his Thompson Vitalizer parlors, received a $5,000 royalty, as usual. He was an infrequent visitor to the offices, and his old remedies were gradually being phased out. Sales of Moxie Lozenges and the Moxie Catarrh Cure for 1902 amounted to little more than pocket change. Soon they would be discontinued completely.

In 1903 the Moxie Society was formed "for social, literary and business development," according to a newspaper article. 'The officers of The Moxie Company have entered heavily into the scheme, and have provided rooms where the members may meet, and will also engage experts in various lines of business who will read papers on different specialties, including business law and various manufacturers. The first course of lectures will take place on the second Tuesday in February."

The notice went on to state: "At each meeting there will be papers given by the heads of departments, and in this manner the company will be able to educate its employees so that when an extension of business is decided upon the promotions will come from the ranks."

The Thompson brothers, Frank Archer, Freeman N. Young and J.L. Beauchain were conspicuously absent from the membership, perhaps because they felt it should be a club by employees and for employees. The officers and charter members of the Moxie Society were: H.C.H. Parker, president; James Mitchell vice-president; Louis E. Green, secretary; Samuel E. Richards, treasurer; and the follow-

THIS picture is taken from life. The young lady is a great lover of Moxie, as is shown by the pleased expression on her face. There is a feeling of satisfaction after drinking a glass of GENUINE Moxie, which has been remarked by all those who use it as a beverage. It satisfies thirst as nothing else can.

These qualities together with its merit of strengthening the nervous system have made Moxie the most popular beverage in this country. It is regarded by many as the American National Health Beverage.

Price 25 cents per bottle, or $2.50 per doz.

There is a rebate for the return of the empty bottles and case.

"A Moxie Girl" appeared in many places during the first few years of the 20th century. Shown here is a page from a fold-out brochure. Although the painting "is taken from life," no specific person was ever identified with it.

Englarged from the Moxie letterhead, these illustrations show the Boston (above left) and New York branches of the firm, circa 1905. Portions of the upper floors of the New York edifice were rented out to various commercial clients.

Above: The entrance to Wonderland, Revere Beach, Massachusetts, sported a Moxie sign when this postcard view was taken, probably about 1905. During the same era two or three Moxie Bottle Wagons were employed during summer months at the amusement park.

Right: Along the Boulevard at Bass Point, Nahant, Massachusetts, the facade of this restaurant advertised fish dinners and Moxie. Massachusetts seacoast and resort towns were popular Moxie outlets, and virtually every thoroughfare had a generous supply of Moxie advertising signs during the first two decades of the twentieth century.

ing additional members—J.A. Penney, A.W. Penney, F.E. Pearse, Charles Beauchain, Charles Carlson, W.F. Rikeman, W.S. Colburn, George Geraty, H.L. Webb, A. MacPhae, A.G. Godfrey, C. Hubbart, F.G. Cunningham, J.H. Gordon, E.L. Parker, W. Wier, C.E. Norton, E.E. Wildes, R.T. Clark, J.H. Adams, C.W. Soares, C.E. Spaulding, C.H. Outland, S.S. Wetherbee, W.W. Tucker, L. St. John, George E. Gale, J.E. Robertson, W.H. Wolffe, A. Barone, E.S. Johnson, and B. Benson.

Louis E. Green, secretary of the group, faithfully kept a file of correspondence with Moxie Society members, some of whom would write to him out of loneliness when staying at distant hotels on Moxie business.

The Moxie Society, also called the Moxie Nerve Food Association, had many social events, with a New Year's Eve party being the highlight each year. Although he was not a member, Freeman N. Young acted as master of ceremonies.

Freeman N. Young was an inventor nonpareil. His automatic bottle rinsing, soaking and labeling machines were manufactured in a Lowell machine shop and used at the Moxie facilities in Boston and New York. The label "Yousay" was given as the trade name to these devices, a name taken from a summer camp formerly located on the grounds which later became Freeman Young's home in Arlington, Massachusetts.

In 1903 additional automobiles were acquired—more Stanley Steamers and, in October, a Knox auto, the latter costing $1,300. During the year Frank Archer was kept busy traveling, including journeys as far west as Detroit and as far south as Norfolk. He was often on the road for weeks at a time.

Ever on the lookout for Moxie imitators, the firm purchased competing products for study. On May 5, 1903, 10 cases of Moxie were delivered to an agent, Rood & Woodbury, in exchange for 10 cases of Phenix Nerve Food. Phenix was a copycat in more than just the "nerve food" part of the name; they had an equivalent to the Moxie Bottle Wagon, the Phenix Tumbler Wagon, which was a horse drawn vehicle in the form of a large tumbler or dispensing glass of Phenix. Like the Moxie wagon, the Phenix unit featured a uniformed attendant who dispensed the beverage for a nickel a glass. "Very Healthful," a catch phrase used by Moxie, was employed by Phenix Nerve Food as well.

Dr. Augustin Thompson passed away in 1903, and following his death, his widow, Flora L. Thompson (nee Forbes) was paid $10,500, such "amount allotted in consideration of the release by Flora L.

glasses, and in a majority of instances all broken ones have been replaced, only in rare instances should glasses be allowed on these orders."

Moxie at the wrong temperature was not appealing to customers, and in 1905 200,000 circulars were printed with the notice: "Never serve Moxie by the glass unless it is ice cold, unless you want to drive your Moxie trade to the other fellow." In the same vein, another massive printing of circulars admonished: "Do you see to it that Moxie is ice cold before your serve it? Do you keep the bottle tightly stoppered when it has been partially emptied? If you do you will get more and more business every day. People may judge your entire business by the manner in which you serve Moxie."

Although Moxie was advertised on billboards, inside and on the outside of streetcars, on wagons, and in many other public places, the main advertising thrust over the years was in newspapers. It was common practice at the time for newspaper editors to return the favor by running "news articles" which in reality were simply advertisements in disguise. Thus, in 1905, one of Moxie's advertising agents, Wood, Putnam & Wood, sent out a notice to different periodicals in which Moxie advertised, suggesting that they run a "news" article as follows:

"A UNIQUE PROCESSION. A few days ago The Moxie Nerve Food Company started from their home in Boston a procession of 14 automobiles. The objective points of this parade are the principal cities and towns of a large part of the United States. The automobiles will keep together from Boston to New York, at which point they will separate, some of them traveling to the far South, while others will continue their journey to different points in the West.

"These 14 automobiles are only a small part of The Moxie Nerve Food Company's automobile outfit. They are known as their 'Educational Department,' and their mission is to familiarize the public more thoroughly with the virtues of Moxie and to impress upon the minds of the American people that Moxie is really the great national temperance beverage, a drink that is healthful and delicious because it contains no alcohol, narcotics, poisonous drugs, or chemical preservatives. In this connection it is interesting to note that The Moxie Nerve Food Company owns and operates in this way and for other advertising and delivery purposes more automobiles than any other concern in the world. It will be interesting for us to watch the coming to this city of the Moxie automobile, which in a short time should arrive here after its long journey, and we hope in as good condition and looking as trim and natty as it did when it left Boston."

These Rambler automobiles, each sporting the Moxie trademark in gold, were photographed in February 1906 in front of the block which included the Rambler automobile showroom of Thomas B. Jeffery & Company. Note the Moxie pennants on the automobiles, a popular feature on all of the delivery cars.

Newspaper editors picked up the hint, and dozens of these notices appeared. In later years, as other Moxie innovations were introduced, news releases often were printed in their entirety.

The pureness of Moxie ingredients was continually featured in an era in which adulteration, harmful ingredients and other food topics were very much in the public mind, culminating in the passage of the Pure Food and Drugs Act in 1906. Whenever an article unfavorable to a competitor appeared in print, a copy was pasted in a scrapbook at company headquarters. Coca-Cola in particular received much adverse criticism at the time, primarily due to the allegation that it contained cocaine and caffeine. As an example, an article in the Newark (New Jersey) *Evening News*, July 9, 1907, noted in part:

"COCAINE IS SERVED AT SODA FOUNTAINS—Two dangerous drugs contained in Popular 'Temperance' Summer Drink. INGREDIENTS OF COCA-COLA.

"Government Authorities Investigating Effects of Use of Beverage, War Department Bars It from Army Canteens—Concoction Asserted to Contain Not Only Cocaine and Caffeine, but Also as Much Alcohol as Beer—South Has the Habit.

"Cocaine, as an ingredient in a popular drink, is sold openly at most of the soda fountains in Newark and elsewhere through the country. This startling and sensational charge is made by Mrs. Ella B. Carter, an active W.C.T.U. [Women's Christian Temperance Union] worker of the city. Mrs. Carter has taken the lead, locally, in a crusade being organized throughout the country by the W.C.T.U. against the sale and use of Coca-Cola, a widely advertised and popular beverage generally sold and consumed as a temperance drink. According to prominent authorities, Coca-Cola contains cocaine, caffeine, and alcohol. This assertion, made by competent government chemists and others, is backed by the admission of the lawyers of the company manufacturing the drink that such is the case...

"It is admitted by the manufacturers that its name is derived from the names of the two substances alleged to be the principal ingredients. 'Coca' is the name of a South American plant, the active agency in which is cocaine. 'Cola' is taken from the cola (or kola) nut, which is said to be used in the preparation of the decoction. So pernicious are the effects of drinking this beverage, it is said on good authority, that its use becomes a habit, and those who drink it habitually and in large quantities develop the symptoms of cocaine and caffeine poisoning. Travelers say that in prohibition towns in the South the drugstores do an enormous business in the sale of Coca-Cola, and those who drink it become slaves to the Coca-Cola habit. Their appetite craving more and more of the stuff, the more they drink, until its victims are unable to get along without it. In an Army order issued June 24, Brigadier-General Myer, of the Department of Texas, with the approval of the Secretary of War, forbade the further sale of Coca-Cola in post exchanges..."

Undoubtedly, Coca-Cola had not been a major advertiser in the paper in question, for if it had been, chances are good the article, a small portion of which is quoted here, would have been omitted or revised. Such was journalism practice throughout much of the era. The more things change the more they are the same, and over a half century later, when cigarette smoking was determined to be harmful to one's health, scarcely an unfavorable article concerning the effects of cigarette smoking could be found in the numerous magazines which depended heavily upon cigarette advertising revenue. New England newspapers in particular, which were the main recipients of Moxie's advertising budget, glorified Moxie in countless articles.

Whether or not Moxie was a cure for alcoholism is debatable. In that it contained no alcohol it was a "temperance drink" and was in favor with the W.C.T.U. and other crusading organizations.

In 1905 Moxie concentrated its efforts on the following outlets in particular, according to a directive to salesmen: druggists, confectioners and confectionery shops, fruit dealers, grocers, restaurants, department stores, saloons, hotels, pleasure parks, and clubs. Saloons were urged to feature Moxie by prominently displaying signs, thus giving an air of respectability to a class of establishment which was in increasing disfavor (culminated by the nationwide adoption of Prohibition years later in 1920). On city skylines, along streetcar and railroad rights of way, and in other places large 24-sheet posters proclaimed the virtue of Moxie and encouraged the population to eat, sleep, and feel better.

Activities continued apace at the Moxie factories on Haverhill Street in Boston and at the corner of Varick and Laight streets in New York City. There was much left-over space in the large New York city building, and the upper floors were rented out to tenants, including the Lash Bitters Company, which rented loft space to store its flavored-alcohol product.

Automobiles continued to be bought, sold, and exchanged. An Oldsmobile which cost $765 earlier was sold in August 1905 for $100, a new Knox was acquired at $750, and a deposit of $600 was paid

Residents of Webster, Massachusetts who enjoyed bowling took time out for Moxie, according to the sign posted above the alley. Not everyone liked Moxie at first, and this was recognized. Moxie was an acquired taste, as the "Learn to Drink MOXIE" lettering of the sign notes. The photograph is probably circa 1905-1910.

"YES, We Sell MOXIE," proclaims a horizontal oval sign set amidst numerous Moxie bottles in the front window of Lewando & Tilton, a Wolfeboro, New Hampshire store, show in a circa 1903 photograph from the files of the Wolfeboro Historical Society. Horizontal oval signs were issued in limited numbers. Most large oval signs were of the vertical format.

The oval metal Moxie sign, usually supported on two black wooden legs, was popular circa 1906-1910. The scenes above and below are of two different refreshment stands in Savin Rock, Connecticut, while the lady standing to the right was photographed in South Weymouth, Massachusetts.

In the time prior to about 1904, before Moxie developed its fancier trademark styles, the word MOXIE was often emblazoned on drugstore, soda fountain, and other windows in uniform block letters. Above is shown the village square, Brookline, Massachusetts, circa 1900-1905. To the left is an unidentified store window, probably in New England, circa 1905. Below is shown the front James Egan's store in North Wilbraham, Massachusetts, about 1906.

A "foxtail" Moxie sign is in the right-side window of G.J. Whitney & Company, Center Barnstead, New Hampshire, in this photograph taken on December 9, 1905. This style of Moxie trademark was in use during the 1904-1907 period, after which time it was replaced by the trademark (with distinctive lower left and upper right crossbar to the X) used frm 1907 onward. Like many stores of its time the Whitney business also served as a post office.

for a Panhard. Two of the Company's Moxie Bottle Wagons suffered extensive damage in Newark when the building in which they were stored caught fire. Profits were good for the year 1905 and amounted to $65,098.08.

Frank M. Archer, the man responsible for much of Moxie's growth and, especially, the proliferation of Moxie advertising, was a subject of discussion at the February 15, 1905 Board of Directors meeting. In recognition of his service for the years 1901 through 1904 his salary was retroactively increased to $5,000 per year, and for 1905 it was posted at $6,000. The difference between these amounts and the sums earlier paid to him came to $4,094.84, a check in which amount was given to Archer. In a token gesture, 25 shares of the Moxie Nerve Food Company of New England were sold to Archer for $250. Although Archer became increasingly important and within a few years was doing the lion's share of the work, his stock ownership in the early years never amounted to more than 1%. Time and time again he requested the opportunity to enlarge his interest, but the Thompson brothers and Freeman N. Young steadfastly refused. Still, the main stockholders were generous to Archer in terms of salary, and a number of years later a business magazine was to report that he was the highest-paid executive of any firm in New England.

The following year, 1906, was a good year—a very good year— the best yet under the management of the Thompson brothers, Freeman N. Young, and Frank Archer. A record number of freight car loads of Moxie left the factories during the month of August. Things were so good that a dividend to stockholders in the amount of $60,000 was paid on September 6th, and by year's end the ledgers showed a record profit of $97,412.71.

Frank Archer devised many forms and procedures contributing to the firm's efficiency. Profit and loss records showed, for example, that a case of three dozen Moxie pint bottles cost $1.85 to fill, while a case containing a dozen quarts of Moxie cost $1.15. The Philadelphia office, a marginal venture at best, was restructured, and its activities were combined with the New York branch. The Standard Bottling Company, Lowell, remained an active but insignificant part of the Moxie business. Bottling activities there were confined primarily to ginger ale and non-alcoholic champagne cider. The days of Standard were numbered and within a few years it would be closed down. Boston and New York divided territories between the two offices, with the Boston office claiming five of the six New England states, while the New York office handled Connecticut, Delaware, the District of Columbia, Maryland, Michigan, New Jersey, New York, Ohio, Pennsylvania, Virginia, and West Virginia.

Not far from Post Office Square, Holbrook, Massachusetts, F.H. Talcott, druggist, advertised Moxie via a large sign on the side of his store. The text noted in part: "Yes! We Sell MOXIE. The Most Healthful Beverage." Shown are views of the same sign from two perspectives, with the bottom photograph depicting also the porch of the Masonic and Pythian Club House next door. Both photographs were taken on the same day and probably date from the 1900-1910 decade.

Taken at an unidentified location, this snapshot shows a large metal Moxie sign affixed to the fold-up front of a refreshment stand at a fair or outdoor event. Although Moxie is advertised, an examination with a magnifying glass of the original photograph shows that the bottles at the center of the counter are of another product!

On the front porch of the store of Coral E. Jones, Meat & Groceries, location unknown, is a metal Moxie sign showing a crate of the beverage. This is the "Brownie" sign with tiny Brownies cavorting.

Gone were the days when Moxie was distributed in West Coast states and other distant lands, although an active business was recorded for the eastern part of Canada (through the Boston office), and occasional shipments were made to Bermuda.

Counterfeiting and substitution continued to rear its ugly head, and the problem of misuse of Moxie glasses increased. Frank Archer sent out numerous notices, observing, for example: "So far this year, we have ordered over 1,100 barrels of Moxie glasses, and we find that our liberality in connection with Moxie glasses has been very much abused by some of our agents and jobbers and their representatives. It has come to our attention that some of our agents and jobbers and their representatives have suggested to the dealer that he can get Moxie glasses, they will cost him nothing, etc., even when they knew he had sufficient Moxie glasses. This practice we intend to stop." Similarly, controls were set in place whereby the customer had to sign a form stating that he "hereby acknowledges the receipt from The Moxie Nerve Food Company of New England, sole owners and manufacturers of Moxie, of (number to be filled in) distinctive Moxie glasses, and agrees to use the same only for the serving and advertising of Moxie." In a not too subtle statement Archer warned that "orders containing glasses being too frequently submitted will arouse the suspicion of the Moxie Company that its interests are being neglected."

Still, Archer did not want to harm the loyalty of hundreds of faithful Moxie outlets. The "compensation case" program was increased, and free cases of Moxie and in some instances extra Moxie glasses or mugs were given in return for agreeing "to conspicuously display Moxie and Moxie signs in the windows of the store for at least two weeks during the year, and to conspicuously display Moxie signs in and on the store throughout the year." During this period, syrup was not dispensed in wholesale quantities to soda fountains, and Moxie had to be served by pouring from quart bottles. At intervals over a period of years, the firm would change its position and agree to sell syrup, and then retrench in view of counterfeiting and substitution.

Keeping track of bottles remained a problem. Frequent calls were made for outlets to return empties to the factory, and in an era in which glass bottle manufacturing was scattered among many suppliers, new bottles were acquired from several sources. Often, returned crates would contain bottles other than Moxie. Ledgers kept by the company show numerous notations of empty Witch City Appetizer, Chelmsford Spring, Simpson Spring, Cliquot Club and other bottles, which were returned to their rightful owners on an exchange basis.

Advertising efforts were intensified in all areas. Receiving particular attention were translucent signs applied to the inside of store windows. On March 1, 1906, Frank Archer sent the following notice to Moxie agents:

"Our order which we placed for translucent signs in Germany last year has arrived. We are negotiating for hundreds of men, if they can be obtained, to put same up in windows of dealers who sell Moxie. As you know, we have one to meet most all requirements, and we should be the largest translucent sign advertisers in the world this year.

"The Forbes Lithograph Manufacturing Company has our orders for posters on the press, and we are now negotiating with the bill posters in all of our agency cities for these posters to be displayed May 1st... Our new shipping tag, known as the Moxie Shipping Tag, is now in preparation for shipment, and we believe it is going to aid very much in the return of empty Moxie bottles and in full goods breakage... March 1905 was a very good month. Our shipments were a little less than 100 car loads for that month. Let us hope, and the indications are right for it, that there will be over 150 car loads in March 1906."

Although the "hundreds of men" were never hired, over a dozen employees of the New York office alone were kept busy posting the translucent signs, usually working in teams of two men. Each man was paid from 10c to 20c per sign effectively put in place. In addition to signs advertising Moxie, as part of the translucent window decorations other signs were provided with general themes such as "Refreshments," "Restaurant," and so forth. Apparently, some stores would request the general-purpose signs and not want the Moxie advertising! Frank Archer prepared an instruction book which noted in part:

"These [translucent] signs are intended to be placed in store windows... MOXIE SIGNS MUST BE PLACED FIRST. A translucent sign No. 46, 60, 61, or 63 must be the first sign that the advertising man puts into the dealer's window. Never put on any other number until one of these numbers has been put on.... The advertising man is to use good judgment and only put signs on such stores that handle Moxie and then only in reasonable numbers. You must never, under any circumstances, leave any translucent signs with a dealer to put on himself.

Made and Sold Since 1885.

During the early days The Moxie Nerve Food Company of New England and its successor, The Moxie Company, advertised that the beverage had been sold since 1885. In later times advertising copy writers pushed the date back to 1884. The bottle illustration to the left is a picture of a large and colorful cardboard cut-out produced around the turn of the century. An enlargement of the label is shown above, with the caption "Made and Sold Since 1885."

Lovers of Moxie often submitted photographs to
The Moxie Company. Shown here is a young girl
"wearing" a Moxie sign, standing next to a Moxie
Cooler, with another Moxie sign on the grass to the
right, next to a teddy bear and a cat.

Drugstores mounted many Moxie exhibits. In the above snapshot W.A.
Burton, an Athol, Massachusetts pharmacist, proudly displayed Moxie to the
exclusion of any other products. A faded sign to the right on his building notes
that he also sold Hood's Sarsaparilla. Below, another drugstore window shows
a Moxie exhibit, this one shared with a display for Orangeine Soda, which
was billed as a pain reliever, bracer, and cure.

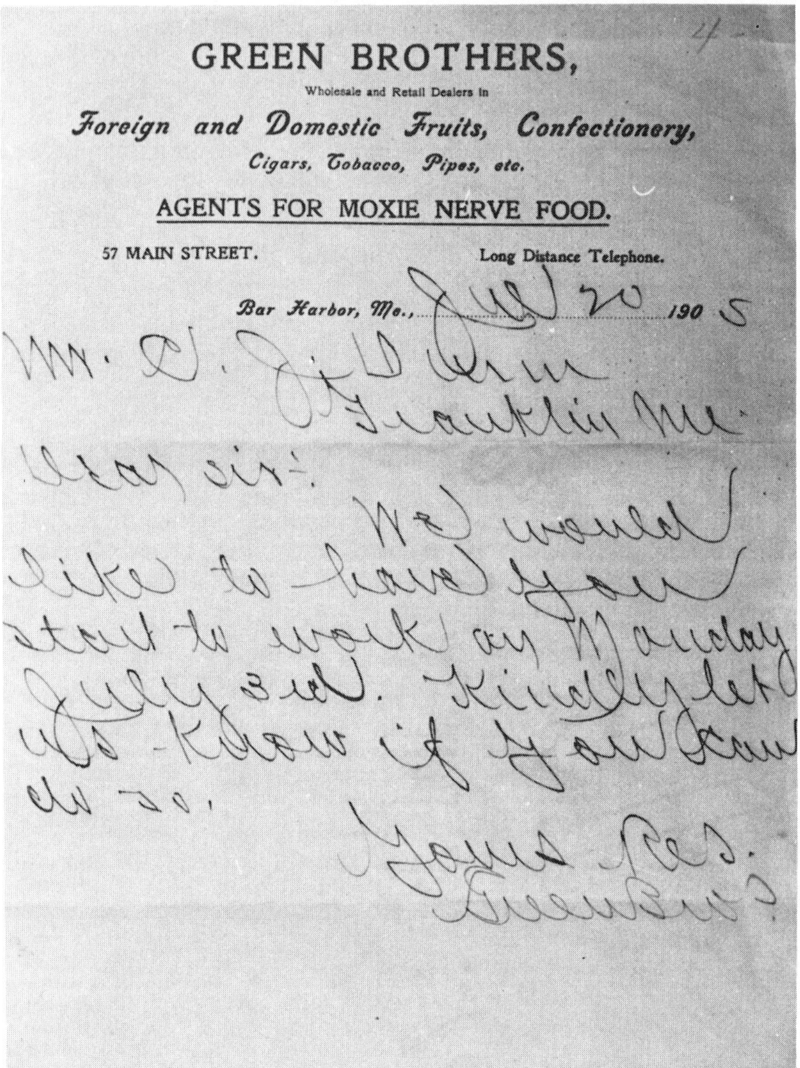

GREEN BROTHERS,

Wholesale and Retail Dealers in

Foreign and Domestic Fruits, Confectionery,

Cigars, Tobacco, Pipes, etc.

AGENTS FOR MOXIE NERVE FOOD.

57 MAIN STREET.   Long Distance Telephone.

Bar Harbor, Me., _____ 190 5

Mr. D. J. D. Orm
Franklin Me.

Dear sir:-

We would like to have you start to work on Monday July 3d. Kindly let us know if you can do so.

Yours res.
Green Bros.

Moxie was distributed by dozens of different agents. The above letter is from Green Brothers of Bar Harbor, Maine.

Above: Several Moxie signs adorned the post office at East Windham, New York, including the large red, black, and white pressed metal sign in the foreground.

Below: Main Street, South Bristol, Maine, in the 1910 era.

"Any signs except signs No. 46, 60, 61, or 63 are given in payment to the dealer in consideration that he keeps up signs 46, 60, 61, or 63 as long as he keeps up signs of other numbers. No charge is to be made to the dealer for any of these signs.

"As a general rule there must be as many Moxie signs put on a dealer's window as there are signs of the other kind. That is, one Moxie sign for each of any other kind that is put on... Always put Moxie signs on first. Be sure to always put on a translucent sign with the word Moxie on it in the dealer's window first, as it has been found by experience that if you do not do this, and if you put on first some of the signs that do not have the word Moxie on them, the dealer will say, 'I guess I will not have any more put up.' The way to overcome this is to never put any sign until you have put on the sign with the word Moxie on it first."

Agents were instructed to put translucent signs on the window as near as possible to the level of the eye. It was noted that the average level for pedestrians and streetcars was five feet, six inches from the sidewalk.

An idea of the omnipresence of Moxie advertising in 1906 is gained by such notations as 16,840 framed metal signs shipped to the firm by the Eureka Sign Company in March 1906, 9,450 cardboard cutouts in the shape of a Moxie bottle shipped by Forbes during the months of September and October, and quantities of such diverse items as "brass checks," "aluminum steel openers," and large 24-sheet posters. Newspaper readers were treated to an interesting campaign featuring spritely Brownie figures.

Vehicles continued their prominence. Moxie Bottle Wagons were active throughout the Northeast, with Wonderland Park at Revere Beach, near Boston, having three of them simultaneously during the summer. Each was equipped with a special curved electric sign measuring three feet wide by one foot high. Horse teams and wagons were gradually phased out in favor of electric and gasoline delivery trucks. Rapid delivery of fresh Moxie was especially important, for Moxie, if kept warm and not sold for a period of time, was apt to turn sour. There are numerous accounts of sour Moxie being poured down the drain.

Company records and scrapbooks for 1906 reveal many interesting incidents. L.A. Hager was fined $9.62 for driving too fast on June 29, 1906. The company reimbursed him for he was on Moxie business. J.L. Beauchain, who managed the Boston facility, realized that the Standard Bottling Company in Lowell could not make Moxie as effectively as the Boston plant. Accordingly, 14 large wooden

Moxie at Coney Island: Along Surf Avenue, the main thoroughfare of this famous New York seaside amusement park area, an ice cream stand dispensed Moxie circa 1905.

Right next to the Old Mill, also on Surf Avenue, a prominent Moxie sign was displayed during the same period. New York State was second only to New England in terms of Moxie popularity during the early years of the present century.

Above: The front of a dance hall, location unknown but probably in New England, circa 1905-1910. "This is the dancing pavilion between the store and the house. It is large enough to dance six sets," notes an inscription on the photograph in the author's collection. Near the door is an oval metal Moxie sign (of the type that measures slightly larger than thirteen inches wide by nine inches high).

Below: Extending out into Lake Winnipesaukee at The Weirs, New Hampshire, this pier featured Moxie along with other items in a concession operated by Otto Kelley of Laconia (a nearby town). The photograph dates from the summer of 1908.

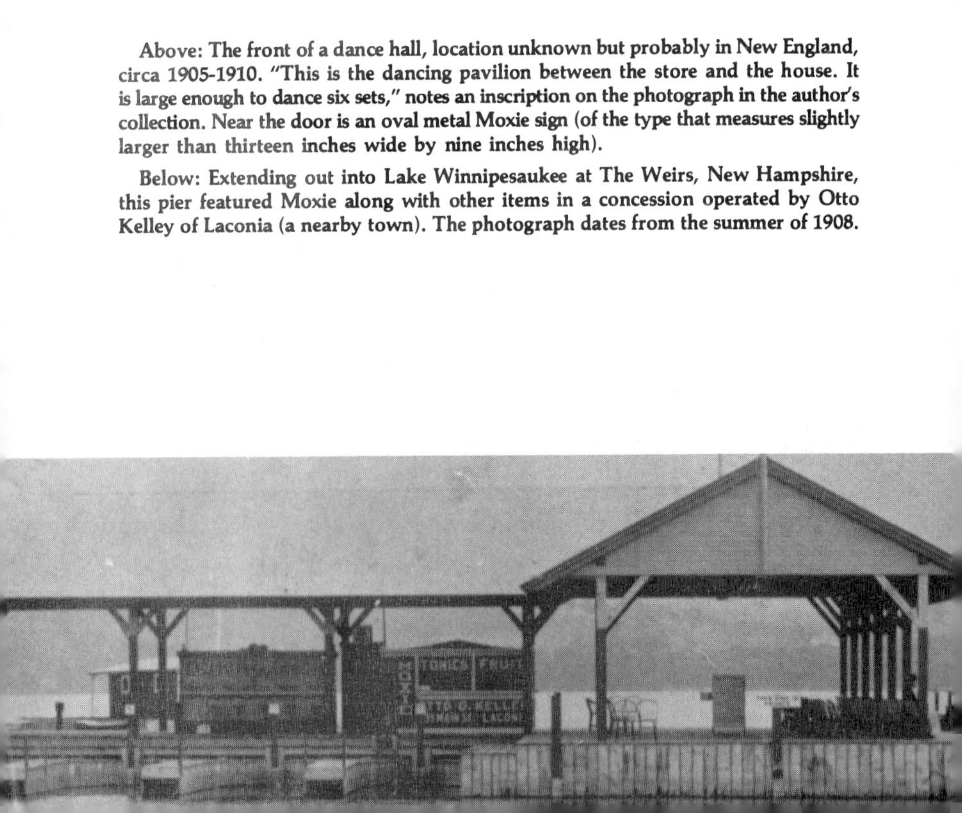

![A bearded man in a hat seated behind a large bear, in front of a store with Moxie signs reading "MOXIE" and "YES! WE SELL MOXIE VERY HEALTHFUL FEEDS THE NERVES."]

Above: M.E. Robbins, a Vermont bear hunter, is shown with his 101st prize in this photograph taken before 1910. In the background is a metal Moxie sign, while in the store window are other Moxie items.

Right: This sign, on the porch of Buttnar's store, Londonderry, Vermont, offers soft drinks of various types, including Moxie, which heads the list.

Moxie in the home at the turn of the century. The Moxie Nerve Food
Company of New England sold wooden cooler cabinets, of which
presumably this is one, for use in restaurants, hotels, and fine homes.
In addition, commercial dispensing coolers boldly emblazoned with
Moxie insignia were produced in several varieties.

tanks, tens of thousands of Moxie bottle labels bearing the Lowell address, and other things were destroyed. Investigating the feasibility of dispensing Moxie in syrup form, the firm shipped two gallons of syrup to the Charles L. Bastian Manufacturing Company, Chicago, "for experiments." On December 17, 1906, a dozen Moxie bottles were found missing in the stock room of the Boston plant. A ledger note tells the tale:

"Empty box found under the No. 2 receiving run. It is presumed that the contents of this box were taken by the electricians that worked here Sunday, December 16th. Charged to profit and loss."

Around this time, a newspaper article related the fate of a competitor:

"A truck load of bottles shaped like the well-known Moxie bottle was removed Tuesday from the premises of the Lynn Bottling Works, a concern run by Clarence Coates of this city, in order that they might be broken up by the Moxie Company pursuant to an order of the Supreme Court. As is well known in the trade, The Moxie Company employs inspectors to visit stores handling beverages for the purpose of seeing that nothing other than Moxie is served to customers as and for Moxie.

"It was found that a beverage put up by Coates in a bottle like the Moxie bottle in shape and size was being marketed and that owing to the similarity of the package to the Moxie package, retail dealers were able to substitute this Coates production when Moxie was called for..

"[The court] submitted a decree against the defendant, preventing him from selling beverages in bottles shaped like the Moxie bottle and from refilling empty Moxie bottles, and further commanding Coates forthwith to deliver up to the complainant for destruction all such bottles in his possession. The decree also provided that complainant recover of the defendant damages in cost of suit. It will be of interest to manufacturers and dealers to know that the destruction of packages made in infringement of trademark rights, under an order of the court, is becoming increasingly common in the United States. It has long been practiced in England, where it is found to be an effective deterrent to fraud. Imitators find the risk of investing capital in imitative packages for probable destruction too great to be faced and dislike the ridiculous notoriety that ensues..."

Another article noted that Vice-President Freeman N. Young and Joseph T. Brennan of The Moxie Company visited the plant of the Lynn Bottling Works on Saratoga Street "and there officially received

Freeman N. Young (left) and Joseph T. Brennan of The Moxie Company engage in a bottle-smashing party at the Lynn (Massachusetts) city dump. It happened that Clarence Coates, owner of the Lynn Bottling Works, engaged in some naughty practices, including refilling empty Moxie bottles with Coates Nerve Food Appetizer, which may have tasted like Moxie but wasn't the real thing, and also putting up his beverage, correctly marked, but in a bottle resembling that of Moxie.

Moxie took the matter to court, Coates lost, and an article in the Lynn "Item" newspaper related: "[The court] submitted a decree against the defendant, preventing him from selling beverages in bottles shaped like the Moxie bottle and from refilling empty Moxie bottles, and further commanding Coates forthwith to deliver up to the complainant for destruction all such bottles in his possession." It was further noted that "Brennan and Young, at the request of Mr. Coates, who did not desire to witness the destruction of what was formerly his personal property, refrained from carrying on the work at the plant on Saratoga Street, where the bottles were received, and willingly consented to the proposition to smash the bottles into smithereens at the city dump."

from the proprietor, Clarence B. Coates, 37 full cases of bottles, shaped like the Moxie bottle, which by order of the court, the complainants in the civil action were bound to destroy." The tale continued:

"The wholesale destruction of the bottles, which have been used by Mr. Coates in retailing 'Coates Nerve Food Appetizer,' claimed by the Moxie people to be an imitation of their well-known nerve drink, which has been sold by storekeepers during the present summer in lieu of Moxie, was completed at the city dump at the foot of Shepard Street, in the presence of a small but interested gathering of spectators and an *Item* [Lynn newspaper] photographer, who snapped the picture which is reproduced herewith. Messrs. Brennan and Young, at the request of Mr. Coates, who did not desire to witness the destruction of what was formerly his personal property, refrained from carrying on the work at the plant on Saratoga Street, where the bottles were received, and willingly consented to the proposition to smash the bottles into smithereens at the city dump... Mr. Coates admitted that he possessed 100 cases of bottles, and the first installment of the lot to be destroyed was the 37 cases— less than one-half the number to be smashed. As soon as the remainder can be collected they will be conveyed to the dump and broken into bits."

Chapter 7

Moxie
Newspaper Campaigns

Around the turn of the century, newspapers were one of the main advertising media for spreading the Moxie message. On the following pages is reproduced the Moxie advertising campaign for the year 1899. Then, as now, newspaper advertising was measured in terms of column inches. The series of 22 advertisements was comprised of 13 15-inch ads, 8 5-inch ads, and 1 6-inch ad. For reproduction in the present book, larger advertisements have been reduced to conform with the present page size.

For *daily* papers, Pettingill & Company, the advertising agency for Moxie, instructed:

"This series consists of 22 advertisements... Run these in order— as they are numbered—each advertisement appearing but one time. We wish you to run these advertisements for nine consecutive weeks, two of them a week, selecting such days as will be the most convenient for you to give us good position, providing, however, two days intervene between insertions. At the end of nine weeks, and after 18 advertisements have been inserted, you will continue for four more weeks, running one advertisement a week, thus completing the 22 advertisements in the series in a period of 13 weeks... Be sure that a copy of every paper containing this advertisement is sent to The Moxie Nerve Food Company, 68 Beverly Street, Boston, Mass., as well as to us, Pettingill & Co."

For *weekly* newspapers the instructions were as follows:

"Run only the 5-inch, 3-column advertisements [occupying a total of 15 column inches], one each week, omitting all smaller advertisements. There are 13 of these advertisements in the series, and this will cover the period of the 13 weeks for which we have contracted to run space in your paper..." (The 13 advertisements scheduled for the weekly papers were those with the following numbers in the series: 1, 3, 5, 7, 9, 11, 13, 15, 17, 19, 20, 21, and 22.)

1899 was in the era of Moxie as a patent medicine which had become more prominent as a beverage. At the time, the label on the Moxie bottle was titled Beverage Moxie Nerve Food, to indicate that it was more than just a medicine. Moxie was depicted as essential in everyday life. Children loved it, golfers needed it, doctors wouldn't be without it. By implication, *you* needed it too.

"Men of science know the value of Moxie," noted the first advertisement in the series. "Chemists find upon analysis that it is a pure, healthful, nerve-creating beverage. They readily determine the fact that not a single injurious ingredient is used in its composition. Because such men know this, they drink Moxie themselves, and enjoy this most refreshing of beverages, and are benefited by its nerve-creating properties." At the time, complaints about patent medicines were appearing with increasing frequency in many publications, so Moxie was quick to point out that it was free of "injurious" ingredients, presumably referring to cocaine, morphine, and other substances found in certain competitive products.

Today, if a doctor endorses something it must be beneficial, for nothing helps sell a remedy for coughs, an aid to sleep, or other nostrum than a white-jacketed doctor beholding The Product with a serious gaze. Things haven't changed much, and back in 1899 the second advertisement in the Moxie series noted:

"The reason doctors endorse Moxie Nerve Food is that they are assured of its healthfulness and of the fact that it is scientifically prepared. That Moxie is a result of a discovery of a regular physician of high standing [a reference to Augustin Thompson] is in itself an endorsement in its favor." Of course, it can be argued that Thompson did not *discover* Moxie, for it did not exist earlier. Rather, he formulated or invented it.

"A wise golf player is this man who stops at a critical place in the game and refreshes himself with Moxie," the third advertisement in the series noted. "Because Moxie is a nerve food it is invaluable where a clear head and a steady hand are needed. Professional athletes appreciate Moxie on account of its strengthening properties." Significantly, this advertisement notes that "Moxie is a nerve food, a recognition that it is but one of many nerve foods. Years later, The Moxie Company was to take the position in numerous legal actions that "nerve food" was its private term, and any other beverage calling itself thus was apt to be pounced upon by Moxie's aggressive lawyers! In practice, there were indeed many nerve foods and nerve tonics during the last part of the 19th century.

Cyclists, particularly older ones (for some unknown reason), liked Moxie, according to the fourth advertisement in the series:

"Bicyclists know the value of Moxie. It refreshes, quenches thirst and as it is nourishing to the nervous system it does much to lessen fatigue. Old bicycle riders when asked what they will drink, will invariably answer, if they are on their wheels, MOXIE."

While adults formed the main market for Moxie at the time, the ingenious copy writers for Moxie did not overlook the fact that little kids had brains and nerves which might benefit from the tonic:

"Children love Moxie. They would rather drink it on a warm day than eat. Nothing strange about this. Instinct teaches them what is good for them. Moxie nourishes their nervous system. It is as valuable a food for their little brains and nerves as bread and butter is for their body. Give the little ones all they want of it. It will keep them well, make them vigorous, cheerful, robust, healthy, and happy," according to the fifth advertisement in the 1899 series.

"Do not be deceived, get the genuine. Genuine Moxie is always served from a bottle like this, in a Moxie glass. Never in any other way," petitioned the sixth advertisement in the series. "The genuine is healthful and nerve-strengthening, so be sure you get it."

This was a sensible precaution, for druggists and others were always endeavoring to serve "Moxie" without actually buying the genuine product. Various pharmaceutical digests of the era were filled with analyses of patent medicines, colas, tonics, and other substances, often in response to queries from readers who wanted to know how to compound the product for sale in their stores. For example, in the May 1897 issue of *The Western Druggist*, published in Chicago, by G.P. Engelhard & Company, 358 Dearborn Street, the following formula was given:

MOXIE SYRUP

Sarsaparilla flavor . . . . .2 fl. oz
Tincture Nux Vomica . . . . .1 fl. oz
Citric acid solution . . . . .fl. dr. 4
Egg mixture . . . . .1 fl. oz
Syrup . . . . .1 gallon

Such formulations were often wide of the mark. The preceding omits gentian root, the most prized "secret ingredient" of Moxie at the time. When the preceding formula was read to Mrs. L.S. (Virginia) McElwee, granddaughter of Augustin Thompson, she stated that it in no way resembled the early Moxie formula with which she was quite familiar. *The Western Druggist* in the same era informed its readers how to make Coca-Cola, listing as one of the ingredients "wine of coca," a mixture of cocaine and alcohol!

The housewife was a candidate for Moxie, and the seventh advertisement in the 1899 series suggested that: "A happy restful minute comes in the midst of a hard morning's work about the house to the tired, thirsty housewife when she stops to refresh herself with that thirst-quenching temperance beverage—Moxie Nerve Food. It gives strength to the nerves and gives fortitude and vigor to all—especially to women." Shown in the advertisement is a standing

Above: I.E. Harriman's store in Barnstead, New Hampshire, displays a round metal Moxie sign (against the column at the right side of the building) in this October 1908 photograph. This particular type of sign seems to have been especially used in Vermont, New Hampshire and Maine, but not to the exclusion of other states.

Left: This faded photograph, taken in September 1906, shows a similar round metal Moxie sign, with a smaller oval sign hanging over it, on the porch of Brown's store, Bridgewater, Vermont.

housewife pouring a glass of Moxie, while on the floor a little girl drinks a glass of The Product while a cat watches.

No need to take sleeping pills when Moxie is at hand, as the eighth advertisement noted: "Before going to bed it is a good plan to drink a glass of Moxie. It refreshes one wonderfully. It acts beneficially upon the stomach; it nourishes the nervous system so that quiet, refreshing sleep will follow its use."

While lesser tennis players might be satisfied with Coca-Cola, Hires Root Beer, or some other tonic, "A *champion* tennis player who realizes the necessity of a clear head, an accurate eye and steady nerves, to obtain all of these—drinks Moxie wherever he may be. It is good for his stomach. It is refreshing, it is thirst-quenching, but above all it strengthens the nervous system. Athletes everywhere drink Moxie in preference to any other beverage." And, the ninth advertisement in the series shows, sure enough, a bottle of Moxie and a glass on a table right on the tennis court!

Exactly what constitutes a *sloppy* drink is unknown today, but Moxie apparently felt them competitive, as the 10th advertisement noted:

"Why do you put cheap, sloppy drinks into your stomach, that do you real injury? Moxie Nerve Food is healthful, refreshing, made in a clean, scientific manner, and does good to whoever drinks it, because it strengthens the nerves."

A primary ingredient of the picnic basket pictured in advertisement No. 11 is Moxie, and in the offing a dashing young man offers a bottle of Moxie to the object of his affection seated nearby under a parasol. The text notes:

"A perfect picnic is that where the Moxie has been brought, no matter what else has been forgotten. Because it is refreshing and a wonderful nerve food, it is invaluable. It is a necessity to perfect enjoyment on a day's outing."

Intelligent readers take note: "Hard head work is made much easier when an occasional rest is taken and a glass of Moxie drunk. Nothing is so refreshing and thirst-quenching. Brain-workers realize better than anyone else that Moxie does nourish the nervous system," noted the 12th advertisement in the 1899 series.

Then it was back to the doctor, a recommendation that always was convincing. The 13th advertisement featured a distinguished physician near a seated lady: "The doctor says to the convalescent patient, 'all you need now is plenty of Moxie Nerve Food. Nothing else will help you to restore your shattered nerves as quickly as will Moxie. I drink it myself, and I use it in my home because I know that it is helpful as well as delicious.' Then, too, Moxie was discovered by a brother physician of a large practice, extending over many years. It is therefore scientific, pure, safe, and an enjoyable preparation." Again, reference is made to Augustin Thompson's *discovery* of Moxie. But, then, discoveries were nothing new in the field of patent medicine, for another advertiser of the era, Dr. Sanchez, advertised the "discovery" of a product called Oxydonor Victory, which was just about the best thing ever for mankind. Similarly, pages of just about every newspaper and magazine at the time were filled with like claims.

"You will find your wife better in every way if she drinks Moxie Nerve Food. This is the experience of hundreds. The reason for it is that Moxie nourishes the nervous system and enables women to forget they have such a thing as nerves," proclaimed the 14th advertisement in the series.

We've all heard of people *dying* for a drink, figuratively speaking, but the 15th advertisement in Moxie's 1899 series seems to encourage this in the literal sense: "Don't jump off!... the wise conductor says to the passengers preparing to leave the train after it has started. There is but one thing that would induce this naturally sensible man to thus risk life and limb. He has forgotten to order a case of Moxie Nerve Food sent to his house. He does not know how he can get along without it over Sunday. He has learned that there is nothing as thirst-quenching and refreshing as Moxie. He has also learned that on account of its nerve-strengthening properties how valuable it is in the house and how much better his wife has been since she has been drinking it." (Again a reference to keeping the wife happy.)

In later years Dr. Pepper, the popular cola, suggested that the hours of 2, 10, and 4 o'clock were ideal for drinking it. The 15th advertisement in Moxie's 1899 series encouraged a similar activity:

"Moxie Nerve Food should be drunk frequently. It strengthens and makes new nerves, as food makes blood and flesh. Besides being beneficial, it is delicious and thirst-quenching."

The sensible employer might find that Moxie pays for itself, or at least this is the suggestion of the 17th advertisement in the series: "A respite from work—Moxie Nerve Food. Stop long enough from your work to drink a glass of refreshing Moxie. See that you have it in your office for your clerks and stenographers. They enjoy it and it does them good on account of its strengthening properties. A hard day's work is lightened when Moxie is used. More work can be done by those who drink Moxie because their nerves are strengthened, their stomachs are kept in good condition and there is a certain refreshfulness about Moxie that appeals to all brain

Above: Moxie was advertised on an awning in West Chester, Pennsylvania, circa 1910. Very few photographs of Moxie awnings survive today.

Right: In Rochester, New Hampshire, an agent for Moxie was P.J. Rumazza, who conducted his business on North Main Street. The Rumazza family, which had recently immigrated from Italy, was primarily in the fruit and vegetable trade, but at another location in the same town. This picture dates from about 1905.

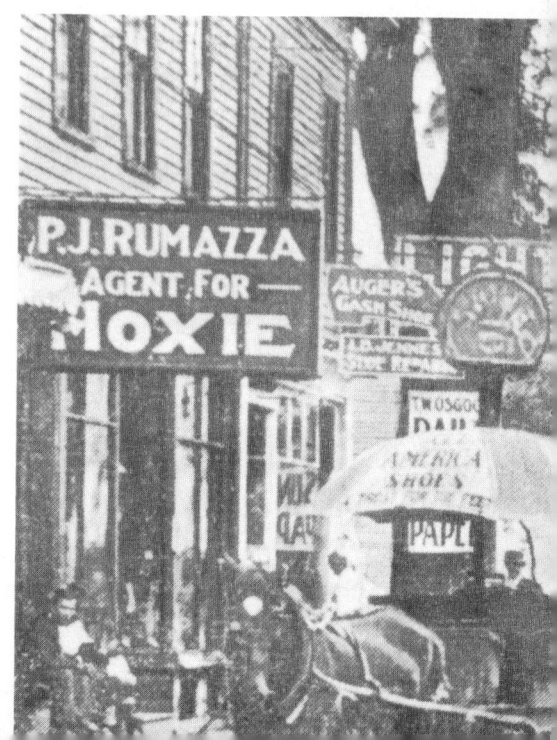

workers. Moxie will pay for itself on account of the extra amount of work that can be accomplished when it is used, if you have it always on hand in the office."

Children recur as a theme in the 18th advertisement: "Children love it and should be encouraged in having all they want. There is nothing that does the growing boy or girl so much good as Moxie. The reason for this is that it is a REAL FOOD for the nerves, and so acts beneficially in aiding to develop their nervous system in a healthy manner."

And, at the end of a day, what better drink than Moxie? The 19th advertisement: "After a hard day's work nothing can bring more joy to man's heart than a cool, refreshing glass of Moxie, on his return from the noise and worry of a business day down town. Besides being refreshing, it is restful because it nourishes the nervous system."

The wife's tiring activities during the day are not forgotten, as the 20th advertisement noted: "Nothing is so worrisome and nerve exhausting as a hard day's shopping. Women, exhausted after shopping, appreciate Moxie. It restores their worn out nerves quicker than anything else will, as it is a genuine nerve food. It refreshes as nothing else will, and quenches the thirst in a marvelous manner. Try a glass of Moxie the next time you are worn and tired."

In the era before the Pure Food and Drugs Act of 1906, popular beverages and tonics were apt to contain all sorts of things, especially alcohol. Indeed, the general class of tonics known as bitters contained alcohol as the primary ingredient. Moxie was an exception and was billed for its temperance qualities. This and the perennial theme of avoiding substitutes and imitations formed the text for the 21st advertisement: "Just indignation should be expressed when a dealer imposes on you by suggesting any other temperance beverage when Moxie is called for. Moxie is a genuine nerve food, healthful and refreshing. There is only one Moxie, and you should insist upon having it every time, and always refuse worthless and perhaps harmful imitations. Get the genuine that comes in regular Moxie bottles, and should be served to you in the Moxie glasses."

The final advertisement in the 1899 series, No. 22, stressed the importance of Moxie on shipboard, perhaps inspired by Augustin Thompson's sons, who loved sailing and who owned large yachts: " 'Already to start now, sir!' announces the captain, as he apologizes for the delay getting under way. 'We could get along without anything better than Moxie. Because it was late in arriving we were obliged to wait for it.' The fact that Moxie is refreshing and thirst-quenching, while at the same time it strengthens the nerves, makes it invaluable for a day's outing on the water. Its beneficial action upon the stomach and nerves does much to prevent sea sickness."

When the curtain came down in 1899, America looked forward to the 20th century. Although scholars were quick to point out that the new century officially began in the year 1901, and 1900 was the last year of the 19th century, the public paid no attention to such technicalities, and the moment 1899 ended, celebrations were staged everywhere.

Although the emphasis of Moxie as a nerve food and palatable medicine was to continue for a few more years, the direction gradually shifted from health to enjoyment. The 1890s ended, Moxie had been established as a prominent tonic on the American scene, but the best years were yet to come.

1899 Moxie Advertising Campaign—Advertisement No. 1

Advertisement No. 2.

MOXIE
Nerve Food
A Wise . .
Golf Player

Is this man who stops at a critical place in the game and refreshes himself with MOXIE. Because Moxie is a nerve food it is invaluable where a clear head and a steady hand are needed. Professional athletes appreciate Moxie on account of its strengthening properties.

MOXIE
Nerve Food

Druggists everywhere sell Moxie by the glass. Grocers everywhere deliver Moxie to the home by the bottle or case.

1899 Moxie Advertising Campaign—Advertisement No. 3

MOXIE Nerve Food
➤ Bicyclists

Know the Value of Moxie.

It refreshes, quenches thirst and as it is nourishing to the nervous system, it does much to lessen fatigue. Old bicycle riders, when asked what they will drink, will invariably answer, if they are on their wheels, MOXIE.

All druggists sell Moxie by the glass.
Any grocer will deliver it to your house by the bottle or case.

Advertisement No. 4

Children Love

Moxie. They would rather drink it on a warm day than eat. Nothing strange about this. Instinct teaches them what is good for them. Moxie nourishes their nervous system. It is as valuable a food for their little brains and nerves as bread and butter is for their body. Give the little ones all they want of it. It will keep them well, make them vigorous, cheerful, robust, healthy and happy.

Your Druggist sells Moxie by the glass. Your Grocer will deliver it to you by the bottle or case.

MOXIE
Nerve Food

1899 Moxie Advertising Campaign—Advertisement No. 5

Do Not Be
DECEIVED

GET THE Genuine

GENUINE...
MOXIE

is always served from a bottle like this, in a Moxie glass. Never in any other way. The genuine is healthful and nerve-strengthening, so be sure you get it.

All druggists sell Moxie by the glass. Any grocer will deliver it to your house by the bottle or case.

Advertisement No. 6

A HAPPY RESTFUL MINUTE comes in the midst of a hard morning's work about the house to the tired, thirsty housewife, when she stops to refresh herself with that thirst-quenching temperance beverage—

MOXIE
Nerve Food

It gives strength to the nerves, and gives fortitude and vigor to all—especially to women. Sold by Druggists and Grocers. *Get the Genuine.*

1899 Moxie Advertising Campaign—Advertisement No. 7

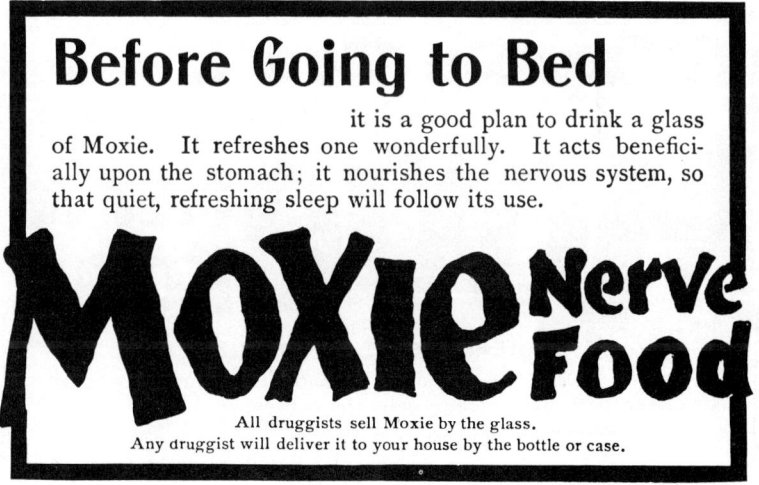

Before Going to Bed

it is a good plan to drink a glass of Moxie. It refreshes one wonderfully. It acts beneficially upon the stomach; it nourishes the nervous system, so that quiet, refreshing sleep will follow its use.

MOXIE Nerve Food

All druggists sell Moxie by the glass.
Any druggist will deliver it to your house by the bottle or case.

Advertisement No. 8

A Champion

tennis player who realizes the necessity of a clear head, an accurate eye and steady nerves, to obtain all of these—drinks Moxie wherever

MOXIE Nerve Food

he may be. It is good for his stomach. It is refreshing, it is thirst-quenching, but above all, it strengthens the nervous system. Athletes everywhere drink Moxie in preference to any other beverage. All Druggists sell Moxie by the glass. Grocers everywhere will deliver Moxie to your house by bottle or case

1899 Moxie Advertising Campaign—Advertisement No. 9

Why Do You ...

put cheap, sloppy drinks into your stomach, that do you real injury?

MOXIE Nerve Food

IS HEALTHFUL, REFRESHING,
made in a clean, scientific manner, and does good to whoever drinks it, because it strengthens the nerves.

All druggists sell Moxie by the glass.
Any grocer will deliver it to your house by the bottle or case.

Advertisement No. 10

MOXIE

Nerve Food

A Perfect Picnic ..

Is that where the Moxie has been brought, no matter what else has been forgotten. Because it is refreshing and a wonderful nerve food, it is invaluable. It is a necessity to perfect enjoyment on a day's outing.

Sold by Druggists and Grocers. *Get the Genuine.*

1899 Moxie Advertising Campaign—Advertisement No. 11

MOXIE

Nerve Food

HARD HEAD WORK

is made much easier when an occasional rest is taken and a glass of Moxie drunk. Nothing is so refreshing and thirst-quenching.

Brain-workers realize better than anyone else that Moxie does nourish the nervous system.

All druggists sell Moxie.
Grocers will deliver by bottle or case.

MOXIE

Nerve Food

Advertisement No. 12

The Doctor Says

To the convalescent patient, "All you need now is plenty of Moxie Nerve Food. Nothing else will help you to restore your shattered nerves as quickly as will Moxie. I drink it myself, and I use it in my home because I know that it is healthful, as well as delicious." Then, too, Moxie was discovered by a brother physician of large practice, extending over many years. It is therefore a scientific, pure, safe, and enjoyable preparation.

Druggists everywhere sell Moxie by the glass. Any Grocer will deliver it at your home by the bottle or case.

MOXIE
Nerve Food

1899 Moxie Advertising Campaign—Advertisement No. 13

YOU WILL FIND

your wife better every way if she drinks

MOXIE Nerve Food

This is the experience of hundreds. The reason for it is that Moxie nourishes the Nervous System and enables women to forget that they have such a thing as nerves.

All druggists sell Moxie by the glass.
Any grocer will deliver it at your house by the bottle or case.

Advertisement No. 14

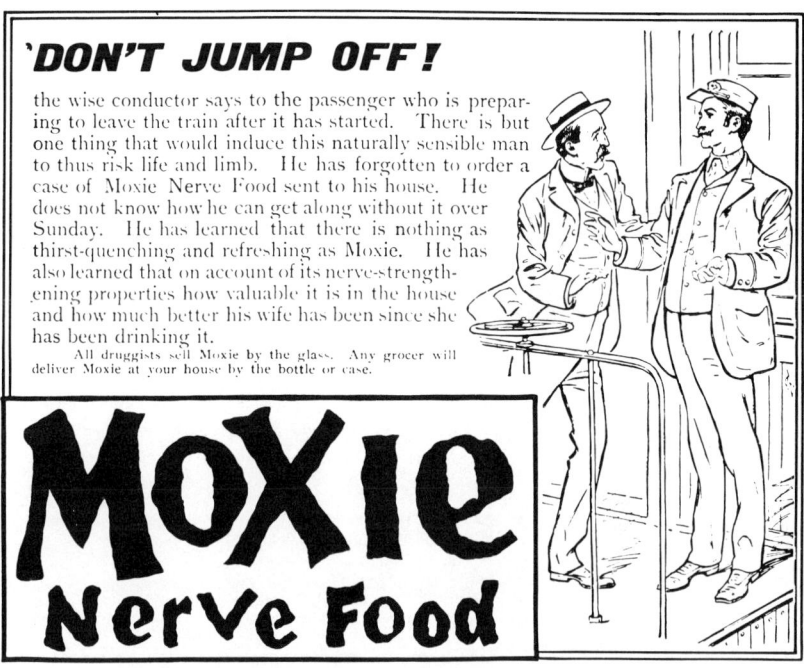

'DON'T JUMP OFF!

the wise conductor says to the passenger who is preparing to leave the train after it has started. There is but one thing that would induce this naturally sensible man to thus risk life and limb. He has forgotten to order a case of Moxie Nerve Food sent to his house. He does not know how he can get along without it over Sunday. He has learned that there is nothing as thirst-quenching and refreshing as Moxie. He has also learned that on account of its nerve-strengthening properties how valuable it is in the house and how much better his wife has been since she has been drinking it.

All druggists sell Moxie by the glass. Any grocer will deliver Moxie at your house by the bottle or case.

MOXIE
Nerve Food

1899 Moxie Advertising Campaign—Advertisement No. 15

MOXIE Nerve Food

Should be drunk frequently.

It strengthens and makes new nerves, as food makes blood and flesh. Besides being beneficial, it is delicious and thirst-quenching.

Any grocer will deliver it to your house by the bottle or case.
All druggists sell Moxie by the glass.

Advertisement No. 16

A Respite From Work

MoXie
Nerve Food

Stop long enough from your work to drink a glass of refreshing Moxie. See that you have it in your office for your clerks and stenographers. They enjoy it and it does them good on account of its strengthening properties. A hard day's work is lightened when Moxie is used. More work can be done by those who drink Moxie because their nerves are strengthened, their stomachs are kept in good condition and there is a certain refreshfulness about Moxie that appeals to all brain workers. Moxie will pay for itself on account of the extra amount of work that can be accomplished when it is used, if you have it always on hand in the office.

All druggists sell Moxie by the glass. Grocers everywhere will deliver Moxie to your house by the bottle or case.

1899 Moxie Advertising Campaign—Advertisement No. 17

Children Love

it and should be encouraged in having all they want. There is nothing that does the growing boy or girl so much good as Moxie. The reason for this is that it is a REAL FOOD for the nerves, and so acts beneficially in aiding to develop their nervous system in a healthy manner.

All druggists sell Moxie by the glass. Any grocer will deliver it to your house by the bottle or case.

Advertisement No. 18

After a hard day's work Nothing can bring more joy to man's heart than a cool, refreshing glass of Moxie, on his return from the noise and worry of a business day down town. Besides being refreshing, it is restful because it nourishes the nervous system.

Grocers everywhere will deliver Moxie to your house by the bottle or case. All druggists sell Moxie by the glass.

1899 Moxie Advertising Campaign—Advertisement No. 19

TIRED ... SICK Nothing is so wearisome and nerve-exhausting as a hard day's shopping. Women, exhausted after shopping, appreciate Moxie. It restores their worn out nerves quicker than anything else will, as it is a genuine nerve food. It refreshes as nothing else will, and quenches the thirst in a marvelous manner. Try a glass of Moxie the next time you are worn and tired.

Druggists everywhere sell Moxie by the glass. All Grocers deliver Moxie by the bottle or case.

Advertisement No. 20

Sold by Druggists and Grocers.
Get the Genuine.

JUST INDIGNATION

should be expressed when a dealer imposes on you by suggesting any other temperance beverage when Moxie is called for. Moxie is a genuine nerve food, healthful and re-

MoXie Nerve Food

freshing. There is only one Moxie, and you should insist upon having it every time, and always refuse worthless and perhaps harmful imitations. Get the genuine that comes in regular Moxie bottles, and should be served to you in the Moxie glasses.

All Reliable Druggists sell Moxie by the glass. Any Grocer will deliver it to your house by bottle or case.

1899 Moxie Advertising Campaign—Advertisement No. 21

"All Ready to Start Now, Sir!" announces the captain, as he apologizes for the delay in getting under way. "We could get along without anything better than the Moxie. Because it was late in arriving we were obliged to wait for it." The fact that Moxie is refreshing and thirst-quenching, while at the same time

MoXie Nerve Food

it strengthens the nerves, makes it invaluable for a day's outing on the water. Its beneficial action upon the stomach and the nerves does much to prevent seasickness.

All druggists sell Moxie by the glass. Grocers everywhere will deliver Moxie to your house by the bottle or case. *Get the Genuine.*

Advertisement No. 22

From the 1890s through the 1920s the main thrust of Moxie advertising was the medium of newspapers. Each year a distinctive campaign was created, with those from the late 1890s through about 1910 being the most imaginative. Sketches rather than photographs were used, for they reproduced better in newsprint.

In the next several pages are shown imaginative cartoons signed by artist D'Emo, part of a series of over twenty subjects used in the year 1900.

Such campaigns were run in areas in which Moxie was distributed. In this way an audience could be pinpointed. As Moxie was not nationally distributed, magazines represented a wasted effort so far as many readers were concerned. Accordingly, magazines were used sparingly in Moxie advertising campaigns, exceptions being certain New England publications such as *Youth's Companion, Cape Cod Magazine,* and others.

The man who keeps cool, looks well, and keeps well, no matter the wilted condition that others may be in, is the man that drinks **Moxie Nerve Food.** Stick to Moxie in hot weather. You will have no stomach disorders. You will be refreshed as by nothing else. You will be invigorated in a healthful manner, for Moxie does nourish the nerves.

All druggists sell Moxie by the glass.
Grocers sell Moxie by the bottle or case.

MOXIE

Trying housework is particularly fatiguing in hot weather. It is a wise woman that fortifies herself by drinking Moxie Nerve Food. Not only is it refreshing and most palatable, but it is a great nerve strengthener and a nerve creator. Housewives who drink Moxie owe health and freedom from nervous exhaustion to this delicious temperance beverage.

Sold by all druggists by the bottle or glass
Kept by grocers everywhere.

MOXIE

MOXIE

Brain workers, professional men, business men, have learned by experience the value of Moxie Nerve Food as an aid to them in their labors. Nothing will invigorate the nerves and the brain like that Temperance Beverage, Moxie. That it is delicious to the taste and marvellously thirst-quenching is also highly in its favor.

Sold by all druggists by the glass. Your grocer will deliver it to your home by the case.

The sea-shore would be as devoid of its charm without the sea as without that most delicious and thirst-quenching of all beverages, **Moxie Nerve Food.** Moxie is drunk at all sea-shore and summer resorts, and does much in adding to the pleasure of the sojourners to these places, as well as giving to them vim and vitality, on account of its nerve-nourishing qualities.

All druggists sell Moxie by the glass. Be sure you get the genuine. Grocers everywhere sell Moxie by the bottle or case. Order it in your house.

A **Moxie child** is easily recognized. Children who are given **Moxie Nerve Food** are healthy, strong, and happy. The summer heat fails to wear them to a shadow. Moxie fortifies and strengthens the nerves of the little ones as food does their bodies. Children love this temperance beverage.

All druggists sell Moxie by the glass.
Your grocer has Moxie by the case, and will deliver it to your home.

From the **start** the favorite is the athlete who, when he trains, drinks **Moxie Nerve Food.** Moxie keeps the stomach in good condition. It is a delicious beverage. Above all, Moxie nourishes the nervous system, and, being a nerve food, gives endurance where endurance is needed.

Ask your druggist for a glass of Moxie.
Served always in Moxie bottle.
All grocers sell Moxie by the bottle or case.

In the hospitals the value of **Moxie Nerve Food** has been acknowledged. Doctors give Moxie to their patients, for they know that it nourishes the nervous system, and thus invigorates the entire body. After the use of anesthetics Moxie has been found to be the only liquid that can be retained on the stomach, and but little of it is necessary to quench the most feverish thirst. People who drink Moxie can keep well at all times, and in all climates.

Druggist everywhere sell Moxie by the glass.
Your grocer will deliver Moxie to your home by the bottle or case.

MOXIE

The prosperous druggist is he who advocates Moxie and knows no substitute for that refreshment-bringing, thirst-quenching, temperance beverage. That **Moxie Nerve Food** does good by keeping the stomach in good condition in hot weather, and prevents fatigue by giving vitality to the nerves.

Druggists everywhere sell Moxie by the glass. Your grocer will send it to your home by the bottle or case.

MOXIe

The Woman can shop without fatigue no matter how hot the weather, if she drinks **Moxie Nerve Food.** Such women are the envy of their tired, jaded sisters who continually approach collapse in warm weather. Moxie should not be a secret to any one. The good it will do and the pleasure it will give in drinking it can easily be determined by a trial. Moxie is not a medicine, but it nourishes the nervous system.

Any druggist will sell you Moxie by the glass. Your grocer will send Moxie to your home by the bottle or case.

On the next several pages are Moxie advertisements from several different campaigns from the turn of the century. The Moxie logotype, with the large X in the center, as shown on the preceding and following pages, was used extensively in newspaper advertisements but not in many other places.

Children Love It, and it does them good, for it nourishes the nervous system and is refreshing and thirst-quenching.

MoXie Nerve Food

PLEASES THE PUBLIC

more than any other beverage on account of its usefulness. It quenches thirst as nothing else can, and the way it nourishes the nervous system increases its popularity.

Druggists sell Moxie by the glass.
Any Grocer will deliver it to you at your house by the bottle.

As Any Dispenser of Temperance Beverages will tell you, is the most popular of all drinks for is quenches thirst, nourishes the nerves and overcomes fatigue. . . . .

Druggists sell it by the glass. Grocers by the bottle. Get the Genuine.

In Demand. The above is an actual scene, showing the crowd around the MOXIE Wagon at the Worcester Mass. State Fair, in their eagerness to get a glass of this delicious, refreshing beverage after the fatigue of sight seeing. All Druggists sell it by the glass. Grocers by the bottle and case. Get the Genuine.

When Fishing will be found to be an enjoyable thirst-quenching drink that gives strength to the nerves and lends zest to the sport. Druggists, Grocers and Dealers in Temperance Beverages everywhere sell it. Get the Genuine.

When on a Bicycle Ride proves to be the most enjoyable and refreshing of beverages, for it quenches thirst and by nourishing the nerves it creates a feeling of vigor that adds keener enjoyment to the exercise. Sold by Druggists and Grocers. Get the Genuine.

BETTER THAN PLAY

To the children is that delicious temperance beverage—

MoXie

A drink th...
summer, f...

YACHT AHOY!

Can you spare us some of your

MoXie
Food

Coaching Joys

Are multiplied when a supply is on hand of that delicious, healthful beverage,

...g, and nerve
... glass.

M
N

Will que...
besides
stimulat...

JUST A MINUTE,

And when you are dressed you can have a glass of

MoXie
Nerve Food

A reward worth trying for. The little ones love this delicious beverage, and because it is a *nerve maker*, many summer ills are avoided by its use.

Druggists and Grocers.

Palmer Cox, born in Canada in 1840, early developed a flair for cartooning and writing. His best-remembered creation, the Brownies, first appeared in 1880 as part of illustrations made for a poem by Arthur Gillman which featured each letter of the alphabet supported by one of these diminutive figures. Accompanied by verses penned by Cox, the Brownies appeared in *St. Nicholas* and *The Ladies Home Journal* magazines. In 1887 *The Brownies: Their Book* was published by the Century Company, New York, setting the stage for many repeat appearances in book form of these lovable cartoon characters.

Cox described his creation: "Brownies, like fairies and goblins, are imaginary little sprites who are supposed to delight in harmless pranks and helpful deeds. They work and sport while weary households sleep, and never allow themselves to be seen by mortal eyes."

In 1906 The Moxie Nerve Food Company employed Brownies to cavort among the letters in the word MOXIE, to lift crates of the beverage, and to otherwise frolic and sport across the page.

The series of advertisements was heralded by a notice: "SPRING is here. With it begins the 22nd year of Moxie. The merit of Moxie will be maintained during our 22nd season—21 years of increasing custom and popularity. REAL MERIT—the perfect cleanliness of manufacture—the tonic quality—the delicious satisfying taste—will still be distinctive of Moxie; will still make new friends for Moxie and new customers for Moxie dealers during the season of 1906."

This was in the era when Moxie still celebrated its founding date as 1885, for considering 1885 as the first year, and 1905 as the 21st year, spring 1906 was indeed the beginning of the 22nd. In later years someone overlooked the actual history of the firm and pushed the date back to 1884, where it has been maintained ever since in advertising.

Many of the motifs in the 1906 advertising campaign repeat earlier themes. The Moxie Bottle Wagon was in evidence, joined by some new conveyances, a Moxie automobile (with a cooler on the back) and a Moxie delivery truck. This was the era of the "Moxie Makes You Eat, Sleep, and Feel Better" slogan, and this was shown. Interestingly, the Brownies, omnipresent throughout the campaign, were not specifically mentioned by name, nor was Palmer Cox identified as the inspiration for the little creatures.

"WOMEN EVERYWHERE are enthusiastic advocates of Moxie," one advertisement began. "They have learned to love it because of its delicious taste... Give them all they want of it. It will always do them good... "

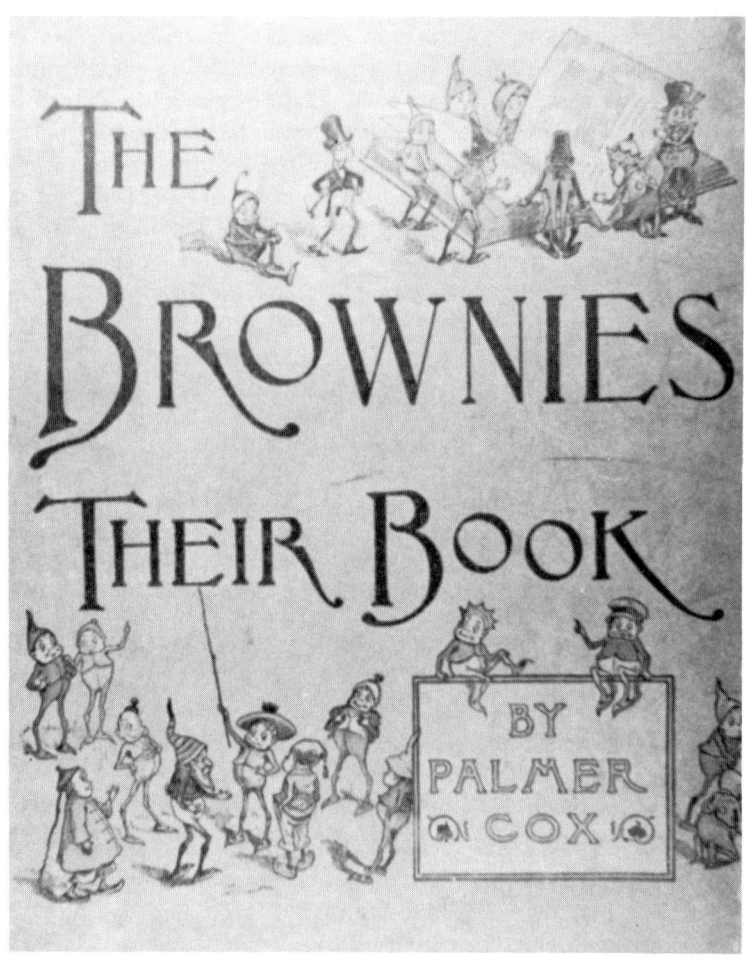

Brownies, elfin creatures devised by artist Palmer Cox, cavorted across the pages of many books, including the one whose cover is shown above. Brownies were often used in advertising for various products, including Moxie (in the 1906 advertising campaign and elsewhere), Brownie soda, and others.

Another advertisement, one featuring a Brownie standing next to a large bottle of Moxie, and with a Moxie "foxtail" sign hanging against the mirror above, was an early appearance of the "being particular" theme that Moxie was to intensely use a decade later: "We don't blame you for being particular, for Moxie, besides being refreshing, is a genuine nerve food." The same advertisement had the Brownie, who really should have been invisible, answering a customer at the soda fountain who pointed to the bottle of Moxie and asked: "Is this the genuine Moxie?" "Of course it is," the Brownie replied. "You don't suppose for a minute that we, or any other reputable druggist would trifle with the health of our customers by serving them with anything but the genuine. Just look at that label! You may be sure that when a druggist gives you Moxie from the original bottle with the label intact, you are getting the genuine... "

"PHYSICIANS RECOMMEND MOXIE" was the title of another advertisement in the series. "The modern doctor fights shy of alcoholic beverages as well as the unnecessary use of powerful drugs," the copy noted. Right next to the good doctor's medicine bag was—you guessed it—a bottle of Moxie Nerve Food!

Another advertisement featured a physician in the form of a Brownie, standing on a table next to a Moxie bottle nearly his size, speaking to a tired woman who buried her face in her hands: "Moxie! Yes, madam, that's what we up-to-date physicians now recommend for that spring tired feeling. We drink it ourselves and give it to our families... "

City folk back in 1906 yearned for weekends and holidays when they could leave the hustle and bustle of commercial activity. "OFF FOR THE COUNTRY—Be sure that you order a good supply of Moxie. See to it that it is properly addressed and shipped so that you will find it waiting for you on your arrival at your summer home. You will take it just as soon as you arrive..." While few readers of Moxie advertisements actually possessed separate summer homes, there is no doubt that this advertisement, as well as advertisements featuring automobiles, yachts, and other luxuries, contributed to the image of the Moxie Nerve Food product.

Still another advertisement in the series features a paunchy businessman leaning back in his chair near a roll-top desk. In his hand is a glass of Moxie. He addresses a seemingly distraught man who approaches him, as a Brownie with a telegram comes through the door in the background: "DON'T GET EXCITED—The man who succeeds in business keeps a cool, clear head on his shoulders. He knows the importance of being careful about what he drinks. The keen, progressive, up-to-date business man of today drinks Moxie

Nerve Food. He keeps it handy to his desk..."

Not only did businessmen like Moxie but, according to another advertisement, "ALL KINDS OF MEN in various walks of life, whose desire it is to get the most good out of their existence, will be found to be habitual drinkers of Moxie... Moxie drinkers eat better, sleep better and feel better for its use..." The same notice further advised: "Drink Moxie on the street."

At least two advertisements featured sign posts pointing the way to "Goodtown," noting that "YOU CAN GET MOXIE THERE." At the time Moxie, ever alert to innovative advertising, had posted signs along well traveled routes. The copy observed: "Note when automobiling the reliable mile posts which will not only show you your way, but tell you where you can renew your supply of Moxie." And, another advertisement suggested that Moxie was even more important than fuel: "Don't start on a long run without a case of Moxie. When you are sure that it is aboard, then look to the gasoline and other necessary adjuncts for the trip." Similarly, another advertisement related that "THE CHIEF NECESSITY FOR A YACHTING TRIP is a good supply of Moxie."

Brownies made a short-lived appearance on the stage of Moxie advertising. In later years the little cartoon characters were all but forgotten, although a few metal outdoor signs featuring Brownies on a crate of Moxie still were to be seen here and there.

SPRING
IS HERE
WITH IT BEGINS
THE 22D YEAR OF

MOXIE

The merit of MOXIE will be maintained during our twenty-second season — twenty - one years of increasing custom and popularity spell REAL MERIT — the perfect cleanliness of manufacture — the tonic quality —the delicious satisfying taste — will still be distinctive of MOXIE; will still make new friends for MOXIE and new customers for MOXIE dealers during the season of 1906.

MOXIE
MAKES YOU
EAT, SLEEP
AND
FEEL BETTER.

This and the next nine pages feature panels from Moxie's 1906 newspaper advertising campaign, proclaimed as the 22nd year of the beverage. Shown above are symbols of the era, including the automobile (first employed by Moxie about 1902), the familiar Bottle Wagon (first used in 1886), a motorized delivery truck, and a typical billboard. Among the letters are Brownies, mythical leprechaun-like creatures devised by Palmer Cox, who featured them in cartoons and, in 1887, a volume, "The Brownies—Their Book," the first of many illustrated texts telling of the exploits of these little elves.

In the words of Palmer Cox: "Brownies, like fairies and goblins, are imaginary little sprites, who are supposed to delight in harmless pranks and helpful deeds. They work and sport while weary households sleep, and never allow themselves to be seen by mortal eyes."

Brownies appeared in Moxie advertisements briefly, primarily in these and related newspaper advertisements and on a variety of metal sign showing a wooden Moxie crate and several of the elfin creatures.

In 1906 The Moxie Nerve Food Company of New England used 1885 as the inception of the beverage, as implied by stating that prior to 1906 there were 21 years of "increasing custom and popularity," the number of years from 1885 through 1905 inclusive.

WOMEN EVERYWHERE

are enthusiastic advocates of Moxie. They have learned to love it because of its delicious taste. It is refreshing and thirst-quenching. Moxie is good for the children. It is as good for their nerves as food is for their growing bodies. Give them all they want of it. It will always do them good.

Fatigue arising from housework, social duties or athletic pursuits vanishes before a glass of Moxie. This is because it sustains the nerves.

Women who keep Moxie in the ice-chest at all times eat better, sleep better and feel better for its constant use.

The trying days of summer have no terrors for the woman who drinks plenty of Moxie.

Have you a case in your house now? If not, it would pay you to order one immediately.

Sold by all Grocers, Druggists and Dealers in temperance beverages
$2.50 a case, 25 cents per bottle, 5 cents a glass at all fountains

07A3058

"Is this the genuine Moxie?

"Of course it is. You don't suppose for a minute that we, or any other reputable druggist would trifle with the health of our customers by serving them with anything but the genuine.

"Just look at that label! You may be sure that when a druggist gives you Moxie from the original bottle with the label intact, you are getting the genuine.

"We don't blame you for being particular, for Moxie, besides being refreshing, is a genuine nerve food. The most careful and rigid analysis shows it does not contain a particle of alcohol or any narcotic, poisonous drug, or chemical preservative.

"What's more, when I get thirsty I drink Moxie in preference to anything else I have in the fountain."

$2.50 per case; 25 cents per bottle; 5 cents per glass at all fountains.

— 252 —

MOXIE
PHYSICIANS RECOMMEND MOXIE
The modern doctor fights shy of alcoholic beverages as well as the unnecessary use of powerful drugs. The fact that Moxie is non-alcoholic and does not contain a particle of any ingredient that is injurious accounts for its popularity with the medical profession. Thousands of them drink it and recommend their patients to use it as often as they may desire, for they have learned that it really is sustaining to the nerves, and for this reason those who drink it experience nights of sweet, restful sleep and days free from many of the little ills that mar the pleasure of living.
Moxie drinkers eat better, feel better and accomplish more and better work because of its use.
A case kept in the house at all times will be found to be a source of pleasure and benefit.
Sold by all Grocers, Druggists and Dealers in temperance beverages. $2.50 a case, 25 cents per bottle, 5 cents a glass at all fountains.
MOXIE
07A1000

MOXIE
"Moxie! yes, madam, that's what we up-to-date physicians now recommend for that Spring tired feeling. We drink it ourselves and give it to our families.
"Moxie is better for you than any Spring medicine, for it contains no poison ous drugs or alcohol.
"Moxie nourishes the nerves, tones up the stomach and generally refreshes the entire body. Drink it and housework is more easily performed.
"Get the Genuine. Order a case from your grocer today and keep it in the house all the time."
$2.50 per case; 25 cents a bottle; 5 cents per glass at all fountains.
MOXIE

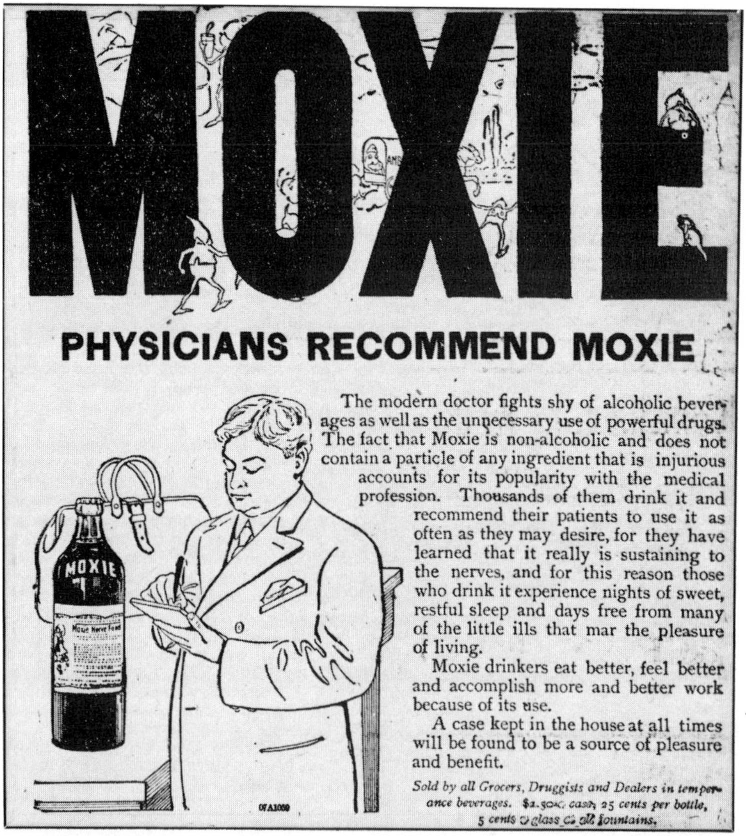

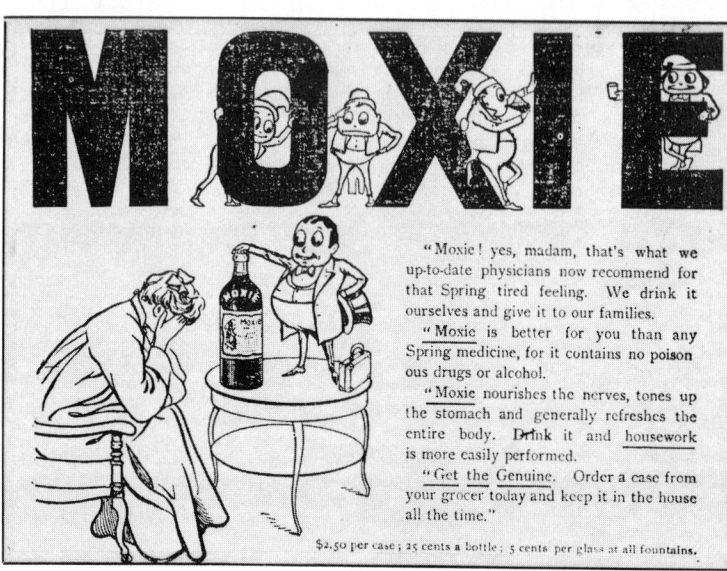

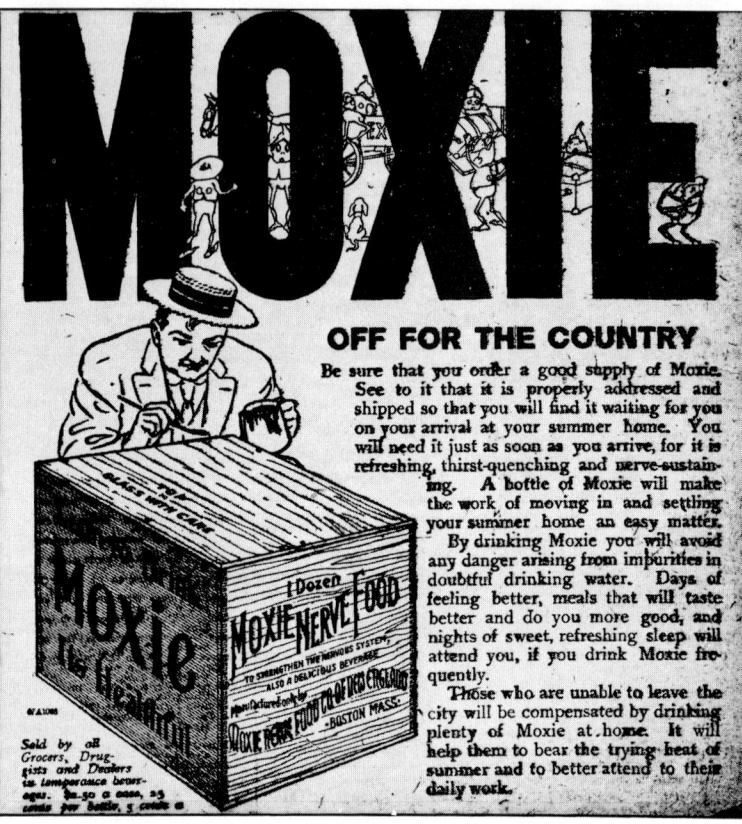

Moxie themes in the 1906 newspaper advertising campaign were familiar and were similar to those used years earlier. "Off For The Country" notes that before going to one's summer home a supply of Moxie should be ordered. Few readers of New England newspapers possessed summer homes, but showing the habits of the wealthy—their activities, their pleasures, and other trappings—has long been a way to sell merchandise to everyone. Moxie was egalitarian. It appealed equally to the lowest-paid worker as well as owners of country homes, yachts, and other luxuries.

WHEN TRAVELING

"Hurry up! Have you got your ticket yet? The train is almost ready to start."

"It is more important to be sure we have a good supply of Moxie."

"I never start on a long journey without that. There is nothing that is so thirst-quenching, refreshing, and because it is a real nerve food, it invigorates one so that the tedium of a long journey is lessened, and it prevents car sickness."

"Furthermore, one never knows what kind of water may be had on the trains or in the places we are to visit."

"Frequently it is dangerous to drink it. Most always a change of water has a bad effect."

"With plenty of good Moxie one may travel comfortably and with impunity."

"That is why I consider Moxie most essential for a long journey. After you have bought your Moxie then it's time to see about your tickets."

Sold by all Grocers, Druggists and Dealers in temperance beverages.
$2.50 a case, 25 cents per bottle, 5 cents a glass at all fountains.

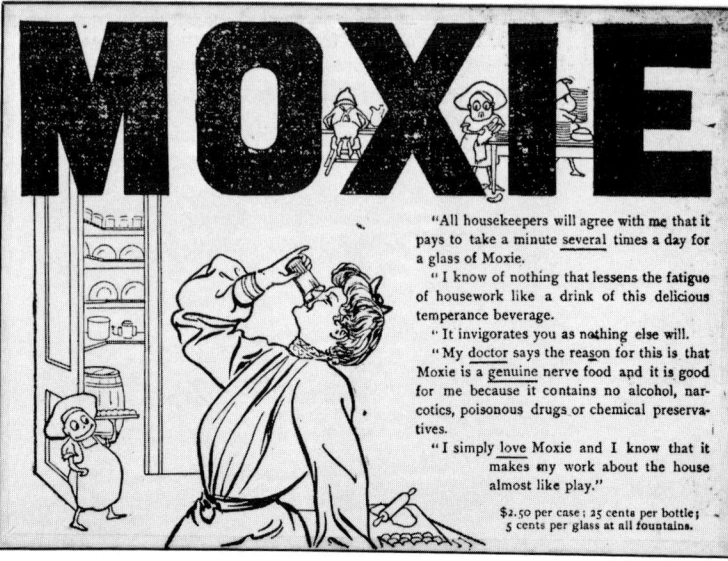

"All housekeepers will agree with me that it pays to take a minute several times a day for a glass of Moxie.

"I know of nothing that lessens the fatigue of housework like a drink of this delicious temperance beverage.

"It invigorates you as nothing else will.

"My doctor says the reason for this is that Moxie is a genuine nerve food and it is good for me because it contains no alcohol, narcotics, poisonous drugs or chemical preservatives.

"I simply love Moxie and I know that it makes my work about the house almost like play."

$2.50 per case; 25 cents per bottle; 5 cents per glass at all fountains.

DON'T GET EXCITED

The man who succeeds in business keeps a cool, clear head on his shoulders.

He knows the importance of being careful about what he drinks. The keen, progressive, up-to-date business man of today drinks Moxie Nerve Food.

He keeps it handy to his desk.

He enjoys it because of its thirst-quenching, delicious properties.

He appreciates it because it nourishes his nerves and enables him to do more and better work.

Sold by all Grocers, Druggists and Dealers in temperance beverages.
$2.50 a case, 25 cents per bottle, 5 cents a glass at all fountains.

The portly businessman shown above, holding aloft a glass of Moxie in one hand and with a crate of Moxie at his elbow, apparently owes his success, at least in part, to drinking New England's favorite beverage.

His visitor, hat in hand, obviously comes seeking information, if not inspiration, while a Brownie in the background delivers a telegram to the important and obviously successful captain of industry.

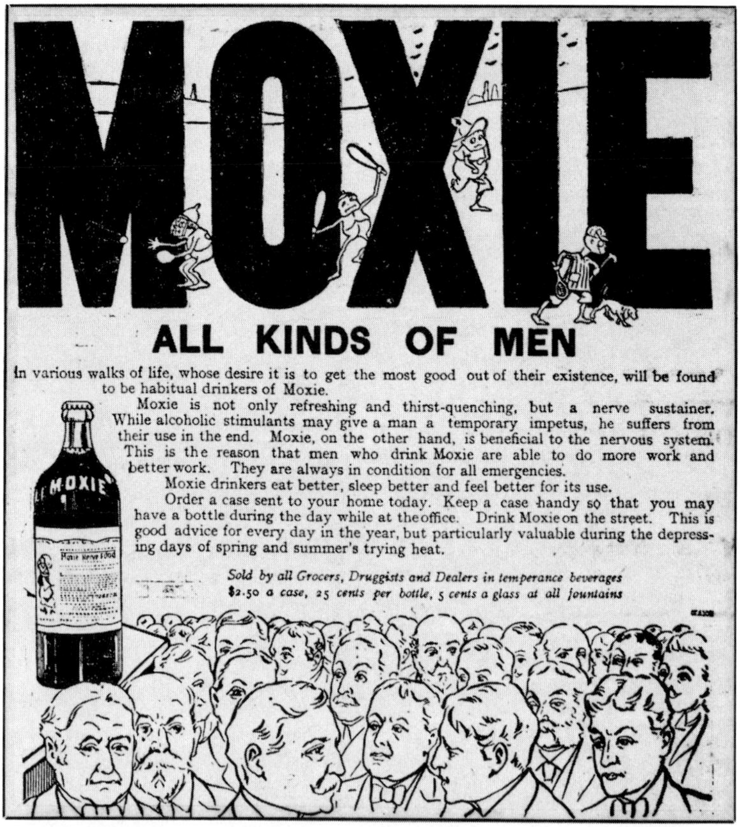

MOXIE

ALL KINDS OF MEN

In various walks of life, whose desire it is to get the most good out of their existence, will be found to be habitual drinkers of Moxie.

Moxie is not only refreshing and thirst-quenching, but a nerve sustainer. While alcoholic stimulants may give a man a temporary impetus, he suffers from their use in the end. Moxie, on the other hand, is beneficial to the nervous system. This is the reason that men who drink Moxie are able to do more work and better work. They are always in condition for all emergencies.

Moxie drinkers eat better, sleep better and feel better for its use.

Order a case sent to your home today. Keep a case handy so that you may have a bottle during the day while at the office. Drink Moxie on the street. This is good advice for every day in the year, but particularly valuable during the depressing days of spring and summer's trying heat.

Sold by all Grocers, Druggists and Dealers in temperance beverages
$2.50 a case, 25 cents per bottle, 5 cents a glass at all fountains

MOXIE

"This man has a serious business problem that needs his best thoughts.

"A glass of Moxie first is what will enable him to do justice to it and help him to overcome all difficulties.

"Moxie, besides being refreshing, invigorates one as nothing else will, and this is because it is a genuine 'nerve food.'

"The fact that it contains no alcohol, narcotics, chemical preservatives or poisonous drugs insures its consumers against feeling any bad after-effects from its use.

"I notice the 'boss' always keeps Moxie in the office, as well as at his home, and I have seen him frequently stop at the soda fountains for a drink of it when he is on the street."

$2.50 per case; 25 cents per bottle; 5 cents per glass at all fountains.

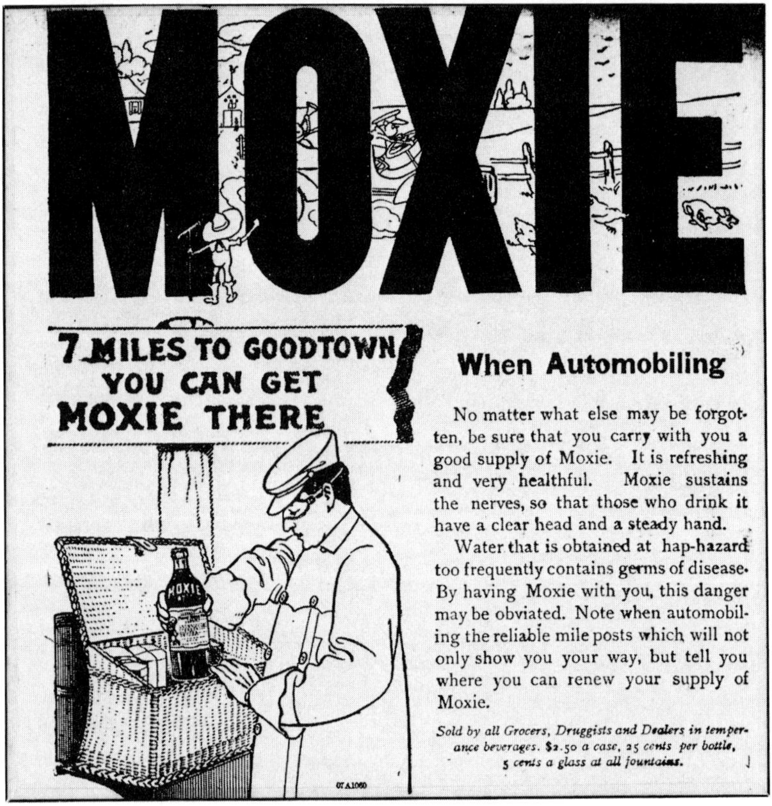
MOXIE
7 MILES TO GOODTOWN
YOU CAN GET
MOXIE THERE
MOXIE
When Automobiling
No matter what else may be forgotten, be sure that you carry with you a good supply of Moxie. It is refreshing and very healthful. Moxie sustains the nerves, so that those who drink it have a clear head and a steady hand.
Water that is obtained at hap-hazard too frequently contains germs of disease. By having Moxie with you, this danger may be obviated. Note when automobiling the reliable mile posts which will not only show you your way, but tell you where you can renew your supply of Moxie.
Sold by all Grocers, Druggists and Dealers in temperance beverages. $2.50 a case, 25 cents per bottle, 5 cents a glass at all fountains.
07 A1060

1 DOZEN
Learn to Drink
Moxie
very Healthful
MOXIE
When Moxie comes in at the door is the time that care flies out of the window.
It is a great convenience to go to the ice-chest when one is tired or thirsty and get a nice cold drink of refreshing and invigorating Moxie.
Moxie is a genuine nerve food. Those who drink it eat better, sleep better, and enjoy life to its fullest extent.
To Moxie drinkers cares that to others seem mountain-high, sink into insignificance. Health waits on people who drink this delicious beverage, that contains no alcohol, narcotics, poisonous drugs or chemical preservatives.
$2.50 per case; 25 cents per bottle; 5 cents per glass at all fountains.

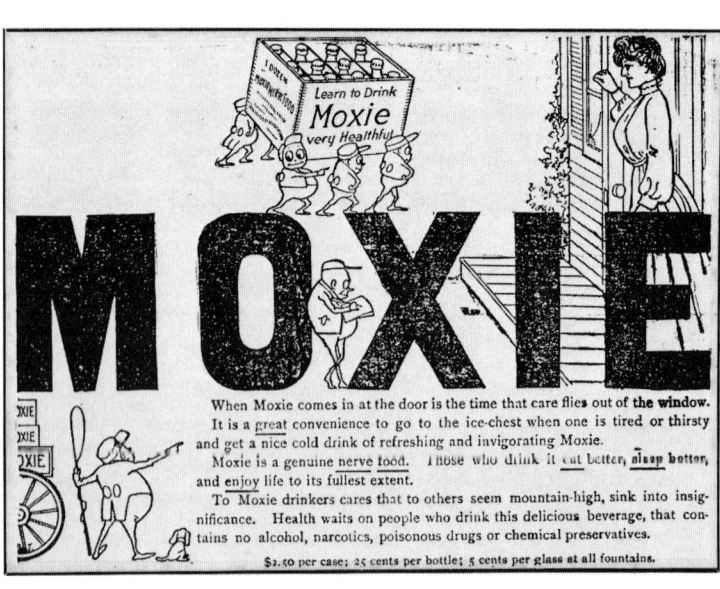

MOST IMPORTANT OF ALL

for an automobile trip is a case of delicious, thirst-quenching Moxie.

This great temperance beverage nourishes the nerves so that the auto-mobilist who drinks it always has a keen eye, steady hand and clear brain.

Don't start on a long run without a case of Moxie. When you are sure that is aboard, then look to the gasolene and other necessary adjuncts for the trip.

Sold by all Grocers, Druggists and Dealers in temperance beverages.
$2.50 a case, 25 cents per bottle, 5 cents a glass at all fountains.

06A1027

No wonder children love Moxie. They will leave their play any time for a glass of this thirst-quenching, delicious beverage. There is nothing in the world better for them.

Moxie is the food their nerves require, and the little ones' nerves need nourishing as much as their bodies do.

The fact that there is no alcohol, narcotics, poisonous drugs or chemical preservatives in Moxie makes it a safe and most desirable drink for every member of the family.

This is the reason that physicians use it in their own homes and recommend it to their patients.

$2.50 per case; 25 cents per bottle;
5 cents per glass at all fountains.

The Chief Necessity for a Yachting Trip

is a good supply of Moxie. It is nerve-sustaining and delicious. Drinkers of Moxie eat better, sleep better and feel better for its use. Moxie drinkers are noted for their steady nerves, clear heads and happy, contented dispositions.

When traveling by sea or land, Moxie should be used rather than water obtained from sources you are unfamiliar with, which too frequently contain germs of disease.

Moxie will be found an excellent preventative for sea-sickness. This is because of its beneficial effect on the nervous system.

Keep Moxie in your house when you are at home, take it with you when you travel. It will add much to your enjoyment and health on all occasions.

Sold by all Grocers, Druggists and Dealers in temperance beverages; $2.50 a case, 25 cents per bottle, 5 cents a glass at all fountains.

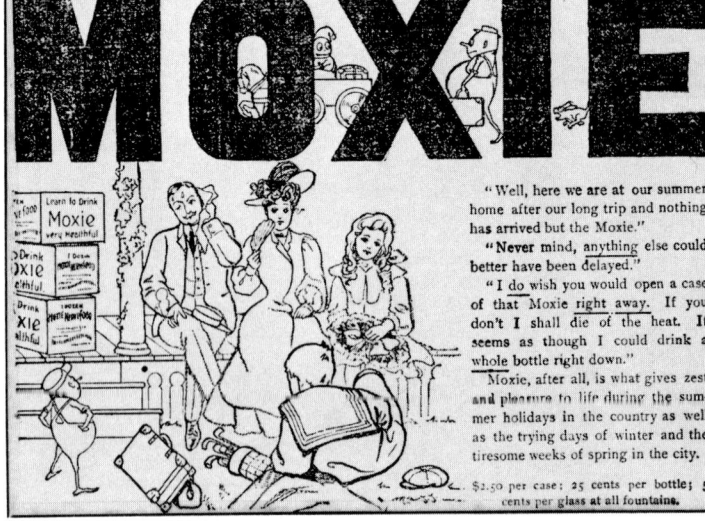

"Well, here we are at our summer home after our long trip and nothing has arrived but the Moxie."

"Never mind, anything else could better have been delayed."

"I do wish you would open a case of that Moxie right away. If you don't I shall die of the heat. It seems as though I could drink a whole bottle right down."

Moxie, after all, is what gives zest and pleasure to life during the summer holidays in the country as well as the trying days of winter and the tiresome weeks of spring in the city.

$2.50 per case; 25 cents per bottle; 5 cents per glass at all fountains.

— 260 —

In 1907 Snow's Ice Cream Rooms, a Massachusetts soda parlor, handled various beverages bottled by Ephraim Provo, including Provo's Witch City Appetizer, according to the sign on the left side of the porch.

Witch City Appetizer, put up by the Witch City Bottling Works, 4-6 Sewall Street, Salem, Massachusetts, was packaged in a bottle similar in size and shape to Moxie, leading the attorneys for The Moxie Company to bring action against the proprietor, Ephraim Provo, in the Supreme Judicial Court of the Commonwealth of Massachusetts, with the following result:

"Defendant enjoined from selling any beverage having the visual appearance of 'Moxie' in a bottle having substantially the shape of the 'Moxie' bottle or labeled and wrapped substantially like the 'Moxie' bottle.

"Ordered that the defendant deliver up for destruction all bottles as above described in his possession."

Of all of the Moxie imitators, none was more successful than Modox, which achieved a wide sale in the New England states in the years prior to 1907. Although there was not much similarity in the glass bottles used by the two products, the names were confusing. And, like Moxie, Modox printed its label in black on an orange background. Following a court fight, Moxie obtained an injunction against Modox, which was prohibited "from using the word 'Modox' on bottles, labels, signs, or advertisements in connection with the marketing of a beverage..." Subsequently, Frederick B. Thatcher, who furnished bottles of unusual shape to Modox, filed a petition of intervention claiming that the court decision deprived him of business. His petition was denied, and the court noted that Thatcher "cannot be said to have any legal interest in the question of whether the defendants are using these bottles as an instrument of deception." An earlier suit against Modox was dismissed when the judge found that Moxie itself was deceptive in its advertising in that the Lieut. Moxie "legend" apparently had no basis in fact.

Provo selected for his label an orange background with black letters. This was his undoing, and The Moxie Company, noticing the similarity in the color and shape of the Witch City Appetizer bottle to that of Moxie, wasted no time in filing suit. The unfortunate defendant was ordered to have all of his bottles *publicly destroyed*, according to the Moxie recitation of the case. How many people attended this bottle-smashing event was not recorded.

The color of the Moxie label and the shape of the bottle were irresistible to the Visner Bottling Company of Gloucester, Massachusetts, which noted that its Nox-All Nerve Food was "More Palatable if Served Ice Cold—Keep in a Cool Place." The only trouble was that Moxie's label also suggested that The Product was "More Palatable if Served Ice Cold—Keep in a Cool Place." Again, vengeance was swift, and in the Superior Court of the Commonwealth of Massachusetts it was decreed:

"Defendant enjoined from selling a beverage called 'Nox-All Nerve Food' or any other beverage as and for 'Moxie' or from suggesting or facilitating its substitution by retail dealers... Ordered, that the defendant deliver up for destruction counterfeit bottles and labels used in marketing 'Nox-All Nerve Food.' "

If surviving photographs and other memorabilia are any indication, the most successful Moxie imitator was Modox, which, apparently, was supposed to be an Indian name, for an Indian chief was used prominently in its advertisements. There was a Modoc Indian tribe at the time and, presumably, a group of such Indians would have been called Modocs, but where the X came from in MODOX was a mystery unless it could just have happened that it was inspired by the middle letter of MOXIE.

On May 20, 1907, the Circuit Court of the United States, District of Rhode Island, enjoined The Modox Company, of Providence, Rhode Island, and its officers and directors "From manufacturing, selling, or offering for sale any beverage so packed or dressed, as to be likely to deceive purchasers of 'Moxie,' and more particularly, from selling or offering for sale, any beverage other than 'Moxie,' resembling 'Moxie' in appearance, put up in bottles like or similar to that of 'Moxie,' or 'Modox,' or in bottles so similar thereto as to be likely as to deceive purchasers, or from selling or offering for sale 'Modox' or any beverage other than 'Moxie,' having the distinctive color, appearance, and flavor of 'Moxie,'... or from using the word 'Modox' on bottles, labels, signs, or advertisements..."

In retrospect, at least part of this decision seems to be unfair, for the Modox bottle was distinctively different from that used for Moxie and had a design with a distinctive band or ring around the shoulder.

The Modox Company, 233-239 East Exchange Street, Providence, Rhode Island, on May 20, 1907, was enjoined from further selling the beverage, due to its similarity to Moxie. The above photograph was probably taken a few months earlier and shows Barre's Business Bazzar (sic), a meat, grocery, and beverage store. Modox's sales must have been successful at this outlet, judging from the tall stack of wooden Modox crates behind the gentleman.

Modox, the famous Moxie imitator, featured an Indian chief in its advertising, noting that the product was "Made from Indian herbs." At the time the art of the Indian medicine man was viewed as a strong selling feature by many patent and proprietary nostrums.

Shown above is an unusual metal tip tray faced with applied lithographed paper (rather than the usual enamel), while at the right is shown an empty Modox bottle produced by the Nickel-Tone Mfg. Company, Providence, R.I. (part of the inscription on the other side can be seen reversed through the glass).

And, further, it was furnished with a wire-type closure (unlike the crown seal used by Moxie at the time).

Frederick B. Thatcher, supplier of glass bottles to The Modox Company, petitioned to intervene in the decision, but this was to no avail, for the same court noted:

"As patentee [of the unusual Modox bottles], the petitioner stands no better chance than as a mere manufacturer or seller of glass bottles; and if he should be permitted to intervene, it would seem to follow also that all those who supply The Modox Company with parts of its package—the printers of labels, the vendors of caramel for coloring the contents of the bottles, etc.—would have a similar right to intervene on the ground of the threatened loss of a customer by an injunction against The Modox Company..."

The cases against Toxie, Rixie, Hoxie, Noxie and Proxie, all of which have a sound similar to Moxie, were decided in favor of the latter firm. The Proxie decision in particular was involved and went through the court of appeals.

In November 1915 the Wacker & Birk Brewing Company, Chicago, began marketing "Proxie," a non-alcoholic carbonated beverage. The general type was and is known as "near beer," a class of liquid refreshment resembling beer in color and taste but differing from beer in that it contains less than one-half of one percent alcohol.

H.E. Stauffer, the Patent Office examiner, commenting on the phonetic similarity of Moxie and Proxie, stated succinctly: "As has so often been said, it is difficult to understand why a newcomer in an established line of business selects a mark quite like that of a well advertised mark if he really wishes to distinguish his goods from those of a competitor. There is no necessity for so doing. The field of distinctive marks is limitless, yet the applicant has apparently selected a mark as near like that of a well known and extensively advertised mark in the same line of business as it was possible to do and avoid exact duplication. It is therefore concluded that the goods are alike and the marks are so similar as to lead to confusion."

The Proxie case was appealed, and the defendants lost again. A telling paragraph appeared in the record: "Applicant in his testimony explains that he hit upon the word 'Proxie' to indicate that his beverage was approximating without actually being ordinary beer, carrrying out the idea of what is expressed in 'near beer,' but applicant *has not* satisfactorily explained why he spelled this word 'Proxie' instead of 'Proxy.' "

Note: When the author was reviewing certain of Frank Archer's correspondence files of the 1910-1920 decade, he noticed an in-

Three Moxie imitators are shown above. The Universal Appetizer, made by the Lynn Bottling Works in Massachusetts, was packaged similarly to Moxie Nerve Food and bore a black and orange label. Toxie Hyball, made by the California Fruit Beverage Company in Los Angeles, was too close in name to suit Moxie, and an injunction was obtained. Bo-La, made in Manchester, New Hampshire by Daniel Daoust, did not resemble Moxie in name, but apparently Bo-La was served in place of Moxie by many restaurants, druggists, and other vendors. Lawyers for Daoust noted that the defendant was "not responsible for the fact that tricky retailers represent his manufacture as that of The Moxie Company, provided he has done his legal duty in distinguishing his product." Notwithstanding this, an injunction against Bo-La and its maker was obtained. However, Bo-La went on to another generation of sales, presumably with care being taken not to confuse it with Moxie at the retail level.

teresting coincidence. Archer's secretary, in referring to stockholders' meetings, often misspelled "proxy" as "proxie"!

Despite the fact that numerous beverages, elixirs, and potions had "nerve tonic" or "nerve food" as part of their name before Moxie did (for example: Ellis' Nerve Tonic was registered in the Patent Office under label trademark No. 3,291 on June 12, 1883), by the early 20th century The Moxie Company presumed that it had exclusive right to such designations, especially for use in the field of beverages, and various courts seemed to agree. Thus, Standard Nerve Food, Imperial Nerve Food, East India Nerve Food, Excelsior Nerve Food, Coates Nerve Food Appetizer, and Nerve Tonic were all struck down as illegal infringements on the all-powerful Moxie Nerve Food name.

Still other cases took a different tack. An example is the litigation between The Moxie Company, plaintiff, versus Daniel Daoust, defendant, in the United States Circuit Court of Appeals. Daoust concocted a beverage sold as Bo-La, a name that could hardly be confused with Moxie. The label noted that Bo-La was a "Tonic for the Blood and General Health" and was "Highly recommended by able physicians." The bottle, however, was the general size and shape of the Moxie container, and, like Moxie, Bo-La had a dark molasses-like color. Apparently the difficulty arose with soda fountains and stores which would dispense Bo-La in glasses over the counter, pouring the substance directly from the Bo-La bottle but without the label being observed or studied by the customer. When a patron stated, "I'll have Moxie," he was served something else.

In addition to remedies in the courts, Moxie mounted a defense against this common practice by boldly embossing on its soda fountain glasses the statement "LICENSED ONLY FOR SERVING MOXIE." Substitution has been a continuing concern for other beverage manufacturers over the years, and in 1984 the author was reminded of this when he stopped at a popular fast food restaurant and asked for a Coke. "Will Pepsi do?" was the reply by a counter attendant who obviously had been trained in the dos and don'ts of trademark confusion.

Substitution was the focus of a complaint voiced in a letter sent to The Moxie Company by Miss S.F. Shaw of Cathance Lake, Cooper, Maine, in the eastern part of the state near the Canadian border:

"On August seventh I bought three bottles of Moxie at Harry Lombard's store in Meddybemps, Maine. When I got them back to the camp I noticed they were *without* labels and each bottle had the same sort of cap to it. (I am sending you one of the caps.) One of the

The Moxie Nerve Food Company of New England was constantly on the lookout for Moxie imitators. When a suspected look-alike or taste-alike product was noticed, often a case or two would purchased for testing and evaluation. The above photograph from the archives of the firm shows a bottle of Ver-best to the left of a bottle of Moxie, set up and ready for photography. Ver-best, which used the motto "Nerve rest, Ver-best," was produced by H.P. Morris & Co., Boston, and was billed to be "Unequalled as a Nerve Food" and "Unexcelled as a Wholesome, Safe and Pleasant Beverage." The trademark of the product showed a young girl drinking a glass of the substance.

A post card, circa 1906, showing a bottle wagon made for Noxie-Kola, a Canadian drink with a name imitative of Moxie.

The residence of F.B. Perkins, the manufacturer of Noxie-Kola, as shown on an early post card.

bottles was without doubt a regulation Moxie bottle, stamped with your mark, but the other two were marked 'For Crown Soda Water, Clark's Harbor, N.S. [Nova Scotia], M.A. Nickerson.' They all contained the same kind of drink (imitation Moxie) which made two members of the party extremely ill for about six hours.

"We have been drinking Moxie all our lives and it has never before made us ill.

"I do not wish to make any claims but I do hope you will follow this up, for the vile stuff was bottled in one of your bottles which I will be glad to send to you upon request. My reason for writing this is to save someone else a similar experience."

Oliver Mitchell of Mitchell, Chadwick & Kent, attorney for The Moxie Company, leaped into action and hastened to advise Miss Shaw:

"We immediately sent an inspector to interview Mr. Lombard, and learned from him he was selling a beverage put up by Walter J. Commins, of Calais, Maine, which has the appearance of genuine Moxie. Of course, as is usual in such cases, he denied having sold any of the Commins beverage upon a call for Moxie. After the preliminary investigation, Mr. Brennan of this office went to Calais on August 25th, and there conferred with Mr. Commins and his attorney... The result of this visit is that we have put a quick and effective stop to this case of infringement on The Moxie Company's rights. We have the signed admission of Mr. Commins that he made and sold the infringing beverage, and we also have his agreement to immediately stop the putting up and sale of such beverage, coupled with the provision for the destruction of the imitation Moxie bottles. The conclusion of this matter is as effective as an injunction of the court, and we have no doubt but what, under the advice and guidance of his counsel, that Mr. Commins will keep his promise. We have also communicated with Mr. Lombard and have a similar statement from him. We have told him that a letter of apology is due to you and if you have been put to any expense for medical service or otherwise, on account of the sale of this spurious beverage to you, that he should properly compensate you. For this purpose we have given him your name and address, and we shall be interested to know whether he does in fact adopt our suggestion... Your action in this matter has been of great benefit, not only to The Moxie Company, but to the general public, because by putting a stop to Mr. Commins' fraudulent dealing, you have doubtless saved many other persons the unpleasant experience which you had, following the drinking of the inferior imitation of Moxie."

Not content to let the matter rest there, The Moxie Company

printed in *This Book About Substitution Law* a letter from Commins in which he promised to discontinue his naughty activities, the subject of such activities occupying three pages in the Moxie booklet. *This Book About Substitution Law* concluded with a warning, then an invitation to visit Moxieland:

"Moxie is inimitable, for its formula is secret. Many have attempted to imitate it and have tried to simulate the name, the bottle, the package and other distinctive features so well known and recognized as indicative of the genuine. But substitutors make little headway in the market even before we discover them. After we discover them they make no progress at all, as the numerous judgments, decrees and injunctions printed in this book well attest.

"Moxieland is open to everybody; pure food experts, doctors, chemists, bottlers and other trained observers are especially welcomed. The sanitary process of producing Moxie is as essential as the formula itself and therefore all Moxie extract is made solely at the Moxieland laboratory, under strictly hygienic conditions. The secret formula is a scientific compound of distinctive ingredients and the result is an absolutely safe and wholesome tonic beverage for all."

Although readers of *This Book About Substitution Law* no doubt enjoyed learning of the various Moxie skirmishes and, if they were potential imitators, were suitably frightened off, the problem of copycats continued long after Vol. III of the aforementioned booklet went out of print.

In 1939, by which time Frank Archer had been in his grave for two years, the affair of Moxie vs. Noxie came up again, this time in the courts of New York. Decades earlier a Canadian firm marketing Noxie Kola had been enjoined from using the "Noxie" name. In 1939 a New York outfit, claiming to have a license from the Canadian firm, aggressively marketed Noxie Kola in the northeastern states. In a re-enactment of the earlier situation, The Moxie Company was ingranted injunctive relief for infringement, and the new Noxie Kola passed from the scene.

The related matters of Moxie imitations, products with confusing names, counterfeiting of the Moxie product, and other concerns occupied the attention of Moxie officials from the earliest days onward. Scrapbooks maintained by the firm include numerous court decisions not only involving the Moxie firm but those pertaining to others, which Moxie felt might be useful in its own cases some day. Labels of competing and look-alike products were also preserved. If a product had "Nerve Food" or "Nerve Tonic" as part of its name, it was a candidate for Moxie scrutiny!

Phenix Nerve Tonic, which was said to "Remove Sleeplessness,

DRINK
NOXIE
TRADE MARK
KOLA

In Bottles Only
Splits—
1 glass 3¢
Club—
2 glasses 5¢
Family Size—
5 glasses 10¢

During the early 20th century, a Canadian beverage named Noxie achieved a wide sale. There was even a Noxie Bottle Wagon! A bottle which once held the Canadian product is shown to the right.

In 1939 an American firm claiming to have a license from the Canadian outfit started producing Noxie Kola and distributing it intensely in the eastern part of the United States. A metal advertising sign from this era is shown above. The Moxie Company went to court and in the same year the reborn Noxie Kola met its demise. Over the next several decades the Moxie vs. Noxie and the much earlier Moxie vs. Modox court decisions were cited as precedents in many other cases, a computer search of litigation records revealed during the course of research for the present book.

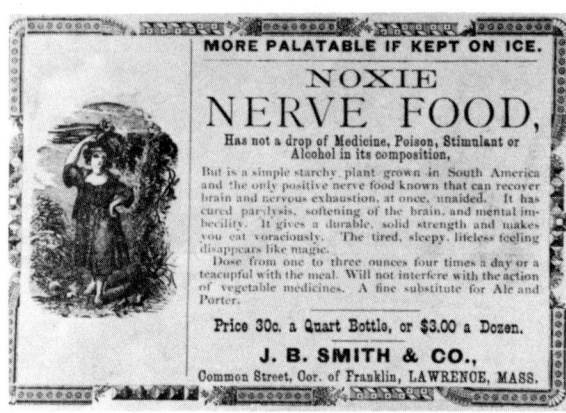

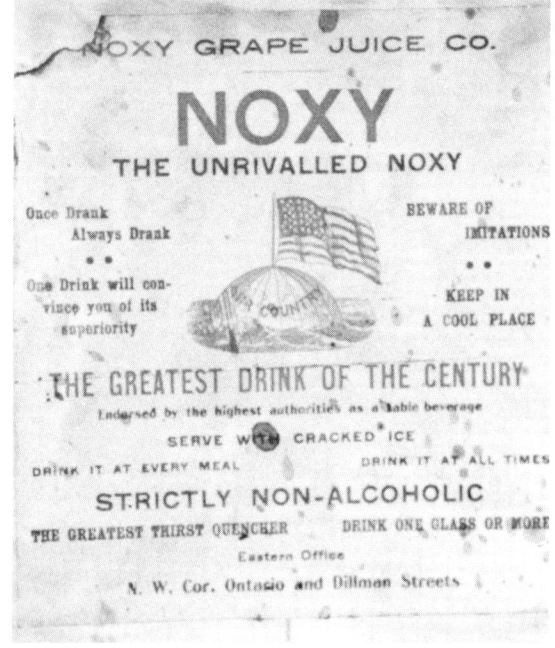

NOXIE

Nerve ☀ Food.

O. A. SMITH & CO.,

32 Orchard St., Haverhill, Mass.

Noxie of two different manufacturers and Noxy were obvious copycats of the Moxie name. Note that Noxie Nerve Food made by J.B. Smith & Co. also featured copycat graphics and printing on the label.

Nervousness, Nervous and Mental Exhaustion, Improves the Appetite, Aids Digestion," was billed as "The Best Tonic Known." Standard Nerve Food, another competitor, deemed it advisable to package their product in a paper wrapper with letters arranged similarly to those on the Moxie Nerve Food beverage. Apparently Tongo Tonic was viewed as a threat to Moxie, for several clippings were saved concerning it. An obvious imitator was Foxie, described as "Delicious, Healthful, Invigorating" with a further notation that "Everybody Drinks It." Not much other information has survived concerning this ephemeral beverage.

Then there was Noxy, more fully known as "The Unrivalled Noxy," which brazenly warned its customers to "beware of imitations"! Noxy, which immodestly noted it was "The Greatest Drink of the Century, and was "Endorsed by the highest authorities as a table beverage" had one of its several mottos: "Once Drank, Always Drank." The emblem of Noxy, a product of the Noxy Grape Juice Company, was a globe nearly completely submerged in an ocean, but with the American flag flying proudly from the North Pole.

Less threatening, but still worthy of keeping tabs on because it featured the famous sinking globe-with-flag engraving and was sold from the same Philadelphia address (but by the Tobasco Fruit Wine Company) was Kola Celery and Pepsin Compound, which was billed as "The Greatest Tonic and Appetizer." A wineglassful three times a day, "in whiskey or plain," was the recommended dosage. The product was said to "make muscle," "quiet the nerves," and "aid digestion."

Ver-Best Nerve Food, bottled by H.P. Morris & Company, Boston, had as its catchy sales pitch "Nerve Rest, Ver-Best." Simpson Spring Nerve Tonic, bottled by Simpson Spring, South Easton, Massachusetts, was also viewed as competitive. Ironically, in 1912 the Simpson Spring Company became a Moxie agent!

In the early years the word "Noxie" was appealing to more than one individual, and another Noxie product, not Noxie Kola as bottled in Canada in early times and in New York later, but Noxie Nerve Food bottled in Massachusetts, appeared. J.B. Smith & Company, Lawrence, Massachusetts, contrived Noxie Nerve Food, and bottled it with a label almost identical to that used by Moxie. On the left was the standing figure of a woman holding a sheaf over her head. Whereas the Moxie label said "More Palatable if Served Ice Cold," Noxie advised that the product was "More Palatable if Kept on Ice." Moxie advised that it "Contains not a drop of poison, stimulant or alcohol," while Noxie "has not a drop of medicine, poison, stimulant or alcohol in its composition." There were numerous other similarities as well. At least one other Massachusetts imitator also used the Noxie name.

Moxie sprang into action, and J.B. Smith & Company with its Noxie Nerve Food and others were brought to justice in the Circuit Court of the United States, District of Massachusetts, with an opinion rendered on January 2, 1888. The court decision noted, in part:

"The above cases [involving eight different defendants] were heard together... The complainant manufactures and sells a beverage called Moxie Nerve Food, and it seeks to restrain these defendants from the use of its trademark and from an imitation of its labels, bottles and wrappers.

"The registered trademark of complainant is simply the word 'Moxie.' The complainant insists, however, that it is also entitled to a trademark in the words 'Nerve Food.' It appears from evidence that these words had been previously applied in several cases to medicinal compounds, but never before to a beverage. All of the defendants use the term 'Nerve Food' on their labels. In [some cases] the defendants called their article the Standard Nerve Food, while in others the defendants term it Imperial, or East India, or Excelsior, or Noxie Nerve Food. The evidence shows that these defendants sell their preparations for the genuine Moxie Nerve Food made by the complainant. In the labels, bottles and wrappers there is an evident attempt on the part of the defendants to imitate those used by the complainant. Some of the labels are closer imitations than others. In two cases the defendants go so far to adopt the name Noxie in place of Moxie. In several cases apollinaris bottles are used in place of Moxie champagne bottles. But it does not seem to be important to closely analyze the different labels or bottles used by defendants, for I am satisfied that the labels, wrappers and bottles of all the defendants bear so close an imitation to those of complainant that the public are deceived in consequence..."

A preliminary injunction was granted in favor of Moxie, followed by a permanent injunction later the same month.

Seizing an advertising opportunity, Augustin Thompson printed facsimiles of the court decision, adding his own commentary:

"It is the purpose of the Moxie Nerve Food Company to enforce their rights to the bitter end by means of detectives.

"This decision gives the Moxie Nerve Food Company a monopoly of the markets of the United States on the word 'Moxie,' or 'Nerve Food,' when they are used alone or with other words, on labels, packages, bottles or wrappers covering a fluid like the Moxie Nerve Food, or an imitation of it sufficient to deceive the unsuspecting, and proprietors and retail dealers will have to quit or go to prison.

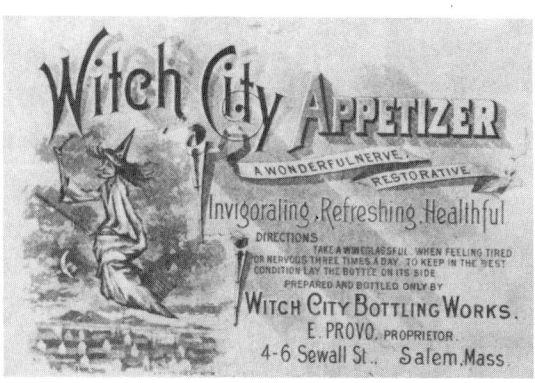

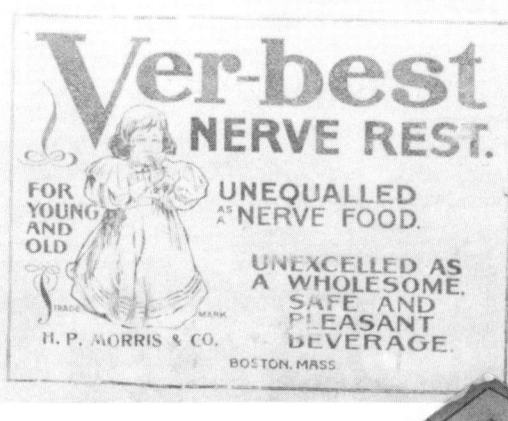

From the scrapbook kept by The Moxie Nerve Food Company of New England come these labels of products that Moxie felt to be threatening. Any label with the word "nerve" as part of the inscription was a candidate for close scrutiny.

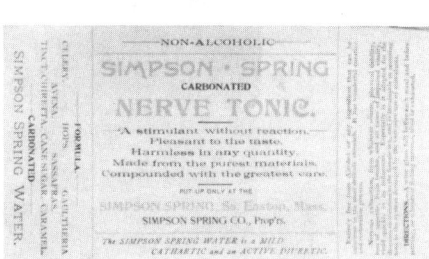

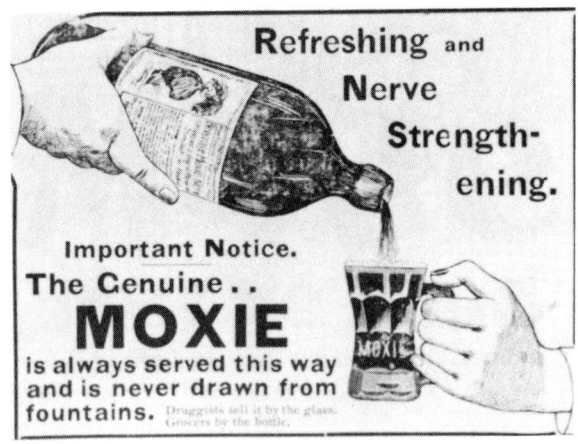

Refreshing and Nerve Strengthening.

Important Notice.
The Genuine..
MOXIE
is always served this way and is never drawn from fountains. Druggists sell it by the glass. Grocers by the bottle.

MOXIE
IS
THE ONLY REAL NERVE FOOD.

Druggists sell Moxie by the glass. Any Grocer will deliver it to you at your house by the bottle.

OXIE

ONE DOLLAR BOX OF OXIES.

Two genuine Moxie advertisements and two advertisements of competitors, with the curious "Oxie" pills featured to the left and Phenix Nerve Tonic shown below. Phenix had the audacity to note that it was "The Original Moxie Compound"!

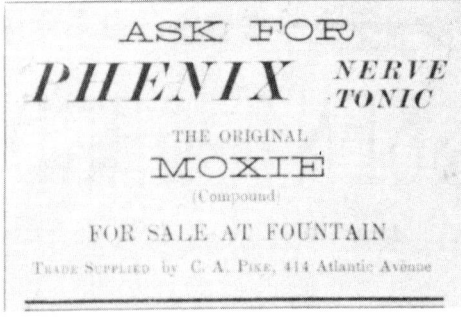

ASK FOR
PHENIX NERVE TONIC
THE ORIGINAL
MOXIE
(Compound)
FOR SALE AT FOUNTAIN
Trade Supplied by C. A. Pike, 414 Atlantic Avenue

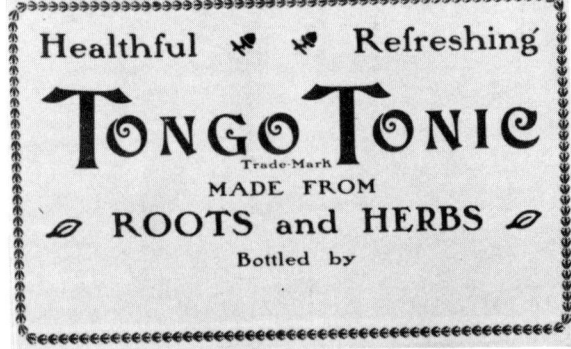

Foxie, a Moxie imitator, was made by the Liquid Carbonic Acid Manufacturing Company, a large firm that should have known better. Tongo Tonic was apparently viewed as a Moxie imitator as well, for several Tongo labels were saved in The Moxie Company archives. At the bottom of this page is shown a genuine Moxie label issued by the Moxie Company, Atlanta, Georgia branch, late 19th century.

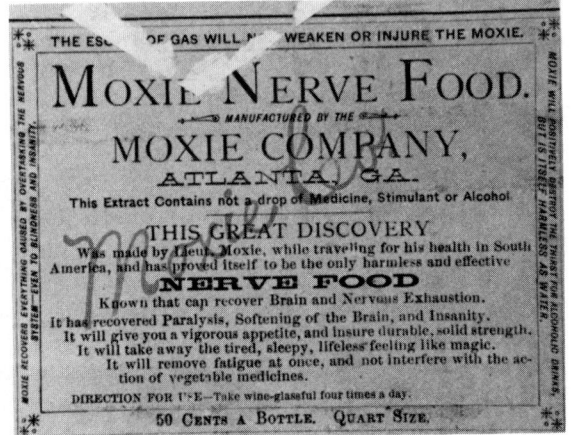

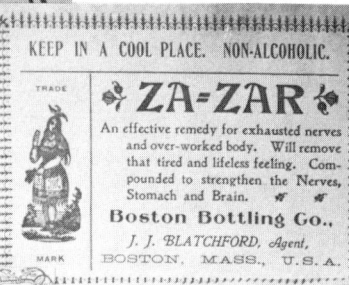

Some labels from the Moxie scrapbook: Photographs of labels in the scrapbook kept by the Moxie Nerve Company of New England. Shown are products of some of Moxie's competitors. Below and to the left is an old tintype, reversed, of a Phenix "bottle wagon," actually a vehicle that seems to be in the shape of a large Phenix Nerve Tonic serving glass. Obviously an imitation of the Moxie Bottle Wagon, the Phenix attraction had a man within who dispensed beverages.

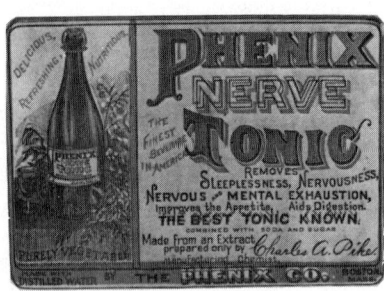

"Through this action of the United States court, the Moxie Nerve Food now becames one of the most valuable articles of commerce in this country, and the decision settles forever the right of the Company to the exclusive use of their own specific invention."

Thompson also noted that frauds occurred soon after Moxie Nerve Food was first put on the market:

"August 13, 1885, the Moxie Nerve Food Company, incorporated under the laws of Maine, put an original trademarked beverage upon the market called 'Moxie Nerve Food.' Its popularity was so large, counterfeits and imitations began to flood the markets, from the hands of soda bottlers, under the title of almost any kind of a Nerve Food but Moxie, until the Company appealed to the courts for protection. Decisions were obtained against these frauds in Texas and Massachusetts to the number of ten. The great value of the market for this most popular beverage ever known caused the most stupendous legal fight ever witnessed in Massachusetts, drawing out some of the first lawyers in the state."

In New Orleans, John T. Shaw, general Moxie agent for the State of Louisiana, ran a prominent advertisement titled "DON'T BE SWINDLED BY FRAUDS ON MOXIE NERVE FOOD." Prospective purchasers were implored to "protect yourselves by inspecting labels, and see that they bear the names of A. Thompson, M.D., General Manager, Lowell, Mass., and Moxie Co., Atlanta, Ga., who guarantee it to be a sparkling, harmless beverage, and the best nerve tonic on the market. Any imitation is a dangerous cheat and fraud upon the consumer and does not contain a particle of Moxie..."

For use in various newspapers around the United States, Moxie prepared an ad headed "FRAUDS" warning citizens that 'Your city has been flooded with fraudulent imitations of the 'Moxie Nerve Food' to steal a market on its remarkable reputation. Buy neither the bottled goods or at the soda fountain unless the dealer is supplied with the appended certificate, showing he has been appointed our special agent to sell pure goods," to which was added a reproduction of a small notice appointing various agents.

Particularly obnoxious to Augustin Thompson and his fellow entrepreneurs was a product known as Gloria or Gloria Nervine, which brazenly claimed that the good reputation of Moxie in the Chicago area due to the fact that Gloria was being sold as Moxie! A small poster with the title "A WARNING TO THE BOTTLING TRADE" was issued by Thompson in an effort to forestall further incursions:

"You are hereby notified that the circular issued to you by the Beverage Supply Co., of Lowell, Mass., is untrue. The making of their goods and imitation of the flavors of Moxie, and their issue of the following circular is a part of a conspiracy to get a sale of their stuff when Moxie is called for by the glass, thereby robbing us of the fruits of our costly advertising, and the high reputation of our goods.

"CIRCULAR ISSUED BY THE BEVERAGE SUPPLY CO. 'The syrup now called 'Gloria,' or 'Gloria Nervine,' was so sold by various Moxie Companies in Chicago, and for seven or eight years as Moxie, and made its reputation. Certain eastern parties claimed they had a different Moxie and wanted the old kind stopped, so 'Gloria' appeared to be a good name and the thousands who were accustomed to its taste for years will agree that it has no superior. 'Gloria' is for sale everywhere.'

"The cowardly sneaking liar does not dare sign his name to it.

"The above circular issued by the Beverage Supply Co. is a whole cloth falsehood. Its author was arrested in Chicago and stripped of $60,000 worth of property by legal process, for cheating and counterfeiting with the stuff. The reputation of the Moxie obtained all the sale for it that was ever obtained, and when the cheat was discovered by the public, they threw it into the street. Sixty-one of this man's accomplices were arrested at the time he was, and heavily fined. We hereby notify bottlers and dealers, that if our detectives shall find them selling the stuff when Moxie is called for, no mercy will be shown to them. They shall be dealt with for a conspiracy to defraud, and pushed to the penitentiary, if possible."

More on the same subject, and a surprising revelation concerning the Chicago Moxie Nerve Food Company, was contained in still another circular issued by Thompson:

"623 ARRESTS FOR COUNTERFEITING MOXIE. We do not send this out as a threat, for we are sure that a large majority of the trade would disdain to trade under fraud if they knew it. This heading is to draw your attention and to prevent the summary mode of consigning it to the wastepaper basket without reading, as is the custom. The West has been ravaged by counterfeiters of MOXIE. These arrests were a necessity. The genuine Moxie bears a tan-colored label, has 'Moxie Nerve Food Co., Lowell, Mass.,' blown in the bottle, and my name—Augustin Thompson, M.D.—and vignette is on a white, red and black printed label, pasted across the mouth of the bottle. The Chicago Moxie Nerve Food Company has ceased to do business, because it was originated to counterfeit our goods—we suppressed it. The old counterfeit was sold in a similar mode as our own; only the forged side label was white. The cork label was an exact counterpart of ours. My name on it was a forgery, and its use in sales was a forgery.

623 Arrests for
Counterfeiting "Moxie."

WE do not send this out as a threat, for we are sure that a large majority of the trade would disdain to trade in a fraud if they knew it. This heading is to draw your attention and prevent the summary mode of consigning it to the waste paper basket without reading, as is the custom. The west has been ravaged by counterfeiters of MOXIE. These arrests were a necessity. The genuine MOXIE bears a tan-colored label; has "Moxie Nerve Food Co., Lowell, Mass.," blown in the bottle, and my name—Augustin Thompson, M. D.—and vignette is on a white, red and black printed label, pasted across the mouth of the bottle. The Chicago Moxie Nerve Food Co. has ceased to do business, because it was originated to counterfeit our goods—we suppressed it. The old counterfeit was sold in a similar mode as our own; only the forged side label was white. The cork label was an exact counterpart of ours. My name on it was a forgery, and its use in sales is a forgery. My detectives find an imitation of the flavor of MOXIE, called "*Gloria*," which is sold by the glass when MOXIE is called for. Here is where the trade are liable to arrest. My detectives are scouring the cities in the United States, and have orders to arrest all who pirate the market we have made, bought and paid for with expensive advertising. This market, the law says, is ours, as much as is our other property. The man who originated this "*Gloria*" is now in the hands of the law. We now have a sale of nearly 500,000 cases annually. Such a business is worth defending. We *shall* defend it, *bitterly* if need be. We give the trade a profit of 200 per cent in glass sales. The public soon detect a fraud, and refuse to patronize such dealers, reasoning well, that a man who will defraud in one thing would in another, and could not be trusted to put up a prescription for the sick wife or child. Such a distruction of confidence cannot be mended. I believe the intelligent trade have my view of the results of such a business. We shall protect you to the utmost. Genuine MOXIE can be had by addressing the **MOXIE NERVE FOOD CO.**, 513 Wash St., St. Louis, Mo.; 14 Charles Place, Chicago, Ill.; 126 Plymouth Avenue, Minneapolis, Minn.; 209 Market Street, Pittsburg, Pa.; Des Moines, Iowa, and General Office, 68 Beverly St., Boston, Mass.

AUGUSTIN THOMPSON, M. D.,
General Manager Moxie Company.

A scandalous episode in the history of Moxie was the operation of the Chicago Moxie Nerve Food Company (earlier called the Western Moxie Nerve Food Company, the same name used for the St. Louis branch at another time), which did business for several years. At the same time that G.P. Walker, manager of the Chicago enterprise, was buying token amounts of extract from the Moxie Nerve Food Company of New England in Lowell, he was purchasing large quantities of an imitation syrup from another Massachusetts source! This deception was discovered by Augustin Thompson's detectives, and arrests were made. The above notice tells the tale.

DON'T

BE SWINDLED BY

FRAUDS ON MOXIE
NERVE FOOD.

None Genuine without this Trade-Mark.

Trade-Mark (Copyrighted)

PROTECT YOURSELVES

By inspecting labels, and see that they bear the names of A. THOMPSON, M. D., General Manager, Lowell, Mass., and J. J. SCHOTT MF'G Co. Galveston, Texas, who guarantee it to be a Sparkling, Harmless Beverage, and the Best Nerve Tonic on the market. Any imitation is a dangerous cheat and fraud upon the consumer, and does not contain a particle of Moxie.

The plant we extract from has never before been used in pharmacy, and is too expensive to be used in cheap stuff called Nerve Food, and sold in imitation of Moxie.

Don't drink the villianous compounds put up by some unscrupulous and irresponsible bottlers, when you can get genuine Moxie, put up under the personal supervision of MR. J. J. SCHOTT, whose experience of twenty-eight years in the drug business has gained for him a national reputation for the highest standard of excellence.

Price 50 Cts. per Bottle or $5 per Dozen

Sold by Retail Grocers, Druggists and Saloons, all over the Country, and in Soda Water by all Leading Fountains.

J.J. Schott, the Galveston agent for Moxie, issued this warning against imitations of the beverage. Information concerning the mysterious secret ingredient of Moxie is given: "The plant we extract from has never before been used in pharmacy and is too expensive to be used in cheap stuff called Nerve Food and sold in imitation of Moxie."

Many were the posters, notices, and advertisements warning the public to beware of counterfeit Moxie and putting bottlers on their guard that vigorous prosecution would follow any evidence of fraudulent activities.

"My detectives find an imitation of the flavor of Moxie, called 'Gloria' which is sold by the glass when Moxie is called for. Here is where the trade are liable to arrest. My detectives are scouring the cities in the United States, and have orders to arrest all who pirate the market we have made, bought and paid for with expense of advertising. This market, the law says is ours, as much as is our other property. The man who originated this 'Gloria' is now in the hands of the law. We now have a sale of nearly 500,000 cases annually. Such a business is worth defending. We shall defend it *bitterly* if need be... Genuine Moxie can be had by addressing the Moxie Nerve Food Co., 513 Washington Street, St. Louis, Missouri; 14 Charles Place, Chicago, Illinois; 126 Plymouth Avenue, Minneapolis, Minn.; 209 Market Street, Pittsburgh, Pennsylvania; Des Moines, Iowa; and General Office, 68 Beverly Street, Boston, Mass.— Augustin Thompson, M.D. General Manager, Moxie Company."

More information on the Chicago Moxie Nerve Food Company was provided in a circular addressed to "Dealers in the Northwest," which stated, in part:

"January 29, 1889, this company leased the right to bottle Moxie in the Northwest to George P. Walker, who, in turn, a few days later, assigned the said lease, by our consent, the Chicago Moxie Nerve Food Company, whose business passed under the control of Walker... The said Walker and his company have defaulted in every agreement under said lease, and it has been annulled. We have obtained evidence that 'Moxie' sold by that company during the last 12 months, perhaps longer, is but a fraudulent imitation of our flavor. You are requested to return to the said Chicago Moxie Nerve Food Company all the 'Moxie' you have on hand, bottled within the last year... We have taken possession of our property in Chicago...and have sued for return of the plant. Pending a reorganization of the business there, under the direction of this Company, genuine Moxie can be obtained from Peter Van Schaack & Sons, 40 Lake Street, Chicago..."

The Chicago Moxie Nerve Food Company was not the only outfit wanting to make its own "Moxie" and sell it as such. C.A. Pike made Phenix Nerve Tonic, billing it as "The Original MOXIE Compound," with expected consequences once Moxie learned of it! A similar fate awaited the proprietor of "Conklin's Moxie."

A scrapbook of clippings from the Moxie archives has more entries bearing the 1900 year date than for any other time, indicating that the earlier court decisions did not deter those who sought to trade on the Moxie name. So bad was the situation in 1900, that one newspaper reporter wrote: "The Moxie people are on the war-

A cock fight is shown in this Moxie advertisement of the 1880s. The rooster "Moxie" triumphs over the dead rooster "Anarchist-thief" with "Imitation Nerve Foods" lettered in the background. The caption notes that the advertisement is "Dedicated to the men who attempted to rob my roost in the dark; who never felt the throb and satisfaction of business honor; who interpose a counterfeit to prevent it, when the drunkard would save himself with Moxie; who asked the debased dealer to give the same to the poor worn out working girl, because his profit would be one cent more. To the Texas and Boston thieves who thought justice could be bought or lied to death."

The last sentence refers to two Texas and eight Boston imitators who were brought to justice in 1888.

path after imitators. It is said that they have the best combination of legal talent it is possible to secure and also have one of the best organized forces of investigators, including men and women in all walks of life of any concern in the world that caters to the public..." Moxie paid for large advertisements in *The Pharmaceutical Era* and elsewhere to warn dealers, druggists, store owners, and others against "serving an imitation of Moxie when Moxie was called for," noting that all caught in the act would be prosecuted.

Moxie also took notice of a curious imitator, not a beverage or Nerve Food, but a product put up in pills and sold for $1 a box. The name was Oxie, and the advertising showed a caveman-type of individual with the head of a bull, "OXIE" lettered on his chest, holding aloft a club. The proprietor was the Oxie Company, Augusta, Maine.

It is to be surmised that Augustin Thompson may not have enjoyed the various legal fights involving infringement, but he certainly enjoyed publicizing the results, as Frank M. Archer did in later decades. Indeed, Thompson would have enjoyed reading Archer's *This Book About Substitution Law* publication.

Noxie, Proxie, Foxie, Hoxie, Toxie—the world would little remember them today were it not for the publicity given to them by Moxie.

MOXIE vs. NOXIE, 1939

Of all names imitators concocted to challenge the Moxie trademark, none was more popular than "Noxie," a style used several times from the 1880s onward. In 1939, Noxie reared its head once again. The Moxie Company brought action against the Noxie Kola Company of New York in the Federal District Court of that state on June 13, 1939. The following is an excerpt from the federal transcript of the case:

Action by The Moxie Company against the Noxie Kola Company of New York, Incorporated, and another to enjoin infringement of a trademark competition, and use of infringing words as part of defendant's corporate titles...

By the motion, plaintiff seeks a preliminary injunction in a suit to enjoin infringement of plaintiff's registered trademark "Moxie" and to restrain unfair competition by the defendants because of the use by them of the name "Noxie Kola" on a similar and competing product. Plaintiff also seeks to enjoin the use of the word "Noxie" by the defendants as part of their corporate titles.

Plaintiff, The Moxie Company, is a Massachusetts corporation engaged in the manufacture and sale of a carbonated beverage and a syrup for making the same, under the registered trademark "Moxie."

In connection with such manufacture and sale the plaintiff and its predecessors have made continuous and exclusive use in the United States of the name "Moxie" from the year 1885. The word "Moxie" was first registered in the United States Patent Office in 1885... The affidavits and exhibits indicate that the "Moxie" trademark has been for many years one of the best known trademarks for soft drinks in the United States. Since the year 1908 the gross receipts from the sale in this country of bottled "Moxie" and "Moxie" syrup have exceeded $35,000,000 and more than $6,000,000 has been spent in the same period to advertise the name "Moxie" and the product which it identifies. Plaintiff's beverage is sold at retail, principally at soda fountains and drug stores. It is ordered by both the retail dealers and the purchasing public by the name "Moxie." The name "Moxie" is accepted by the general public as the badge of the beverage of plaintiff's manufacture.

The defendant, Noxie Kola Company, Inc., is a Maryland corporation and the defendant, Noxie Kola Company of New York, Inc., is a New York corporation. Both have an established place of business in the Borough of Manhattan, City of New York, where acts complained of are alleged to have been and are being carried on. It appears that both the defendants' corporations were incorporated in January of the present year [1939]. The defendants manufacture and sell in interstate commerce a carbonated beverage made from an extract of the cola nut and leaves. Defendants claim the drink is made under an old recipe formerly the property of the Crystal Spring Bottling Works of Waterloo, Province of Quebec, Canada. It is stated that this beverage has been sold in Canada under the "Noxie-Kola" trademark since the year 1900. Defendants' predecessor registered the name "Noxie-Kola" in Canada on or about June 28, 1906 for "a certain beverage, a temperance drink—nerve tonic and blood purifier." Defendants acquired their interests in the Canadian drink and the Canadian trademark "Noxie Kola" by virtue of a recent assignment bearing date the 4th day of February 1939. The papers before me [District Judge Leibell] are barren of any claim that the beverage "Noxie Kola" was ever sold in the United States prior to the incorporation of the defendants in this country.

The governing personnel of both defendants were, prior to the year 1939, officers or employees of the Pepsi-Cola Company, another manufacturer of a carbonated beverage of the same general class as that of the plaintiffs and defendants. By reason of their previous connections, these individuals were familiar with the various carbonated beverages of national reputation sold in the United States, as well as the trade names or trademarks under which they were merchandized. The words "Noxie Kola" are applied or affixed to defendants' bottles or receptacles by placing thereon a printed label prominently bearing the words "Noxie Kola." Like the plaintiff's beverage, defendants' drink is sold at retail and is similar in appearance and taste to that of the plaintiff.

During the short period of their operation the defendants have circularized the soft drink trade advertising the advent of "Noxie Kola" in the United States. In all their advertisements, letterheads and labels, and on their bottles and caps the word "Noxie" is given a prominent place. For example, upon their bottle label the defendants use the word "Noxie Kola," the word "Noxie" appearing above the word "Kola" and the words "trade mark" appearing beneath the word "Noxie." In one of their advertisements defendants refer to the syrup as "Noxie" alone and say "No mixing required. Noxie is a finished syrup ready for bottling." These are typical instances of the use of the word "Noxie" by the defendants in connection with the marketing of their beverage. In addition, the word "Noxie" is employed by the defendants as the first word of their corporate titles.

Plaintiff contends that the use of the words "Noxie" and "Noxie Kola" by the defendants upon their beverage and advertising materials infringes plaintiff's registered trademark "Moxie" and that the use of the word "Noxie" by the defendants constitutes unfair competition...

Defendants in opposing this application for preliminary injunction argued that it should not be granted because (1) defendants' assignors used the name "Noxie Kola" before plaintiff and its predecessors used the name "Noxie"; (2) that the names "Moxie" and "Noxie Kola" are totally dissimilar and cannot possibly lead to confusion in the beverage trade so as to result in a diversion of profits from the plaintiffs to the defendants; (3) the word "Moxie" is (a) descriptive (b) is the name of an individual, Lieutenant Moxie, and (c) is geographic, the name of a Maine lake.

As to prior use—the use of the words "Noxie Kola" upon which the defendants rely, is the use made of the words by the defendants' predecessor. Defendants' own use of the words dates only from January of this year [1939] at the earliest. The use of the words "Noxie Kola" by defendants' predecessor from 1900 was confined to the Dominion of Canada and probably only to the Province of Quebec. That the words "Noxie Kola" were never employed by the defendants' predecessor, or anyone else for that matter, in the United States until defendants adopted the name in January of this year, does not appear to be in dispute...

The prior use of the words "Noxie Kola" in Canada by defendants' predecessor, who never sold his product under that name in this country, cannot be urged to protect the Canadian name in the United States, when that name conflicts with a trademark otherwise properly registered here and applied to and identifying a product of similar class sold for many years in the United States. On the question of use therefore, the defendants must rely only upon their own use thereof in the United States for a period not exceeding five months, and that is of no avail in this case...

I now pass to the defendants' second point of opposition, namely that the words "Noxie" or "Noxie Kola" are not so similar in appearance or sound to plaintiff's trademark "Moxie" as to justify a finding that confusion will result in the beverage trade and in the public mind from their concurrent use. Plaintiff and defendants are in the same type of business. Both sell a non-alcoholic, carbonated beverage of practically the same color and appearance. Both cater to exactly the same trade. Both sell the beverage of their manufacture in glass bottles upon which there are displayed their respective marks on labels affixed to such bottles. Both employ their names upon the bottle caps, the plaintiff "Moxie," the defendants "Noxie Kola." Both claim their names to be trademarked. Plaintiff's label bears the notation "Trademark. Reg. U.S. Pat. Office" directly under the word "Moxie." The defendants do not announce on their label that their trademark is of Canadian origin. They simply display the words "Noxie Kola," with the words "Trade Mark" under the word "Noxie." A person seeing the latter label would undoubtedly infer that the trademark of the defendants was a duly registered United States trademark. There is no reason why he should think otherwise.

However, it is urged that the plaintiff markets its product under the single word "Moxie," whereas the defendants market theirs under the double word "Noxie Kola." This, defendants contend, is difference enough. They say that addition of the word "Kola" to the word "Noxie" eliminates the possibility of passing off their beverage as "Moxie," the beverage of the plaintiff. With this contention I cannot agree. "Kola" is purely a descriptive term. It signifies the cola nut or an extract of it. There are any number of Kola drinks upon the market such as "Coca-Cola," "Royal Crown Cola," "Pepsi-Cola," "Cheri Cola," "Double Kola," "Nichol Kola," "Twin Cola," "Yankee Kola," "Lola Kola," "Lime Cola," "Cleo Cola," "Cana-dry Cola," and "Pop Kola". In all of these the distinguishing or identifying word is the first word. The only arbitrary or distinctive portion of "Noxie Kola" is the word "Noxie."

Defendants' own advertisements clearly show that the "Kola" portion of their mark is merely descriptive of the type of drink. In one of their advertisements defendants state, "Today, more five-cent kola drinks are sold in the United States than all other flavors combined." "Noxie Kola is a full-bodied, full strength kola drink with an abundance of delicious stimulating flavor. It gives great value to the consumer and an honest profit to the dealer and bottlers. The truth of this statement will be discovered instantly by comparing Noxie Kola with every other kola drink on the market."

Is the word "Noxie" so similar to the word "Moxie" as to mislead purchasers of "Noxie Kola" into the belief that they are buying a drink of the plaintiff's manufacture? There is no difference between the two words except in the initial letter. The spelling is otherwise identical. There is practically no difference at all in sound. The plaintiff's "M" is changed by the defendants' "N". No two letters in the English alphabet are more similar in sound or appearance than "M" and "N". Both are labials. From a distance the letter "N" might be very easily mistaken for an "M".

Why did the defendant corporations deem it necessary to their future success to use the word "Noxie" as the identifying mark of their product? Why do they insist upon the use of the word "Noxie" as part of their corporate titles? Plaintiff's old and established product is known as "Moxie." Plaintiff's corporate title is "The Moxie Company." There is no legitimate reason why out of the myriad of names that might be applied to their product the defendants had to select one that looked the same, which was practically spelled the same, and sounded the same as that used by a competitor established for a long time in exactly the same line of business in the United States. I am of the opinion that the defendants purchased the Canadian trademark "Noxie Kola," adopted the name "Noxie" and applied it to their product, for the purpose of appropriating in this country some of the plaintiff's goodwill. If defendants had wanted only the formula or the recipe of the Canadian company, that would have been bought for use in the United States without the name "Noxie Kola." Defendants bought both. I am convinced that what they really wanted was the name "Noxie Kola" and their advertising so indicates.

The word "Noxie" is so close an imitation of the word "Moxie" as to not permit a sincere argument in its defense. No reasonable explanation is suggested why the word "Noxie" need be used. The fact that the word "Noxie" may be known in Canada, especially in the Province of Quebec, did not make it of any real commercial value here, where it was not known at all. On the other hand the fact that "Moxie" is well known here lends strength to the claim that its goodwill is coveted...

I shall not consider defendants' claim that the word "Moxie" is descriptive and should therefore have been denied registration. The general rule is that a word which is descriptive of the article upon which it is used, of its ingredients, qualities or characteristics could not be employed as a trademark... Defendants referred the court to the original trademark No. 12,565, registered by plaintiff's predecessor in the United States Patent Office in the year 1885... It appears to be a label, on the left hand side which is pictured a woman carrying a bundle of flax, wheat, grain, or some other product of the field. To the right of this picture appear the words "Moxie Nerve Food, Has not a drop of Medicine, Poison, Stimulant or Alcohol in its composition, but is a simple starchy plant grown in South America," etc. Defendants contend therefore that the word "Moxie" is a descriptive term, descriptive of "a simple starchy plant grown in South America."

Certainly the word "Moxie" is not a word in general or common use in this country, except insofar as it has been known by application to plaintiff's beverage. To the man in the street the word "Moxie" does not mean "a simple starchy plant grown in South America"—it means the beverage of The Moxie Company. A search of several standard dictionaries does not reveal the word "Moxie" at all. Obviously it forms no part of the English language. Being unknown to our tongue it could not of itself be said to be descriptive of anything. In my opinion the word "Moxie" is an arbitrary and fanciful term which plaintiff's predecessor undoubtedly applied in 1885 to a certain so-called nerve food which he then put upon the market, one of the major elements of which was a simple starchy plant of unknown or unmentioned name grown in South America. This is the only fair and sensible construction to be placed upon the words quoted above and which appear in the old 1885 trademark, for it was clearly a beverage to which the name "Moxie" was applied by plaintiff's predecessor, not to a plant...

The further objection of the defendants to the original registration of "Moxie" on the ground that it is the name of an individual or geographic in character, is under the facts of this case and the present state of the law without merit. Even assuming that word "Moxie" was both geographic (the name of a Maine lake) or the name of an individual (Lieutenant Moxie), the papers before me clearly establish that the use of this mark by plaintiff and its predecessor was actual, exclusive and continuous since the year 1885. Because of that circumstance alone the mark "Moxie" was entitled to registration... and is now entitled to protection from infringement. On the basis of the foregoing I conclude that plaintiff's trademark "Moxie" is a valid trademark. I have already indicated that such trademark, if valid, has been infringed by defendants.

The sole question remaining is that of unfair competition. Facts which support a suit for infringement and those which form the basis for unfair competition are substantially the same... Where, as here, a clear case of infringement of trademark is shown by a competitor's adoption of a similar name on a product of the same general class, unfair competition naturally results. This is especially so where the infringer employs the offending name as part of its corporate title...

Thus I have reached the conclusion that the defendants have infringed and are infringing upon plaintiff's registered trademark.

Plaintiff, through its attorney, sent the defendants a formal notice on February 21, 1939, that the defendants in using the name "Noxie Kola" were infringing plaintiff's trademark and invading plaintiff's trade rights. Defendants disregarded this notice and went ahead with their preparations to put on the market a beverage product, similar to plaintiff's and bearing the trade name "Noxie Kola." Plaintiff filed its complaint and obtained an order to show cause on April 21, 1939. Defendants were served with these papers April 25, 1939. On that date defendants could have had no doubt about plaintiff's intention to enforce its rights and to seek an order of the Court to restrain defendants' use of the name "Noxie Kola."

On February 21, 1939, according to defendants' report to the Court, they had no finished "Noxie Kola" syrup on hand, but did have the equivalent of 47,107 gallons of simple syrup. On April 25, 1939 they had on hand 44,551 gallons of finished "Noxie Kola" syrup and 3,100 gallons of simple syrup. There is dispute as to whether the finished "Noxie Kola" syrup deteriorates rapidly. Defendants claimed to have had on hand on May 22, 1939 approximately 100,000 gallons of "Noxie Kola" syrup valued at $75,000 and 25,625 gross ($4,100 value) "Noxie Kola" cork inserted crowns... The cork insert is claimed to be subject to shrinkage by drying. In view of defendants' deliberate and continous infringement of plaintiff's trademark and invasion of trade rights, of which they must have had knowledge because of the experience of their officers in the beverage field and of which they were formerly notified February 21, 1939, I have concluded that defendants' investment at the time of the argument of the motion on May 22nd should not be considered in fixing the amount of the bond plaintiff shall be required to file an issuance of the preliminary injunction herein. Further, this preliminary injunction will not prevent defendants from disposing of the finished syrup and the simple syrup they now have on hand, using some other name than "Noxie Kola."

Chapter 9

1907 Onward

On April 20, 1907, The Moxie Nerve Food Company of New England secured trademark registration No. 62,295, for Moxie, a "non-alcoholic carbonated beverage and syrup for making the same." The Pure Food and Drugs Act had been passed a year earlier, and as the earlier (1885) trademark registration was for a medicine, a change was desired. Separately, around 1907 the Moxie logotype trademark was revised to what became the standard form used from that time onward, a distinctive representation of the Moxie word with letters slanting slightly to the right and with a distinctively long crossbar to the X. Previously, the word appeared in a variety of styles, including a popular logotype with flares or "foxtails" above and below. Use of the new logotype was not exclusive and occasionally earlier styles were reverted to or something else was tried.

Early in the year, notices were sent out stating that the Secretary of Agriculture of the United States had assigned the company serial No. 1799, after the following guarantee was made:

"The undersigned, Moxie Nerve Food Company of New England, does hereby guarantee that the articles of food or drugs manufactured, packed, and distributed and sold by it, such as Moxie Nerve Food, are not adulterated or misbranded within the meaning of the Food and Drugs Act, June 30, 1906."

This registration number was proudly added to Moxie bottle crates and certain advertising. Pure food became a popular subject, and the newspapers were full of revelations concerning the previously-unsuspected contents of one type of food or another. Moxie emerged with a clean bill of health, for it never possessed substances considered deleterious (although much later, in 1960, sassafras, a Moxie ingredient, was banned). Food fairs multiplied, and purveyors of food and drink were invited to exhibit at shows, often under the "Pure Food Fair" banner.

The left front window of the Miller & Olson Cash Market, location not known, displayed a Moxie sign in this early (probably circa 1908-1910) photograph. "Very Heathful—MOXIE—Feeds the Nerves" is the inscription.

At the time Moxie offered retailers a choice of many different cardboard signs, translucent and adhesive signs and other advertising aids. At one time, the Moxie firm claimed that nearly 1,000 people were kept busy calling on customers and posting advertising, but this figure undoubtedly included employees of the various distributors who handled Moxie.

Open invitations were given to physicians, newspaper writers interested in the subject of pure food (a specialty of numerous journalists at the time), and others to visit the Moxie facilities to inspect for cleanliness. Many favorable newspaper articles appeared, some of which were duly reprinted in the firm's advertising.

The turnip-tasting, or asparagus-like, or sugar cane-like mystery plant of Dr. Augustin Thompson's time was forgotten, and visitors to the Moxie facilities were told that gentian was the key ingredient. Long rows of sparkling white vats in which essence of gentian root was extracted were shown to journalists. Unlike the legendary plant of Lieut. Moxie, which grew in South America near the equator (or was it near the Strait of Magellan?), gentian apparently was imported from France or Spain, for later Moxie advertisements said it came from the Pyrenees, the mountain chain dividing the two countries. "The root is tough and flexible, brownish in color, and spongy in texture. It has a bitter taste and faint distinctive odor, and was used in medicine in ancient times," notes the *Encyclopaedia Britannica*.

In 1907, production of Moxie was primarily centered in Boston and New York. Lowell continued its minor role. In August 1907, 48,403 dozen quarts of Moxie were made in New York, 73,569 dozen in Boston, and just 589 dozen in Lowell. No pints were produced that month. Pint Moxie was never important in the early years, except for use in sampling and for gifts to physicians, newspaper editors, and others of influence. After 1906, regular shipments to doctors were restricted, for the medical claims of Moxie were no more. Apparently efficiencies in manufacturing were realized, for the cost of manufacturing a dozen quart bottles of Moxie had dropped to just 96c at the Boston facility.

Frank Archer continued to create a dazzling variety of Moxie posters, metal signs, tip trays, and other material, stating in a form letter dated May 1, 1907:

"We have caused to be shipped to you, freight prepaid, from the H.D. Beach Company, Coshocton, Ohio, and the Forbes Lithograph Manufacturing Company, Revere, Massachusetts a quantity of advertising matter... This advertising matter is more expensive than any we have ever had and really is designed for the best class of stores. [I trust] you will distribute this advertising matter in a manner you believe will be productive of the greatest results to us both."

In an August 1907 interview with Francis E. Thompson, writer Albert Payson Terhune told of Moxie business and advertising, with emphasis on newspapers:

"[Francis E. Thompson said:] 'The output for this past year, by the way, is 1,000,000 cases, and we will employ a force of 300. That will give you some idea of the rate of increase during the past 22 years.

"Today, Moxie is sold as far west as Indiana, and as far south as North Carolina. Freight rates make it inadvisable just yet to spread the territory further.

"In that district our annual 1,000,000 cases are sold. At $2.50 per case, that brings a total gross receipts up to $2,500,000. We spend from $400,000 to $500,000 a year in advertising. The largest proportion of this sum goes to newspapers.'

" 'How much to magazines?'

" 'None of it. We do not advertise Moxie in the magazines. We have found the newspapers by far the best means of reaching the public, and I speak from experience, for we have tried every method you could think of.'

" 'Including magazines?'

" 'Yes. We gave them a fair trial. There are a number of reasons why we found newspapers better. For one thing, people whose time is limited will read only what is thrust before them. Everybody reads newspapers.

" 'A busy man opens his paper. There is my advertisement staring him in the face. He can't miss it. He sees what I have for sale and why he ought to buy it.

" 'That same man, in order to see an advertisement in the magazine must, first of all, be a magazine reader. Then he must go through many advertising pages to find it. He may be a man who is interested only in the reading of a newspaper or magazine. If so, he won't explore the magazine pages beyond that reading matter in search of Moxie.

" 'But, in the case of newspapers, the advertisement often stands out, prominent, next to the reading matter, where he can't miss it. Even a small, continuous advertisement in a newspaper will often catch the attention of the casual reader, by being so frequently seen.

" 'People are apt to judge the size of a man's business by the size of his advertisements. It would take two or three pages of ads in a magazine to attract the eye as does a 'display ad' in a newspaper, besides entailing the extra task of looking for it.

" 'At our main entrance [to the Boston office and factory] you perhaps noticed a big sign that reads: Notice to Advertising Solicitors:

Moxie on the Rooftops: Above and below are two of several rooftops depicted
in the author's collection of early Moxie postcards and photographs. Above is shown
the trolley car station in Arlington Heights, Massachusetts, circa 1909. The photograph
below, believed to have been taken in Clifton, Massachusetts, dates from August
1906. "Drink MOXIE. It Feeds the Nerves" is the inscription on the shingles. Moxie
rooftop signs were particularly popular on boathouses and concessions by the shore.

Positively no Advertisements placed in Programs, Souvenirs, Catalogues or other Publications except Daily Newspapers. It became necessary to put that sign there to make our position in regard to advertisements clear.'

"There could be no doubt whatever as to the 'clearness' of the notice. Big, terse, emphatic, it greets every visitor who sets foot in the Moxie Building. A 'Beware of the Dog' sign could scarcely be more final. The magazine catalogue or program advertising solicitor who could pass it unflinchingly might possess a stock of nerve which would be invaluable in facing the traditional cannon's mouth or in approaching the same rustic twice with an aureate [gold] brick proposition.

" 'There is another reason why we do not advertise in magazines,' resumed Mr. Thompson. 'As I told you, Moxie goes no further west than the Ohio borders of Indiana. Suppose we advertise it in a magazine that circulated as far west as the Pacific Coast.

" 'Not only would much of our outlay go for nothing and we would create a demand we cannot supply, but some fakirs in the far West might get out an imitation of Moxie and, by selling it, would reap the profit of our magazine ad and do us incalculable injury. That is a plain proposition, isn't it?

" 'We do our heaviest advertising in the spring and early summer, for it is then that the thought of a cool drink is likely to appeal most to perspiring humanity. But we keep our advertising to a large extent all year round.

" 'An advertisement's timeliness is one of its chief advantages. Shove a 'cooling drink' ad in front of a thirsty man on a hot day and it is bound to carry conviction.'

"Of course this latter suggestion of Mr. Thompson's (as he proceeded to point out) cannot be carried on as satisfactorily in a magazine (where the advertising pages are 'made up' long before hand) as in a daily newspaper, where, if necessary, an advertisement can be timed to suit the weather, and· the reminder awoke a memory of an advertisement that appeared in some of the magazines during the cold, damp days of late May and early June. It announced the reader was hot, consumed by thirst, wilted from perspiration and at that moment in dire need of a certain cold beverage."

The preceding Terhune article, which appeared in the *Pittsburgh Press*, is not so much an interview as it is a testimonial to the virtues of newspaper advertising. Over the years, Francis E. Thompson and Frank Archer both issued many statements concerning the

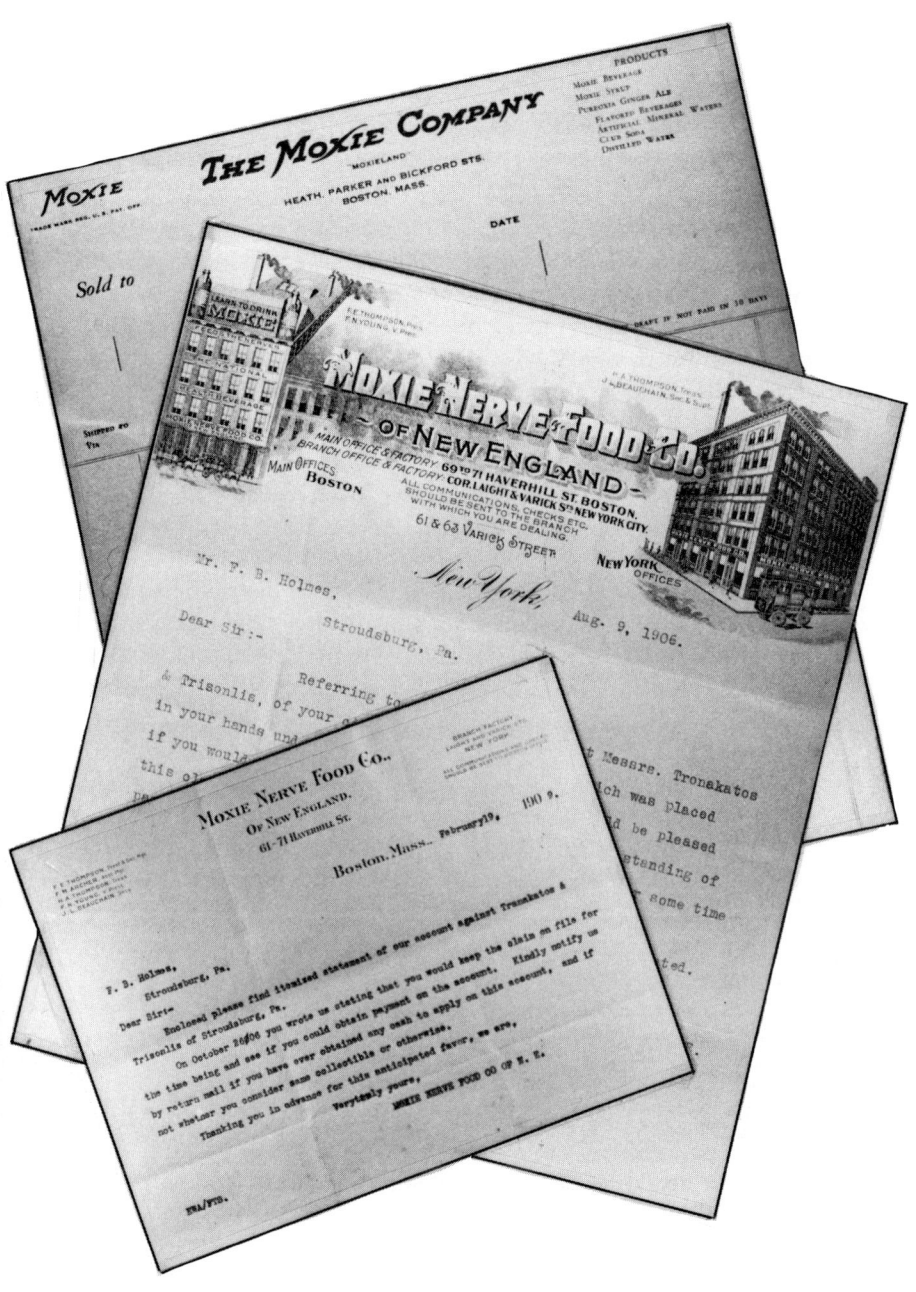

A montage of Moxie letterheads from over the years.

effectiveness of newspaper advertising. In turn, newspapers rewarded them with many favorable news articles. At the same time they *did* advertise in magazines and programs, but on a limited basis.

Moxie representatives were prone to exaggeration. While the firm may have had a *capacity* of a million cases a year, and may have *desired* total gross receipts up to $2,500,000, company ledgers reveal that true sales were but a small fraction of this figure. At the end of the summer season, September 10, 1907 a dividend amounting to $35,000 was paid, and when the figures for the year's operations were added up, $600,000 worth of sales yielded a profit of $61,987.94.

It may have been in 1907 that the Moxie Boy made his initial appearance. In that year so-called "man and box" cardboard cut-outs of various sizes, including large-format pieces about three feet high, made their debut. Depicted was the Moxie Boy facing forward, holding a crate of Moxie. The head of the same boyish figure was separately available on metal lapel pins, wall hangings, and other formats. Company nomenclature of the time dictated that this lad was known as the Moxie *Boy*, while various traveling representatives, particularly those manning Bottle Wagons or automobiles, were each known as the Moxie *Man*. Indeed, the "boy" terminology extended for more than two decades. In later years, the terminology became fuzzy, and the former boy became known as the "Moxie Man." The image of the Moxie Boy changed, and about 1911 the original lad was replaced by a new version showing the Moxie Boy dressed as a soda fountain attendant, with his right hand pointing toward the viewer in an admonishing "Drink Moxie!" manner. In 1917, James Montgomery Flagg's "I Want You!" poster, with Uncle Sam pointing, undoubtedly was inspired by the Moxie Boy, as were several other copycats (examples of which were carefully saved in a scrapbook by Frank M. Archer).

The fleet of Moxie automobiles continued to grow, and Moxie representatives caused a stir when they visited remote villages. Cars were still a novelty in 1907, and the horse remained the staple means of transportation in all but the largest cities. Moxie Bottle Wagons continued their appearances in fairs, parades, expositions, and other gatherings. At the end of the year, eight such units were on hand in Boston, and additional Bottle Wagons were in New York.

Other uses of the Moxie word were fascinating to Frank Archer and other company executives, who kept dozens of newspaper clippings pertaining to events at Moxie Lake or Pond, Moxie Woods, and other Maine locations. Inspired by the beverage, pet owners ap-

The Moxie Boy was featured on cardboard cut-outs made in various sizes. Shown here is one of small format designed for use on a soda fountain counter. Several varieties were made, including the style in which the Moxie Boy is wearing a cap (as shown above), one without the cap, and others with different lettering variations at the bottom. The particular piece offered here was kept as a souvenir by a person who attended the Food Fair in Boston on October 22, 1907. The inscription reproduced to the left is printed on the back side.

A shop proprietor stands with a cardboard cut-out of the Moxie Boy. Note the window signs.

This Providence, Rhode Island window is crammed with Moxie advertisements and products, including bottles wrapped in paper, large cardboard
cut-outs, crates, and miscellaneous signs.

This Moxie exhibit, photographed around 1904, offers visitors a
"Moxie Song Free to Every Purchaser." Shown along the bottom of
the counter are framed pictures of "A Moxie Girl" with the Moxie "foxtail" logotype above her head (such inscriptions were later effaced from
undistributed examples) and a framed item with Roosevelt standing
to the left and a Moxie bottle to the right. There were two separate
captions on the single sign: "The Leading Exponent of the Strenuous
Life" and "The Necessary Support of the Strenuous Life."

plied the Moxie name to dogs, cats, rabbits, and other creatures, notice of which occasionally made the newspapers. "Old Moxie," a famous Maine moose, reached print as well. At the Grand Opera House a play, *Broadway After Dark*, featured the character of Abe Moxie at the top of the bill. In an issue of the *Morning Telegraph*, New York City, an article appeared about Moxie Michelson, a ticket-scalper whose domain was in front of the Amsterdam Theatre. This particular account was unfortunate, for through it Mrs. Moxie Michelson, who had been seeking her errant husband, located him and was able to collect six months of back alimony! Unfortunate was the case of Moxie Schonberg, an accused robber who was found drowned in the Hudson River off Edgewater, New Jersey, according to an article in the New York *World*.

It seems as though many people named Max took Moxie as a nickname, although at least one individual, Moxie Craus, a Texan, was given the name at birth. Moxie was a favorite appellation for small pleasure craft, lobster boats, and the like, and a number of newspaper clippings in this vein were preserved, including an account of an unfortunate instance in which several young boys drowned on their boat, *Moxie*, near Boston.

Diverse Moxie names continued to make the news, and during the next 20 years there were frequent mentions of Moxie named-likes in the press. Moxie Manuel, formerly of the Chicago White Sox, was a regular, as were the towns of Moxie, Tennessee and Moxee (*sic*), Washington. When Indian Head, a resort just above North Woodstock, New Hampshire, obtained three 14-month-old bears, names given were Moxie, Roxie and Coxie.

Moxie was not the only soft drink whose name was copied. Although no accounts were preserved of anyone named Coca-Cola, the tale was told of Ida Modox, an artists' model, a young lady about 20 years of age who married a clerk in the Charlestown (Massachusetts) Navy Yard, later suing him for divorce, giving drunkenness as the reason. Mrs. Leslie, the former Miss Modox, left her husband but enjoyed sending him clever postcards, including one with a verse that went something like: "I am out of the grip of my master; he can run fast, but I can run faster."

Along the road of Moxie history there are many prominent landmarks. What the firm called the "big Moxie bottle" epitomizes this. At least two, possibly three or four giant Moxie bottles were constructed, the first in 1907. An article in the *Boston Traveler*, October 19, 1907 illustrates the bottle, taller than a building, and tells the story:

MOXIE CRAUS must have been an interesting individual back about 1907 when he issued a postcard depicting his two-story brick residence, his picture, the caption "Yours Truly at Home," and the notation: "Printed especially for Moxie Craus, McKinney, Texas." Seeking to learn more, the author dispatched a letter to the authorities in McKinney. A few weeks later a reply was received from Denton, Texas:

"Your letter requesting information on Moxie Craus has reached me by very a circuitous route, but I'm happy to furnish the information requested. My father was Moxie A. Craus of McKinney, Texas. His father was from Germany by way of Berlin. He was a brew meister. My grandfather wanted to name my father Maxie, but he didn't want it to be pronounced with the short 'a' which would make it rhyme with 'taxi.' So he changed the spelling to Moxie. There was no connection with the soft drink Moxie nor with the popular term moxie, which they tell me might be translated 'smarts.' Coincidentally, my grandfather was the pioneer Coca-Cola bottler in this area of Texas, with his plant in McKinney until his death. So it isn't likely that he even knew about the competitive drink Moxie. But I have known about it all my life and remember being posed beneath the sign advertising the drink on a billboard for pictures to be made.

"The 'mansion' on the postcard you have seen was my grandfather's house next to the Coca-Cola bottling works in McKinney and also next to the Craus Ice Cream Factory. You can imagine that my grandfather was very popular with all the town children! The house was sold at his death and turned into an old folks home and has only recently been razed."

—Sincerely,
MOXIE CRAUS.

"MOXIE SHAFT OVERTOPS ALL. Monument to Nerve Building Striking Feature of Big Food Fair.

"Every monument that has been erected in America stood for something great. Bunker Hill Monument is visible for miles around; it stands for liberty... The Washington Monument in the national capital calls to mind the first leader in war and peace, the father of his country. But there are others. Right here in Boston there is one that stands for nerve-building. While it is not in the open where it can be seen by all men, it has been viewed by the hundreds of thousands who have visited the food fair since the opening.

"This great monument stands for Moxie, a drink whose fame is known in every home in America, and which has extended to the uttermost parts of the earth. Wherever civilized man is found, there also is found Moxie. Its fame is monumental, and that is why this massive shaft has been set up in the main exhibition hall. And it is massive. Not of dazzling marble or enduring granite, but of a substance that faithfully reproduces the ordinary Moxie bottle of commerce.

"This great shaft, which brings to mind the household, nerve-strengthening beverage, towers above everything in the building, and go wherever one will it is visible. From the floor to the apex it rises 42 feet, while its diameter is about 16 feet, equal to a house of six stories, with rooms seven feet high. Such a unique exhibit cannot be imagined. It must be seen to be appreciated...

"The thing is actually alive. As a rule, a bottle has an opening only at the top, but this has two on the side, not the front side, because the bottle has no front side. At these openings, which are on the surface of the abnormal bottle, two attendants are earning their salaries—and incidentally working overtime—in an attempt to assuage the intense thirst which the patrons of the fair seem to have when they reach this fountain of youth. The crowd around this novel attraction stands six and seven feet deep all the time, awaiting a turn to get at the faucet of the elixir..."

After its stint in Boston, the big Moxie bottle was exhibited in several other places, including at Luna Park, Coney Island, finally coming to rest at Pine Island, an amusement area near Manchester, New Hampshire. After a few years of exhibit there, during which time numerous postcards of it were sold (with the caption "32-foot Moxie Bottle, Tall as a Three Story House"), it saw a renewed life in another mode, as an article in the *Boston Traveler*, May 20, 1920, related:

"Mr. and Mrs. Louis F. Messier of Manchester, N.H., are about to start housekeeping in a 33-foot bottle, now standing in the heart of a summer colony on the shores of Pine Island Lake in the suburbs of Manchester.

"Mother Goose's shoe, the House that Jack Built, or the Flying Carpet have nothing on Messier's bottle residence.

"Recently transported from its previous location in Pine Island Grove, a Manchester recreation park, the bottle is now undergoing a metamorphosis under the direction of the Messiers and an assistant carpenter.

"Completed, the bottle home will contain six windows, two on each floor, three doors, a cap on the neck of the bottle, awnings, and electric lights. In a few days the Messiers will move in with adequate furnishings, sleeping cots, hammocks, rugs, tables, student lamps, library of books and all of the equipment for household comfort and utility. They have figured with mathematical accuracy just what can be squeezed into the bottle and leave sufficient breathing space for the Messiers.

"Asked how he came to decide upon the bottle for a home, Mr. Messier said he thought a bottle could be used to as good a purpose as half the minature buildings now being utilized by small families to reduce the cost of living."

Another contemporary article on Messier's novelty observed that: "The first floor of the bottle is used as a dining room, the second and third floors, each nine feet [high] are sleeping rooms, which are reached by the use of ship ladders. All of the rooms are comfortably furnished and the bottle has electric lights, telephone service and all the accessories of a comfortable summer camp. Entrance to the bottle is from a door cut through the north side."

The fame of the big Moxie bottle did not diminish, and numerous notices of it were printed from time to time. On September 11, 1977, *Grit* magazine interviewed the owners at that time, Mr. and Mrs. James Todd, who stated they had been living in the Moxie bottle for 55 years.

Todd related that he had received dozens of offers for the house but had turned them all down. "After all, how many people can own a Moxie bottle house? Besides, it is easy to give directions to the place. All you have to do is tell friends to look for the Moxie bottle."

Four years after the advent of the 1907 big Moxie bottle, another bottle, even larger, appeared. By that time the 1907 monolith had been forgotten by all but a few. Early in August 1911, The Moxie

One of the most famous icons was the huge reproduction of a Moxie bottle, "32 foot Moxie bottle, tall as a 3-story house," according to the caption on this photograph. The overgrown bottle, from which an attendant dispensed Moxie, saw service for many years at Pine Island Park, Manchester, New Hampshire. In later years it was moved a short distance away, shingled, and was used as a bedroom facility for a private summer residence.

Facing page: Another big Moxie bottle, circa 1911, which differs in architectural details from the Pine Island Park example.

Company sent out news releases to papers in the eastern states. Dozens carried the information, and the clippings were subsequently pasted in a "Big Moxie Bottle" scrapbook at Moxie headquarters. Typical of many notices was one in the Tiffin (Ohio) *Daily Advertiser*, August 5, 1911:

"LARGEST BOTTLE IN THE WORLD. Will Be Exhibited by The Moxie Company in Madison Square Garden, New York City.

"President F.E. Thompson of The Moxie Company has recently designed what is unquestionably the largest bottle of its kind in the world. The purpose of this is that it may be used in the exhibit at the Domestic Science and Pure Food Exposition to be held in Madison Square Garden from September 23rd to October 4, 1911.

"This big bottle requires a floor space practically 20 feet square. It is 36 feet in height, 12 feet in diameter and almost 38 feet in circumference and is made as to form, color and general appearance like the regular distinctive Moxie bottle.

"This bottle will be so arranged that the patrons of the Exposition can pass through it and while within it will be afforded an opportunity to see the unique arrangements of storing Moxie, icing Moxie, serving Moxie, cleansing Moxie glasses, etc. Patrons on the outside of the bottle may be served also through specially designed serving windows. We believe these arrangements are fully up to date and will measure up in advance to all the hygienic conditions which should and must (but which usually do not) surround the handling of food products.

"The electric arrangements of the big Moxie bottle will be unique and interesting and, so far as we know, nothing like this has ever been attempted by anyone.

"Owing to the enormous size of this bottle a building of unusual height is required for its construction, and even then it must be built in seven sections, one section at a time, each of course fitting its companion section with the most exact nicety. After it is built, set up, and the electric, icing and Moxie-glass cleansing apparatus installed, and after it has been painted and labeled exactly like a Moxie bottle, the various sections are taken apart and crated separately for shipment to New York, its erection at Madison Square Garden being accomplished with special staging and erecting apparatus..."

Other notices published in connection with the oversize bottle related that in the decade preceding 1911 the name Moxie had been featured more than 884,000,000 times in advertising and "if all these 'Moxies' were lumped together into one big word, it would be more

White City, an amusement park at Savin Rock, Connecticut, featured a giant Moxie bottle in this February 1915 notice. At least two, possibly three or four such units were made and attracted wide notice wherever they were set up.

 Moxie Billboards: Above is a Moxie sign on a fence next to the Herbert Hotel, Canal Dover, Ohio, circa 1912-1914. To the left is a Moxie sign on the wall of the building next to the First Baptist Church, Everett, Massachusetts, 1906-1907, while the scene below is of a corner on Center Street, Ashland Pennsylvania, 1907-1910. Poster and billboards were an important part of Moxie advertising campaigns from the earliest years onward.

than 34,000 miles long and more than 7,800 miles high." In connection with the giant bottle, two booklets were prepared, *The Big Moxie Bottle* and *About Moxie 1911.* The final demise of the 1911 bottle is not recorded in the Moxie archives. A comparison of photographs of the 1911 bottle with the 1907 version shows a number of minor structural differences in addition to differing dimensions. A giant Moxie bottle similar to the 1907 version was exhibited at White City, Savin Rock, Connecticut, in 1915, and may have been a third bottle.

1907 marked the end of the Standard Bottling Company relationship with Moxie, at least as reflected in the Moxie records. While the Lowell branch was still operating in the summer of 1907 and producing ginger ale, a small amount of Moxie, and several other products, mention of it did not appear in ledgers after this year. As in preceding times, most Moxie was produced in 26-ounce "quart" bottles, with relatively few accompanying pints. Coastwise steamers were used to transport Moxie up to Maine and from New York to points to the south, as well as up the Hudson River, in addition to standard shipments by the usual method, railroad cars. On April 5, 1907 a fire on the steamer *City of Troy* destroyed 25 Moxie Coolers and 50 packages of advertising matter.

While the following year, 1908, was successful, profits represented a reduction from previous times and amounted to just $17,035.13. This did not keep the firm from paying out a dividend of $55,000 for the year to various officers, not including Frank Archer. Perhaps as compensation for this, Archer received a lump sum bonus of $12,000, representing an extra $4,000 retroactively for each of the years from 1906 through 1908. His pleas to purchase a substantial position in company stock were ignored.

The days of the "Nerve Food" part of Moxie's name were numbered, and many old bottles, labels, and other things bearing this designation were destroyed (over 120,000 pounds of obsolete bottles were sent to the Cumberland Glass Manufacturing Co. from Lowell on July 9th alone). The company received $5 per ton for their use as cullet. Nearly three tons of old 12 and 24-sheet posters were sold to a scrap dealer for 10c per 100 pounds, and an immense quantity of old-style translucent signs went to the junkyard. It was a tough year for the Moxie Bottle Wagons, and five of them were destroyed in a fire at E. Teel's livery in nearby Medford, Massachusetts. A miniature version, Pony Wagon No. 1, which had been shipped from New York City to the distant island of Trinidad a few years earlier, was "lost track of and probably destroyed." Valued at $250, it was

Above: This row of billboards, snapped by a photographer in 1907, features an early appearance of the distinctive Moxie logotype with a long crossarm to the lower left and upper right of the X.

Below: A cardboard placard from the same era features the Moxie logotype in a slightly different form (notice the lower left and right of the M, for example). The "Eat Better, Sleep Better, and Feel Better" slogan was popular and was used for many years.

Millions of People
Eat Better, Sleep Better and Feel Better
Because They Drink
MOXIE
REGULARLY
Millions of Bottles Consumed Annually

One of the most colorful Moxie themes of the 1908 era is that which some collectors have designated as "The Feather Tickle Girl." The above illustration is enlarged from a postcard, but the design appeared in other forms, including a colorfully lithographed cardboard cut-out measuring slightly over three feet high.

Photographed on the front of a summer cottage at Horse-Neck Beach, South Westport, Massachusetts, this couple had little idea that many decades after the circa 1910 picture was taken, collectors would look wistfully at the "The Feather Tickle Girl" cardboard cut-out sign visible at the upper left.

This photograph, submitted to Moxie headquarters, shows a 1910 display at a church fair. At the lower left is a "Feather Tickle" sign, while another Moxie sign is shown at center left against the back wall.

"The Universalist Church gave a carnival the other evening and we gave them a little ad on Moxie. We got first prize. Yours, Stevens & Robinson, Auburn, Me.," is the caption on this photographic post card sent to The Moxie Company.

Moxie ordered by you. This advertising matter embraces a complete assortment of everything we have for 1908 and is packed in a sign carton so that when the advertising matter is removed, the sign carton that contains the same makes an extremely strong sign and should be held or tacked in a very conspicuous place.

"The window display is one of the most effective ways for the retailer to advertise Moxie. From six to 25 cases of Moxie in the window together with large and small cut-outs, signs, etc., furnished by us, conspicuously shown, make a display that attracts the greatest attention. It will increase your Moxie trade surprisingly, as has been proved by dealers all over the country. Display your Moxie signs prominently as they will serve to draw customers to your store."

Moxie customers took Archer's advice. Contemporary picture post cards of the era show Moxie signs of all kinds conspicuously displayed in store windows and fronts, often near advertising for competitors such as Coca-Cola, Pepsi-Cola, Whistle, and others.

Cardboard placards measuring seven inches square were printed in yellow, blue, and black on white for ice distributors who wished to give them to retail customers. Posted in a window, they advised the passing iceman of the quantity needed, while on the back side of the placard appeared an advertisement for New England's best-loved beverage. For S.M. Hill and Company, Wenham Lake, Massachusetts, 10,000 such cards, printed on yellow cardboard, were ordered. Other cards were sent to other outlets.

The popular baseball score cards, a 1908 novelty, were used in a variety of ways. For the annual picnic of the Lowell Pharmacists Association, held at Willow Dale, a local amusement park, on Tuesday, June 9th, round score cards were perforated at the top and overprinted with a special "MEMBER L.P.A." designation. In the days when newspaper reading was a habit for most of the educated population, even the tiniest tidbit—such as the construction and appearance of name badges—was apt to find its way into print, as did the description of these baseball score cards in an issue of the Lowell *Sun*. A cartoon describing this otherwise forgettable event noted that drugstores in Lowell were closed, everybody in town was crying for soda, but out at Willow Dale a Moxie Bottle Wagon was doing a land office business under the direction of George Evans.

As years went by the Moxie Bottle Wagons received fewer and fewer newspaper notices, and the fleet of Moxie automobiles received more. The *Boston Herald* ran a large headline stating "Frank E. Thompson of Arlington is a Most Enthusiastic Motorist," under which was a large picture showing Thompson and noting:

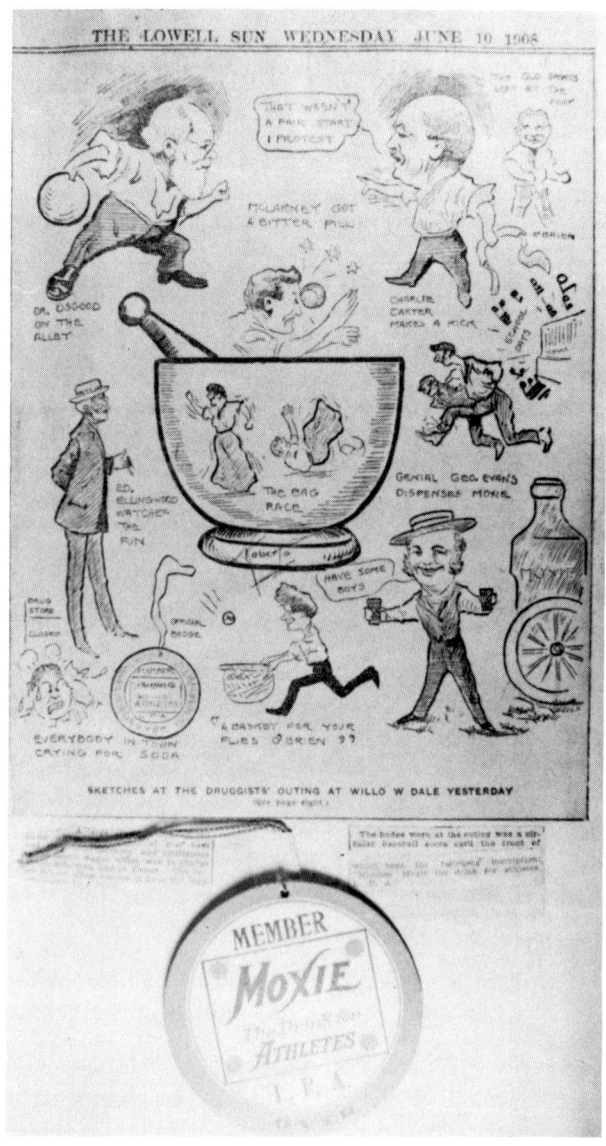

On June 9, 1908, the druggists of Lowell took a day off for an outing at Willow Dale Park. This page from a scrapbook kept by Frank Archer shows a newspaper cartoon featuring the Moxie Bottle Wagon and also a special membership badge printed for the occasion.

"One of the most enthusiastic of local motorists is Frank E. Thompson, of Arlington, who, as head of one of the larger houses of this city, has established a stable of something like 35 automobiles which are used daily in his business. Mr. Thompson is himself a motorist of exceptional ability, and seldom a day passes but he covers something like 100 miles in his car. This is done as a matter of business and pleasure, and, according to his own statement, since he has been using the motor vehicle in the business way he has covered twice the territory in one day than he was previously able to do.

"Mr. Thompson is one of the most active members of the Bay State Automobile Association, a member of the race committee having charge of the tournament at Readville on Memorial Day, and the donor of the $500 trophy offered to the winner of the two-cylinder car class race. His present car is a Locomobile, a picture of which is herewith published."

Another article of the same period differed slightly in the number of cars owned by Moxie and reiterated the usefulness of motor vehicles to the firm. Appearing in the *Ithaca* (New York) *Daily News*, August 28, 1908, the text read:

"That the automobile has made the traveling salesman independent of railroads and time tables was the declaration of P. St. Armor, W.J. Neely, and L.A. Hager, three Boston salesmen who were in the city. They arrived yesterday in a 30-horsepower touring car, carrying a powerful search light. Mr. Neely was formerly a newspaperman who worked for several years on the *New York Journal.*

"He did most of the talking, as he said he had stopped writing for several years in order to give his vocal organs a chance.

" 'It is certainly true to be a successful salesman today a man need no longer be a knight of the grip. Nor need he wear a flashy vest or loud checkered clothes. A pair of goggles, storm coat and a strong leather cap—this is the garb needed by us. Our company has 40 autos on the road and with them we are covering a large portion of the United States.

" 'Is it quicker? Well, I think so. Why, we make as high as 10 and 15 towns a day. That is the advantage of the auto. We can get in and out of small places with ease and not lose a whole day waiting for the next train. Moreover, our railroad fares are nil.

" 'As far as accidents are concerned, we meet with few. Using a powerful search light we can see ahead of us for a great distance, and when going around corners the light serves as a warning.'

"Mr. Neely and his companions appear to be in rugged health and they said that dusty, choky, over-heated or freezing railroad coaches are no longer their trouble since 'king of the road' has come into his own. The knights of the auto left later for Syracuse. They will travel as far west as Chicago."

The idea of a turning automobile searchlight formed a Thompson patent a few years later. Much of Francis ("Frank") E. Thompson's spare time was spent tinkering with automotive ideas. At other times, especially during the summer, he was apt to be found aboard a large yacht, one of several he owned over the years.

After the passage of the Pure Food and Drugs Act, 1906, the beverage industry awaited government action. In 1908 the first prosecution came. Robert N. Harper, of Washington, D.C., purveyor of a product called "Braine Fude," was charged with misleading the public. Braine Fude or, generically, brain food, was dangerously close to "Nerve Food," and Moxie officials kept track of the case as it was reported in newspapers. Harper was convicted and sentenced to pay a fine of $700 for "manufacturing and selling an allegedly mislabeled pharmaceutical compound." President Theodore Roosevelt, who personally chaperoned the Pure Food and Drugs Act through its passage, was disappointed, as he had hoped for a jail sentence.

Another article told of a young Springfield, Massachusetts woman "who contracted the morphine habit by taking a so-called nerve tonic during convalescence; and so strong a hold did it get upon her that she was discarded by her family and, after threatening to take her life, was put in a sanitarium, where she is today a physical and mental wreck." Another scare for Moxie Nerve Food, which did not contain morphine but which had a name dangerously close to "nerve tonic."

Still, Moxie was advertised as being good for the nerves, as a contemporary notice observed:

"THE MOXIE WAGON. Starting on the first day of June the Moxie advertising wagon left headquarters and has been traveling along the coast from Maine to New York ever since, advertising Moxie, the standard family beverage...

"The wagon, which carries the largest bottle of Moxie in the world, arrived in town a few days ago and attracted a great deal of attention. The wagon, with its gray running gear, trimmed in polished

This ornate Moxie Bottle Wagon rig departed on June 1, 1908 for an extensive tour which saw it visit Maine, New Hampshire, Massachusetts, Rhode Island, Connecticut, and New York. All along the way it was heralded by Moxie advertisements and chronicled by admiring newspaper reporters.

The Coburn Press was commissioned to print messages on the back of several different varieties of Moxie post cards, as shown in this 1908 page from the company archives.

brass and carrying a large bottle of Moxie, is drawn by a team of gray horses. All yesterday they were at the fairgrounds advertising the drink that is good for the nerves."

Toward the end of 1908, Archer sent out a directive concerning the advertising campaign for the coming year, 1909:

"For some months we have been hard at work on our campaign for 1909. It's going to be greater than for any year for the past quarter century. Our advertising matter will make them sit up and take notice. Our 'Man and Girl' cut-out will be much talked of and sought after, as well as our original and distinctive fountain sign. Our tray is said to be a work of art, and so on."

This theme was continued by a notice dated November 18th and directed to customers:

"You will be interested to learn that our famous Moxie 'Boy and Girl' cut-out has been finished by the artists and lithographers and is now on the press. The hat worn by the Moxie Girl in this cut-out will, we believe, owing to its simplicity and great beauty, supersede the 'Merry Widow' and all others. Our representatives will start to solicit for Moxie 1909 Spring Display orders in January and at that time will make deliveries of this cut-out of all who avail themselves of a display order."

The year closed with a Christmas party tendered in honor of Freeman N. Young and others at Boston's North Station Restaurant on December 24th by members of The Society for the Study of Human Nature. Young, vice-president of the Moxie firm, was loaded down with favors which ranged in variety from a jumping jack to a live lobster, while Frank Archer received a toy village and a live bantam hen. "Mr. Archer's knowledge concerning hens being limited, he gave the bird to a more experienced friend," a notice in the *Boston Post* related.

The year 1909 saw several changes. John L. Beauchain, who had been connected with the Moxie enterprise since its early days and who in 1909 served as secretary of the firm, passed away on May 25th. Beauchain, a Canadian born in 1868, moved to Lowell as a child. He entered the employ of The Moxie Nerve Food Company in 1886, where he worked his way up from salesman to superintendent of the factory. In 1896 he secured an ownership interest and became a director. Upon his death he left a widow, three brothers, and one sister. The widow was to make her own headlines in newspapers from Florida to Boston a few months later. A typical notice concerning her was carried in the *Boston Globe*, October 27, 1909:

Christmas Tree for Vice-President of Moxie Co.

MR FRED M YOUNG WAS SHOWERED WITH GIFTS

DR TUTTLE WAS NOT FORGOTTEN BY SANTA.

MR HARRY SHAW

FREEMAN N. YOUNG, vice-president of the Moxie Nerve Food Company, was tendered a Christmas tree yesterday noon at the North station restaurant by the members of "The Society for the Study of Human Nature." Lunch was served, but the piece de resistance was the tree loaded with gifts for the popular guest of honor.

The members of the society are evidently students of "human nature," as was shown by the type of gifts and particularly the works of art exhibited in the form of miniature pictures, recent importations from Paris.

Mr. Young was loaded with favors ranging in variety from a jumping jack to a live lobster.

Frank M. Archer was remembered by a toy village and a live bantam hen to dwell therein.

Mr. Archer's knowledge concerning hens being limited, he gave the bird to a more experienced friend.

C. W. Post of Pittsburg was particularly well remembered, receiving several articles of a useful as well as an ornamental nature.

George Dempsey, who is at the head of one of the largest distilling concerns of the country, was given a "Happy Hooligan" that would not stand up.

Others who were recipients of gifts were Dr. Albert H. Tuttle, Roy A. Fay, P. W. Gibson, Raymond L. Moxon, Lott Mansfield, P. E. Moller, Robert L. Woods, Jr., Frank Bennett, Louis Knowlton, Ben Johnson, J. R. Stewart, J. H. Ordway, W. M. Robinson, Joseph Buckley and Harry Shaw.

Freeman N. Young was the featured attendee at a Christmas party held in Boston, December 24, 1908, described in the newspaper article shown here.

"Jacksonville, Florida, October 26th. Mrs. Maybelle A. Beauchain of Boston, a widow, committed suicide in her room at the Aragon Hotel this morning by cutting her throat with a razor belonging to Dr. E.E. Banker of New York, who accompanied her here and occupied a room across the hall. She obtained the razor in Dr. Banker's absence from his room.

"It was reported that Dr. Banker and Mrs. Beauchain were soon to have been married. The suicide was attributed to despondency and the fear of an operation.

"Mrs. Beauchain was about 33 years of age and the widow of John L. Beauchain, for years secretary and superintendent of The Moxie Company. He died May 25, 1909, leaving an estate between $50,000 and $60,000, of which his widow was to have the income during her life. At her death the estate was to revert to relatives of her husband...

"James H. Vahey, Democratic candidate for governor of Massachusetts, was Mrs. Beauchain's counsel and represented her in the matter of the settlement of her husband's estate. Mr. Vahey was about to be appointed trustee for Mrs. Beauchain by the probate court but the estate will now go to the relatives of her deceased husband.

"Some weeks after the death of her husband, Mrs. Beauchain went to Florida for the benefit of her health, as she was in a highly nervous condition and run down physically.

"Dr. Banker has a home in New York, but formerly lived in Florida. A friend of the dead woman said yesterday afternoon that Dr. Banker has a wife, but that he either had begun or was about to institute a suit for divorce in Florida, intending to marry Mrs. Beauchain when he got it."

Toward the end of October 1909, Frank Archer contacted Josiah H. Drummond, a prominent Portland (Maine) attorney, to ask if he would be in Boston soon, for Archer desired to take up the matters of transferring the company's legal office from Saco, Maine to Portland and "with changing the name, or shortening our present title."

Discussions were held with Drummond. Hampden Fairfield, the Saco attorney who had managed the legal affairs of The Moxie Nerve Food Company of New England since 1892, was asked to resign. Frank Archer delicately wrote to him:

"The changes that have taken place in our business and the contemplated changes will necessitate our establishing an office in

Delivery of Moxie: The old and the new. Above is a 1909 snapshot of a Moxie delivery truck, actually a car modified by adding a cooler to the back. On the running board is a cardboard cut-out. Typically such cut-outs were prominently displayed just before the photographer clicked the shutter, for numerous illustrations of Moxie vehicles of the era show them. Below is the old way, a delivery wagon of Thomas J. Bannon, Westerly and Watch Hill, Rhode Island, about 1904. Dobbin wears a horseblanket prominently lettered "MOXIE."

Above: The standard type of horse-drawn Moxie delivery wagon used in New York and Boston during the first decade of the 20th century featured four replica Moxie bottles as posts on each wagon corner, as shown above. Time and time again Moxie would take something ordinary—a delivery wagon being an example—and turn it into something distinctive and memorable.

Below: This advertising card, issued early in 1909, shows Moxie bottle cases in the form of corrugated fibre boxes, a short-lived experiment. From the earliest days through the 1950s, standard bottle cases were made of wood.

Above cut shows the immense advertising effect that can be produced on H. & D. Corrugated Fibre Boxes manufactured by

THE HINDE & DAUCH PAPER COMPANY

Boston   New York   Philadelphia   Pittsburgh   Sandusky, O.   Chicago   St. Louis   San Francisco

Portland. We shall undoubtedly establish it in the office of Josiah H. Drummond, Esq., 396 Congress Street, in that city. We would thank you very much if you would on receipt of this send the records of our company to him in order to enable him to take such steps in the matter as are proper... This change is due solely to the changing conditions, etc. And it is in no manner any reflection upon you as our relations have always been the very pleasantest and your services in every respect have been most satisfactory..."

After appointing Josiah H. Drummond as the firm's attorney and establishing a new legal address (for Maine was a favorable haven for corporate activity at the time; more so than Massachusetts), Archer wrote with instructions, noting a name change:

"As we shall have to file with the different states where we have leaseholds, etc., copies of the change of name as well as with the states where we have to get permission to do business, the secretary of agriculture as to our guarantee, and perhaps the various accounting clerks, we shall have to have a fixed form of notice... We imagine we would have to have 12 certified copies.

"We have already started to print some of the stationery with the new title so as to have it ready to use; that is, 'The Moxie Company' with 'The' to begin with a capital, as we told you over the phone.

"Our seal now reads 'The Moxie Nerve Food Company of New England,' with the date 1892. We thought of changing it to read The Moxie Company with the date 1909. We do not know if this would be correct or not; that is, the year of changing the name or whether there is any materiality of having the year of its incorporation. Whatever you suggest it is agreeable. Kindly let us know so we can order a seal."

A meeting of shareholders was held on December 16th, and on December 17, 1909 a certificate noting the change of name to The Moxie Company was filed with the Secretary of State of Maine. "Nerve Food" was no more.

The financial results for 1909 were not equal to a few years earlier, but still they were satisfactory to the principals. A dividend of $40,000 was declared for the shareholders. At year's end a profit was registered in the amount of $30,944.23.

Who was who in The Moxie Company in 1910 is revealed by the distribution of the 5,000 shares outstanding:

Francis E. Thompson . . . . .2,418 shares
Harry A. Thompson 1,094

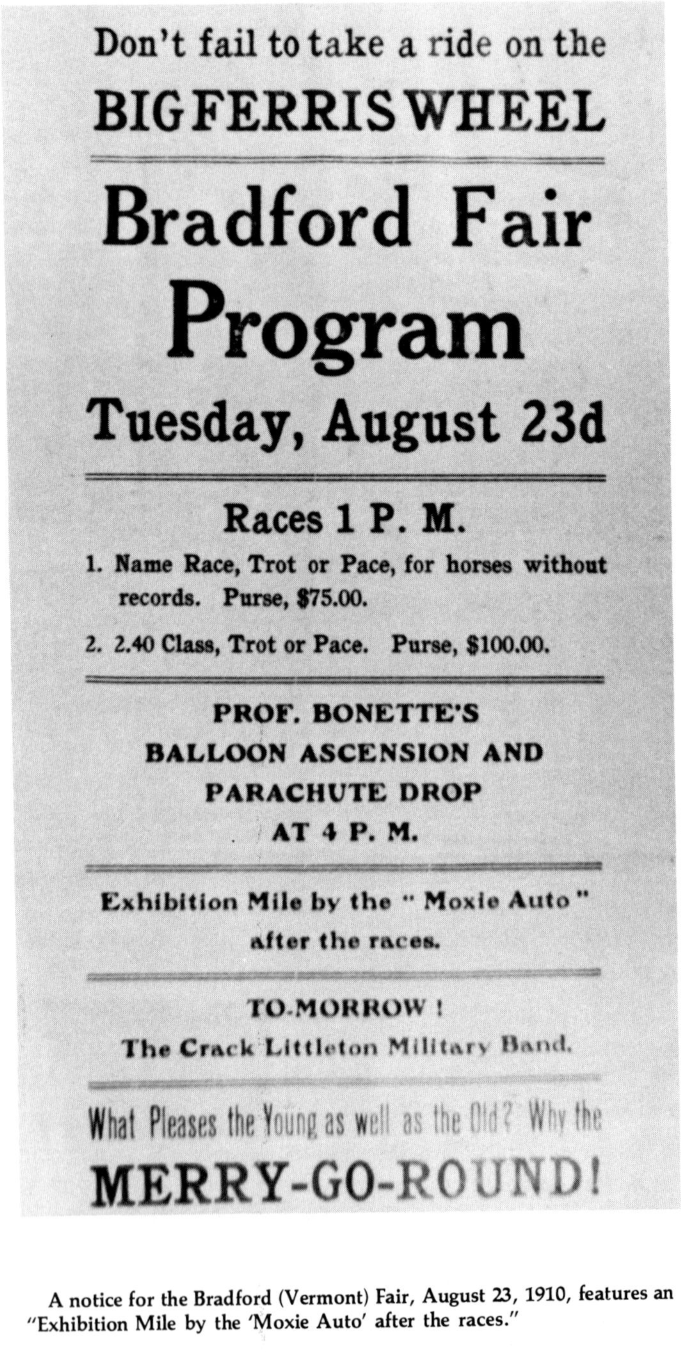

Don't fail to take a ride on the

BIG FERRIS WHEEL

Bradford Fair

Program

Tuesday, August 23d

Races 1 P. M.

1. Name Race, Trot or Pace, for horses without records. Purse, $75.00.

2. 2.40 Class, Trot or Pace. Purse, $100.00.

**PROF. BONETTE'S
BALLOON ASCENSION AND
PARACHUTE DROP
AT 4 P. M.**

Exhibition Mile by the " Moxie Auto "

after the races.

TO-MORROW !

The Crack Littleton Military Band.

What Pleases the Young as well as the Old? Why the

MERRY-GO-ROUND!

A notice for the Bradford (Vermont) Fair, August 23, 1910, features an "Exhibition Mile by the 'Moxie Auto' after the races."

At county fairs and racetracks, Moxie drivers would often do an "exhibition mile" in one of their delivery vehicles, typically taking local reporters along for a ride. The photographs on this page date from 1910 and were used in a booklet published by The Moxie Company on the subject of automobiles.

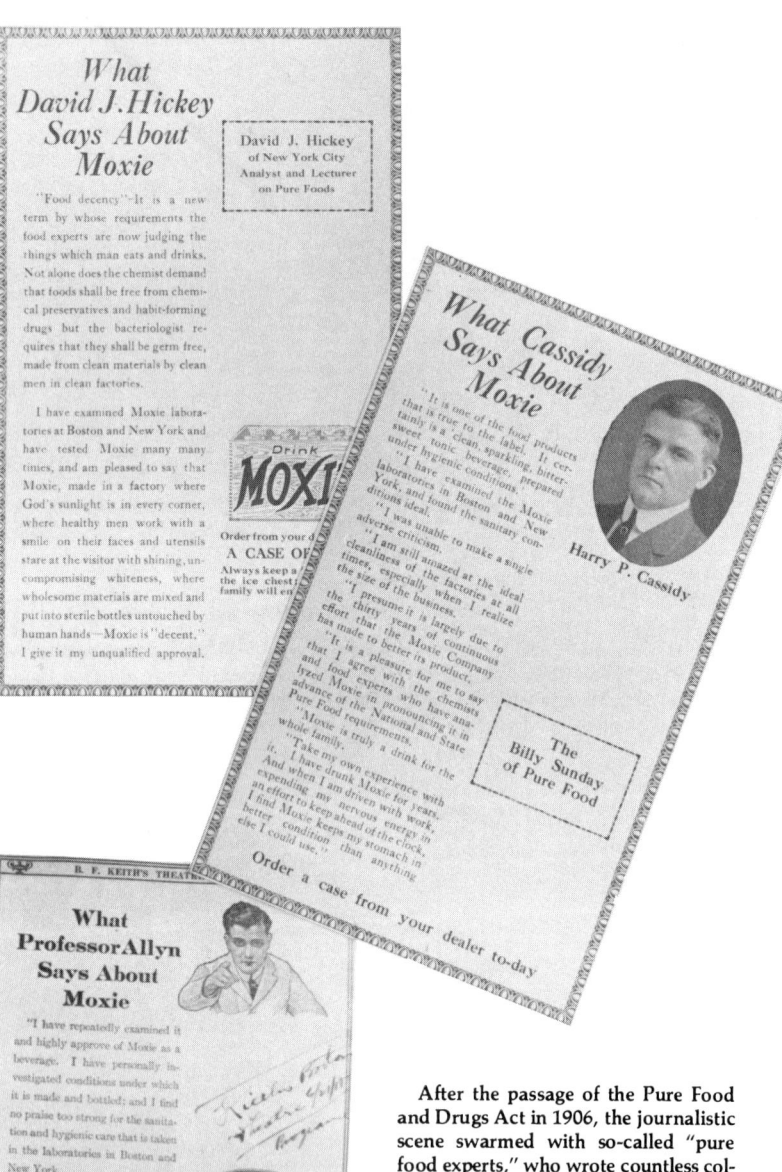

After the passage of the Pure Food and Drugs Act in 1906, the journalistic scene swarmed with so-called "pure food experts," who wrote countless columns on the merits or lack thereof of various products which caught their eye. Moxie always emerged with a clean bill of health and reciprocated by featuring writers in Moxie advertisements which, in turn, brought forth still more articles praising the purity of the Moxie product—a symbiotic relationship.

Above: The refreshment stand at the Centennial Grove, Essex, Massachusetts, was decorated with numerous Moxie signs. On the original photograph, a sharp eye can pick out a Moxie Boy cardboard cut-out (boy holding a case of Moxie) to the left at the side of the standing man; an identical cut-out in the background in front of the counter, and three different Moxie signs above the counter, one of which (to the right between the two trees and above the lady) features a case of Moxie with "Brownies"—a popular motif of the era. The picture was probably taken around 1908-1910.

Right: A metal Moxie sign supported on legs stands in front of Ferguson's store, located at 79-83 Main Street, Greenport, New York.

Not that outhouses were considered by The Moxie Company to be prime places for advertising The Product, but somehow someone affixed a large sign to the side of this one. Or, more charitably, perhaps it was a storage shed of some sort. The sign dates from the 1910 era and features multi-pointed printed "seals" in the corners.

Probably taken around 1910, this photograph shows an unidentified lady, who moved slightly while the picture was being taken, in front of a store advertising "Moxie" on one sign and "Cigars" on the other. Actually, both signs were issued by The Moxie Company. Above the "MOXIE" sign to the left, and in very small print, appear the words "Ice Cold," while below is found "Very Healthful." Above the "CIGARS" word is "Imported and Domestic," while "Also the Celebrated Moxie" appears below.

Below is a close-up view of two similar signs in a window of C. Vaughn's store, Cato, New York, December, 1909.

Above and Below: Views of Moore's Summer Ball Room, which offered "Dancing Every Evening" with the refreshment of Moxie, circa 1910-1912. Moore's was located at The Square, Houghs Neck, Quincy, Massachusetts. Not far from Moore's establishment, another purveyor of Moxie advertised on the side of a building (see illustration below).

At the main business office, 61-71 Haverhill Street, Francis E. Thompson served as president and general manager, Frank M. Archer as assistant manager, Harry A. Thompson as treasurer, and Freeman N. Young as vice-president. During the early part of the year, new stationery had not yet arrived, and old letterheads of The Moxie Nerve Food Company of New England were used with the old name crossed out and The Moxie Company overprinted above.

In 1910, Moxie was the feature of a lengthy article in *Printer's Ink*, the advertising trade magazine, which studied the so-called temperance drink market. It was noted that Coca-Cola planned to spend $600,000 advertising while Moxie was set to go with $300,000. A bit of Moxie history, including an interesting observation concerning an early bottle shortage, was presented to readers:

"In the case of Moxie [in contrast to Coca-Cola, a nationwide beverage], which was a pioneer in the field, having been before the public in excess of 25 years, operations have been purposely limited to that portion of the country bounded on the west by Indiana and on the south by Virginia, due to freight rates both ways, that is on the full and empty bottles. Moxie is invariably put up in a regulation Moxie bottle.

"In this rather limited territory something over $300,000 will be spent this year in advertising Moxie. $40,000 is the sum being spent on one ad alone. The sales of this drink now mount up to 1,500,000 cases a year, which represents 18 million quart bottles! Moxie is always sold at fountains in a special Moxie glass which is moderate in size so that five glasses can be poured out of every quart, which means that 90 million glasses of Moxie are served. The Moxie territory includes less than half the total population of the country, so that the Moxie sales represent more than two glasses per capita.

"This monstrous sale has not been developed without the hardest kind of work and eternal vigilance to offset the continual inroads of unfair competitors, substitutors and imitators. Moxie has been imitated in color and taste and the Moxie bottle has been simulated as regard to shape and general appearance, label and color...

"Back in the early eighties, Dr. Augustin Thompson, a practicing physician of Lowell, Mass., had for years been prescribing a formula of his own making to nervous patients with considerable success. It was in concentrated form and not entirely pleasant to take.

While The Moxie Nerve Food Company of New England was quick to utilize motorized transport, the faithful horse was not overlooked, as the illustration below shows.

A close-up view of a Moxie delivery truck, with a cooler on the back and with a cardboard cut-out of the Moxie Boy holding a case, as enlarged from the photograph shown below. At the time, 1910, Moxie maintained a fleet of several dozen vehicles, primarily in the Boston area. Moxie drivers were instructed to be courteous and to explain to interested onlookers the operation of the car or truck—in an era when motorized transport was a novelty in America.

Several Moxie trucks, each with a cardboard cut-out on the running board (displayed briefly while this photograph was taken). Each truck carried a supply of the Moxie beverage as well as cut-outs, advertising matter, and other promotional items for use by retailers.

The idea came to him that this same concoction, after being diluted and carbonated, would make an excellent temperance drink. The experiment was forthwith tried, the beginnings of the present Moxie business came about. Those men in the company, which was formed in Lowell, when they tasted the drink were skeptical about it ever becoming popular, but it did 'take hold.'

"Lowell was naturally the first distributing center. On March 18, 1885, F.E. Thompson, now president of The Moxie Company, and a couple of companions hired a horse and wagon and started out to peddle their wares. The new drink had been put up in regulation champagne bottles. The Lowell stores were visited and handbills were distributed. Undoubtedly the dealers took to the drink much more readily than they would if it were first put on the public now, because the trademarked drink field was then a new one.

"From the very first, Moxie advertising tended strongly to the newspapers. The first ads were small reading notices in the Lowell newspapers. As the fame and popularity of Moxie spread, orders began to come in from wholesalers in Boston, Worcester, and other nearby centers. By July, four months after the start was made, the sale had jumped so that it was well nigh impossible to obtain champagne bottles. The latter had jumped in value from 18c to 80c a dozen. By August the Moxie workers were hard at it night and day, and still no extensive advertising had been done. When the latter was started in earnest, about the only available precedents at hand were in the cases of Ayer's and Hood's sarsaparillas, the advertising methods of which were followed rather closely, beginning in 1886.

"The trouble getting champagne bottles naturally led to ordering special Moxie bottles. The success in later years in preventing much unfair competition and substitution has largely been dependent upon this move, for without the special Moxie bottle the task would have been much more difficult...

"Several merchandising principles in the case of Moxie will be of interest. 'We have made it our rule never to claim too much in our advertising,' says President Thompson. Practically the same price is charged the small dealer as the large, the price per case up to 60 being $2.10 and over 60 only 10c less. Free coupons have been religiously left alone as being unnecessary and, in any event, expensive and likely to cheapen the product in the eyes of the public. Large spaces in the newspaper have been the general rule about this time of year, backed up by simultaneous billboard advertising. The $40,000 which is being spent upon the two insertions of the current ad, which runs five columns and reads simply: 'Moxie is the Best

A Moxie sign that was custom-made adorns the façade of the store of C.D. Albani, owner of the Bedford Fruit Company in Bedford, Massachusetts, probably circa 1910.

MOXIE GIRLS IN OFFICE MARCH 1909

May Crafts
Ella Garrity
Tessie Silverman
Mabel Robinson
Louise Webber
Florence Schafer
Sue Blanchard
Minnie Gordon

Elizabeth Willard
Belle Shepard-Voge
Della Thomas
Flora Guyer
Alice Finnigan
Grace Lindberg
Laura Prior

This photograph taken in March 1909 at the Boston office shows women employees. Belle Shepard (married name, Belle Voge) was Frank Archer's secretary for many years. She is shown in the bottom row, second from the left.

Producing Moxie at the Haverhill Street, Boston facility during the early part of the century. Certain items of bottling equipment were invented by Freeman N. Young, who received several patents for bottle-rinsing and bottle-labeling devices. Most of these were produced in a machine shop in Lowell and were designated with the "Yousay" brand name. Yousay was the name of a summer camp formerly located on the ground on which Young built his residence on the shore of Spy Pond, Arlington, Massachusetts.

In April 1910 an article was published concerning a sportsman who spent several days in the woods, for him an unfamiliar experience. Among the things he had with him were—you guessed it—a bottle of Moxie Nerve Food, shown here in his right hand.

First prize at the Ellenville (New York) Fair, 1911, was captured by this Moxie salesman who decorated his truck with patriotic bunting and large Moxie cardboard cut-outs.

Another car decorated with Moxie cut-outs. Moxie salesmen were proud of their vehicles, and numerous snapshots were forwarded to company headquarters.

Many were the varieties of Moxie booklets printed with trimmed upper left and lower right corners and with a cover design giving them the appearance of a thick book. "This Book About Substitution Law," which went through three editions, is shown at the upper left and was the most widely distributed of any.

The "Moxie Inspectors Everywhere" cover was used to enclose notices of successful prosecutions of Moxie imitators. Numerous varieties were published over the years, the one above being designated as "No. 51."

Three high school girls in Massachusetts pose with a cardboard cut-out featuring The Moxie Boy with a pointing finger, probably sometime around 1915. Each of the girls imitates the pointing finger pose. At the home office of Moxie, scrapbooks were kept with clippings, photographs, news announcements, and other items pertaining to Moxie and Moxie publicity. Moxie had a loyal following, a fan club of sorts, and often Moxie drinkers submitted pictures of themselves, their children, and even their pets with Moxie bottles and signs as part of the scene.

This photograph, taken in the summer of 1915, shows the veranda of a soda shop in Emery Mills, Maine. A Moxie Boy cardboard cut-out is on the railing, while smaller Moxie signs are under the lip of the porch to the left and right.

This refreshment stand in Bennington, Vermont was photographed shortly before 1910. Displayed are several small Moxie signs plus a larger sign (variety with pointed "seals" on the corners) and, to the right, a cardboard cut-out of the Moxie Boy holding a case, with his head missing. Possibly it was decapitated during an earlier closing of the hinged front.

ing eyes, the Moxie Boy pointed his right hand and index finger in a commanding gesture.

Frank Archer, Jr. later recalled that the model for this version of the Moxie Boy was spotted in a New York City barbershop by a Moxie official. A painting of the new Moxie Boy was then commissioned, and from this painting the advertising material was created.

"When I was a little boy we used to go to Portland [Maine]," related an old-timer to the author. "On the side of one of the buildings was the Moxie Boy in gigantic form, his finger pointing right toward *me*. I was afraid of the Moxie Boy, and my friends were too. He just kept looking at us—staring—he wouldn't stop."

Within a few years, the Moxie Boy became a subject of nationwide discussions. Newspaper articles, often placed by Moxie's advertising department, debated the identity of the Moxie Boy. Later, after about 1919, Frank Archer often put his name on signs next to the Moxie Boy portrait, stating, for example, "Frank Archer says: Drink Moxie 100%." But, the portrait was not of Archer. In 1916, in 1921, and again in 1930, a Moxie Boy identity contest was proposed, but nothing ever came of it. In 1921 on the back of a piece of sheet music Archer told of the by then famous advertising figure:

"The Moxie Boy compels attention. It's his eyes. They follow you everywhere.

"The clear, friendly eyes of the Moxie Boy have made him the most famous advertising figure in the world.

"College professors and scientists have lectured about him. Technical magazines, books of wonder, scientific works in many lands and languages have reproduced pictures of the Moxie Boy. He is famous as a most compelling advertisement because he illustrates a peculiar phenomenon.

"Anywhere within sight of the Moxie Boy and from any angle, his eyes gaze directly into yours in a straightforward, honest-and-true manner that is as clean, sincere, and wholesome as the beverage he recommends—Moxie.

"Books, modern advertising, business colleges, and schools of advertising use the Moxie Boy to illustrate his eye-compelling power. It is based upon a fundamental principle of optical science and draughtsmanship.

"People have used the Moxie Boy cut-outs for countless purposes all the way from the questionable practice of advertising some totally different product to putting him near a house window to discourage tramps by acting the part of the man of the family.

The Moxie Boy with his pointing finger, an authentic example of which is given below, appeared on the scene in 1911 and created a sensation. Before long, numerous copycats emerged, including examples used by Burroughs (office machines), Bunte (marshmallows), and F.T. Rosback Company (wire stapling machines). The Rosback imitation is virtually a dead ringer, except that he wears an R on his tie instead of an M!

DOES your Wire Stitcher ever kink the wire?
Do the legs of the staple ever turn the wrong way?
Top of staple ever break down?
Ever refuse to stitch hard paper?
Wouldn't you like to overcome all this trouble? If so, write

F. P. Rosback Company
Benton Harbor, Mich.

The Largest Perforator Factory in the World.

I WANT YOU
FOR U.S. ARMY
NEAREST RECRUITING STATION

The famous "I Want You" World War I recruiting poster, by James Montgomery Flagg, 1917, probably traces its inspiration to the Moxie Boy, although Flagg credited the idea to a work he observed earlier by a British artist.

Over the years, the piercing gaze and pointing finger popularized by the Moxie Boy was used in many other places by various firms. At Moxie headquarters in Boston, Frank M. Archer pasted illustrations of such copycats in a scrapbook of clippings.

"In almost every town and city in the United States there is someone who believes they know the original of the Moxie Boy. In view of the many thousands of different opinions on the subject, we may offer a prize to a person who picks the actual boy, furnishing us photographic proofs, etc. As a climax to this contest, if we stage it, there will be millions of surprised people, we are sure, when we publicly announce to them the Moxie Boy, and now a man (and some man at that), who posed for this picture many, many years ago, in fact before some of the readers of this article were born.

"The Moxie Boy still goes on, and will go on forever, in his clean, wholesome, sincere way, advising his millions of friends everywhere to drink Moxie, the clean, wholesome, refreshing beverage."

In 1916 an article, "To Hunt Boy with Leveled Finger," appeared, asking readers, "You've all seen him; would you know him if you met him on the street?" The article went on to relate that The Moxie Company, which had brought forth many dazzling novelties, planned "a hunt for the Moxie Boy, with a string of prizes."

In Albany, New York, a patrolman reported that he had discovered a man in the rear of Honickle's Drug Store on Central Avenue. A newspaper clipping continued the story:

"A brother copper of the name of Feeley was advised of the discovery. Feeley grabbed for his revolver and hurried to the rear of the drug store. The store was open, Feeley approached cautiously from the rear and three officers swooped down on the man—a big human appearing figure..."

You guessed it—the figure was a cardboard cut-out of the Moxie Boy! Similarly, Archer reported that cardboard portraits of the Moxie Boy were an effective aid to shoplifting in outdoor fruit stands, in Woolworth stores, and other places where young boys (in particular) gathered.

Noted humorist Robert C. Benchley told of his experience with the Moxie Boy, in an August 1920 article:

"In the window of the grocery store to which I used to be sent after a pound of mocha and java mixed and a dozen of the best oranges, there was a cardboard figure of a clerk in a white coat pointing his finger at the passers-by. As I remember, he was accusing you of not taking home a bottle of Moxie, and pretty guilty it made you feel, too.

"This man was, I believe, a pioneer in what has since become a great literary movement. He founded the 'You, Mr. Business-man!' school of direct appeal. It is strictly an advertising property and has

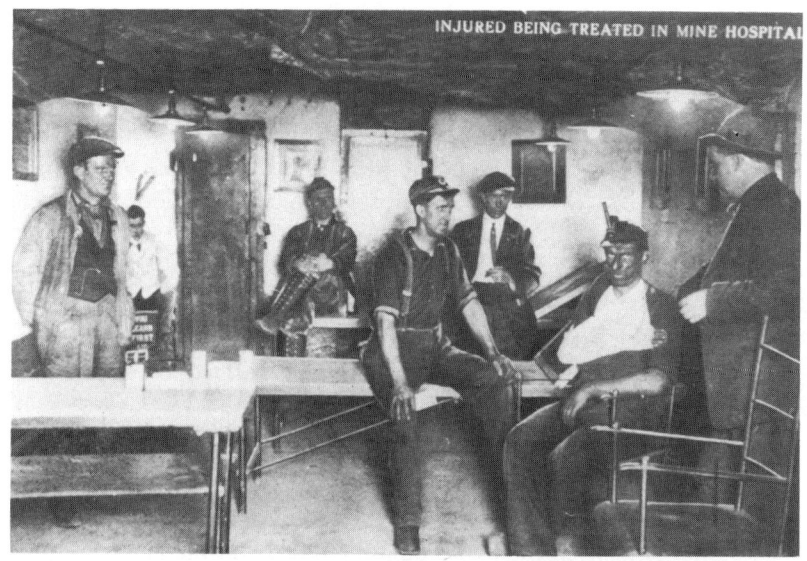

INJURED BEING TREATED IN MINE HOSPITAL

A cardboard cut-out featuring the Moxie Boy can be seen at the left in the above post card photograph—a scene taken 2,000 feet underground in a Scranton, Pennsylvania mine hospital. Literally, the Moxie Boy was everywhere!

ADAGRAM
THE MOXIE COMPANY
LEGAL DEPARTMENT.

Part of a notice from the Legal Department of The Moxie Company featured a fanciful bird-like Moxie airplane!

long been used to sell merchandise to people who can never resist the flattery of being addressed personally."

Although some cardboard cut-outs were nearly life-size and depicted the entire figure of the Moxie Boy, most showed his head and shoulders above a rectangle or oval that commanded the viewer to "Drink MOXIE." This admonition had its funny effects. For example, the *New York Tribune* on February 23, 1918 related a humorous event:

"A man entered a subway a few days earlier calmly smoking a cigar. The guard shouted, 'Say, cut that out! Don't you see that NO SMOKING sign?'

" 'Sure,' said the unperturbed smoker, 'but I don't believe in it. See that one over there?'—pointing to an advertisement placard. 'It says, DRINK MOXIE. Well, do I have to drink Moxie?' "

Soon, the Moxie Boy with pointing finger appeared on post cards as well. On April 11, 1913, customers on the Moxie mailing list were advised that they were each being sent 500 cards, Form No. 508. A related post card, issued in 1914, featured the Moxie Boy with a moisture-sensitive cloth strip below, the so-called "barometer post card," which changed from blue to pink when the weather went from dry to damp. The so-called Moxie Weather Bureau was a cardboard cut-out featuring a sensitive strip of paper between representations of the Moxie Boy with pointed finger and the Moxie Girl.

The Moxie Girl had not yet reached full definition. During the preceding 15 years, many different portraits of girls, some of them "stock" images from the files of German lithographic firms, had been used to sell Moxie. Then came "A Moxie Girl," a winsome young lass wearing a lacy white dress trimmed in purple, who appeared on tip trays, pocket mirrors, and framed signs. She was supplanted by a new Moxie Girl, who faced the viewer and held in one hand a bottle of Moxie and in the other a tumbler. Full-length views of the same person showed a cut glass bowl full of Moxie bottles on a table before her. Intermittently, the Feather Tickle Girl was used— the one with a parasol and ornate hat who stood over an early representation of the Moxie Boy and said, "Wake Up! Send a case of Moxie to our home. Wouldn't that tickle you?" As pretty as these Moxie Girls were to behold, *the* Moxie Girl had yet to appear on the scene. The time for this was not far distant.

For distribution to soda fountains, druggists, and other retail outlets, Frank Archer prepared a booklet, *About Moxie 1911*, which engaged in a bit of puffery and related some past statistics, current activities, and future hopes. 1911 was the year of the second "big

The Moxie Company was always willing to let its suppliers feature Moxie vehicles, bottles, and other items in advertising. P and P, which "takes the place of air in tires," apparently was used by the Moxie Company on certain of its delivery trucks.

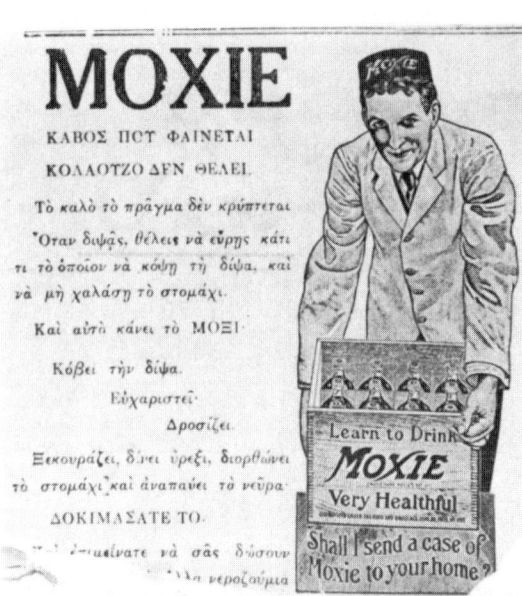

Advertisements appearing in Greek and Hebrew languages reflected Moxie's appeal to various ethnic groups. In an era of recent immigration, many foreign language newspapers flourished in the northeastern part of the United States during the early 20th century.

S.B. Ames, who advertised "Big Bargains In Everything" on the front of his Macwahoc, Maine store circa 1912, had in the front window a cardboard cut-out of the Moxie Boy pointing forward (between the two standing ladies). Maine was one of the most active areas for Moxie distribution and virtually every general store, soda fountain, grocery store, drug store, or other place where food and beverages were served was apt to display one or more Moxie signs.

In 1914 the New York branch of The Moxie Company used White trucks as part of its delivery fleet. Shown above and below are typical vehicles. Note that each of the trucks has cardboard cut-outs displayed on the side, a common situation, especially when a photographer was nearby. The picture below was taken in front of the Moxie building at the corner of Varick and Laight streets, New York City.

Part of the fleet of four White Trucks owned by the Moxie Company, New York City

Moxie bottle." The earlier version was touched upon, as was the new one:

"Some years ago [1907] we built a very large stationary Moxie bottle, about 30 feet high and 24 feet in circumference... This bottle was used for selling and advertising Moxie at fairs and attracted a great deal of attention. We afterward located it at Pine Island Park, Manchester, N.H., where it has been a constant source of interest. Up to this time it has probably been the largest bottle of the kind in the world.

"A few weeks ago we started to build another Moxie bottle of substantially the same character, but larger in every respect. The bottle will be approximately 36 feet high and 36 feet in circumference... The label upon it will measure approximately 13 feet high and 18 feet long."

The Moxie Bottle Wagon, then fading in its glory, was described as "a wagon the body of which is built in the shape of a distinctive Moxie bottle, except that it is many hundred times enlarged. It is large enough to have storage room for a hundred or two regular bottles of Moxie, with ice-tank, glass cleansers, dispensing counters, etc., properly arranged therein, and in addition there is sufficient room for a man to stand or sit within it and through doors located in the rear, serve patrons from a specially designed and constructed serving or dispensing counter." Many millions of Moxie drinkers have taken their first drink from the Moxie Bottle Wagon, the text continued. The Moxie Delivery Wagons, described as "a special Moxie design, representing at the four corners the distinctive Moxie bottle, label, etc.," were described:

"In Boston and New York where we run them, the cities are routed and the men who operate these wagons sell and deliver Moxie, collect Moxie empties, and put out Moxie advertising over a different route each day...

"Some time ago we had prepared some statistics relative to one of these wagons. The results of the sale and delivery of one of our drivers, C.E. Norton, for a period of 16 years, showed that he had put out 2,555,718 bottles of Moxie to the retail trade and that he rebated for and brought back to the factory 2,356,371 empty Moxie bottles. The combined amount of money handled by him during that period was $565,069.25, with a total loss during that time and during that enormous amount of business of only $24. What can speak higher than that of a dealer's honesty?"

Other paragraphs noted that bottles up to 18 years old were still in service, probably a reference to the year 1893, 18 years earlier,

June 24, 1911 in Shaftsbury, Vermont: Several youngsters pose in front of a veranda. In the background are Moxie signs, including one with four "seals" at the corners and, near the center of the picture, a metal sign with a case of Moxie and "Brownies."

This store on Main Street, Fort Fairfield, Maine, displays a metal Moxie thermometer featuring the Moxie Boy at the top and a case of Moxie at the bottom, in this photograph probably taken circa 1912.

This photograph of F.H. Tappan's store in the Lower Corner district of Sandwich, New Hampshire, was taken by the Eastern Illustrating Company (Belfast, Maine) probably sometime circa 1910-1915. A close look reveals two cardboard cut-outs of The Moxie Girl in the window to the right. This building still survives today (1985).

Moxie was the featured attraction at this outdoor stand pictured in a snapshot circa 1905. The Moxie "foxtail" logo, primarily used from 1904 through early 1907, is featured (see lower left).

Storefront window of The Busy Bee, probably 1911-1913. Two large Moxie cardboard cut-outs are featured at the left and center. Advertisements for other products are to the right, although a Moxie bottle, a wall hanging, and a small metal Moxie plaque can be seen in the right foreground.

HE VARIETY STORE.

STATIONERY.

Above: The Variety Store in Bridgewater, Vermont featured a Moxie thermometer (partly obscured by bunting toward the right of the photograph) at the side of the display window. Photograph circa 1912.

Siegel Cooper's Tobacco and Soda Shop, Springtown, New York, 1906, displays a "Yes! We Sell MOXIE" oval metal sign on the front. This style of sign, bowed outward like a shield, was very popular.

around the inception of the crown cork and seal closure. In practice, by 1911 Moxie was phasing out bottles with "Nerve Food" as part of the inscription, and most bottles in circulation lacked this message. It was noted that typical breakage of bottles in transit was about two-tenths of 1%, or one bottle in every 470.

Prospective Moxie agents were advised how to serve the beverage and to attract customers into the store:

"Dealers should have in mind that Moxie is more palatable when served ice cold. Their Moxie trade will grow and incidentally their other business if they are careful in keeping Moxie thoroughly stoppered so that it does not lose the gas; also to always serve it ice cold. Customers calling at your store for Moxie are also apt to make many other purchases. If they do not come to your store for Moxie you may lose their trade on other wares.

"Moxie customers always look for Moxie signs. Dealers should display their Moxie signs prominently. We have found that where a dealer makes a display in his window of from six to 24 cases of Moxie, opening one or more of the cases and standing several bottles of Moxie, both wrapped and unwrapped, on or about them, and arranging them around some of the attractive Moxie signs that we furnish, it serves to attract customers who possibly might have gone to some other store. As a matter of fact it is well understood that attractive window displays of a staple article like Moxie, and especially one widely advertised, is one of the best drawing cards that a dealer could possibly have."

For purposes of window display, dummy bottles of Moxie, sealed but lacking contents, were supplied, after it was realized that full bottles were apt to explode or turn sour if displayed in sunlight for a long period of time.

Appended to the 1911 booklet was a list of states in which Moxie was sold and a list of official distributors therein. Among the Boston outlets were listed Silas Peirce & Co. and the somewhat similarly named, but with a slight twist in the spelling of the last name, S.S. Pierce Co., the well-known grocers. A review of the ledgers of the era show that shipments and bills between the Peirce and Pierce firms were continually confused.

All the while, Moxie continued to build a loyal following. Many were the poems originated and sent to Moxie headquarters by customers who appreciated the product. Many were the snapshots of youngsters drinking from Moxie bottles, or standing next to a cut-out of the Moxie Boy, or otherwise relating to their favorite beverage. At times, the population seemed to be divided into two

Two Moxie displays, circa 1912 (above) and 1904.

categories: those who drank Moxie and loved to tell about it, and those who wouldn't touch the stuff. This sentiment was to linger for decades afterward.

In April 1912, a ball held at Hutchinson Hall featured as its theme costumes made of advertisements. Dancers came dressed to advertise Butterfly Farm, Salada Tea, Worcester Salt, United States Playing Cards, Gold Medal Flour, and numerous other products. Mr. and Mrs. E. Roberts were dressed in Moxie regalia. This ignited a spark of interest, and at once The Moxie Company created a line of Moxie clothing, primarily jackets and caps, but also including capes, dresses, and pants. What better uniform for a Moxie Bottle Wagon attendant or a Moxie car driver?

In 1914, officers of The Moxie Company were: Francis E. Thompson, president; Harry A. Thompson, treasurer; Freeman N. Young, secretary; and Frank M. Archer, vice-president. Of the 5,000 shares issued, Archer had the smallest number of shares, just 50, the same status as in earlier years.

Advertising emphasized the Moxie Boy with his pointing finger. The American Lithograph Company of New York and Boston produced these in vast quantities. From other sources came Moxie thermometers, weather indicators, post cards, openers, and other novelties, including plated knives, forks, and spoons—tableware patented in September 1914. The Moxie Boy was gaining a toehold in the heart of America. He was a familiar sight in dormitory rooms, in places of public amusement, and a post card printed in Scranton, Pennsylvania, showed a large cardboard cut-out of the Moxie Boy in an anthracite mine hospital 2,000 feet underground!

The Moxie Boy and other innovations propelled Frank Archer to the front of the advertising community. Pleased with the recognition, he forthwith announced that in the interest of education he would invite students of advertising in leading colleges—including Yale, Wellesley, Harvard, Cornell, and Brown—to create their own Moxie advertisements, with the reward being an appearance in print. Dozens of different designs were submitted by enthusiastic participants.

Use of the name Moxie for boats, favorite vehicles, horses, and other items increased. Checking on this, A.W. Davis of The Moxie Company wrote to the *American Horse Breeder*, the largest circulation trotting horse journal, to learn that "there are about a dozen Moxies in the yearbook."

Alfred W. McCann, who wrote extensively on the subject of pure drinks and who was a Moxie enthusiast, wrote an interesting article

Two different Moxie exhibits, circa 1911-1914, both featured cardboard cut-outs, including the popular style with the Moxie Boy sitting on a crate with his finger pointed toward the viewer. The unit below features on the right side of the counter a framed cardboard cut-out of the Moxie Girl standing in front of a crystal bowl and holding a bottle of Moxie in one hand and a glass in the other. The counter and backdrop to these exhibits could be easily packed away for transportation to the next scheduled show. Moxie booths such as this were familiar sights in New England Food Fairs, restaurant supplier shows, and other New England exhibitions during the 1900-1920 years. Sample glasses of Moxie were free for the asking.

for *The Globe*, a New York newspaper, which appeared in the May 14, 1914 edition:

"WHY MOXIE IS IN DIRECTORY! Not Loaded With Dope Like Other Beverages—Innocent Hot Weather Drink.

"What business has a beverage like Moxie in a pure food directory? I have been asked questions like that until I find the answers should be written in fire, and hung up as a burning rebuke on the walls of every one of the fake soft drink factories in America.

"Only a few days ago I walked for blocks along the fraud-infested Boardwalk of Atlantic City before I could find a soda fountain where Moxie was served. At last a dispenser was frank enough to say to me in answer to my question: 'I guess they don't make enough on Moxie, and don't like to handle it. We don't have a sign out ourselves. We keep it under the counter.'

"Thousands of gallons of coal-tar nectars flow from expensive marble fountains in all the colors of a Syrian festival during the hot weather season. Not one of them would be possible for if it were not for coal-tar and other chemical frauds.

"It's the money that's in them that inspires their sale, and a childlike love of brilliant colors that inspires their purchase. A drink with anything real in it would not show the 700% profit which these gas-charged shams demand. Hence it is difficult to find Moxie on the Boardwalk.

"There are many drinks on the market which spend thousands of dollars to inform the public that this and that brilliant ball player owes his pink of condition and this and that athlete his marvelous skill to the astonishing virtues of 'so and so.'

"Moxie at least does not claim that it will evolve a third set of teeth or a new patch of moss on a bald dome. When it began its career, under other than its present ownership, it was associated with claims somewhat similar to those now made for the caffeine-loaded waters of youth which are gradually crowding most innocent soft drinks off the market. Mr. Archer, president [sic] of the Moxie concern, is too genuine a friend of the pure food movement to tolerate such nonsense...

"In a plant owned by a New York state senator a load of horse manure was found under the bottling apparatus, and in nearly all the other factories investigated, horses were stabled under the roof where the drinks were mixed. The names of these offenders were published full in *The Globe*, many were arrested and convicted... Now for my reason for admitting Moxie to the *Pure Food Directory*.

"There isn't an ounce of dope in a million gallons of it. Not one of the drugs mentioned, nor any other drug can get into it. It is free from coal-tar, free from ethers, free from alkaloids, free from suds, free from preservatives. Why shouldn't it get into the directory?..."

Moxie repaid Alfred W. McCann's kind words by featuring him in numerous advertisements, noting he was a famous expert and authority.

McCann was not the only person writing about Moxie. An advertisement proclaimed:

"DRINK MOXIE, a beverage that has the fullest endorsement of Professor Lewis B. Allyn, 'Food Authority' of the pure food town of Westfield, Massachusetts, and now food editor of *The Ladies' World*. Professor Allyn has repeatedly analyzed Moxie and has approved it. He has personally investigated the conditions under which Moxie is made and bottled, by numerous inspections of the Moxie plants."

Coca-Cola did not fare as well, and many articles protesting the inclusion of coca leaf extract reached the press. Never mind that the cocaine had been extracted; that did not please the detractors.

H.P. Cassidy was another so-called expert who earned a generous income by speaking to clubs and groups throughout Pennsylvania, New York, and the New England states. Moxie was on his list of favorites, too, and Moxie reciprocated by praising him as an expert of experts. Not only did Cassidy approve of Moxie, he personally used it: "Take my own experience with it. I have drunk Moxie for years. And when I am driven with work, expending my nervous energy in an effort to keep ahead of the clock, I find Moxie keeps my stomach in better condition than anything else I could use," he testified. Further, "I have examined the Moxie laboratories in Boston and New York and found the sanitary conditions ideal. I was unable to make a single adverse criticism. I am still amazed at the ideal cleanliness of the factories at all times, especially when I realize the size of the business. I presume it is largely due to the 30 years of continuous effort that The Moxie Company has made to better its product." Certainly no copywriter paid by Moxie could have done a better job!

In other publicity matters in 1914, the Hearst chain of newspapers, spearheaded by the *Atlanta Georgian*, started a "Buy a Bale of Cotton Campaign" in order to boost the market for cotton, which had sunk to 10c per pound. Although it was unclear what The Moxie Company or Frank Archer would do with the stuff, it was certain that Archer enjoyed the publicity, for he sent out a news release on the subject to the *Boston American,* another Hearst paper:

"It is a great pleasure to honor your request to purchase a bale of cotton. Enclosed find check for $50 covering same. This may be delivered to either our Boston or New York factory.

"We certainly trust that your efforts relative to cotton may be productive. Very truly yours, THE MOXIE COMPANY, by F.M. Archer."

An advertisement and illustration dated February 1915 shows a giant Moxie bottle on view indoors at White City, an amusement park at Savin Rock, New Haven, Connecticut. A comparison of photographs shows that this may have been the unit displayed at Pine Island Park in Manchester, New Hampshire. Perhaps during the idle winter months it was dismantled and shipped down to New Haven, or perhaps it represents a third giant bottle.

In 1915 the Moxie Boy got a girlfriend. Muriel Ostriche, a pert, pretty, and pixyish 18-year-old film star posed in front of the Moxie camera. Soon her likeness appeared on the first of several varieties of hand-held cardboard fans, on cardboard cut-outs, baseball score cards, and numerous other places, including china dinnerware. Muriel, a mischievous lass, was a favorite subject for newspaper reporters, who commented on her activities while filming for the silver screen, her love of life, her romp with a married man, and, eventually, her marriage. When she sued her parents for mismanaging money earned when she was younger than legal age, this made the papers, as did a novel theory in which she stated that after several years of marriage and two children, she found having her husband live in the same house was too restrictive. Accordingly, suitcase in hand he walked out, to return on weekends.

Muriel Ostriche made several trips to the Boston area and appeared on behalf of Moxie, which featured her as the Moxie Girl in numerous advertisements. After 1915, other actresses, including Laura Walker, Frances Pritchard, Lillian MacKenzie, and Eileen Percy, were featured by name in Moxie advertising, although none achieved the acclaim or widespread use in Moxie advertising accorded to Muriel Ostriche. Eileen Percy achieved greater fame as an actress, being the favorite leading lady of Douglas Fairbanks in several films, but her appearance in Moxie advertising was brief. Then there was "Peggy," a seductive young lass of perhaps 14 years of age, whose identity was never stated, if indeed she had a real life counterpart—she may have existed only in the imagination of the artist who painted her image. *The* Moxie Girl was Muriel Ostriche, and Muriel reigned supreme until about 1920.

Muriel Ostriche was a real charmer, and undoubtedly cardboard cut-outs such as these, a familiar sight in restaurants, on store fronts, tacked to fences, and many other places from about 1915 onward, did much to sell quantities of Moxie.

Vitagraph.

MURIEL OSTRICHE.

A Vitagraph publicity photograph of Muriel Ostriche as featured in several newspapers during the height of her Moxie publicity. The picture bears the imprint of Vitagraph, a prominent early motion picture company for which Muriel acted.

Muriel Ostriche was the first Moxie Girl to appear on cardboard fans. That shown at the upper left was the first and was issued in May 1915. The same portrait of Muriel appeared in several other forms—including on a sign showing her peeking over a crate of Moxie and on another sign showing her above a "Drink Moxie" advertisement. Fans such as the four shown on this page were given away free at carnivals, movies, fairs, parades, and other public events.

Muriel was depicted peering impishly from behind a Moxie crate, and sitting on a Moxie crate on a cardboard cut-out, and simply appearing above a "Drink Moxie" ad, in the manner of the Moxie Boy.

In May 1915, the month that the first Muriel Ostriche Moxie advertising fan was copyrighted, Frank Archer pasted a photograph of her in his scrapbook, putting "Moxie Girl" as the caption in pencil above her portrait, and noting in the margin her home address was 565 West 144th Street, New York City. Separately a brief biography was attached to the page:

"MURIEL OSTRICHE has risked her life more than once to add realism to moving pictures, and has been christened the 'daredevil of the movies.' She was born in New York City on March 24, 1897. While in Wadleigh High she began posing for pictures as an extra. Her success was so great that during her second year she left to become a stock member in one of the larger moving picture companies. She has had more than usual success, not only as an actress, but as a writer of scenarios, having written original stories in which she played the lead."

Around the same time, Alfred W. McCann, the pure food writer who idolized Moxie, fired his guns at Coca-Cola. "COCA-COLA ATTACKED AS POISONOUS DRINK BY U.S. GOVERNMENT," proclaimed the headline of one of his articles, which went on to say:

"A lot of Dr. Jekyll and Mr. Hyde questions have been asked me about two mysterious products—Kaffee Hag and Coca-Cola.

"Some people have the idea that the Kaffee Hag concern, which extracts the caffeine from its coffee because it looks upon caffeine as a poison and is engaged in a production of a coffee free from such poison, turns around and sells the Coca-Cola concern this extracted caffeine, so that it may be put back into the popular soda fountain beverage so largely consumed by women, children and temperance advocates.

"When I first heard gossip to the effect that the Kaffee Hag people were pulling off such a hypocritical stunt I made an investigation for the purpose of exploiting the Dr. Jekyll and Mr. Hyde situation.

"Under date of April 2, 1915, I demanded from the Kaffee Hag Corporation access to its books. Through the assistance of Dr. D.M. Dunn I was permitted to go to the limit, with the result that I now know that the Kaffee Hag Corporation does not sell caffeine, either to the Coca-Cola crowd or any other soft drink concern...

Muriel Ostriche was widely featured in Moxie publicity from about 1915
to 1920. Shown here are two china plates and a serving dish. Each is part of
a larger set. Several different border designs were made, as the pieces here
show. Other china was made with the image of the Moxie Boy.

Above: Detail of a photograph showing a cardboard cut-out of the Moxie Boy, probably circa 1915. Another Moxie sign is to the upper right, still another (featuring Muriel Ostriche) is behind the row of bottles to the left of center, and a further sign showing the Moxie Boy is to the extreme left.

Facing page: Another detail of the same photograph, showing Under The Elms, a Maine refreshment stand, shows further Moxie signs, including another of Muriel Ostriche (with a slight light glare on it) to the lower left. An unopened bottle of Moxie sits on the counter along with various other bottles and dispensers.

1916 PROVIDENCE

FOOD FAIR

INFANTRY HALL **FEB. 14 TO 26**
AFTERNOONS & EVENINGS

NOW OPEN

Doors Open 1:30 to 5:30 and
7:30 to 10:30 P. M.
Demonstration Lectures To-day:
3:30 P. M.—"Eggs," Jennie E.
Koehler.
8:30 P. M.—"Pure Candy," Edith
Sickles Wood.
EVERY WOMAN purchasing tickets
after 1 and 7 P. M., daily, will receive
FREE full sized packages of goods exhibited valued at from 10 to 30 cents,
the first 250 receiving an extra number
of packages.
A 41-piece Dinner Set or a Chest
of Silver given FREE daily, donated by THE MOXIE CO.
Admission 25 cents. Partly
paid tickets given free by grocers.
Ask for them.

No food fair in New England was complete without a Moxie exhibit, and the firm attended many of them. Above and below are shown two Moxie setups, while to the left is shown an advertisement for a 1916 event in Providence. The display below notes that a "Moxie Barometer Postcard" will be given free to patrons. On the counter are several Moxie Weather Bureau cardboard cut-outs as well.

Above: This refreshment stand, location unknown, in a circa 1915 photograph, displays several Moxie signs. At the upper left is a cardboard cut-out of the Moxie Boy pointing, in the center near the top is a sign featuring Muriel Ostriche (the actress whose image appeared on several Moxie fans) peering from behind a Moxie crate, while at the center right is a small "Drink Moxie" sign.

Right: This confectionery store, location unknown, advertised Moxie via a well-used metal sign affixed to the woodwork below the window. Presumably it is the proprietor who stands proudly(?) at the door.

New Campaign in the Interest of Moxie

Nine Designs Being Used in Thirteen States.
Posters Produced by a New Method Evolved
by F. A. Archer of the Manufacturing
Company

THE Moxie Company has undertaken an extensive poster advertising campaign this year for the exploitation of the famous beverage of that name, under the direction of Walls' National Poster Service, Inc., official solicitors.

This campaign is a reversion to posting, since the firm was not represented on the boards last year.

It is interesting, and important, too, from the fact that the posters have been produced by a process that is a distinct innovation. They are printed in two colors actually, but by means of the Ben Day process the effect has been obtained of an ordinary four-color poster. This idea was evolved by Mr. F. A. Archer, president of the Moxie Company of Boston, Massachusetts, and promises to create something of a revolution in poster production. The poster has been made by the Forbes Lithograph Manufacturing Company of Boston.

The Moxie posting for this year will include the states of New York, New Jersey, Delaware, District of Columbia, Maryland, Virginia, West Virginia, Connecticut, Vermont, Massachusetts, Ohio, Indiana, Michigan and some parts of Canada, covering each point of any importance in each of the states named.

There are four different designs of 8 sheets, four designs of 16 sheets and the old standard 24-sheet Moxie design.

This campaign may be taken as another illustration of the fact that no other medium can do just what poster advertising does. The patrons of the poster plants increase and multiply. The Moxie campaigns have been successful in the past, and this one bids fair to follow in their footsteps. It is the psychological moment for a campaign in the interest of a popular beverage, and given the Association's new service, with lithographic productions, the result is not for an instant in doubt.

One of the New 8-Sheet Designs.

If at all Particular Drink **MOXIE**

One of the Four New 16-Sheet Moxie Posters.

Drink **MOXIE**
Clean Wholesome Refreshing

In June 1914, "The Poster," an advertising trade publication, featured a forth-coming billboard campaign. "There are four different designs of eight sheets, four of sixteen sheets and the old standard twenty-four-sheet Moxie design," the text notes. From the earliest years onward, posters were an important part of Moxie's advertising budget.

The drugstore counter shown above in a circa 1908 photograph displays a cardboard cut-out of the Moxie Boy holding a case of Moxie. This motif was very popular and appeared in many places, including on postcards and on cardboard cut-outs of much larger format.

The Maplehurst Ice Cream Shop, circa 1915, advertised Moxie by means of two cardboard signs showing actress Muriel Ostriche peering from behind the word MOXIE (to the immediate left and right of the "Maplehurst" sign in the picture above).

Drink **MOXIE**

TO MOXIE DEALERS
Everywhere

The 1915 Moxie Fall Display is now on.

Please call on, phone or write your Moxie jobber at once to submit an order "C" for your signature. If he does not call on you promptly, notify us.

This is the last Moxie display for 1915. Inform us when and through what Moxie jobber you will place order "C."

Is there any attention we can give you that we have not given? We esteem beyond measure your valued patronage for more than a quarter of a century. You have seen us grow from a small beginner to one of the Standard National Products. Your valued co-operation was necessary for this. We owe to you every service we can possibly give you, and it is our aim and ambition to serve you in such a manner at all times as to continue to merit the enormous patronage and loyal co-operation we have enjoyed from you.

To those of you who have not honored us with a call at our Laboratories at Boston or New York and investigated the conditions under which Moxie is bottled (a condition which we are very proud of), may we have the honor of showing you the sanitary and hygienic conditions under which Moxie is handled? Remember you need no appointment. You are always welcome.

We take this opportunity to again thank you, and sincerely trust the high quality of our product, Moxie, will always meet your approval, and we shall be able to give the service you are entitled to. Rest assured our every energy and resource will be directed to that end.

Very respectfully yours,

THE MOXIE COMPANY

"Order C" was the name given to a standard contract and order form for Moxie during the first two decades of the 20th century. The various legal and business aspects of Order C were explained in a special brochure written by Frank Archer. A reminder to place Order C in 1915 was printed on the back of a fan (which featured Frances Pritchard on the front). The above advertisement, also from 1915, encourages Moxie dealers to spring into action.

"The Coca-Cola people do put caffeine into their product, and parents who are wise enough to forbid their growing children the use of coffee, which contains caffeine naturally, permit those same growing children through sheer thoughtlessness to go to the drug store and consume still larger quantities of the same akaloidal drug which is used unnaturally as a business-getting bracer by the Coca-Cola people..."

McCann went on to recite a rumor that Coca-Cola employees spit tobacco into the product during the manufacturing process, later stating that apparently this wasn't true. "The whole Coca-Cola controversy has reeked with dirt and drugs from the time the government attempted to bring it to a head, and it is to be sincerely hoped that the Supreme Court will finally settle the matter one way or another," he noted rather officiously. One wonders why McCann wrote the article in the first place.

Other articles also hammered away at the caffeine theme. One was printed with the headline "Coca-Cola Company Fails to Advertise Dangers of Chronic Caffeinism." The Moxie Company was delighted with all of this adverse Coca-Cola publicity, and as there were so many McCann clippings that the scrapbook could not comfortably hold them, they tucked them into a special folder.

Chapter 11

The Horsemobile

1916 saw another Moxie advertising landmark appear, the Horsemobile. In the beginning of the year there was no hint of it. Early in January, dealers and agents were sent lists of advertising materials that could be ordered or obtained free of charge, including girl thermometers, large and small Moxie Boy cut-outs, large and small Moxie Girl cut-outs, Moxie case cut-outs (with Muriel Ostriche peering over the backside), the head of Muriel Ostriche with "Drink Moxie" cut-outs, metal and fiber fence signs, fans, openers and stoppers, muslin signs, seals, translucent signs, glasses, and more.

Newspapers were full of war accounts. After the incident at Sarajevo in August 1914, the Great War, later called World War I, broke out. By early 1916, numerous shortages occurred in America, due to shipments of material to the fighting factions overseas. Frank Archer advised Moxie outlets:

"We ask for your cooperation and indulgence. The lack of material, the shortage of tools and machinery, the scarcity of labor, the shortage of locomotives and freight cars of every kind, the lack of storage, embargos of all kinds, the unsettled conditions due to the war in every direction, the uncertainties and tremendous difficulties of obtaining our imports, the weather conditions unequaled for half a century—these are some of the things that make these the most unusual times, when foresight cannot compete with hindsight."

Moxie customers were then requested to order sufficient supplies of the beverage far in advance to anticipate all needs.

The fame of Muriel Ostriche spread, and soon the public found her image on china dinner sets. These and other tableware items became popular Moxie giveaways, and much favorable publicity resulted. At the 1916 Providence Food Fair, held February 14-26, each day a 61-piece dinner set or a chest of Moxie silver was given away, donated by the Moxie Company.

Miss Doris Tompkins of Dundee, Michigan, won
a Moxie silver tea set in a 1915 contest. Her picture
was preserved in the Moxie archives.

The Fall River (Massachusetts) *Evening Herald,* March 13, 1916, carried a notice of a similar event:

"A pure food exposition is to be held in Fall River next week beginning Monday evening and closing Saturday... As an added inducement to attract people to the fair, they are to give away six dinner sets, 61 pieces in each set, and three chests of silver, the gifts being made possible by the generosity of The Moxie Company, which is donating them...

"On Monday evening a dinner set will be awarded to the most popular grocer or market man in Fall River. This degree of popularity is to be determined by popular vote. A coupon will be printed in the *Evening Herald* every afternoon, beginning Saturday. All you have to do is clip these coupons and deposit them at the Moxie booth at the fair...

"On Tuesday the dinner set will be awarded to the most popular woman clerk in the city, whether she be employed at a grocery market or any other store in the city, and the chest of silver will be awarded to the woman clerk receiving the second highest number of votes. On Wednesday evening a dinner set will be awarded to the most popular letter carrier. On Thursday evening a dinner set will be given to the most popular woman school teacher and a chest of silver to the second most popular. On Friday evening a dinner set will go to the most popular policeman. On Saturday evening a dinner set will be presented to the most popular woman stenographer and a chest of silver to the one receiving the second highest number of coupons..."

In Rutland, Vermont, on August 31, 1916, it was announced that at the Shrine Theatre on Monday, Wednesday, and Saturday nights The Moxie Company would present the young lady who costumed the most like Muriel Ostriche, the Moxie Girl, a beautiful set of dishes. On Tuesday, Thursday, and Saturday a set of dishes would go to the young man costuming most like the Moxie Boy. "Pictures of the Moxie Girl and Boy are on exhibition at the Shrine and one set will be given out each night. Judges will be local people," a notice observed.

Similarly, in August 1916 the store of Miss Fanny L. Young of Barnstable, Mass., served as the display setting for a 61-piece set of dishes and two 20-piece sets of breakfast dishes to be awarded as premiums at the Barnstable County Agricultural Society exhibits.

Frank Archer enjoyed the company of beautiful women, and if they had red hair, so much the better. His penchant for redheads was mentioned in print many times. In August 1916 the Waterville

(Maine) *Morning Sentinel* wrote of the Central Maine Fairgrounds and the preparation for a forthcoming event, stating in part:

"There probably will be a large attendance of red-haired girls on the grounds on Wednesday, for on that day the Moxie people offer a prize of a 20-piece set of dishes to the prettiest red-haired girl attending the fair between the ages of 20 and 25 years. On Thursday the same rules apply to the prettiest black-haired girl, who will receive a like prize. But whether she is a maiden with black tresses or one with locks of auburn hue, if she wins the first prize of the Girls' Garden and Canning Club she will win a 61-piece dinner set from the Moxie people in addition. Two other prizes are also offered by this company, one for the best looking young man and one for the best looking girl between the ages of 20 and 25..."

A Lewiston, Maine contest noted in the *Daily Sun*, September 13th of the same year, told of six sets of china dishes to be awarded to the best looking red-headed girl, to the best looking lady clerk in the exhibition building, to the homeliest man, to the best looking young lady on the fairgrounds Tuesday, to the best decorated booth in the exhibition hall, and to the best looking fellow in the town. Somewhat similar specifications were given for Moxie china to be awarded at the South Paris (Maine) Fair in the same month. At the New England Fair in Worcester, Massachusetts, in September, seven *camping* sets of 21 pieces each were awarded. "Miss Helen M. Westwood, a nurse at the Red Cross tent, received a camping set for having the prettiest red hair at the fair the first three days..." Seeking variety, The Moxie Company specified that sets of dishes awarded at the Topsham (Maine) Fair in the same year were to go to "the man with the largest family present at the fairgrounds" and another set "to the man with the largest feet."

In April 1917, at a ball and pageant at the Copley Plaza Hotel, Boston, "The Moxie Company offered ten 20-piece breakfast sets, made for them by the great potters, Owen China Company, unobtainable except of The Moxie Company, unique, original, distinctive, rich, disposed of in accordance with the rules laid down by the Boston Women's Publicity Club."

Finally, at the Boston Herald-Traveler Patriotic Food Conservation Exposition during the first two weeks of April 1918, The Moxie Company contributed 25 breakfast sets of china containing 20 pieces per set, 2,000 ice cream dishes, 1,000 ash trays, and 25 dolls each 32 inches tall. The appeal of the dolls was enhanced when it was stated that "at a charity bazaar held in New York City not long ago, Mrs. William K. Vanderbilt entered the bidding when one of these

Menus for Monday

Breakfast

CEREAL	BAKED APPLES, CREAM

CORNED BEEF, POTATO AND GREEN PEPPER HASH
SLICED TOMATOES

| BUTTERED TOAST | COFFEE | MOXIE |

Dinner

FILLET OF BEEF, ROASTED, TOMATO SAUCE
SWEET POTATOES, SOUTHERN STYLE
BOILED CAULIFLOWER, CREAM SAUCE

| GRAPE JUICE WHIP | COFFEE | MOXIE |

Supper

SWEET CORN IN CREAM
SLICED PEACHES

| COOKIES | TEA | MOXIE |

CORNED BEEF, POTATO AND GREEN PEPPER HASH. Chop very fine half or a whole sweet green pepper, from which the seeds have been removed. Melt 3 or 4 tablespoonfuls of butter or choice bacon fat and in it cook the pepper until it is softened and yellowed. (If desired, a slice of onion, chopped fine, may be cooked with the pepper). Add about 1½ cups of cold corned beef and 2 cups or cold boiled potatoes, both chopped fine, and 3 or 4 tablespoonfuls of broth or water. Mix thoroughly, then cover and let cook until it is a very hot throughout and a slight crust is formed below. Remove the cover and add 2 tablespoonfuls of butter, in little bits here and there. With a spatula fold one side over the other, omelet fashion, and turn on to a hot platter.

FILLET OF BEEF, ROASTED. Remove the skin and non-edible portions from a fillet of beef, and wipe all over with a damp cloth. Set on a rack in a pan, spread with butter, drippings or bacon fat, and set into a hot oven (250° F). After 10 minutes reduce the heat and let cook about 15 minutes longer, basting with hot fat every 6 or 8 minutes. Remove the meat to a hot platter and pour off all the fat but 2 tablespoonfuls. Into this put 2 tablespoonfuls of flour and ¾ teaspoonful each of salt and pepper, stir and cook until frothy, then add one cup of tomato purée (cooked tomato pressed through a sieve fine enough to keep back the seeds) and stir until the sauce boils. For a higher flavored sauce, cook 1 slice each of onion, carrot and green pepper with a few bits of thyme and parsley, in butter, until browned; then cook them in the tomato before strained.

SWEET POTATOES, SOUTHERN FASHION. Pare and cut in halves, lengthwise, 5 sweet potatoes of medium size. In an agate baking dish or an earthen casserole dispose a layer of halved potatoes. Over these sprinkle ¼ cup of sugar (brown or maple will be found particularly good in flavor for this use), add 2 tablespoonfuls of butter in little bits, here and there, and dredge lightly with salt. Put the remainder of the prepared potatos into the dish and season as before with sugar, butter and salt. Turn in half a cup of boiling water, cover with dish and let cook about 1 hour, basting the potatoes occasionally with the liquid in the dish. Remove the cover for the last of the cooking, that the potatoes may brown slightly on the edges.

CREAM SAUCE. Melt 2 level tablespoonfuls of butter. Cook in it 2 level tablespoonfuls of flour and ¼ teaspoonful each of salt and pepper; then add one cup of rich milk (or part cream and part milk) and stir until it boils and is thick and smooth.

GRAPE JUICE WHIP. Crush ripe grapes and press the juice through a cheese cloth. To ¾ cup of the juice add ½ cup of sugar, the juice of half a lemon, 1 cup of double cream, and the white of 1 egg beaten until foamy. Beat the mixture with a cream whip and take of the froth as it rises to the top. When all the available froth has been removed, let it chill on ice. Put the unwhipped mixture and that which drains from the "Whip" into 4 tall glasses, then add the froth or whip to the glasses, piling it high in them.

COOKIES. Cream ½ cup of butter; beat in 1 cup of sugar, the beaten yolks of 2 eggs (one left from the Grape Juice Whip and one other), ⅓ cup of milk, the white of 1 egg, beaten dry, 2 cups of flour sifted with 3 level teaspoonfuls of baking powder, and enough more flour to make a dough that can be rolled into a sheet. Cut in rounds or other shapes and set into a baking pan; dredge with granulated sugar and bake in a quick oven.

YOU'LL FIND MOXIE DECIDEDLY REFRESHING AND
STRENGTHENING AFTER A DAY'S SHOPPING

The Moxie Menu Book featured suggested recipes for each day of the week, with Moxie being an ingredient of each meal. Frank M. Archer maintained an interest in things culinary, and later, in the 1920s, hosted a cooking school in Moxieland. In other instances prizes were given to Boston area cooks of special ability.

Moxie bottling facilities were a source of pride to the firm, and the public was invited to inspect the plant. Above is part of the Moxieland building in the late 1920s, while below is shown a production line at the Haverhill Street, Boston plant a couple of decades earlier.

fascinating Moxie dolls was at stake and only succeeded in carrying off the doll when she had extracted $115 from her velvet handbag."

Early versions of Moxie china plates, saucers, cups, and other pieces primarily featured Muriel Ostriche, while most later versions showed the Moxie Boy. Numerous variations in edge designs and decorations were produced.

Garments featuring Moxie advertisements, introduced a few years earlier, came to the forefront in 1916. "The Moxie Company has instituted a unique and novel campaign, conducted by young ladies in a limousine painted pure white," a publicity notice announced. "The young ladies and the chauffeur wear suits made from the famous Moxie cloth. The mission of these young ladies is to call on doctors, lawyers, ministers, dentists, nurses, hospital officials [and others] to extend a personal invitation for them to visit The Moxie Company's laboratories either in New York or in Boston. It is desired to have influential and civic-minded people see the conditions under which Moxie is manufactured."

Many people accepted the invitation, and comments of certain visitors found their way into articles and advertisements. A description of Moxie's headquarters on Haverhill Street noted:

"Those who patronize the elevated railway cars as they pass to and from the North Station are familiar with the four-story white building which is the home of The Moxie Company. There the drink is manufactured, bottled, and dispatched throughout a wide area... By a well arranged system, the receiving and dispatching departments are kept separate. All the empty cases are received at the Beverly Street side of the building, while the filled and wrapped bottles in their wooden cases are sent out from the Haverhill Street side. As the public walks under the runways which extend over the sidewalk to a large Moxie wagon, some idea may be gained of the size of the business by the sight of wagon after wagon. When the empties are received from the Beverly Street side the bottles are put through the most careful system of sanitary cleansing... The bottles are then ready for filling and capping, and by an expeditious system of tracks and runways, the racks of bottles quickly find their way from one department to another. Once capped they are sent to a large circular machine where the labels are automatically applied. It is only a few moments before they are wrapped and placed in boxes which are nailed and given a final inspection before being shipped.

"All of the men handling Moxie wear white suits which are changed each morning. Every afternoon at the close of work all the machinery is subjected to a thorough cleansing... The most interesting section of the whole establishment, perhaps, is the large laboratory at the top of the building, where the various processes of manufacturing the Moxie essence are carried out. Everything is snow white. The many kettles, tanks, vats, and glass jars attest to the vast amount of material that is daily needed to fill the demand.

"It was 31 years ago that Moxie was first made in Lowell. The company's headquarters have been at 69 Haverhill Street for the past 20 years..."

A few years later, Frank Archer developed an ingenious scheme. He enjoyed fraternizing with vaudeville and stage personalities who visited Boston in the course of giving performances. Actors and actresses were invited to tour the Moxie factory. Their comments, if they cared to make them, were reprinted in large advertisements in the Boston newspapers, together with biographical sketches and publicity concerning the stage event in which they were appearing. Thus, Archer received publicity for Moxie, and the stage personalities received publicity for themselves, apparently an ideal equation. This procedure went on for many years and involved many different people.

The cleanliness and purity of the Moxie manufacturing process was a recurrent theme in an era which still was wary of false advertising claims. A stamp of approval was placed upon Moxie by the *Christian Science Monitor*, which, on August 2, 1916, published a Moxie advertisement, the first soft drink of any kind to be featured in that conservative newspaper, according to a note made by Frank Archer in his advertising file.

A Moxie advertising novelty of the time, and one that garnered much newspaper publicity, was the Moxie Stilt Man, Fred H. Wilson. An article in the *Boston American*, August 16, 1916, told of a fanciful dialogue between Fred Wilson and another Moxie publicity-getter, Muriel Ostriche:

" 'Oh, see the Custom House tower,' exclaimed Muriel Ostriche, the celebrated star of the World Film Company, looking out her second-story window right into the eyes of the curious Mr. Wilson.

" 'I am not the Custom House Tower. That has a clock for a face,' retorted Mr. Wilson, who wasn't at all abashed at looking into second-story windows.

" 'Then what are you?' demanded Muriel, as perplexed as Alice in Wonderland. 'You must be something.'

" 'Perhaps I'm a wireless station,' replied the tall person.

" 'Do you hear anything from the *Bremen?*'

A newspaper cartoonist combined photographs of Muriel
Ostriche, the Moxie Girl, with Fred Wilson, the Moxie Stilt
Man, to create a sketch of Wilson engaging in a second-story
conversation with the attractive young actress.

" 'No, but I can hear the wind blowing through huge whiskers.'

" 'I refuse to talk politics,' responded the dainty Muriel. 'I must go now and be thrown over a cliff to be rescued by the hero. Would you like to be a movie actor?'

" 'I tried,' sadly answered Mr. Wilson, 'but they couldn't get all of me in the camera.'

" 'Well, goodbye.'

" 'Goodbye.'

"Golden-haired Muriel, who is known all over the country as the Moxie Girl, left her window and trotted off to the picture studio. Mr. Wilson, known as Moxie's Telegraph Pole, stalked with great dignity up the street in his extraordinary garments that are decorated in the most curious way with Moxie advertisements. Wilson is not a street advertising man. There is as much difference between him and the ordinary sandwich man as between Raphael and a house painter. Wilson is an artist. He spent 12 years learning his trade.

"Lots of people who see him think he is actually a monstrosity, for he walks on his wooden legs as easily as lots of us perambulate on our regular ones. Not only that, he can dance the tango, two-step and fox trot as well as anyone else. Sometimes he steps out in front of a band or procession and dances along to the edification of thousands.

"Wilson's pantlegs measure 120 inches. That's the same length as the wheelbase of the more expensive automobiles. Nonetheless, he can double himself up and ride in an automobile in some mysterious fashion. What his stilts, artificial legs, or whatever they are, look like, nobody knows. It's his trade secret. Recently he went down to Coney Island, but nothing could persuade him to go bathing.

"Wilson is in great demand for country fairs and other outdoor ceremonies. He always attracts attention and starts a Moxie epidemic wherever he passes."

In June 1916, the Moxie Stilt Man was an attraction at a gathering of advertising men who were addressed by President Woodrow Wilson. Although newspaper photographs of the event pictured Wilson as one of many people in a large group, there was no difficulty in picking out the Moxie representative—the Stilt Man was the star of the show.

Fred Wilson sometimes discarded the Moxie costume for regular garb. In 1916 he went to Toronto, Canada, to help sell the Canadian equivalent of war bonds, walking "hundreds of miles through the streets of this city," according to an account.

Fred Wilson, the Moxie Stilt Man, is shown in a candid snapshot taken on May 10, 1916, possibly in New York City, for Wall Street is mentioned on nearby signs.

On June 29, 1916, President Woodrow Wilson addressed a group of advertising men at an outdoor rally in Philadelphia. The most prominent onlooker visible in the distance to the right was the Moxie Stilt Man, who managed to share publicity honors with the President.

An article in a Bangor, Maine newspaper noted that Wilson "has conquered the fox trot, the tango and other forms of modern and popular dances most successfully. He has covered the entire United States for The Moxie Company, leading many prominent parades through the country... He towers 15 feet above the sidewalk."

Archer was proud of Wilson, and in an interview noted that "one of the chief summer amusements is drinking Moxie. But if that isn't enough, Moxie furnishes all sorts of free amusement to the public through its features. There is Fred Wilson, for example. He is the champion stilt-walker of the world, bar none... All Wilson has to do is walk down any street and business and traffic are suspended."

Wilson was not without his problems, for at the Eastern Maine State Fair in the same year a drunken man accompanied by two young women, before whom he apparently desired to show off, seized him by one of his wooden legs and nearly upset him, according to a newspaper account. Fortunately, Wilson kept his equilibrium and no accident resulted. "Mr. Wilson carries a whip as a matter of some protection against animals and some reckless human beings, but has not used it for years," the notice continued. "It seemed he would have been justified in applying it most vigorously to the offender, but he refrained, as he did not desire any unpleasant notoriety. In 12 years the king of stilts has suffered but two serious accidents." In Sacramento, one of the stilts broke and he had an unfortunate fall, which disabled him for 14 weeks, readers were informed. In New York he fell over a wire which laid him up for many days. "He stated that if he had another accident, making the third, he should quit the business. Being a high-salaried man, he contemplates retiring from the business in a year or two. In any event he will then have a competence upon which to retire without financial worries. Mr. Wilson has a flattering offer to join the Ziegfeld Follies next winter, his dancing on stilts being a feature which is considered most valuable by the management of that famous organization."

Wilson, who made his home at 295 Huntington Avenue, Boston, was one of Archer's close friends. When distant from the Moxie office, Wilson regularly sent photographs back to headquarters. A later note, sent with a photograph on October 31, 1920, showed his respect for Archer's advertising ability:

"This picture taken at Market and Broad streets, Newark, New Jersey. Shows good action which is hard to get in a still picture. Wish you were using it in an ad on account of the manner in which you would handle the detail possibilities."

Above: Dorothy Russell, who made many public appearances for Moxie around 1920, is shown wearing a Moxie advertising jacket. Many varieties of these jackets were made during the late 'teens and early 1920s.

Right: A great attraction during the 'teens was Fred Wilson, the Moxie man on stilts, who made frequent public appearances in parades, at fairs, and other events, shown here at the "Stampede" held at Sheepshead Bay, New York, August 12, 1916.

Of all the Moxie publicity endeavors, from the Bottle Wagon to the giant bottles to Muriel Ostriche to the Stilt Man to the Moxie Boy with the pointing finger, none excited the public fancy more than the Horsemobile. This device, which Archer proudly stated was the greatest moving advertisement ever created, consisted of a car chassis on which a plaster, wood, or metal horse was mounted. Guidance was accomplished by a steering wheel mounted through the neck. Extensions made it possible to operate pedals and controls from the stirrups.

Although later stories were to obscure the true origin of the Horsemobile, contemporary newspaper articles, publicity releases, and company records show that the device was originated by Frank Archer early in 1916. It was not Archer's intention to use it in Moxie publicity. Rather, his son, Frank M. Archer, Jr., enjoyed automobiles, and his father created it for his son's use in an automobile parade in Brookline, Massachusetts. "The boy came out first and was awarded the prize. The horse worked so well that it was decided by The Moxie Company to use it as an advertisement. Two others were built," related Joe Doucette, an early Horsemobile driver.

Among the first press notices was an article in the Brookline *Townsman*, July 1, 1916, which noted in part:

"The Horsemobile is the latest thing in motor vehicles and will be seen for the first time by residents of Brookline on the fourth. It will be exhibited by Joe Doucette as a feature of the parade on that day and is sure to attract much attention. The Horsemobile, which was manufactured at a local garage by Mr. Doucette, assisted by J.P. Smith and J.J. Hoffman, consists of a wood and iron horse bolted to a runabout. The right-hand stirrup is the brake and the left-hand stirrup is the clutch. There is an emergency lever on the left-hand side. It is steered by a rod running up through the neck of the horse. The gasoline and spark are also operated through the neck..."

The rider of the Horsemobile was Joseph P. King, also known as "Moxie Joe," a name later given to all Horsemobile drivers. Using the stage name of Gen. Doucette, he had been a showman for many years. A Moxie publicity release noted that he had performed earlier on a unicycle on Boston's Tremont Street, lectured before police departments of large cities concerning the setting up of physical training apparatus, and went through the streets with a carpetbag and straw hat—obviously a colorful character. If that were not enough, he was a stuntman and often jumped from tall buildings without hurting himself.

Two press notices, actually advertisements placed by The Moxie Company, featuring the Horsemobile.

For The Moxie Company, years earlier he manned the Bottle Wagon at such far-flung outposts as Coney Island, Atlantic City, Washington, D.C. and Revere Beach. "In those days The Moxie Company was putting out coins about the size of a half dollar and constructed so as to ring like a genuine coin," a publicity release related. The reference apparently was to aluminum tokens, of light metal and quite unlike silver coins. The recollection may have been faulty, but in print it undoubtedly impressed many readers: "Moxie Joe used to visit the lobbies of the theatres when people were coming out, and drop one of the coins in such a manner that it would ring true. Everyone would fish for their pocketbooks and pockets, and there would be a congestion of people, all hunting for the money that had been dropped. Eventually they would find it, and it was good for a drink of Moxie at the Bottle Wagon. When Moxie Joe was discovered in these acts, he usually was met with courteous but forceful requests to vacate. In some instances, up to date managers, like Al Sheehan of the Tremont Theatre, used to engage him in conversation until the crowd had passed out. In no other way could the congestion be broken."

Apparently the eccentric Moxie representative was well-known to Boston theatre goers, for it was further related that "many first-nighters remember Moxie Joe as he was wont to purchase a front row seat in the orchestra, wait until the curtain went up, walk down the aisle about half way, take off his hat, exposing the illuminated letters DRINK MOXIE. It was often 15 or 20 minutes before he could be persuaded to leave the theatre. All eyes would be centered on him, and no play, however good, could hold the audience while Moxie Joe was performing."

Shortly after the turn of the century, Moxie Joe was a frequent sight at fairgrounds, often as a Bottle Wagon attendant, as noted. A favorite trick was to play the nephew to Reuben Ryder, a naive farmer who was tormented by a youngster and who chased after him, often with a prod used to encourage oxen. Occasionally, Uncle Reuben would appear to punish Moxie Joe severely with the device, causing the watching crowd to protest against Uncle's unfair treatment. "Sympathizing with Moxie Joe, they would lay down their nickels and get their money's worth in a glass of Moxie," it was related.

In one instance, Moxie Joe ventured to play the part of a "wild man" at a fair. He was put on a platform with 50 pounds of raw meat, while a barker told the audience, "We are going to feed the wild man." The crowd, disgusted, began to run in every direction. "In the mixup and excitement they let the wild man loose. He started

Horsemobile which recently created such a sensation in Boston and is now about to break into New York. At a little distance the contrivance looks like a large white horse, ridden by a jockey in his colors, pushing a new 1917 model Horsemobile. The horse, however, is not alive. The rider controls the motor from the horse."

In Lynn, Massachusetts, readers of the *Daily Evening Item* were treated to the following essay in the August 19, 1916 issue:

"Lynn got its first view of the much-heralded Moxie Horsemobile today and was in no way disappointed. Doubtless the Horsemobile is one of the most attractive forms of advertising ever utilized by The Moxie Company...

"The horse, dapple gray in color, and about the size of an ordinary driving horse, is mounted on an ordinarily constructed automobile chassis... General manager F.M. Archer of The Moxie Company is responsible for the idea. The Horsemobile was first constructed as a joke, but its instantaneous hit has so pleased the company that beginning next week it will be exhibited at all the fairs, even going throughout the West. The body of the horse is especially constructed of sheet iron, wood, and plaster and is solid and strong. The bridle, a beautiful piece of harness, was made in Mexico of plaited and colored horsehair.

"Of local interest is the fact that arrangements have been made for one of the young women appearing in the Lynn photoplay, *A Romance of Lynn*, to ride the animal across the range of the camera next week. Throughout the city streets the unique vehicle makes about 12 miles an hour, but it can be made to speed along at more than 40 miles. Thus far it has traveled some 2,000 miles. At the fairs is where it will be exhibited. Arrangements will be made for races between the Horsemobile and real horses.

"The jockey today stated that the Horsemobile was kind and gentle, suitable for a lady to drive, but that it was very difficult to keep clean and had an enormous appetite for high priced gasoline."

The Moxie Company was in its glory at the end of August at the Barnstable, Massachusetts fair. Although the second day of the event was officially designated as Governor's Day, the *Boston Herald* noted that history would remember it as "Moxie Day," for:

"In every part of the spacious grounds one encountered the word Moxie. Invariably a gift went with the name. Hundreds of Moxie bells, the famous stop-look-listen kind, were distributed. Moxie canes of special design were seized eagerly by youthful attendants. They were even more popular than the 'Charlie Chaplin' canes of a year ago. For the fairer sex there were thousands of Moxie fans, with pictures of such famous motion picture stars as Mary Pickford [sic] and Muriel Ostriche, to say nothing of Moxie 'Peggy,' imprinted on them. These, however, were merely souvenirs, compared with the more valuable Moxie Bailey Beach society coats of original designs. Hundreds of these were distributed and worn at once by the proud possessors. Then there was the Moxie Horsemobile, with Joe Doucette, its original jockey-chauffeur."

Among the prizes awarded at the Barnstable Fair were china breakfast and dinner sets, each piece with the portrait of Muriel Ostriche, 100 of the previously-mentioned Moxie canes, and 25 "society parasols." An account noted that "the life-size Moxie Boy cut-out, he of the wonderful eyes, is in evidence on all sides!"

The tried and true Moxie Bottle Wagon, drawn by real horse power, was not forgotten, for in the midst of the Moxie Horsemobile publicity, the *Boston Traveler* reported in August 1916 that during the morning rehearsal of *Very Good Eddie* at the Wilbur Theatre it was so hot that when someone cried out, "Oh, for something to drink!" this is what happened:

"The rehearsal broke up abruptly. To the utter surprise of the stage manager the entire company left the stage, made a dash for the door and hiked up the alley to Tremont Street. There one of the familiar Moxie Bottle Wagons had pulled up outside the theatre. With a rush the 'Very Good Eddies' took the wagon by storm. The genial Moxie Man had his hands full for the next 10 or 15 minutes. Moxie was the favorite beverage of the day. At length, with spirits renewed, the company trailed back to the theatre. There the rehearsal was resumed with such pep and enthusiasm that the deserted stage manager, after his morning work was completed, followed the example of his company, stepped into the nearest drug store, and ordered himself a Moxie."

Before a month had passed, the Moxie Horsemobile developed into a caravan. Accompanying it were two other Moxie cars, a large Buick decorated in green and gold and occupied by L.A. Hager, and a smaller car with A.W. Hodgman, although the drivers often switched vehicles.

On October 31, 1916, the New Britain (Connecticut) *Herald* recited some Moxie history:

" 'MOXIE HORSE' HERE. Famous animal makes his appearance on the city streets and acts like any Kentucky thoroughbred—

The "Very Good Eddie" Company
Stopping to refresh themselves on their way from rehearsal with
VERY GOOD MOXIE

In the midst of a rehearsal, the company of actors and actresses from the stage production "Very Good Eddie" ran out into the street and patronized the Moxie Bottle Wagon. The event was duly recorded by a photographer and used in Moxie advertising, as shown above.

Moxie Horsemobile

EQUIPPED WITH LEE TIRES

A tire performance probably unequalled, because it showed their use under every conceivable kind of condition that a tire could ever be called upon to meet.

This truly most famous publicity feature that has ever been put out by anyone started from Boston, Massachusetts, early in 1916, covering Massachusetts, Maine, New Hampshire, Vermont, Rhode Island, Connecticut, New Jersey, and Greater New York; finally winding up in the middle of December, owing to the weather being rather chilly for the jockey, Moxie Joe.

Besides covering the immense territory and mileage referred to, it was displayed in show windows, and was in most every kind of garage that has ever been built, and of course in conditions of territory where there was no such thing as a garage; parked on fair grounds, village greens, city corners, parks, etc.; up mountains, down gullies, over the latest boulevard roads; over trails, and re-built country roads where they pride themselves on throwing the dirt into the centre of the street and letting the autos tread it down; at fair grounds where special guards were required to keep the crowds at bay, racing for a record at city and country fairs, keeping pace with country bands on their way to the fair grounds, and in various processions in various towns and cities, in which it took part.

During this entire time there was never a change of tires; it wound up with the original tires it started with, and apparently in as good condition as when it left. As far as observation goes, the tires appear to be good for another season.

Probably never were tires subjected to so many conditions and to so hard tests.

If You Desire to Operate Your Car
Without Tire Trouble, *Use Lee Tires*

Geo. W. MacBride & Co., Inc.
N. E. Distributor for Lee Tires and Four-Wheel Drive Trucks

Motor Mart   6 Columbus Ave.   Boston

Write for Details Concerning Open Territory

A Lee Tires advertisement featuring the Moxie Horsemobile.

"At last the famous horse of Church Street has arrived in the shape of the Moxie Horse. His advent has been heralded for the past two weeks in the local papers [by advertisements placed by the Moxie Company] and many were the curious ones that gathered on the street corners to look at the creamy white steed as he rode the streets. The horse with 'Moxie Joe' driving is touring the New England states and has already visited Maine, New Hampshire, Vermont, Massachusetts, and Connecticut, traveling over 8,000 miles. The horse is mounted on the chassis of a small automobile and is driven and controlled by the man known as 'Moxie Joe,' who rides the Kentucky thoroughbred. His mane is braided with red, white, and blue ribbons and he wears a bridle that is woven out of real horsehair at a cost of $75. At the various country fairs that he has visited, many presents of blankets, whips, drinking pails and bridles have been received by his rider and master.

"While in the state of Vermont the keys to the state were presented to the Moxie Horse by the State Fair officials for doing a mile on the track in two minutes. At most of the fairs, exhibition miles are done on the race track in remarkably fast time. It is an easy thing for the horse to make 60 to 75 miles on the road each day. The only advertising matter on either animal or driver is a red sash worn by the driver and containing the word Moxie.

"With the animal on this tour are two sister automobiles, one being the gold-leaf car driven by A.W. Hodgman. This car has been covered with gold leaf at a cost of $1,200 and makes a very smart appearance with its green trimmings. The other is painted a cream color, having a gold strip, and is driven by L.A. Hager. The machines are to proceed from here to New York, where they will stop off on their way to Washington, D.C."

By August 1917, The Moxie Company had five Horsemobiles in service. By that time Joseph P. King had traveled through eight states and covered 12,000 miles in the original Horsemobile unit. Other Horsemobiles racked up additional mileage. It became the custom to herald the Moxie Horsemobile in advance by running "news" articles in local papers and, finally, printing large illustrated advertisements. In some locations, large cardboard cut-outs of the Horsemobile and rider were leaned against the inside of store windows lining the planned Horsemobile route. Text on the back side of the large and impressive placards reprinted earlier newspaper notices. While most areas were delighted to have the Horsemobile, occasionally problems were encountered, as in New York City where a special permit had to be acquired to drive the unit the length of Manhattan down to Wall Street.

In 1919 the H.D. Beach Company, Coshocton, Ohio, made toy Moxie Horsemobiles lithographed on thin steel panels. These two-dimensional toys, lithographed on both sides, were made in two colors, with a black horse and red car (as shown above) and with a white horse and blue car (the lower illustration). The flat panels, which were printed in the same colors on each side, were distributed in kit form. The recipient had to attach the wheels by means of bending flat metal strips in the proper position. In later years, these toys became popular Moxie collectibles.

A September 26, 1917 newspaper clipping datelined Shippensburg, Pennsylvania, told of an unfortunate incident:

"Monday afternoon, about five o'clock, Mr. J.P. King of Boston, Massachusetts, who drives the famous Moxie auto horse, a replica of a horse mounted on a Maxwell chassis, and as well known in the advertising world as the famous 20-mule team, met with an accident near Centerville. As they reached that point, a four-mule team, which was in front of them, suddenly became unruly and in order to avoid killing or injuring one of the animals, if not the driver, Mr. King swerved his machine to one side and in so doing ran into an abutment, badly bending one of the axles. Mr. W.E. Fowle, of Danville, Pennsylvania, the state representative of The Moxie Company, was driving along in his big yellow car and towed the damaged car [to a garage where repairs were made]."

Sometime during this era, Theodore Roosevelt was photographed perched atop a Horsemobile. Perhaps it was this event which inspired The Moxie Company to place advertisements urging the adoption of a nationwide yearly celebration of the former president's birthday.

Horsemobile accessories were devised. Balloons printed with the Horsemobile image and lollipops in the shape of the Horsemobile were popular with kiddies along the route. On February 5, 1919, it was reported that "as fast as conditions, manufacturing, etc. will justify, a miniature Moxie Horsemobile will be created." Made by the H.D. Beach Company of Coshocton, Ohio, miniature horsemobile metal toys in two formats—blue with a white horse and red with a black horse— were widely distributed later in the same year. Still later, in 1925, came crystal set radios adapted by a Boston firm from toy Horsemobiles, but these were produced in small quantities.

In May 1919, the Horsemobile was pressed into service to sell bonds for the Victory Loan. Journeying through Maine, Joseph P. King stated that by the time he arrived in Waterville, $100,000 worth of bonds had been sold to interested spectators. An article published in the Manchester (New Hampshire) *Union* May 19, 1919, noted:

"The Moxie Liberty Horsemobile and [its chauffeur] arrived in the city this morning from Lewiston, Maine for the purpose of boosting the Liberty Loan drive in the city. The Horsemobile attracted a great deal of attention and is entirely new to anything that has ever been displayed in this city. It has been a great help toward putting the loan over the top through the state of Maine and is expected to help New Hampshire a great deal while on its tour. The machine was displayed at the Amoskeag Mills at the noon hour, where large crowds gathered to look it over. This evening the machine will be

The George Wilcox automobile agency afforded overnight storage for the Moxie Horsemobile, here shown with the horse displayed in the front window—a curiosity for passersby.

Moxie Horsemobile on an Essex chassis, circa 1925, photographed in an unknown location. From a scrapbook of various Horsemobile photographs kept by Frank M. Archer.

seen at Lake Massabesic and Pine Island Park. It was displayed at the mills at 5:30 p.m."

On the next day the *Daily Patriot*, Concord, New Hampshire, noted that Joseph P. King, dressed as a cowboy, was the driver of the Horsemobile which "takes the place of war tanks in cities and towns where they are unable to go during this great drive for the Fifth Liberty Loan."

In May 1919, two Horsemobile units left Boston and set out across the country to the West Coast. The Moxie Company planned the route carefully and sent newspaper notices in advance. Drivers were J.S. Mole and Joseph P. King. "Although the riders are real, their mounts were only life-size models of the real things placed upon Maxwell and Dort automobile bodies," noted a Cambridge, Ohio newspaper on August 15th. The trip westward must have taken its toll, for the Dort Horsemobile, Dort factory serial No. 24,114 and Moxie inventory No. 75, on the ledgers at a cost of $1,486.34, was sold for $200 to G.E. Greene on December 30, 1920.

In later years, many New Englanders would have fond memories of the Horsemobile from their childhoods. In 1984, Elizabeth Bywater was one of several such people furnishing recollections to the author. She reminisced:

"I remember the Moxie horse and see it in my mind right now so clearly. Mounted on a chassis was a life-size white horse. A Groton [Massachusetts] man, the late Paul Blood, was the driver. The steering wheel was in the center of the neck, with brake, clutch, and other things worked by hand. Paul was splendid in a uniform of black trimmed with red and gold—such a sight to behold! It was, I believe, around 65 years ago, as I am now 71 years old. His arrival in town was heralded by one neighbor to the next calling, 'Paul and his Moxie horse are coming.' Then everyone would get out of their homes and wave and cheer. Even the shopkeepers would make an appearance. Paul was always so happy to see each of us and would wave and call each by name. It was the big event in town. Then Paul would go to the surrounding areas. If only I had a picture.

"Also, my father was a telephone repairman and used to work on the telephones of Mr. Hager, an important person in the Moxie organization, who lived in a beautiful home in Littleton, Massachusetts. When Papa went to service the phones, many times Mr. Hager would be home. He would have a nice visit with Papa and give him a box of Moxie lollipops. These were all different colors and shaped like animals. Of course they were Moxie-flavored. They were such a nice treat and were shared with our neighbors and children. I truly was never very fond of Moxie—it reminded me of a miserable medicine Mamma insisted I take—perhaps to ward off the 'evil spirits.' "

Another old-timer recalled:

"It was a big day when the Moxie automobile horse came to town each year. It was in a parade, and no matter what else was in the parade, all eyes waited for the Moxie horse and rider to come by. Once the rider was a cowgirl with long flaming red hair. It was truly sensational.

"After the parade ended, the driver would park the car and let children climb up into the saddle where they could have their pictures taken.

"Then there were usually lots of gifts for the kids. I remember lollipops, fans, and balloons. Moxie was wonderful, and the company that produced Moxie always treated the public to a good time. It is a shame that today more companies aren't like the Moxie organization. I suppose that such a thing would be called commercial now, but back then Moxie was a part of our life, and the more Moxie things we saw, the more we liked it."

A 1922 newspaper clipping told of the search for a new Moxie Girl, at a time when Muriel Ostriche was a rapidly fading screen memory:

"Mr. Witschi has just returned to the home office at Boston after a trip which started July 6th, 1921 and terminated July 26, 1922, during which time he covered Maine, New Hampshire, Vermont, Massachusetts, Rhode Island, Connecticut, New York, New Jersey, Pennsylvania, Delaware, District of Columbia, Virginia, West Virginia, Ohio, and Michigan. We will leave to your imagination the thousands of large cities and small towns through which he rode, as no city was too large and no 'four corners' too small for a visit... During this trip, thousands upon thousands of snapshots were taken of men, women, and children of all walks of life, on the back of the famous Moxie Horsemobile, which is admitted to be the moving phenomenon of publicity.

"Mr. Witschi has arrived just in time to start out with new additions to this famous family...which will cover the shore resorts from the Delaware Gap to Bar Harbor. In each and every place he will make a special effort to see the prettiest 'miss' in town, as an effort is now being made to locate a 'little Miss Moxie' who will be 100% American and have all the qualities and qualifications essential to warrant her being adopted as Miss Moxie. That is, she should be

Arnault Edgerly, then vice-president of The Moxie Company, was shown with the Rolls-Royce Horsemobile at the South Shore Horse Show, described in the *Boston Herald*, September 1, 1931. The Rolls-Royce unit was featured in many Moxie advertisements during the period. When the *Moxie Song*, copyrighted in 1930 (an adaptation of an early song by the same name copyrighted in 1921), appeared, it featured on the cover a color representation of the Rolls-Royce Horsemobile. A metallic cigarette lighter produced during the same period also featured this unit, as did a wide variety of metal signs (which showed the Rolls-Royce with a 1933 Massachusetts license plate). The Rolls-Royce had an unfortunate accident and was overturned in a ditch. Repaired, it saw service for a number of years thereafter, finally meeting an ignominious end in a junkyard.

In August 1931, a LaSalle Horsemobile driven by D.J. Callahan visited the Lehighton (Pennsylvania) Bottling Co., a Moxie distributorship owned by Justin Dunbar. The Horsemobile influenced Mr. Dunbar, for soon he fashioned a large wooden two-dimensional horse which he mounted on a truck in front of his factory.

In 1932 a "Horsemobile" trailer was made at a cost of $450. Designed to be towed behind a regular Horsemobile, the unit consisted of a small trailer with a low flat bed on which was mounted a standing horse. The unit failed to excite public curiosity and was used for just a short time.

An article in the *Boston Traveler*, September 19, 1933, noted that "Frank Archer now has a stable of five Moxie Horsemobiles." Not mentioned were two "lame" units stored but not used. In 1935, six Horsemobiles were used, with No. 154, the Rolls-Royce, receiving the most attention (at least the gasoline bills for it were higher, according to the meticulous records entered each month in the company ledgers).

Horsemobiles were last used actively during the early 1950s. Eventually, all went to the scrap heap, except for a single unit, a LaSalle, which was preserved in derelict condition, after having last seen service about 1954. Hoping for a revival of its earlier glories, the Moxie-Monarch-NuGrape Company had it restored by a Massachusetts specialist, and during the 1970s it was featured in many places from Atlanta to Maine. At a July 1984 gathering of Moxie enthusiasts and historians in Union, Maine, the LaSalle was a featured attraction. By the end of the same year, some organizational changes were contemplated, and it was anticipated that the soft-drink branch of the company, by then known as Moxie Industries, would be spun off to Frank Armstrong, earlier chief executive of the company. On

In the 1930s, The Moxie Company used metal cigarette lighters featuring the Rolls-Royce Horsemobile. The above is an enlarged illustration.

The Moxie Horse Trailer, shown in tow behind a Moxie Horsemobile, was used for a short time during the 1930s. Built at a cost of less than $500 it failed to attract the interest of the public and was soon discarded.

Another view of the Moxie Horse Trailer, shown here as part of the Moxie Caravan.

Charles Adams of the Adams Bottling Works is shown astride a Moxie LaSalle Horsemobile in 1931. He also drove a small cyclecar with a Moxie bottle on the radiator and a Moxie sign on the hood.

The Moxie Rolls-Royce Horsemobile is shown in Roxbury on an early spring day.

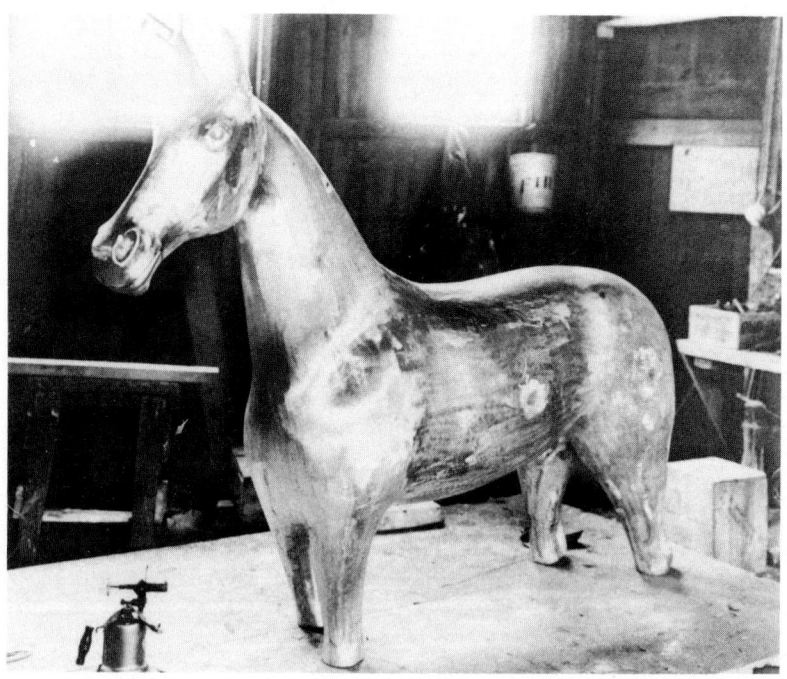

This unusual photograph from the archives of the The Moxie Company shows a newly-molded aluminum horse, a process in the creation of a Moxie Horsemobile, probably in the late 1920s.

Moxie Horsemobiles often traveled in groups during the 1930-1933 period and were referred to as the "Moxie Caravan." Often such a parade consisted of five or six Horsemobiles, but the above photograph shows just three, led by the Rolls-Royce behind a police motorcycle.

Frank M. Archer, Jr. stands beside the Rolls-Royce Moxie Horsemobile, leader of the Horsemobile fleet during the 1930s.

Above: A parade of six Horsemobiles, led by a LaSalle, followed by the Rolls-Royce, in a snapshot taken in the early 1930s.

Right: In downtown Boston a Horsemobile advertises an event at the Tremont Theatre.

Below: An entourage of Horsemobiles calls on a Moxie distributor in the early 1930s.

The Moxie Rolls-Royce Horsemobile, with balding tires, was a featured attraction at an outing held by the Nationwide Service Grocers, Salem (Massachusetts) Division, at Centennial Grove on June 8, 1932.

At the time the Rolls-Royce was the war horse of the Horsemobile fleet. By early the next year the odometer had racked up 100,000 miles! Made at the American Rolls-Royce factory in Springfield, Massachusetts, the unit was No. 154 in The Moxie Company's fleet (such numbers being continuous from the early days and not representing the vehicles in use at any one time). In the 1930s, seven Moxie Horsemobiles were a part of the firm's entourage of motor vehicles, which also included numerous salesmen's cars, delivery trucks, and others.

A scene in the parking lot of Moxieland, circa 1931, shows three of seven Horsemobiles then in use. At the time they often rode in caravans and were familiar sights in Boston and surrounding areas.

An unfortunate incident in Horsemobile history: The Rolls-Royce Horsemobile, pride of the fleet, is shown overturned in a ditch.

A LaSalle Horsemobile in action in Massachusetts in 1930.

Another view of the LaSalle.

December 20, 1984 the remaining original Horsemobile was sold to the author and Eddie Clark, thus starting a new chapter in its history.

Although the Moxie Horsemobile was far and away Moxie's most prominent news subject in 1916 and the years immediately following, other events were worthy of notice.

Due to the exigencies of the war, which resulted in coal and power shortages, shipping restrictions, and other problems, federal fuel administrator Dr. Harry A. Garfield, a very controversial figure, decreed that certain non-essential businesses had to close down at intervals during the winter in early 1918. The Moxie Company on January 17, 1918, posted a notice that all manufacturing and business facilities would be closed from the 18th through the 22nd, and that "only such work will be permitted to be done within the manufacturing establishments as can be done without the use of heat or light... All employees will enjoy full pay at the time."

A couple of months later, Billy B. Van, described as "one of Frank Archer's friends," and as "one of the most prosperous actors in America," and who owned a farm in New Hampshire, took time out from his appearance in the stage production of *The Rainbow Girl* to visit Archer in his office at the Moxie plant. In an advertisement, Archer praised Van's abilities, and in turn the actor, who was not only a comedian but also the operator of "one of the best hygienic dairies in New England," told how sparkling clean the facilities appeared to be. A view of the Moxie enterprise at the time appeared in print in the words of Billy B. Van, undoubtedly coached by Frank Archer:

"I accepted an invitation to visit the Moxie plant. We journeyed to the top floor, a beautiful room with white floors and ceilings and hygienic floors. This was the extract and syrup room where the roots and herbs are prepared. Along one side were immense tanks in which the herbs are assembled. The tanks were white and spotlessly clean. In another section of the room were great percolators suspended from the ceiling, in which the juices of the roots [gentian root] and herbs were being percolated and carried into covered glass carboys. The combining of the simple syrup, extract, roots and herbs, and the burnt caramel was all done here."

He related that a soaking and sterilizing machine could process 48,000 bottles every eight hours, and that a battery of jumbo automatic fillers could handle 1,200 bottles each per hour when working to capacity. During the preceding August the plant took in 1,200,000 empty bottles and filled them with Moxie, working without any overtime. Employee benefits were then discussed by Billy Van:

"Never did I see so much enthusiasm amongst employees who have spent the greater part of their lives in an industry, each trying to do his utmost in the best possible manner, as in this institution only the best counts. During the busiest times, and especially the hot weather, an attendant serves Moxie, ice cream and cake, as the work goes on, without limit. Rest rooms, etc. are provided, as are facilities for preparing meals, etc., for the lunch hours. Phonographs with the latest records, singing, telling stories, and the imparting of up to date news is encouraged."

Around the same time, Laura Walker, who was appearing as the leading lady in *The Man Who Came Back* at the Plymouth Theatre, posed for her portrait to appear on a Moxie hand-held cardboard fan. "Miss Laura during the operation was quite patient and submissive, like the role she plays in the now-famous melodrama," reported a Boston paper.

Another Archer friend, Jack Donahue, was featured as "Jack Moxie Donahue" in a Moxie ad, which helped the actor by depicting him as a cop directing traffic, inviting people to see his production of *Angel Face* at the Colonial Theatre. An article on the same subject noted that Marguerite Zender, who played the leading female part in *Angel Face*, was looking for a stage name and had considered "Angela Moxie," among others. The production was directed by George Lederer, another Archer acquaintance, and the comedy was by Victor Herbert. These two men were the subjects of a Moxie article in the *Boston Post* which noted:

"In a discussion by Messrs. Herbert and Lederer on Moxie and its advertising, each tried to outdo the other in the number of years they had been drinkers of Moxie and familiar with its unique and distinctive methods of advertising distribution and its close association as a beverage with the theatrical profession, which it is fair to say numbers many hundreds of thousands, and that the profession has no peers. A recent Moxie ad, with the famous Moxie Bottle Wagon, started the discussion by Mr. Lederer, who told of the difficulty that was encountered in trying to get one of the famous Moxie Bottle Wagons on the roof of the Casino Theatre in New York at the time when the Casino was the musical comedy center of the world, and when under the management of Canary & Lederer, at the time referred to, that phenomenal success, *The Belle of New York*, was having its introductory production."

July 1933: The Moxie LaSalle Horsemobile and the Moxie car are featured attractions in the Legion Day Parade, Harrisburg, Pennsylvania.

D.J. Callahan drives the Moxie LaSalle Horsemobile in this October 7, 1932 photograph taken at the Forest Festival, Elkins, West Virginia.

1919 was the eve of Prohibition, which became nationwide the following year. An illustrated article in the *Public Ledger Pictorial* depicted the bar in the old King George Hotel, New York City, the first "dry" bar in the town, "now run by the Salvation Army, with everything intact from the bar except the drinks." An attendant was shown pouring Moxie from a bottle, and in the background a Moxie sign appeared prominently on the back mirror.

Someone suggested that with Prohibition coming, the name of the town of Rye, New York should be changed. "It will never do to have a town with a name like that under the dry regime. Such a name would be too suggestive and would bring back memories. Before we change the name of this town we will listen to suggestions for a new name," noted a newspaper article. "Some of these have already been received from readers." Among those submitted was Moxie, New York!

During the war, a tax on sodas, soft drinks, and ice cream was levied when such were served at soda fountains and ice cream parlors. Moxie led the fight in New England for the repeal of this, stating that these were really food items and pointing out the illogic that the same drinks and ice cream were not taxed when served in restaurants.

Sugar was in short supply toward the end of 1919, and rationing was in effect. Frank Archer gained much public acclaim when he announced that he would turn over an allotment of three boxcars full of sugar to the public for distribution among hospitals, families, and small manufacturers. It was midwinter, Moxie sales were at a seasonal low (for the best sales were always in July and August), and "Mr. Archer decided to use it to relieve the shortage which will be felt keenly, especially as Christmas approaches."

The Moxie Bottle Wagon met its demise, and after 1919 the units were simply fond memories, although one or two may have survived in storage. The year before, Bottle Wagon No. 27, in storage in Allentown, Pennsylvania, was ordered broken up on August 3rd, and the value on the books, $186, was written off. In 1919, Bottle Wagon No. 39, valued at $207.50 and stored with C.F. Adams, Lancaster, Pennsylvania, was destroyed. On August 4, 1920 Frank Archer wrote off as "out of use and unsalable" Bottle Wagon No. 31 at Wakefield, Rhode Island (on the books at $450), No. 45 at Ritterville, Pennsylvania ($450), No. 41 at Boston ($385), No. 29 at Boston ($450) and Bottle Wagon accessories for $20. Various horse-drawn delivery wagons were sold for next to nothing or simply scrapped.

An early mention of Frank Archer's son appeared in the same year. The *Boston American*, February 14, 1919, carried this notice:

"Frank Archer, Jr., son of Mr. & Mrs. Frank Archer of 762 Washington Street, Brookline, who has been dangerously ill with pneumonia at the home of his parents, is now out of danger, although he is very weak. Archer, who is 15 years of age and attending preparatory school, is said to be the best amateur shot in the state for his age and is very well known by local enthusiasts of hunting, riding, and fishing. Despite his splendid physical condition this is his second attack of influenza, having been first stricken in September."

The junior Archer, for whom the first Horsemobile was allegedly constructed nearly three years earlier, recovered nicely and went on to engage in many sporting pleasures. The son of a wealthy man, the younger Archer had many opportunities. Several years later, on October 2, 1925, a photograph of him with his horse "Moxie" appeared in the *Boston Globe*. Moxie and his rider were a talented combination and were winners in the jumping class. Automobile racing, polo, and sport fishing were other interests. Unlike his father, who kept his nose to the grindstone and who rarely left the office, Frank M. Archer, Jr. took ample time to pursue leisure activities.

Chapter 12

The TNT Cowboy

In March 1919, Frank M. Archer's rags-to-riches tale, *The TNT Cowboy*, was printed. A slim pocket-size purple-covered volume, *The TNT Cowboy* told the story of Fred, a New York chap with New England forebears, who overcame many adversities and through the dint of hard work achieved financial success and the girl of his dreams.

Shortly thereafter, in May 1919, a second printing appeared with a white covering and gold letters, and the addition of illustrations and the note: "The author is deeply indebted to 'Calder' for the following illustrations..." Depicted were scenes from the melodramatic episode, including "Horsemobile," "Fred Conquers 'Wild Mike,' " "Fred Catching Overland Express," and others.

Copyrighted by Archer himself, the title and introductory pages to the book bear no mention of The Moxie Company. That awaits the story text. Archer was 57 years old in 1919, and around this time he sought to gain personal recognition by featuring his name on all sorts of Moxie Company products, ranging from fans to posters, perhaps as compensation for his trivial 1% stock ownership in the company (he continued to own only 50 of 5,000 shares). The story of the TNT Cowboy is undoubtedly a microcosm of Archer's own life, for when The Moxie Company is mentioned in the text, the Advertising Department of the firm, which in real life Archer so capably headed, is featured as the key to Moxie's success.

There are also parallels between the TNT Cowboy and the life of Theodore Roosevelt. "The strenuous life" described the style of Fred in *The TNT Cowboy*, while the same term was used on a Moxie poster featuring Theodore Roosevelt approximately two decades earlier at the turn of the century. Like Fred, Roosevelt was from the East but went out West, where he engaged in ranching, later returning.

A direct connection can be established with "A Midnight Adven-

THE
TNT
COWBOY

[TRADE MARK]

BY

F.M. ARCHER

Title page of "The TNT Cowboy," written by Frank M. Archer by dictating the text to his secretary, Belle Voge, in little over an hour's time early in 1919. The slim volume, which went through at least two printings, chronicled the exploits of strenuous Fred and the love of his life, Betty. After the book saw print, Archer went on to expand the characters of the book, especially the personality of Betty, far beyond what the printed pages indicated. Indeed, Betty in particular seems to have been Archer's dream girl, and much time, effort, and expense was spent composing advertisements about her. It was said that Betty was inspired by a Chelsea girl, possibly someone admired by Archer, for advertisements about her were placed on many occasions in Chelsea newspapers.

ture," a short tale related in advertisements of The Moxie Company earlier, one appearing in the February 4, 1919 issue of the *Boston American* being representative. This tale told of Fred Stone, an actor who was starring in the stage production *Jack O'Lantern*, who had a ranch on Long Island. "It had been a strenuous day," the tale began. Fred and his consort Violet had been busy with broncos and other animals. On the way home from an evening's relaxation he saw the Moxie Horsemobile ridden by Big Red, a disgruntled cowboy he had earlier discharged. Later in the tale, Fred rescued a lass who had been captured by Big Red, becoming a hero in the process. The story of Fred Stone, and Archer's own ideas, set Archer to thinking. It wasn't long thereafter that *The TNT Cowboy* was written, or, rather, dictated. Archer's secretary, Belle Voge, told a newspaper reporter:

"WORKS WITH DYNAMIC FORCE. Belle Voge, private secretary to F.M. Archer, general manager of The Moxie Company, and author of *The TNT Cowboy*, says that taking Mr. Archer's dictation taxes one almost beyond measure, that the dictation is volcanic, delivered with lightning-like repetity, but in such plain, understandable English as to require practically no changes or modifications. As an illustration she says:

" 'On Saturday morning, March 1, 1919, 10 o'clock I was called to Mr. Archer's office and took the dictation of the story of the TNT Cowboy. Mr. Archer used no notes whatever. The dictation was completed at quarter before 12, only one and three-quarters hours time being consumed. Upon transcribing the notes I found it practically unnecessary to make any changes. That the story is interesting is evidenced from the many personal letters, which are tremendously flattering, received by the author from men and women in every walk of life. I feel honored at being chosen to take this dictation.

" 'While much has been said about Betty, the wonderful character inspired by a Chelsea girl, Fred must not be overlooked, although not a Chelsea boy. That he is a TNT in many forms is putting it mildly. Woe to the white slavers who wait for their prey and live off their earnings and drag them further and further into degradation, if they come within his reach, as manliness, cleanliness and right living constitute Fred's middle name. Remember how he handled "Red" and other gangsters. Later you are to hear of his treatment of the wife and children neglecter.

" 'It is not out of place to say that these stories in a way are a diversion for Mr. Archer from his many important and trying duties. From titles and memoranda I find on his desk, I shall not be surprised any day to be called upon to take dictation for the following:

READ
THE **T.N.T.**
COWBOY

DISCUSSING
STRENUOUS LIFE

A scene from "The TNT Cowboy" is featured on the back of this hand-held Moxie fan from the 1919 period. It could be that the cowboy in fur(?) pants, sitting on the Moxie crates and smoking a cigarette, is non other than Fred, the strenuous hero of the fanciful tale. Actually, a reading of the text of Frank Archer's story does not identify this scenario, nor does this picture appear in the book.

'My Duxbury Girl,' 'Why Mollie Takes Such An Early Car,' and 'White Slavers' Gal.' If titles mean anything, something interesting I am sure is to come. Therefore one must always be steeled to expect a call to take and transcribe matters shot at one with lightning-like repetity and dynamic force.

" 'In closing it seems but natural that I have my say about Vice-President Archer, feeling well qualified to do so on account of my 15 years' association. While he is most resourceful, energetic, inventive, and an original genius who works with dynamic force, back of all of this is manliness, truthfulness, and kindness. It is a matter of public note that there are no 'help' or 'employees' in the Moxie business throughout the United States—from the highest to the lowest position, everyone is an 'associate' and is so regarded...' "

Throughout the balance of 1919, and well into the early 1920s, the theme of *The TNT Cowboy* was carried through to many Moxie advertising and promotional themes. When Ann Pennington, the actress, was scheduled to appear at the Colonial Theatre in 1919, Moxie's advertising copy intrigued readers by suggesting that she *might* appear as Betty, one of the main characters in Archer's story. Similarly, visitors to the Lewiston (Maine) Fair were exhorted to read *The TNT Cowboy* before attending, for a pageant involving the TNT Cowboy theme was scheduled. At one time a musical play based on the book was staged and received mixed reviews.

To further promote the book, Archer caused the popular series of Moxie cardboard fans to be redesigned. Instead of patriotic music on the back of each, for the ending of hostilities in the Great War (World War I) had lessened the fervor, logical replacements were scenes from *The TNT Cowboy*, with one fan showing "Fred Conquers 'Wild Mike', " a bronco-busting episode. "READ THE T.N.T. COWBOY" commanded the inscription on the back of each fan. Whether or not periods should be used, and whether it should be stated as T.N.T. or simply TNT, was never standardized, but the book was done in the TNT (without periods) format.

Notwithstanding the sales efforts of The Moxie Company and Frank M. Archer, *The TNT Cowboy* apparently achieved rather modest sales, as evidenced by the scarcity of remaining examples today. To the present-day reader the text reads jerkily, often skipping from one theme to another without warning.

The tale begins with the early career of the hero:

"Fred was born on the upper east side of Fifth Avenue, New York. His parents were sturdy New England stock. His mother was noted for being the best cook in the neighborhood and also one to be called on and sought after when there was any trouble. His father was a man of great business and mechanical ability and sort of 'Papa' of the neighborhood," the first paragraph relates.

"Fred attended the public schools and developed into a husky, sturdy young fellow. On account of his clean living methods and his love of all kinds of athletic sports he was the life of every party. He also had the many usual harmless schoolboy love affairs. Finally graduating with honors from school, Fred's father and mother strongly urged a college course, but Fred overruled them on this and won them over to his way of thinking so that after graduation the family decided that Fred was to be a statesman and lawyer. His father secured a clerkship for him with one of the great law firms of the metropolis."

Fred approached his new position with enthusiasm, delving into Blackstone and other legal references. As it happened, his first task was to evict a Mr. Cobb from his modest home on New York City's upper West Side. He could not come to throw the parents, a grandfather, and three young children out in the street, especially since the mother was ill and the father had been out of work due to an injury. "The Cobbs had lived in this same house for twenty-four years and enjoyed the respect of everyone except a few tradesmen with whom they had gotten behind in their accounts." In an era in which small-time merchants, particularly those of foreign extraction, were viewed with jaundice, Archer continued the tale: "One of these tradesmen who was pressing the claim was one of the recently arrived merchants in this country, and who believed that the pound of flesh was due him, and that he owed no consideration or thought to the well-being or consideration of others... [Fred visited the demanding merchant] to see if some adjustment could not be made. He had some difficulty in understanding all the merchant said because it required what is called a motion reader as well as a linguist to understand him, that is, the merchant had so many movements of his hands, shoulders, hips, etc., trying to illustrate his language, that it was difficult to understand him. Finally it was apparent to Fred that he would not relent, not give them any extension of time, and would not reduce the account for cash."

True to the theme of a hero, Fred analyzed his own modest savings account balance, withdrew the necessary funds, and paid the Cobbs' debt of two months' rent, "then gave each of the Cobbs enough money to tie them over their difficulties, notwithstanding their most strenuous protestations."

This task awakened hero Fred to the realization that "if it were part of the duties of a lawyer to turn poor people into the street, he had all of the law business he wanted." True to form, he returned to the office, submitted his resignation, and told his family. His

believed that this was good business, and especially necessary as there were two or three of the 'Settee Johnnies' there who could only clean their fingernails and look out at the windows. Fred realized, however, that their small and undeveloped brains were capable of throwing out innuendoes, providing they could do so anonymously. A force of celebrated accountants were called in, and went over the accounts and verified them to the last penny."

The melodramatic tale continues as: "Papa Smith, who had formed an attachment for the 'Non-Highbrow' Fred, felt that perhaps he might have done him an injustice, in a way, and sought to ease his conscience, as it were, by handing Fred his personal check for $2,500, which Fred spurned, but suggested, however, that Mr. Smith apply it to the Salvation Army, Red Cross, YMCA, Knights of Columbus, or some other organization that could use it for the benefit for many needy ones who would probably apply it much more usefully than Mr. Smith, and very much less selfishly."

After some introspection at home, Fred decided to pack up his belongings and follow the course of the setting sun, buying a ticket for Lincoln, Oklahoma, without the slightest idea of what he was going to do upon arrival. When the train halted, he found Lincoln to be little more than a way station with a watering tank, general store, and a few utility shops. It happened to be Saturday, the first day of the month, a time when the ranchmen came to town to arrange for supplies and provisions for the coming weeks. "Fred made known to each one that he was seeking a position as a cowboy. Naturally many of them grinned and pointed at him and called him a tenderfoot." A cowboy who had imbibed too much taunted Fred and with a lariat roped him and dragged him off his feet. Strenuous Fred was not one to take this lying down, so he sprang up and promptly flattened the offender. This put him on equal footing with the bystanders, and Fred became "one of the gang."

Employment was not to be offered, but the suggestion was made that Fred would do well to attend a forthcoming rodeo to demonstrate what he could do.

"Finally, the day of the roundup came and an announcement was made that an eastern tenderfoot would undertake to ride 'Wild Mike,' the wildest, worse, bucking bronco in the world. A great laugh went up from the thousands assembled. They had seen so many tenderfoots try the test and go back East sadder but wiser boys. The bronco was roped, dragged into the ring, promptly tied by the cowboys with their lariats running around the pummel of their own saddles, their broncos being trained to the minute not to move until they said the word. Fred was thrown onto the back of the bronco, the wild

FRED CONQUERS WILD MIKE

Seeking a change in his life, Fred journeyed westward, where he landed a job on a cattle ranch. Scorned as a tenderfoot, Fred proved his mettle by conquering Wild Mike, a bronco which had been the undoing of all those who had tried to ride him earlier.

vicious, bucking bronco, and he bucked as a bronco never bucked before. However, he had Fred on his back, who had been transposed from the ballroom boy of the East to the determined ranchman of the West. His riding in the East and his strenuous exercise and training gave him the agility, nerve, and strength which far exceeded that of the plainsmen who were being saved only from a life of complete breakdown owing to their dissipation, by the outdoor environment. The mad horse tore through the corral, threw himself, reared up, went over backwards, laid down, rolled over, and did the hundred and one things that animal instinct caused him to do in the effort to rid himself of this human sticking plaster. However, when that great horse had his fill of rolling over, going over backwards, etc., and gotten back onto his feet, Fred was right there with a smile. Fred dismounted amid the continued applause of the thousands, and was then and there given the name as 'Mr. Nerve, the King of the Cowboys.' "

Fred decided that being a rancher was for him, and before long he was foreman of the largest ranch in Oklahoma. He was described as being remarkably good to his employees, encouraging them to participate in sports and strenuous activities. At the same time Fred nurtured the desire to own his own ranch.

Back East, Betty had not forgotten Fred. She "cultivated to the fullest extent the acquaintance of Fred's father, mother, brother and sister, and in this way kept a general idea of where Fred was and what he was doing, although they never gave her the exact address or never told Fred of her visits. She was aware, however, that Fred was somewhere in Oklahoma, and she sought in every ingenious way to convey some message to Fred."

Fred's parents told her that he hoped to own his own ranch someday. "Betty thought over the situation in all sorts of ways and remembered that she had a personal fund that her grandfather had left her." She was dissuaded from making a loan, for her parents knew that Fred would not accept charity. As luck would have it, Fred's bachelor uncle passed away, "leaving Fred's father a substantial sum, and leaving Fred, of whom he was very fond, $25,000."

When the news arrived by telegram in Oklahoma, it happened that Fred was with the owner of the ranch, Mr. Bruce, who had been ill for some time. One thing led to another, and the ranch was offered to Fred for $100,000, with $25,000 down and the balance at $10,000 a year.

To abbreviate the story, Betty came to Oklahoma, where she and Fred, not yet married, conducted the ranch in a manner beneficial to all those associated with it. Jealousies sprang up, and Miss Gay,

FRED CATCHING OVERLAND EXPRESS

Red, the desperate villain of the saga, kidnapped Betty and carried her off on the Overland Express. But, not to worry, for daring Fred mounted a trusty steed, overtook the train, climbed aboard, rescued Betty, and put Red in the hands of the local sheriff.

a schoolteacher, was attracted to Fred, while "Red" found Betty to be irresistible. One day Red kidnapped Betty and forced her aboard the Overland Express. Strenuous Fred mounted his steed, Wizard of Oz, and turned loose Betty's famous bronco, Jack O'Lantern, to follow him. Strenuous Fred caught up with and climbed aboard the train, set Betty free, and turned the villain over to the sheriff, Brig Young. He and Betty returned just in time to attend their own wedding.

In the meantime, oil had been discovered on the Oklahoma ranch, and Fred and Betty were rich. All the emoluments of life, including that most marvelous of inventions, the airplane, were at their command. A separate firm, the Betty Oil Company, was formed, and its shares were traded on the exchanges.

Following the wedding, Fred and Betty returned to the East to visit their families and to attend "many balls, dinners, and theatre parties" given in their honor.

True to the hero-and-villain theme, Fred encountered some of the old "Settee Johnnies" of his earlier days, one of whom was a stockbroker and who was unaware of Fred's connection with oil in Oklahoma. Seeking to sell Fred some shares, he gave him a tip on an outfit called the "Betty Oil Company," telling him what it was, what the stock was worth, the money there was to be made in it, and how it was going to jump 20 points in price. Fred decided to play the game and placed orders for many shares, more than the stockbroker and his friends could deliver. Fred demanded the shares he had bought, but the former "Settee Johnny" could not deliver, for, unknown to him, Fred was the majority stockholder of the firm! In what was just retribution, they had to "get down on their knees and beg off with a substantial punishment of dollars and cents. This enabled Fred and Betty to make a lot of personal donations to many of their acquaintances whom the world had not treated as well as it might, and they were also able to make great donations to the Salvation Army, Red Cross, YMCA, and other worthy organizations," upon which words the text of The TNT Cowboy ends.

Oh yes, about the term "TNT Cowboy," the strenuous life of Fred made him "The TNT of the cowboys, with a brain of equal force to the TNT," or dynamite. This reference within a sentence of the text captivated Archer, and The TNT Cowboy the book was named.

The more Archer read his own text, the more he was fascinated with it, and before long actors and actresses were dressed as Fred, Betty, Brig Young, Red, Miss Gay, and various cowboys and other characters. At the time, Frank M. Archer, who enjoyed the companionship of theatrical people, used The TNT Cowboy as a vehicle

FRED AND BETTY LEAVING RANCH TO VISIT NEW YORK

One day Betty dipped her hand into a stream on the ranch and came up with a bunch of goo—oil! From that point, their fortune was set, and the Betty Oil Company was formed. Among the rewards was a modern airplane which Fred and Betty used to leave the ranch to visit their home, New York City, where many gala affairs were scheduled in their honor. The story ends as one of the socialites who had ignored Fred earlier, a so-called "Settee Johnnie," tried to sell Fred stock in the Betty Oil Company, pushing it as a good investment. Without revealing his status as a majority owner of the Betty Oil Company, Fred offered to buy a large amount of shares. The seller could not deliver that much, was caught in a "corner," and had to pay dearly to be extricated, thus giving Fred and Betty an additional sum of money, which they donated to charity.

to commission Ann Pennington and others to appear in different skits featuring segments of the melodrama. The public, it seems, did not share Archer's enthusiasm, and to remedy this he spent money from The Moxie Company's advertising fund to place numerous notices in Boston newspapers, especially in 1919 and 1920. These were in the form of "teasers" which the cognoscenti (those who possessed a copy of the book) would recognize, but others would find mystifying. Samples:

"Betty says—Christmas fans the flame of happy memories and sends a glow of warm goodwill from heart to heart," "TNT Frank Archer now hopes to Personally Introduce Betty and Miss Gay to You," "Was Betty in the Chelsea fire?," "Betty—The type that likes to quarrel for the pleasure of making up," "The Bad Man 'Red' Kidnaps Betty," "Miss Gay is jealous of Betty," "Fred and Betty journey from the ranch to New York and back in their own private aeroplane," and "Betty is in a class by herself."

It is evident that Archer was trying to impress the girl who was the inspiration for Betty, who apparently lived in Chelsea, for more advertisements were run in the Chelsea *Evening Record* than in any other location.

The well-known Moxie Horsemobile was converted to duty for The TNT Cowboy cause, and a new device, the Moxie "Ponycycle," was created, the latter featuring a motorcycle to which a sidecar (on which was mounted a horse) was attached. Typically, "Fred" would ride the motorcycle while "Betty" would be to the side astride the horse. A September 1919 notice in *Motorcycling and Bicycling* magazine gave technical details:

"MOTORCYCLE, WOODEN HORSE AND GIRLS HELP SELL A GOOD DRINK. The Moxie Company has selected a unique means of advertising their product. A motorcycle, fitted up with a wooden horse weighing 350 pounds, mounted on the regular spring suspension of the Henderson sidecar and chassis with angle iron supports running to the body, is their equipment, to which is added two goodlooking TNT cowgirls. With the exception of the girls, the outfit came from the General Motorcycle Sales Company, Boston. They are now on a tour of the eastern states. The only forced stops thus far recorded are occasioned by the crowds which gather to get a close-up of this novel advertising scheme."

Frank M. Archer furnished publicity photographs and news releases to various New England newspapers and was rewarded by seeing "news" of his accomplishment appear in many places. A typical article appeared in Lewiston, Maine:

"MOXIE TNT COWBOY FEATURE ARRIVED IN LEWISTON

The Bad Man 'RED' Kid...Bet...

Betty gathers up all of he... ...onal

BETTY

BETTY

Don't confuse Betty with some vain, wants-to-be social climber, or make-believe highbrow. Think of her as a real honest-to-Godness, goodness girl who is not too proud to join the mart of trade and believes that everyone who is worth while should do something worth while, and that is what she is doing now.

Read T. N. T.

Who Is BETTY?

Read T. N. T.

...S GAY

...s jealous of ...ETTY

TNT BETTY

T N T Betty and Miss Gay made their personal appearance at the Broadway Theatre last night. The enthusiastic reception which they received well repaid for the delay in appearance. This, that and the other one who thought they knew Betty, found how badly they were mistaken. They found that she was the Queen of the great outdoor girls, and still the refined, dignified lady of the city; the kind who does great honor to the marts of trade and to everyone with whom she comes in contact; spreads good cheer, good living, good ideas; worships the man, woman and girl who enjoy everything that is worth living for; truly personifies the joining of the East with the West, and fully lives up to the high ideal of the character of that wonderful story, the T N T Cowboy.

The author, Betty and all concerned desire to thank the Manager, Mr. Green, together with the audience who showed by their enthusiasm, their high appreciation of Betty and Miss Gay.

Drink MOXIE

The "Chelsea (Massachusetts) Record" in December 1920 carried many teaser advertisements pertaining to Betty, heroine of "The TNT Cowboy." Frank Archer, who wrote the copy, furnished an answer of a sort in the advertisement shown to the left. Over a period of time the mythical Betty, who apparently had a real life counterpart, became a goddess in Frank Archer's eyes.

— 478 —

MOXIE
Announcement

★ ★ ★ ★ ★ ★ ★ ★ ★ ★ ★ ★ ★ ★ ★ ★ ★ ★ ★ ★

The Moxie T. N. T. outfit, which by the way has two of the prettiest Cow Girls in the world, will endeavor to do honor to the Boston Alleppo who entrain at Boston, Thursday morning at eight o'clock en route to Lewiston to take part in one of the greatest State Masonic outings that will take place anywhere. This is saying something. The organization is composed of the best fellows in the word on the victrola. Read the T. N. T. Cow Boy and have be congratulated on such a gathering.

The Clans are to proceed in a body to the Lewiston State Fair Grounds on Thursday. This will be a spectacle that will be worth going thousands of miles to see, and anyone is warranted in taking the rubber off the roll to see this event. This is an attraction that will draw blood from a stone and make the tight-wad a careless spendthrift.

There will be refreshments galore—Moxie and Camel's milk predominating.

Get your tickets early, and avoid the rush.

After the stress of the last few years people should let out their pent-up-feelings and let merriment take the place of gloom and sadness. Smiles bring cheer but nowadays not always beer. Get together, cuddle up, be good fellows, forget your troubles, join the procession, make everybody happy, open your heart and your home to the Alleppo boys. Bread cast upon the water in this way will bring you barrels of Camel's milk perhaps. Quench your thirst before it starts by drinking Moxie. An ounce of prevention is worth a ton of cures.

On Thursday night see that every light is burning in every window for the Alleppo boys. Watch for the SPECIAL that leaves Boston at eight o'clock.

Get out the tall hat like papa used to wear. Give the dress suit a shake. Unlock the piano and get a new record on thev ictrola. Read the T. N. T. Cow Boy and have real enjoyment.

See that grandma and grandpa get on their best bib and tucker and have a conveyance on hand to take them in comfort to the great Fair.

Put every kid to bed early Thursday night so that they will be in fine trim for Friday.

Before the curfew gets a chance to ring the bell for eight o'clock everybody in bed, turn the clock back or stop it.

Boys, this is the chance for you to give your best girls the time of their lives. Don't neglect it, don't be a slacker. Get in the front line trenches, and go "Over the Top." Take out your marriage license before there is a War Tax on it. Have the knot tied before there' is any advance in the price of knot tying.

Boston Alleppo sends advanced greetings and are sure of receiving a State of Maine welcome, which is the welcomest welcome of them all.

To promote the "TNT Cowboy" book, Frank Archer spent thousands of dollars on advertisements of various sorts, including the "Moxie Announcement" above, which enticed visitors to go to the Lewiston (Maine) Fair for "one of the greatest state Masonic outings that will take place anywhere." The public was advised to "Read the TNT Cowboy and have real enjoyment."

Numerous people took snapshots of the Moxie Ponycycle outfit. Frank Archer collected some of these in a scrapbook, and the examples shown on this page are from that source. The year is 1920, a crisp day in the photograph above, a warmer day for the lariat twirler shown to the left, and a snowy winter day for the pair pictured below. Mr. Charles Moxie, who had recently returned from the war in Europe and who had achieved distinction there, is pictured as the horserider.

THURSDAY. On arrival the TNT outfit came directly to the *Sun* office. The Moxie Company has put over another advertising feature. The people of Lewiston and the suburban towns will have the opportunity to witness this feature at the fair grounds again today. Arrangements have already been made with the Lewiston Fair officials to have the Moxie Ponycycle do an exhibition mile on the track previous to the start of the races. During the day the Moxie TNT Cowgirls distributed beautiful fans and other valuable presents to the patrons attending the fair.

"The Moxie Company has engaged the services of Miss Edith Hutton and Miss Mildred Farrar to portray the characters of the TNT Cowboy girls. These ladies are well known in the theatrical profession in all of New England. Miss Hutton has appeared in Lewiston several times at the Empire Theatre and Music Hall in this city.

"Mr. Charles Moxie, who has just returned from overseas and who has won honor as a skilled mechanic in France, has been especially engaged by the Moxie Company to operate this wonderful advertising feature, 'The TNT Cowboy Outfit.' There are six beautiful Moxie babies [dolls] on exhibition at the fair grounds and are to be given away to the children of Lewiston and Auburn. The judges have been selected by the fair committee. Mr. Gebow, the State of Maine representative of Moxie, is traveling with the TNT Outfit."

This article, from the Fall River (Masschusetts) *Daily Globe,* is typical of many:

"THE famous Moxie horse that has for several years toured the country mounted on a small automobile is in town today, but now the horse is mounted on the Moxie Company's 'Ponycycle.' The most pleasing feature is the fact that the jockey who formerly rode the horse during its perambulations about the country has now been displaced by two beautiful cowgirls.

"Miss Edith Hutton, formerly well-known in Providence theatrical circles, and is also well known in Fall River, having appeared here in the local theatres several times, is portraying one of the famous TNT Cowgirls. She appears with Miss Mildred Farrar, motion picture actress, and the two cowgirls have spent the greater part of the day visiting all the points of interest in the city. Miss Hutton is known to theatre goers as a clever comedienne and is something of an athlete.

"The whole advertising feature is known as 'The Moxie TNT Outfit.' The outfit visited the office of the *Daily Globe* today, where a big crowd gathered to cheer the cowgirls."

As time went on, Archer increasingly identified himself with the hero of his tale. An article appearing in a Boston newspaper in December 1919 told of an apparent car theft and identified Archer in an unusual way:

PAUL MILLER, "the T. N. T. cowboy," who entertains thousands by skill with lariat.

DARING COWBOY SKILFUL ROPE PERFORMER

Paul Miller Tours Country as Hero of Frank Archer's Novel

All good actors are not on the stage. Paul Miller, an excellent performer, both in the movies and on the boards, is doing a fine job on the streets of Boston and New York as Fred the T. N. T. Cowboy.

Fred, the T. N. T. Cowboy, is the hero of a book or dime novel of that name written by Frank Archer, vice-president of the Moxie Company, in two hours one afternoon when his foot was asleep.

The original of the book is no less than Fred Stone, the comedian, whose acrobatic stunts and fondness for Moxie so endeared him to Mr. Archer that he inspired him to write a novel. The book, by the way, was written before July first.

As Fred, the T. N. T. Cowboy, whirling his rope and riding on a horse tricycle affair spattered all over with Moxie labels, Paul Miller travels through the big cities, and ever and anon performs daring stunts, which justify his title of "T. N. T." He even darts by a traffic cop after he has been ordered to stop, and thus Moxie gets advertised in courtrooms and jails.

MOXIE T. N. T. COWBOY FEATURE ARRIVED IN LEWISTON, THURSDAY

On arrival the T. N. T. outfit came directly to the Sun Office. The Moxie Company has put over another advertising feature. The people of Lewiston and the suburban towns will have the opportunity to witness this feature at the fair grounds again today. Arrangements have already been made with the Lewiston Fair officials to have the Moxie Ponycycle do an exhibition mile on the track previous to the start of the races. During the day the start of T. N. T. Cowgirls distributed beautiful fans and other valuable presents to the patrons attending the fair.

The Moxie Company has engaged the services of Miss Edith Hutton and Miss Mildred Farrar to portray the characters of the T. N. T. Cowboy girls. These ladies are well known in the theatrical profession in all of New England. Miss Hutton having appeared in Lewiston several times at the Empire theatre and Music Hall in this city.

Mr. Chas. Moxie who has just returned from overseas and has won honor as a skilled mechanic in France has been specially engaged by the Moxie Company to operate this wonderful advertising feature, "The T. N. T. Cowboy Outfit."

There are six beautiful Moxie babies on exhibition at the Fair grounds and are to be given away to the children of Lewiston and Auburn. The judges have been selected by the Fair committee.

Mr. Gabow the State of Maine representative of Moxie is traveling with the T. N. T. outfit.

The TNT Cowboy, inspired by a booklet of that name written by Frank Archer, was close to Archer's heart. The Ponycycle outfit and Fred, the TNT Cowboy, toured New England, New York, and other northeastern areas. To help with the publicity, Archer furnished stock photographs to newspapers, the most popular such picture being that shown to the left.

"F.M. Archer, Sr., of The Moxie Company, better known as T.N.T. Archer, author of the story The TNT Cowboy, and his son, F.M., Jr., had a bad scare yesterday when they thought that F.M. Junior's automobile had been stolen.

"Early last night, T.N.T. sent his chauffeur on an errand, telling him to take F.M. Junior's car instead of the family auto. An hour later when Archer, Jr., entered his garage he found a strange car there. He immediately informed T.N.T., who called up the Brookline police station. The sergeant who answered the telephone said that a lady had called up to say that someone had taken her car from Coolidge Corner and left another one in its place.

"Upon receiving this news, T.N.T. and his son hurried to Coolidge Corner and there found son's auto unharmed. The young woman who had lost her car also appeared upon the scene. Her description tallied with that of the strange machine in the Archer garage, and a trip to the garage revealed that it was hers. According to T.N.T.'s theory, the chauffeur stepped into the wrong machine when he left Coolidge Corner and drove it home."

Despite heroic promotional efforts, the TNT Cowboy flopped. The Ponycycle didn't help, numerous mentions of the TNT Cowboy on fans didn't help, the extensive advertising campaign didn't help. By 1923, the TNT Cowboy was forgotten by nearly everyone, although mention of him cropped up in a few scattered later references. It is not recorded how many copies of the book were published, but sales undoubtedly were disappointing. Indeed, during the preparation of the present book, the author was not able to locate an example until he visited the Library of Congress, Washington, D.C. and examined the very specimens of the first and second printing editions that Archer had deposited in the copyright files many decades earlier.

The Moxie Horsemobile was sidelined for a time, but after the Ponycycle and The TNT Cowboy book were forgotten, the Horsemobile went on to entertain another decade of onlookers.

There is no question, however, that Archer satisfied his desire for publicity and nurtured his ego with the TNT Cowboy publicity and personal identification with it. At a time in which Archer was an insignificant shareholder in the company but was the main driving force behind the Moxie advertising and sales efforts, this reward of fame, albeit short-lived, was undoubtedly deserved.

Chapter 13

The Glorification
of
Frank Archer

At the beginning of 1920, 5,000 shares of The Moxie Company were owned by the same people as they were over a decade earlier, with the exception that the holdings of John Beauchain, long deceased, had been distributed among various beneficiaries. Frank M. Archer had 50 shares, and, despite his entreaties to acquire more, the opportunity to buy additional shares was denied him. The main owners of the company were Francis E. Thompson with 1,218 shares, his wife Mabel with 1,200, Harry A. Thompson with 1,094, and Freeman N. Young's holding of 844 shares. By the start of the 1920s decade, Archer had sipped the wine of fame, was a friend of numerous actors and actresses, and had derived a large measure of enjoyment from the publicity he generated for his own book, *The TNT Cowboy*. The next step was to further his public image.

Before long, virtually anything having to do with Moxie had Frank Archer's name connected with it. "Frank Archer Says: If at all particular, Drink Moxie," "Frank Archer Says: Drink Moxie 100%." The explanation of the image of the Moxie Boy with pointed finger as printed on the back of the 1921 sheet music edition of the *Moxie Song* was prefaced by "Frank Archer Says..."

Unlike its 1904 predecessor, *Just Make It Moxie For Mine*, the *Moxie Song* achieved a measure of popularity outside of Moxie's own advertising circles. Following the publication of the tune in sheet music form on August 19, 1921, the melody was recorded on at least two phonograph record versions. Player piano owners, whose numbers were increasing yearly, had their pick of either an American arrangement on a Connorized brand roll or an English product on an Artona roll. On May 19, 1930, the same song, with slight revisions, was published under a slightly different title, illustrated with a color picture of the Moxie Rolls-Royce Horsemobile on the cover.

After the publication of *The TNT Cowboy*, Archer's hobnobbing with stage personalities increased apace, and one Boston newspaper

Photographs of a Moxie delivery truck, December 1919, taken at the Moxie factory at Varick and Laight streets, New York City. This factory was maintained through the mid 1920s, at which time it was replaced by a Brooklyn facility operated by the short-lived Moxie Company of America and, farther to the north, The Moxie Company's Roxbury, Massachusetts "Moxieland" domain.

In the scene below a conveyor is set up, presumably to load crates filled with Moxie into the back of the van. It is a snowy day, and the truck is equipped with chains. The top photograph, taken on December 22, 1919, shows a slightly warmer situation—no accumulated snow. The old factory in New York was demolished later to make way for a motor vehicle tunnel.

The Latest Mode of Travel !
Miss Grace Nolan, a Boston girl, now starring in "A Prince There Was" at the Tremont Theatre

A GEORGE M. COHEN PRODUCTION

Drink MOXIE

Frank Archer's show business friends were often featured in newspaper, magazine, and souvenir program advertisements in the Boston area. On this page are shown three of many stage personalities: Grace Nolan, Raymond Hitchcock, and Ed Wynn.

What Raymond Hitchcock Says About Moxie

"I began using Moxie years ago— in the old 'King Dodo' days. I discovered then how it quenched my thirst and relieved my fatigue; and it has never disappointed me since.

"There is nothing too good to say for Moxie—certainly it was a happy thought to blend the bitter with the sweet into such a truly delicious beverage as Moxie.

"Only one other adjective describes it properly—'wonderful.'

"When one is worn out, perhaps with a dry throat—as in my case with the results of strenuous thought and action, required in rehearsals and performances—I have always found Moxie extremely beneficial.

"It is invigorating in a constructive fashion.

"Moxie is really an indispensable support of the strenuous life."

Order a case from your dealer to-day

"I may be 'A Perfect Fool'
but I'm very particular"

Ed. Wynn
In The Grab Bag— appearing at the Tremont Theatre under the direction of A.L. Erlanger

Phone your dealer to deliver a case today

Some of the patents issued to Frank Archer in the 1920s are shown together with a patent issued in 1926 to Harry A. Thompson for a beverage vending device.

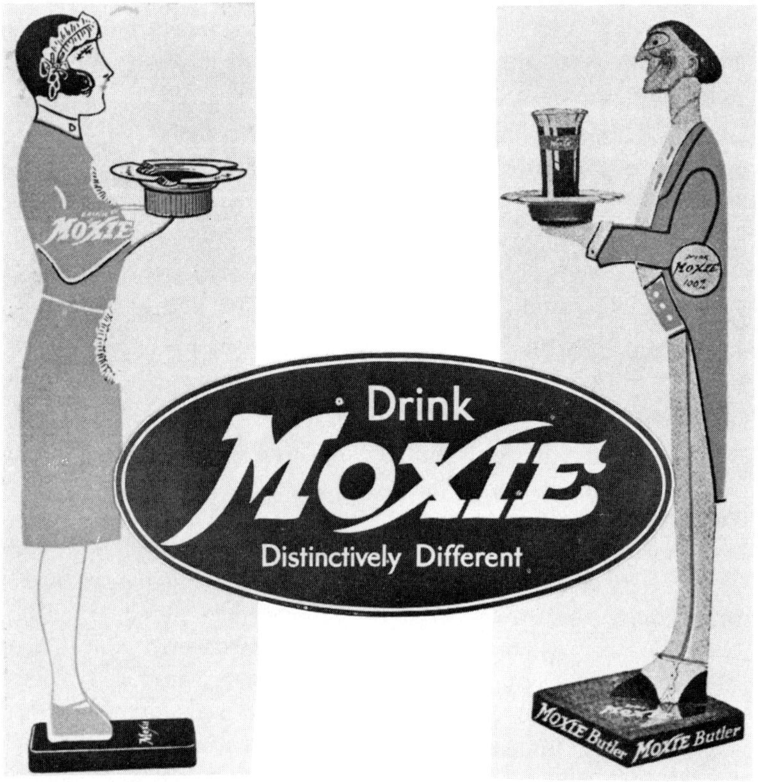

Moxie items from the 1920s: Above are the Moxie Maid and the Moxie Butler, wooden silhouettes, the latter featuring the image of actor Raymond Hitchcock, whose image is also found on the Moxie Candy Man lollipop shown at the lower right. "Distinctively different" was a popular Moxie theme.

for the country generally if Plymouth Rock had landed on the Pilgrim fathers and squashed them good and proper, commented the comedian.

"He said that Prohibition not only does not prohibit, but it allows the rich to drink all the whiskey, champagne, wine, cordials, and even beer, while the poor must make their own hooch and run the risk of getting arrested or patronize bootleggers at $18 a quart..."

Hitchcock went into deeper water and attacked the United States Constitution, stating it was a relic of the dark ages.

What happened to the Archer-Hitchcock relationship after that is not recorded, at least not by newspaper clippings in the Moxie archives.

Although very few girls actually appeared on Moxie fans after the days of Muriel Ostriche, Lillian MacKenzie, Frances Pritchard, Eileen Percy and Laura Walker, all of whom appeared before 1920, the enticement of being a publicized Moxie subject was extended by Archer to many attractive lasses. "You are pretty enough to appear on one of our fans," said Archer to pretty girls he encountered, especially redheads. For example, a press notice mentioned that Violet Mersereau, who appeared in *Finders Keepers*, produced by the Eastern Feature Film Company, was selected "as the prettiest girl to decorate their posters and fans." If she indeed appeared in print, apparently her name was not part of any caption, or at least the author has never located such an item.

In 1985, Frank M. Archer, Jr. recalled that he was about 10 years old when he first met Raymond Hitchcock. Whenever George M. Cohan, Ed Wynn, Billy Van, Fred Stone, Mary Pickford, or Douglas Fairbanks were in Boston they would be entertained at the Archer home in nearby Brookline. Joseph Kennedy was a frequent guest as well. When Frank, Jr. was 16 to 18 years old he would chauffeur these and other celebrities around Boston and show them the sights. "I got to know them very well," he related. "They were happy to pose for Moxie pictures and conduct interviews without charge.

In January 1921, Frank Archer, together with B.H. Green of the Broadway Theatre, visited the dancing school of Miss Helena Hipwell at Fraternity Hall in Chelsea. He told the children that at the forthcoming May festival he would give prizes to students showing exceptional abilities. He distributed Moxie lollipops to all present and said there would be a beauty contest, noting that "the winner of this contest will have her photo placed upon Moxie fans, and it will also be made possible for the young lady to appear in person in several of the Boston theatres, so that if the girl has ability of any kind this

Two of many Moxie advertisements featuring theatrical personalities. Archer made it a point to cultivate friendships with actors and actresses who appeared in Boston. Many were prominently featured in Moxie advertisements. In turn, his friends often mentioned Moxie or used Moxie props on stage.

Following the lead of Muriel Ostriche, numerous movie stars, stage personalities, contest winners, and other girls posed before the Moxie camera. The girl shown above was used on a cardboard fan in the early 1920s.

will be a good opening for her to make good in the profession she may have in mind, and show her the way to a successful career."

In 1919 Ann Pennington had been mentioned as a subject for Moxie fans, but, like so many such publicity notices, reality may have differed from hope. No fans bearing her name as part of a caption have been seen by the author, although it is possible that she may have posed for an unnamed portrait. On March 28, 1921, a newspaper article told of a gift to Pennington from Archer:

"Ann Pennington got a present yesterday. It was a large silver bowl full of American beauty roses, and it was presented by Frank Archer of The Moxie Company. Miss Pennington is one of the Moxie girls. Her beautiful countenance may be seen on many of the souvenirs given out in various places by the enterprising concern. Every time one of the ladies so distinguished by the company comes to Boston they are the recipient of some special attention... Miss Pennington's happened to be a silver bowl as large as her own self, almost."

And then there was the real-life counterpart of "Betty," the heroine of *The TNT Cowboy*. As noted, Betty apparently lived in Chelsea. Archer spent countless hours dreaming up advertising copy which extolled the virtues of Betty to the skies, expanding her personality and virtues far beyond the information given in his book. Before long, Betty became a divine goddess in Archer's eyes.

In February 1921 another of Archer's stage friends, George M. Cohan, the celebrated Irish songster, playwright, and comedian, was featured in Moxie advertisements in the Boston area. It was stated, apparently without Cohan's knowledge, that both Cohan and the leading figure in his new play, *Mary*, were avid Moxie drinkers. "George M. Cohan is not going to sue Frank Archer, the Moxie Man, for buying big advertising space to declare that both Cohan and 'Mary' drink Moxie," a newspaper article stated:

" 'Since Prohibition, I don't care what I drink,' declared Cohan. 'Moxie is all right, it has it on home brew, anyway.' Cohan came to Boston to get his new company started in *Mary*. It took courage to bring a new troupe back to Boston after the original company had spent 20 weeks there, but Cohan's middle name is courage..."

On April 10, 1921, the *Boston Post* carried this notice:

"On the arrival of Mr. Abraham Erlanger, who is here for the purpose of producing for the first time on any stage *Two Little Girls In Blue*, Frank M. Archer, one of Erlanger's great admirers, presented him with a very unique and novel cane, the handle of which represents one of Mr. Erlanger's famous stars, 'Hitchy.' The sculptor who prepared this unique head is of national fame. The alloy is of bronze and other metal, which together with the plating and finishing, is the work of several of the most experienced artists in this line."

The number of Moxie novelties, especially children's toys, proliferated. Added to the metal pull-toy Horsemobiles were numerous other items, many of which were distributed free, as in a Christmas party hosted by Archer:

"The children of Chelsea were given a Christmas party with about 1,500 presents given free on Christmas morning donated by Frank Archer of Moxie. For the last two weeks Mr. Archer has visited the different theatres of Chelsea and has given as his opinion that there could be no better place than the Broadway Theatre for the distribution of such toys to the young people.

"As a result of the above decision, Mr. Archer met Mr. Green yesterday, and in the presence of the board of directors of the Black Theatre Company and those of The Moxie Company a contract was closed by where 1,500 presents are to be given away free at the Christmas morning show for the children, with the distinct understanding that everything is to be free, and no charge whatsoever is to be made for any article...

"The presents to be distributed consist of all kinds of whistles, games, Moxie Horsemobiles, ice cream dishes, guns and other toys that will please the hearts of little ones... We think that the city of Chelsea owes a great deal to the Moxie people for what they have done and also what they are doing at present..."

A follow-up article in the Chelsea *Record* noted that 2,200 people came to the party and that "the children had a fine time, and when a picture of Mr. Archer was shown on the screen, they made the house ring with their cheers..."

An article published a few months later illustrated a wide variety of Moxie toys, including statues of Raymond Hitchcock in several sizes and formats, a see-saw, sled, elephant pull toy, two-wheel pull cart, toy Horsemobile with Hitchcock, blackboard, three-wheel tricycle, four-wheel baby carriage, pony on four wheels, balloons, whistles, and paper popguns. In 1921 the horse on the Ponycycle, used in T.N.T. Cowboy publicity, carried on the company books at a value of $18, was transformed into a pony rocking horse!

Frank Archer continued his generosity to employees. In 1920 each worker, called an "associate," received a sum equal to one week's salary, together with a personal commendation for good work. Each

office headed for Canobie Lake. "The outing is held annually in pursuit of the Moxie management belief that all work and no play makes both Jack and Jill dull," noted Archer, in apparent contradiction to his own personal habits.

Similarly, at Christmas time Archer wanted all of Boston to know that "for the purpose of our associates to have an opportunity to do their Christmas shopping in an orderly and practical way, this Christmas shopping day is given with full pay."

In 1921 at a lobster banquet served in the North Station Restaurant for Moxie employees, each department head received a souvenir book as a personal gift from Archer. A 26-piece silver set, originally made for "TNT Betty" as part of her Ponycycle tour, was given to Mr. L. Dahl, while Betty's mirror was won by Mr. A. Godfrey, and Betty's silver fruit bowl was claimed by James Penney. The silver tea service made for Betty went to Miss A. Thompson, her silver nut bowl to Mrs. Alice Stiegler, while a framed portrait of Frank Archer was the reward of Mr. C.A. Burke.

Archer captured the lion's share of Moxie publicity. One can scan Boston and other newspapers and find only isolated, scattered references to the Thompson brothers and Freeman N. Young, Moxie's main stockholders. More often than not, when Francis ("Frank") E. Thompson or Harry A. Thompson reached print in the 1920s, the subject was their luxurious yachts.

Occasionally an article about Freeman N. Young would be written, especially when he hosted annual reunions of the Junior Baseball Players of Massachusetts, an association of players from the 1873-1875 years. One article discussed his suburban Boston estate in Arlington:

" 'Yousay,' the private club of Freeman N. Young, prominent citizen of Arlington and the leading director of the Middlesex Sportsmen Association, which has its home on the shores of Spy Pond in this town, henceforth will have an annex on a small island in the middle of the pond. For many years the island, comprising about two acres of picturesque timber and greenery, was the property of the Boston and Maine Railroad...

"Recently the railroad communicated with the Middlesex Sportsmen Association, offering the island to the association for something like $2,000. The association did not feel like purchasing the island. Mr. Young is much interested in the association, although he maintains his private club, 'Yousay,' in this town near the Winchester line. He has provided the club with a moving picture theatre and

This snapshot from the 1920s shows a Moxie canoe on Spy Pond, Arlington, Massachusetts, at the home of Freeman N. Young, a major stockholder of the firm.

interesting films and also an elaborate wireless radio station. Mr. Young purchased the island, and the deeds and transfer papers are now being prepared."

The *Boston Globe* on January 1, 1926, noted that Freeman N. Young on his 70th birthday dedicated an addition to the Middlesex Sportsmen Association building. "In real life he is called Freeman N. Young, but to members of the club and to his friends he is just 'Brig.' Yesterday Mr. Young was 70 years old, and about two weeks ago he issued invitations for members of the club and his friends to come to his clubhouse and help him celebrate." It was noted that he paid for an addition 35 feet long and 50 feet wide complete with a motion picture theatre.

"Mr. Young is a former Lowell boy and the story of his life is that of a self-made man. Starting, in under conditions that made it necessary for him to go to work when young, he used his brain toward bettering himself all the time. He took up various activities, played professional baseball in the 1870s, and is now head of the well known Moxie Company of Boston," the narrative continued.

Still another article told of a problem in Young's backyard: "Shall the ducks be driven from Spy Pond or pulled under and eaten by the turtles? Those who know say there are turtles in that harmless looking pond 50 or more pounds in weight... Freeman N. Young is thoroughly alive to the menace of these turtles, and for some time he has been offering a cent a pound to the boys who will catch them. Frank Webb has earned a considerable sum by his catch."

Still another article told of Young's unique home:

"A worldwide traveler and a big game hunter, his bungalow adjoining his residence is running over with trophies of prowess and personal contact in the many countries where he has explored. The heads of rare animals, stuffed birds and reptiles and objects of art as well make this not only a museum but a collection appealing particularly to a man with sportsman's instinct. On one wall is portrayed in bas-relief the discovery and working of a California gold mine in which Mr. Young is interested, while billiard tables and indoor games of great variety attract the interest of the visitor."

Freeman N. Young and Archer were close friends. Sheriff "Brig" Young in Archer's *TNT Cowboy* book was named after him.

It was inevitable: Frank Archer wrote a play. As part of an article about Moxie lollipops given away at the Broadway Theatre, Chelsea, Mrs. Isabel ("Belle") Voge, secretary to Frank Archer for 15 years, was quoted as saying some nice things about the theatre and the management:

"So much impressed was she that if a certain play is produced by the Moxie associates, which play has recently been written by Mr. Archer, and is now being illustrated by one of Boston's greatest artists, they will give the performance there. The title of the play, however, at present can only be made known by initials—H.M.V.

"As a crude synopsis it can be said that this play deals with a somewhat high-strung girl, very beautiful and intelligent, from a splendid family. One of the scenes illustrates a sojourn of the heroine in New York City. It illustrates several of our Cape Cod sections, Boston—particularly Scollay Square, and one of the great New England fires. This play would be interesting to our readers because it particularly takes in Chelsea, East Boston, Cambridge, Somerville, and one of the plants in Boston of one of New England's greatest corporations. On account of the stress of the Moxie business, etc., the associates may not be able to produce it for some time, but if it is produced, manager Green has assured them that for rehearsal purposes as well as production, he will consider it an honor to place the Broadway at their disposal."

The Chelsea *Evening Record*, February 15, 1921, gave away the title as *Her Master's Voice* and noticed that a key line was "Mamma, why do you have to give him all your money?"

What may have been a "teaser" advertisement for the same production, a notice in the Chelsea *Record*, November 30, 1921, posed Frank Archer's question, "Do you know why girls leave home?"

Of all Moxie promotions, none caused more problems than Frank Archer's brainchild of the Moxie Candy Man—the lollipop molded in the image of Raymond Hitchcock. Notations in the company's records tell the story:

"August 29, 1921: 28 cartons containing 1,400 Candy Men were returned for rewrapping because they were 'sticking to bags.' " Many other notices were made concerning the same problem.

"August 31, 1921: 22 boxes equalling 1,100 Candy Men at 2½c each are to be distributed free by the Bonyea Candy Company, as they cannot sell them."

Autumn 1921: "7,450 Candy Men were considered to be soft and unsalable and were sent to Winchester's"—which made all the Moxie Candy Men at the time—to remelt. These were on the books at $141.55, but the salvage value came to just $8.40. A further deluge of unsatisfactory Candy Men were returned for melting.

Archer was especially proud of the Moxie Candy Man and, as noted earlier, applied for a patent, which was granted a year later

Francis Edward Thompson, one of two sons of Augustin Thompson, shown here in later life. For many years he served as president of The Moxie Company.

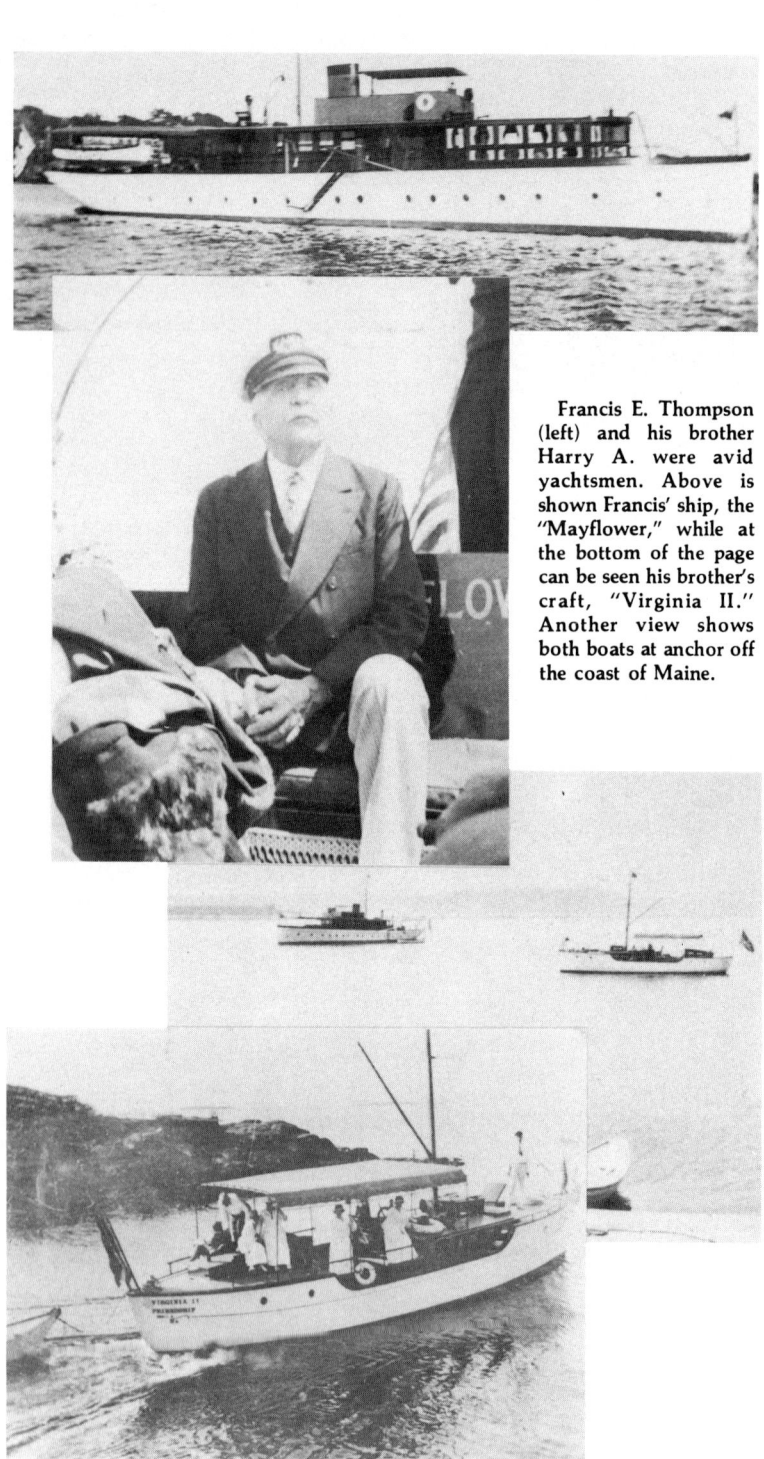

Francis E. Thompson (left) and his brother Harry A. were avid yachtsmen. Above is shown Francis' ship, the "Mayflower," while at the bottom of the page can be seen his brother's craft, "Virginia II." Another view shows both boats at anchor off the coast of Maine.

Above: Visitors to the birthplace of President Calvin Coolidge, which saw service as Florence V. Cilley's store circa 1926 when this picture was taken, were able to buy Moxie per the large sign on the building near the gas pumps. In this very same store Coolidge ordered glasses of Moxie for himself and his companions shortly after learning of Warren Harding's death and of his own succession to the presidency in 1923.

Below: In the 1920s a large Moxie billboard overlooked a busy commercial intersection in Waterville, Maine.

President Calvin Coolidge and Moxie: Coolidge, standing on the White House lawn, holds a Moxie magazine advertisement featuring the Moxie Kid and the Moxie Pup, in this 1926 photograph. He is flanked by Captain David B. Phillips and Captain George C. Cahoon, who were visiting Washington courtesy of "Cape Cod Magazine," which subsequently reprinted the illustration. In a ceremony they presented some Cape Cod clams to the president.

Several of "The Moxie Maids" are shown on a Boston stage in the 1920s. Frank Archer had close theatrical connections, and many vaudeville skits and other routines featured Moxie antics.

As might be expected, this "endorsement" of Moxie aroused criticism. *The Boston Review* sought an explanation. None was forthcoming, according to a notice in that publication:

"I regret to record the fact that the spokesman for the President has not yet explained why he recently allowed the President to act as an advertising agent for Moxie. It was on the occasion of a visit to Washington by two eminent Cape Codders who carried to the President as tokens of esteem from the Cape a fine selection of the Cape's very best clams... They had their 'pictures tooken' with the President, the captains carrying their pails of clams and the President holding in his hand a copy of *Cape Cod Magazine*. Reproductions of that photograph printed in daily papers were not clear enough to show just what it was the president carried, but the *Cape Cod Magazine*, which is printed on excellent paper, published the photograph and it shows the President holding a copy of the magazine. Curiously enough, he did not hold it with the front cover out, but held the back cover in full view, and the full-page advertisement of Moxie shows very clearly.

"Just who arranged for the President thus to give his tacit approval of Moxie has not been explained. There isn't any doubt... that it was his intention to hold the magazine just as he did. And the proprietors of Moxie, which is *not* a Cape Cod institution, get a fine advertisement without paying a cent for it—at least they didn't pay the President a cent for it. Will the spokesman for the President kindly tell us how the game was pulled off?"

Chapter 14

Moxieland

In June 1925 Frank Archer, Jr., following in his father's footsteps, was named as a beauty contest judge:

"Miss Massachusetts, fairest of the fair, will be selected from a group of girls who have been picked by Elks of every seat in Massachusetts at the New Ocean House, Swampscott, Monday. The judges will be Sturges Rice and Frank M. Archer, Jr. of the Moxie Company."

A later article noted that the winner was Miss Thelma Todd of Lawrence, who was chosen from 24 contestants.

The story had an unhappy ending, for an article in the *Boston Post* a decade later, December 16, 1935, noted:

"Hollywood's latest tragedy, the death of Thelma Todd, former Lawrence girl, is an ironical gesture of fate. Winning fame and fortune as a screen comedienne, the lovely Thelma, who was indisputedly one of the film capital's most beautiful blondes, met a tragic and mysterious death...

"At 18, when studying in the Lowell School to become a school teacher, Thelma won an Elks beauty contest and became known as Miss Lawrence. A short time later at a much larger Elks beauty contest at the New Ocean House in Swampscott, she was chosen Miss Massachusetts. This was no fixed affair nor idle honor, for the harassed judges, Frank M. Archer, Jr., James A. Travers, and Sturges Rice, spent literally hours trying to decide whether Thelma, the blonde, was more beautiful than the two brunettes, Ann Galloway of Lowell and Alice Debury of Newton... She went to the Paramount Picture School in 1925 and was in a picture released by 'students' in 1926..."

New Moxie novelties continued to appear. One of the most curious was a crystal set radio in the form of a Horsemobile, made by adding components to a metal Horsemobile toy of the style earlier released in 1919. Advertisements placed in July 1925 showed a listener using earphones attached to terminals at the bottom. In December of the same year, Frank Archer, Jr., distributed Moxie radios to Western Union messengers and *Boston Herald* news people at a party hosted by The Moxie Company. Scattered presentations were made at other events around the same time.

Another Moxie novelty of the time was a mantle or shelf clock made in Winsted, Connecticut and bearing the Moxie label on the face. Apparently these were distributed in relatively small quantities. Wall-hanging versions were also produced in limited numbers.

In 1925, newspaper ads featuring the old Moxie Bottle Wagon appeared as did some advertising featuring the portrait of Dr. Augustin Thompson, a reflection on nostalgic earlier times.

An event in Boston society was chronicled in November 1925:

"The wedding of Miss Virginia Stewart Thompson, daughter of Mr. and Mrs. Harry A. Thompson of 684 Westford Street, and Mr. Leland Stanford McElwee of Boston, was one of the largest of the season thus far. The ceremony took place at the home of the bride's parents on Saturday evening at six o'clock...

"Mr. McElwee is a graduate of Bowdoin College, class of 1916... Mrs. McElwee is a graduate of Rogers Hall School of Lowell and of the Garland School of Boston. Mr. and Mrs. McElwee left later in the evening for an extended wedding trip by automobile and will make their home in this city this winter."

Mr. McElwee, a banker by profession (with the Old Colony Trust Co., Boston), and Mrs. McElwee were never active participants in the Moxie enterprise, although they had a stock ownership interest.

A mini-campaign of sorts was launched in 1925. When the Horsemobile was paraded through a town it was billed as "The Modern Paul Revere." Newspaper advertisements suggested that a Paul Revere cocktail, consisting of a half glass of ice-cold Moxie and an equal quantity of milk, would be invigorating, healthful, and delicious. "Even those who don't like milk will love it this way."

Moxie was having problems. Although Archer's advertising and innovations had propelled it to the forefront in New England, particularly around Boston, elsewhere sales were languishing. Hindsight provides several explanations:

At a time when Coca-Cola and many other branded soft drinks were available for a nickel a bottle, Moxie was sold only in the cumbersome 26-ounce size, enough for five glasses to be sure, but

Moxie was an advertisement for the automobile, and the automobile was an advertisement for Moxie—a symbiotic relationship. Moxie was a willing contributor to advertising for automobile salons and displays, with Boston Auto Show program covers of 1925 and 1926 being representative.

The Moxie Bottle Wagon was put into use in the eighties and is still going strong. It is unique as a publicity feature and practical to display and serve Moxie for which it was designed. This wagon was invented by Mr. Francis E. Thompson, President and Mr. Freeman N. Young, Secretary, who obtained patents on it in the United States and foreign countries. This picture will bring back fond recollections to the many who were wont to patronize it.

The Moxie Bottle Wagon, an anachronism after 1920, was featured in the 1926 advertisement shown above, which noted that it "is still going strong." By that time, nearly all such units had been abandoned or destroyed, although it is possible that one or two stray vehicles may have survived. "This picture will bring back fond recollections to the many who were wont to patronize it," the caption notes.

not the right size for quick refreshment, for the unused portion had to be recapped and put on ice.

The Moxie bottle, with its medicine-like orange label with black printing and rather plain appearance, was no match for the artistic bottles of Coca-Cola and others.

While Frank Archer implored the public to "Learn to Drink Moxie," the fact was that a significant percentage of the population simply did not like the beverage. Its bittersweet flavor was not appealing to palates which preferred a sweet refreshment.

In mid-1925, the old facility at Laight and Varick streets in New York City was on its way out. Soon it would be demolished to make way for a vehicle tunnel entrance. Most Moxie was shipped from Boston. The Moxie Company had an ambivalent attitude toward syrup. It was sold sparingly, and only to soda fountains and other dispensers. Gone were the days when quantities of syrup would be shipped to dozens of bottlers in distant states. The net result was that bottled Moxie had to be shipped by rail or truck from Boston or New York. Freight rates and the risk of damage and spoilage were such that the sales territory was confined primarily to the northeastern states. By contrast, Coca-Cola readily shipped large quantities of syrup and materials to a wide network of regional bottlers all over America.

Archer's oft-stated request for increased stock ownership continued to fall on deaf ears, and while he was drawing a generous salary, he did not have the satisfaction of significant stock participation in the firm to which he contributed a majority of the ideas. Increasingly, his attention turned to civic affairs, appearances at clubs, and his friendship with theatrical personalities. At the same time he certainly was "minding the store," but the flow of fresh advertising ideas slowed down, leading to the conclusion that his heart was not in it, at least not to the extent it was earlier.

Still, there were some changes in the wind, and it was hoped that Moxie's fortunes would improve. In May 1925, The Moxie Company bought a derelict brewery in the Roxbury district from John F. Moors and others, trustees of an estate holding the property. Bounded by Parker, Old Heath, Heath and Bickford streets, the new purchase was assessed at $180,300 at the time, of which $43,100 represented the tax assessor's estimate of the worth of 86,299 square feet of land. "New owners plan extensive improvements," a May 29th article commented.

In autumn 1925 a renewed sense of energy pervaded the Moxie organization. On November 24th a special announcement was sent

This Moxie advertisement from the late 1920s features a slogan, "OK'D BY MILLIONS," that was used in numerous advertisements and on various placards of the era. The Moxie Kid is shown holding the Moxie Carrying Bag, which bears yet another "advertisement" for F.M. Archer, who was fond of putting his name on various Moxie products of the 1920s and 1930s. The omnipresent Archer's name also appears on the sign being carried by the Moxie Dog.

to dealers, noting that a new seven-ounce size, to be known as "Kid Moxie," would be made available at $2.50 per case of 24 bottles. A pint-size bottle was announced, also sold with 24 bottles to a case. The standard Moxie, the 26-ounce style which in earlier times was referred to as a "quart," remained the largest format. Dealers were advised that 900 cases of the seven-ounce size, 650 of the 16-ounce type, and 650 of the 26-ounce Moxie would fit in a boxcar. Indeed, boxcars were a symbol of success, and over a period of time numerous pictures were taken of boxcar-loads of Moxie shipped to Douglass, Four, Smith, and other distributors.

The advertising writer for Moxie did not have a very good sense of history and apparently had forgotten the "pint" size of Moxie distributed earlier in the century, primarily as samples to physicians, restaurants, newspaper editors and others, for an announcement observed:

"1926 is the first time of our putting out other than the 26-ounce size. As you know we have been putting out all that our capacity is able to produce of the seven and 16 ounce size..."

To promote Kid Moxie a new advertising gimmick was devised— you guessed it—the Moxie Kid, a young chap who was later portrayed with a Moxie Carrying Bag (devised by Frank Archer and bearing his name prominently on it) or the Moxie Pup.

An advertisement in the *Boston Traveler*, December 24, 1925, featured the new Moxie Girl wearing an "M" lapel badge and was "the first appearance in any paper" of the new girl, according to a note made by Frank Archer on a scrapbook page. Elsewhere it was stated that the young lady in question represented the end of a long search for a perfect companion to the Moxie Boy.

The Moxie Boy remained a fixture of the firm's advertising. His piercing eyes were familiar to visitors to Times Square and Columbus Circle in New York City, bathers at Revere Beach in Massachusetts, and to summer people at Ogunquit, Maine. His identity remained a mystery, but speculation surfaced from time to time. The Portland (Maine) *Evening Express*, November 17, 1926, featured William E. Lawrence, a young man who was then playing at the Jefferson Theatre:

"Mr. Lawrence, it appears, posed for the well-known poster which is familiar to the patron of every drug store in the universe: a poster of a young man with the admonitory finger raised advising people to drink Moxie and to lead the strenuous life. There is practically no one who ever reads advertisements of any type who does not know this particular poster, and there is certainly no well-groomed

This Moxie advertisement features an ice box, a household item that was being rapidly supplanted by the electrical refrigerator. The "All Sizes Now" notation refers to 7-, 16-, and 26-ounce bottles which were sold during the period.

An aerial view of Moxieland shows the rooftops painted with guide signs for pilots. Before Moxie moved there in 1926, the complex served as a brewery, inactive since the advent of Prohibition.

A ground view of Moxieland taken about the same time—in the late 1920s.

"How Many Please"

The Treasurer—

He knows the chorus
And the 'stars";
That's why he stays
Behind the bars;
He faces mobs
That want to fight

BUT—

"A glass of MOXIE sets him right"

Left: The treasurer or ticket agent at a busy theatre calms his nerves by drinking Moxie, according to this advertisement. This apparently happens after he says: "Rows A to C reserved for life, rest of the house sold out. Standing room $20—don't crowd."!

Below: The creation of an Easter cocktail was an innovative use for Moxie. Break a fresh egg into a bubbling glass of Moxie—shake vigorously and serve. "It'll put pep and sparkle into your whole day."

The Easter Cocktail

Do This With Your Easter Egg

Break it fresh into a bubbling glass of Moxie—shake vigorously and serve. It'll put pep and sparkle into your whole day. You'll feel every bit as well as you look.

It's invigorating—healthy and delicious

Phone your dealer to deliver a case today.

"The Moxie Company also has on the road three Horsemobiles, two advertising cars in each state, 31 advertising cars in all, then there are the Moxie Man lollipops, napkins, balloons, smoking stands, and other novelties quite off the beaten path of general advertising...

"The visitor to Moxieland is taken first to the 5th floor of the plant. This floor is under lock and key for it is here that the extract of the beverage is compounded... 26 herbs and oils are compounded by two expert chemists, who alone comprise the force of the 5th floor. They work daily from 5 a.m. to 9 a.m. The rest of the day is devoted to cleaning... The compound is placed in large suspended tanks, and the extract is allowed to drip drop by drop into five-gallon glass containers. It takes from four to six weeks for one of these tanks to fill, and the contents, when syrup and carbonated water are added, will make a carload of Moxie...

"The [Rockland] *Independent* reporter was allowed to taste a drop of this extract on his finger. Take it from him—it is the taste that lingers, bitter—more so than wormwood. One is impressed with the fact that it is really medicinal, healthful, and will sweeten and tone up a sick stomach and create an appetite. On this floor are three 1,000-gallon extract tanks,... There are three large syrup tanks, and with the carbonated water the product is pumped under 65 pounds pressure to the bottling room downstairs... The visitor of course is interested in the actual bottling operation. The men come dressed all in white, with their hands encased in rubber gloves and their face protected with wire screen from flying glass from broken bottles, to work at the bottling machines in 30-minute shifts. The Moxie plant is turning out 5,200 cases of Moxie a day. The product is now put up in three sizes of bottles. The men are not kept at the bottling continually but are shifted to various operations. Three carloads of new bottles from the American Bottle Company, Toledo, arrive every week. Special machinery sticks on the labels, labels bought in 10-million lots from the Forbes Lithograph Company in Revere...

"Over 100 employees are on the job daily in Moxieland with 23 young ladies in the office. Members of the Moxie family are contented. The turnover of help is less than 1% per year. One man has been in the employ of the company 34 years and one veteran is still on the job at age 85. The company formerly operated a similar plant in New York, but the site was taken over by the city for a new vehicle tunnel. A fleet of trucks operates within the city limits, and direct truck service is to be instituted between Boston and New York. Eight trucks are used for delivery in New York and 11 in Boston.

The MOXIE Boy

For the last eighteen years the Moxie Boy has pointed the way to Millions of Thirsty Buyers, and is recognized universally as one of the outstanding trade figures.

The MOXIE Girl

After months of searching we have found the Girl to present Moxie and assist the Moxie Boy in dispensing to particular people a Refreshing Drink.

Part of an advertisement of 1926 by the American Lithographic Company, "Makers of Colorgraphic Advertising," with offices in Boston and New York. The firm printed the cardboard cut-outs shown here. The Moxie Girl at the bottom of the illustration, a 1926 version, apparently was inspired by a model hired by the company. She was the latest in a long line of Moxie girls which began several decades earlier.

Front and back of a
cardboard cut-out
from the 1920s.

Drink
MOXIE
IF AT ALL PARTICULAR

"There are 36 agents in Boston and a grand total of 750 agents under the careful supervision of the main Boston office. Last year the company used $600,000 worth of sugar, and as further evidence of the output, let it be known that one chain store alone last year bought $80,000 worth of Moxie. There are no special discounts offered, just two prices, one for agents and the other for stores. The store using only a few cases a week can buy just as cheaply as the chain store with the $80,000 business.

"And this gigantic business has flourished under the management of Frank Archer, the man behind the guns, who came to the concern in its infancy as general manager when the product was made on North Washington Street at the rate of 25 to 30 cases a day. This was in the days when Moxie was a tonic. And the dream of Mr. Archer continues to form in the announcement that in the middle of next month the firm will start manufacturing Moxie at their new plant in Heath Street, Roxbury. It will remain an annex to the main Moxie plant on Haverhill Street."

Dictating to his secretary, Frank Archer produced a news release early in 1926 which told of some of his philosophies. Written in the third person, the text appeared to be the work of another individual:

"It took 50 long years to get it, but it is worth it. You have all heard of the boy who left home with nothing but an appetite and who came to the big city with ambition to make money. Well, some 30 years ago there was a certain boy with a good appetite and two plans. One was to make money and the other to help the other fellow. He eventually had the opportunity of doing both, and now his position in this line of endeavor ranks first.

"He believed that employees should be given opportunities in the business in which they are associated. He not only believed this plan, but he did give them the opportunity. Today, his associates are part of the successful business which has been built up and which is renown throughout the world. He created a working Utopia for them. The workplace had walls of white enamel, and those were kept spotless at all times, the red tile floors were always immaculate. Windows there were galore and there was plenty of light and sunshine.

"For equal ability in similar lines they are paid several times more than others are. Every employee is considered part of the firm, and the cooperation given by the associates has been a big factor in putting their product and their organization where it is today—in a class by itself...

Look at the lower part of the window carefully and you will see the Moxie Girl, with finger pointing toward the viewer, displayed in this circa 1926 (the copyright date of the cardboard sign) view of the Lake View Ice Cream Parlor, probably in Vermont. Also featured are Coon's Ice Cream, NuGrape, and other treats.

The ice cream parlor of H.A. Kittredge, of Wells, Maine featured Moxie, according to a large sign to the right of the door. Also offered were Havana Ribbon cigars and Apollo chocolates. The photograph probably dates from the 1910-20 decade.

MOXIE with Duck Sandwich

A Duck sandwich always tastes more delicious when you drink Moxie. There's a flavor and tang to Moxie that adds zest to any lunch.

And now Kid Moxie—the generous single-drink size—makes it convenient and handy to carry and serve. Moxie with outdoor lunches.

With Roast Lamb,-hot or cold-*Moxie* is delicious

After the introduction of Kid Moxie, The Moxie Company mounted an extensive newspaper advertising campaign to show the versatility of the drink, especially with lunch or dinner. Here are shown the advantages of consuming Moxie with such diverse items as a duck sandwich, roast lamb, steamed clams, and a lobster sandwich.

With Steamed Clams *Moxie* is unsurpassed!

With a LOBSTER Sandwich, *MOXIE* is wonderful!

"Frank Archer is that Maine boy. He thinks of the other fellows too. Last year he distributed over 1,500,000 toys throughout the world, and has without a doubt given away more toys than any man alive. Who is there that hasn't enjoyed reading his ads and seeing his unique attention-appealing devices throughout the country.

"Frank Archer and his associates will within a few days go into the new Moxieland..."

In 1926, Moxie lollipops were back on the scene. Apparently the production and shipping problems had been straightened out. On April 12th it was noted that in less than a week 300,000 cherry-red suckers had been distributed and that more than 2,000 Moxie songs had been given away.

An advertising program featuring Moxie as the ideal beverage to go with other things was instituted in the summer of 1926. Newspaper readers saw Moxie in combination with duck sandwiches, hot dogs, lobsters, steamed clams, fish dinners, roast beef dinners, roast lamb, ice cream, spaghetti, hot blueberry pie, chop suey, chicken sandwiches, steak dinner, ham and cheese sandwiches, Indian pudding, vegetable salad, hot biscuits, oysters, waffles, and minced pie.

Moxie was a sponsor of the Herald Traveler Cooking School instituted by the newspaper of that name. Contests for cookies and cake recipes appeared in the *Herald Traveler* pages, and, for a time, daily prizes included a Moxie tricycle. So that their mothers could attend the cooking school, a nursery was established for the children. "The Moxie Company, always generous where little ones are concerned, contributed Moxie lollipops, Moxie balloons, and Moxie tricycles for the enjoyment of very small guests," a notice related.

A special event was announced: "There is to be an added feature in the gift line today. Frank Archer, of Moxie fame, who has already sent Moxie tricycles for the nursery, besides lollipops and other goodies, announced that he will present 20 crystal radio sets to the holders of lucky numbers in the nursery this afternoon."

Frank Archer was a marble shooter from way back, according to several contemporary articles. Each year in the mid-1920s he opened an annual tournament, donating 100,000 or more marbles each time to the event. "An old ringer player himself, Frank M. Archer knows the benefits which youngsters derive from this skillful sport." It was related that during his childhood in Lincoln, Maine, Archer was school champion.

By the summer of 1926 the new seven-ounce size, the Kid Moxie, was joined by another Archer innovation. An August 9th notice stated:

"The newest thing—the new handy Moxie Carrying Bag snuggly holds just six Kid Moxies. The rush of dealer demand is being met as rapidly as this famous bag can be manufactured."

This particular bag style bore an illustration of the Moxie Kid holding a bagful of Moxie in his right hand and with the Moxie Pup under his left hand.

More on the Carrying Bag appeared in a notice to dealers sent on August 24th:

"You also will want to have in mind that the Moxie Carrying Bag for six of the Kid Moxies is the knockout of the year as a container. Such quantities as you can use to advantage will be supplied to you. If you put these in the hands of the dealer and put into each bag six Kid Moxies from the stock, you will find that by his displaying them it will increase his sales, as it has many others, at least 10 times.

"It is particularly important for you to bear in mind that the new single drink Kid Moxie, seven ounce size, is the recognized single drink bottle of the world... It is important that you place your order for Kid Moxie to take care of the enormous demand that you will get now that people are returning from their country homes and schools are opening. This Kid Moxie is going to be a knockout for schools, offices, restaurants, and the home. You will see them being carried through the streets in the Moxie Carrying Bag by people going to work as well as to pleasure."

There was only one problem: Kid Moxie was priced 10c at retail, at a time when numerous competitors, including Coca-Cola, were available for a nickel.

A promotion, Moxie Week, was instituted. For example, the Brockton (Massachusetts) Public Market at its two branches observed this celebration, selling the pint-size (16 ounces) Moxie for 14c. "With every bottle of Moxie sold this week we will give free a souvenir— hundreds of fans, hats, balloons, toys etc. that will please both children and grownups. See our window display," exhorted newspaper advertisements.

The Moxie Maid, the companion to the Moxie Butler (the latter featuring the caricature of Raymond Hitchcock, but now modified to a silhouette rather than a carved head), was a popular feature in numerous advertisements. Some illustrations showed her holding an ash tray, while others showed her with a bottle of Moxie, and some showed four wheels on the bottom of her wooden pedestal.

Frank M. Archer, Jr. received frequent newspaper notices for his public relations activities, benefit concerts, charities, and the like.

tlers, particularly those located in areas other than New England, might have been unfamiliar with Moxie, a "What Is Moxie" page furnished details:

"Moxie is a pure, wholesome and refreshing carbonated beverage—a sparkling, healthful blend of root and herb essences. Moxie has an aromatic tang, a delicious, thirst-satisfying, bitter-sweet taste that is distinctly different from all other beverages.

"Until this year only about 10% of the people of the United States, living in a comparatively tiny northeastern section of the country, have ever had a real chance to enjoy Moxie." At this point Archer apparently forgot that in the 1880s and 1890s Moxie was distributed all over America, with bottlers and franchisees in St. Louis, Chicago, Los Angeles, Cleveland, and elsewhere. 'These good people and their sons and daughters have bought more than $75,000,000 worth of Moxie because *they like it*," Archer continued.

"New England is the birthplace of Moxie, where for many years it has enjoyed the widest distribution and largest sale among all proprietary bottled beverages. It is estimated that 5,000,000 people from other states and foreign countries annually visit New England. Among these visitors are countless thousands who will greet Moxie as an old acquaintance when it comes to their home towns, for Moxie makes friends quickly and holds them long.

"Every bottle of Moxie is composed of a score of separate and distinct elements. It is a pure food product in which every ingredient is of the finest quality. Moxie extract and Moxie syrup are compounded, blended, aged and put in containers for shipment by the most modern scientific methods, under carefully supervised hygienic laboratory conditions.

"In its keen, appetizing effect as a thirst-quencher, Moxie is unique, distinctive, different. Public speakers, grand opera singers, theatrical stars, and athletes have found Moxie very soothing, re-vivifying, and satisfying in the course of their most strenuous efforts." Here Frank Archer's favorite word, "strenuous," appears again!

"Doctors, surgeons, chemists, pure-food experts and dietitians have long given Moxie the highest rating, constantly using Moxie themselves and suggesting its use to others, because Moxie is a complete, satisfying and effective thirst-quencher in itself...

"*The Moxie Company of America* is extending the distribution of this delicious and beneficial beverage to the world through the manufacture and sale of Moxie Fountain Syrup and by the awarding of exclusive territorial franchises to leading local bottlers everywhere, except in the New England states. The tremendous capacity of the new Moxie Syrup Plant, the rapid and systematic

THE FAMOUS *MOXIE*
HORSEMOBILE

This is "Moxie Joe" and the latest model of what has long been called "The Most Famous Mobile Advertisement in the World." When the first Moxie Horsemobile was built, the automobile was almost as much of a rarity on city streets as the horse is now.

The Moxie Horsemobile goes everywhere Moxie goes. But that has been only the beginning of its travels. In motion pictures, newsreels, newspapers, magazines, and learned books on the subject of advertising, the Moxie Horsemobile has literally "gone around the world." Stories about it have been translated into all languages throughout the world.

Every year and everywhere on his travels, "Moxie Joe" and the Moxie Horsemobile are at the disposal of all civic and charitable organizations for publicity stunts, field days, parades, children's outings, etc. For years the Moxie Horsemobile has "done his bit" every summer to aid Uncle Sam's army recruiting work. All the time this leader of the Moxie Advertising Parade is enlisting customers for the dealers who sell Moxie.

"The Famous Moxie Horsemobile" headlines this page in The Moxie Company of America's brochure for the 1929 advertising campaign. In its era, which lasted for several decades after 1916, the Horsemobile was one of the most famous advertisements America has ever known. Crowds would flock to see it, and clippings concerning its appearance filled a large scrapbook at Moxie headquarters. Drivers of the several different Horsemobiles were generically known as "Moxie Joe," after Joseph P. King, the first Horsemobile driver back in 1916.

Ask your Dealer to deliver a Bag of Moxie today

Moxie Carrying Bag holds 6 Bottles of *Kid Moxis* the new single drink size and has a hundred later uses. Devised by FRANK ARCHER Exclusively for MOXIE. REGISTERED

Drink MOXIE

More advertising items from the 1929 era: Above is shown a Moxie Horsemobile with a bottle on the back, an artist's conception combining the old and the new. To the right is a distinctive Moxie bottle carton, while below is one of several posters. These and numerous other advertising pieces of the era featured the Horsemobile as a central theme.

Drink MOXIE Distinctively Different

NOW- at soda fountains *and* in bottles

Three Moxie signboard posters, an official Moxie bottle cap, and the familiar Moxie Boy cardboard cut-out are shown from the The Moxie Company of America's brochure for its 1929 advertising campaign. "Drink Moxie 100%" was a prevailing theme of the period.

franchising of territory, the perfection of plants for equipping bottlers, and complete arrangements for intensive advertising in every franchise territory throws open immediately to leading bottlers the greatest time-tested and profit-proven opportunity in the carbonated beverage field!

"New England's greatest popular-sale and profit-making beverage is now ready to start making new business, new sales records, and *greater profits* in your territory. We of *The Moxie Company of America* greet you with this message. You will find that our friendly, four-square way of doing business and the methods we use in bringing the merits of Moxie to the attention of the public will always be distinctively different, diverse, novel, and appropriate to this delicious drink which for nearly half a century has been in a class by itself."

Archer was a master at the publicity and promotion game, and any survey of the great names in advertising of the early part of the present century should rightfully include him near the top of the list. The Horsemobile, the Ponycycle, the ephemeral TNT Cowboy, the celebrity fans, the puzzles, the children's toys, the man on stilts, and other gimmicks and novelties made Moxie a household word throughout its trading area. These successes were not forgotten in the 1929 advertising campaign. Although Archer stated that "the main foundation of [Moxie's] success has been newspaper advertising," the 1929 booklet devoted an entire page to the Horsemobile. By 1929 the Horsemobile had sired many offspring, and enough duplicate examples were available that virtually any fair, parade, or other gathering in New England was apt to see "Moxie Joe" —the generic name given to all Moxie drivers—very much in evidence. The quality of the cars on which the horse was mounted changed, and by the late 1920s and early 1930s such marques as Rolls Royce and LaSalle were in evidence. While in 1916 and subsequent years the Moxie name did not appear on the car itself (but was very much in evidence on distinctive jackets worn by the drivers), by 1929 advertising appeared on the running boards and cowl. At that time Archer noted:

"This is 'Moxie Joe' and the latest model of what has long been called 'The Most Famous Mobile Advertisement in the World.' When the first Moxie Horsemobile was built, the automobile was almost as much of a rarity on the city streets as the horse is now.

"The Moxie Horsemobile goes everywhere Moxie goes. But that has only been the beginning of its travels. In motion pictures, newsreels, newspapers, magazines, and learned books on the subject of advertising, the Moxie Horsemobile has literally 'gone around

Moxie was an attraction at the soda fountain as well as in the home, as shown in these 1928 illustrations made for The Moxie Company of America.

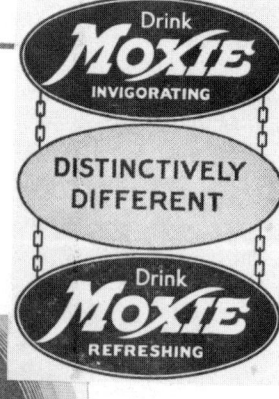

For many decades Moxie had a close relationship with the automobile. The 1929 advertisement above suggests that Moxie insures steady nerves, a clear brain, a quick eye, and other attributes necessary for safe driving. To the right and below are shown Moxie signs of the 1928-1930 period.

Moxie items: Above is a sample label issued by The Moxie Company of America, 1929, with a space for the imprint of a franchisee, while to the left is shown a circa 1935 bottle bearing the imprint of the Aliquippa (Pennsylvania) Sanitary Bottling Works. Below is a filled crate of Moxie from the same period, while to the lower right is a Moxie Bottling Co. of Lehighton (Pennsylvania) bottle of the time.

More 1929 items: Moxie syrup was sold in several forms, including gallon jugs (of several varieties, one with a stippled surface, unlike that shown here) and 50-gallon barrels. Apparently barrels could not be made to hold precisely 50 gallons, for shipping records of the time show they contained from about 48 to 51 gallons. Below is shown a metal Moxie sign of the period.

the world.' Stories about it have been translated into all languages throughout the world.

"Every year and everywhere on his travels, 'Moxie Joe' and the Moxie Horsemobile are at the disposal of all civic and charitable organizations for publicity stunts, field days, parades, children's outings, etc. For years the Moxie Horsemobile has 'done his bit' every summer to aid Uncle Sam's army recruiting work."

Archer pinpointed newspapers as the main advertising vehicle for the planned 1929 campaign, noting:

"We use daily newspapers first and principally for Moxie advertising, simply because daily newspapers in every household in the neighborhood are as much a part of intimate family life as good pure food and drink. They get results. In daily newspapers we are able to concentrate the influence of Moxie advertising within the territory where it will be most effective in backing up the sales efforts of Moxie bottlers, retail dealers, and soda fountain dispensers.

"Daily newspapers are read by all classes, old and young, and everyone who has a dime is a Moxie prospect. Moxie advertising catches the eye and can be read at a glance, even by hurried readers. There can be no doubt that wherever bottlers and dealers work together to push Moxie, Moxie newspaper advertising will help tremendously to increase sales year after year.

"Now, Moxie is coming into *your neighborhood*, and all the neighbors who go to the drug and grocery stores, soda fountains, restaurants, refreshment stands, and such are going to see Moxie advertisements in the newspapers."

In combination with the newspaper campaign other media were used. Archer noted that "millions daily hear Moxie radio advertising," a commentary on a current campaign in the Boston area. Further, "the President of this Company has had many years of successful experience in combining newspaper advertising with Moxie billboards, posters, wall signs, radio, dealer-helps, the famous Moxie novelties, and Moxie sales promotion service."

Since the 1880s, Moxie carefully prepared newspaper advertisements each year. The 1929 versions were much different from those of a few decades earlier, but still many of the familiar Moxie symbols were retained. First and foremost, the Moxie name, in the form of the distinctive trademark devised in 1907, appeared as a major feature. The slogan "drink Moxie 100%" was popular, as were the tribute to Moxie's taste, "Distinctively Different." The Moxie Horsemobile, a fixture since the summer of 1916, appeared in new form, this time with the car sporting a 1929 Massachusetts plate with

Advertising items from the 1929 period include the Moxie Carrying Bag at the upper left, a Moxie bottle carton that could be made into a puzzle (upper right), a cardboard cut-out of the Moxie Kid and the Moxie Pup (lower left), and a tally card featuring the Moxie Pup.

Three posters, each of 24-sheet size, are shown for the Moxie advertising campaign for the year 1929. "Thousands of them" were planned, according to a promotional brochure.

The Moxie Bottling Company of Lehighton (Pennsylvania) had its own version of the Horsemobile, a wooden silhouette of a horse and rider mounted on the back of an open-bed truck. This agency was very active in the 1930s and distributed Moxie in specially-molded glass bottles unlike those used by The Moxie Company.

September 1930: The young daughter of E.L. Hinds poses for a snapshot in the saddle of the Rolls-Royce Horsemobile.

Above and left: Cleveland, Ohio store windows photographed on August 19, 1930 by a Moxie representative.

Below: Display in the window of "The Los Angeles Times," 1930. In this year Moxie was heavily advertised in Southern California.

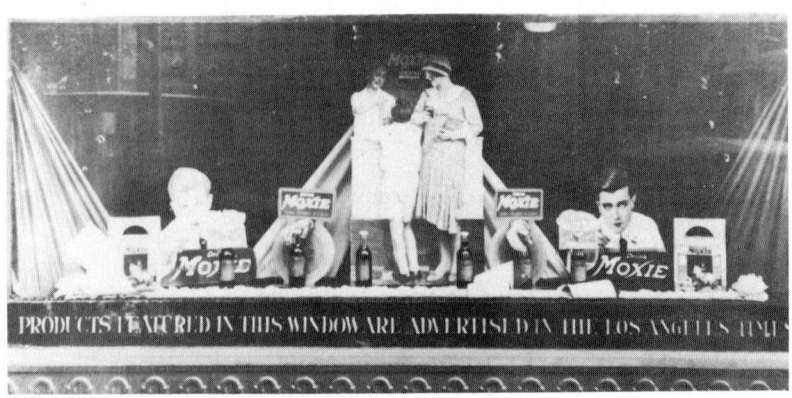

stock, the Moxie story might have been different. Still, the advertising part of the business was nothing less than spectacular.

This huge billboard greeted automobilists at the exit of Holland Tunnel, Jersey City, New Jersey, linking that city with Manhattan. Frank Archer was especially proud of this presentation, circa 1929, in one of the New York area's most prominent advertising locations.

Delivery truck of the Seilheimer Beverage Company, Hackensack, New Jersey, Moxie Division, as photographed in August 1930. This unit has the inscription "OK'd BY MILLIONS" in a starburst on one door and "In a Class by Itself" on the other (not visible in the photograph).

1929 Moxie Billboards

Shown on this and the next few pages are snapshots of Moxie billboards taken during the 1928-1930 years, but mostly 1929, by a traveling representative. The territory depicted is primarily Massachusetts, Rhode Island, and Connecticut.

Although a few billboards show the Moxie Boy with his pointing finger, most are of geometric designs. The motto "Ok'd by Millions" is seen frequently, as are "Distinctively Different," "Clean, Wholesome, Refreshing," and "Delightfully Refreshing."

These billboards were posted by The Moxie Company, Boston, at the same approximate time Frank Archer was launching his Moxie Company of America venture.

1929 MOXIE BILLBOARDS

1929 MOXIE BILLBOARDS

1929 MOXIE BILLBOARDS

1929 MOXIE BILLBOARDS

1929 MOXIE BILLBOARDS

Chapter 16

Moxie in the 1930s

Despite great expectations, The Moxie Company of America did not prove all that Archer hoped it would be. Perhaps part of the problem was that Archer spent much of his time in Boston, while the main facilities were located in New York City. There were some successes, however, and over 300 new distributors and bottlers were signed up, extending the Moxie product westward and southward. In the meantime, the New England company, separate from Archer, missed his guidance. Thus the stage was set in 1930 for a merger that would satisfy everyone.

Toward the end of December 1930 it was announced that on December 31st a special meeting of the stockholders would be held to vote on a plan of merging the businesses and activities of The Moxie Company (the New England company guided by the Thompsons), The Moxie Company of America, and the Pureoxia Company. "The majority of the stock of The Moxie Company and the Pureoxia Company, which are closely held, has already agreed to the merger," according to a notice which appeared on Christmas day 1925 and which continued:

"The plan would join the three businesses under the name of The Moxie Company, which concern would increase its capital stock to 58,500 shares of Class A stock without par or voting power, and 517,000 Class B stock with full voting power, 400,000 shares of which are to be issued and 117,000 to remain in the treasury to provide for a conversion of Class A stock. The A stock would be entitled to cumulative dividends at the rate of $3 annually.

"The merger would be accomplished solely on an exchange of stock basis. 31,333 shares of A and 235,000 shares of B stock should go to present stockholders of The Moxie Company; 16,667 shares of A and 140,000 shares of B will go to The Moxie Company of America [on the basis of one-third of a share of A stock and one share of B stock for each share of Moxie Company of America A stock, and

A Moxie advertising truck with two oversized bottles shown in Portland, Maine in the 1920s.

A Moxie delivery truck of the Sweeney Bottling Works, Middletown, New York, as photographed on April 9, 1930 by George Demers, a Moxie Horsemobile driver.

nine-tenths of a share of B stock for each share]; and 10,500 shares of A and 25,000 B shares will go to the Pureoxia Company, for all of its assets except real estate on Norway Street, Boston. The Moxie Company of America is the only one of the three which has stock publicly owned. It now has outstanding 50,000 A shares and 100,000 B shares.

"The Moxie Company of America was formed about two years ago for the purpose of manufacturing and distributing Moxie syrup in territories outside of New England under a license and royalty agreement with The Moxie Company. Pureoxia manufactures and distributes, mainly in eastern Massachusetts, ginger ale and allied beverages. The business has been established more than 30 years and has been steadily profitable."

In the new firm, the board of governors and officers consisted of Frank M. Archer, chairman; Frank M. Archer, Jr., vice-president; Benjamin B. Avery, vice-president; B. Devereux Barker (of the law firm of Barker, Davis & Shattuck, Boston), board member; Arnault B. Edgerly, vice-president; William E. Stanwood (partner, Spencer, Trask & Co., Boston), director; Francis E. Thompson, president; and Harry A. Thompson, treasurer.

At last Archer achieved the corporate position of his dreams. He was chairman of the board of The Moxie Company. He also drew the most generous salary in a compensation schedule which gave him $30,000 per year, his son $20,000 per year, Francis E. Thompson $20,500, Harry A. Thompson $18,000, Benjamin B. Avery $20,000, and Arnault B. Edgerly $8,000.

The Pureoxia Company, whose primary products were ginger ale and soda water, had been formed by Harry A. Edgerly in 1899. Years earlier, in 1895, he owned several hotels in Florida. An account noted: "There, in an atmosphere of gracious hospitality, you would have found your comforts and needs eagerly anticipated. And it was there that Mr. Edgerly first became interested in the beverage business." The story continued:

"Always alert to provide the best of everything for his guests, he imported the finest ginger ales obtainable in those early days. Mr. Edgerly personally tested and tasted the known beverages of the time, and undoubtedly was one of America's first expert connoisseurs of ginger ale. As a businessman Mr. Edgerly foresaw the great and growing popularity of this beverage. He had sprung from a family of bankers and professional men descended from early New England pioneers. He saw an opportunity before him, had faith in himself, and made his decision promptly. In 1899 he disposed of his successful hotel business and set out to blaze new trails in the manufacture of first-quality ginger ale.

"He built a beverage plant that through the years has been a model for the whole industry to pattern after... In Pureoxia he was sure he had achieved such a beverage, and New England agreed with him. Many other ginger ales have been introduced since Pureoxia pioneered the way in 1899, but none has ever threatened its leadership in its home territory. It was typical of Mr. Edgerly that when his health failed about a year ago [this account was written in 1931] he worried not about himself but about the future of the product. So he called upon another leader in the beverage business, a man whom he had never before met but for whom he had great admiration, Frank M. Archer, the Moxie Man.

"Inviting Mr. Archer to examine his business books, Mr. Edgerly said, 'Mr. Archer, many bankers and beverage companies have sought to acquire Pureoxia. But I want you to have it. Yours is the only company with the ideals, the plant, the equipment and high standards of excellence to carry it on as I want to see it carried on.'

"The story of Frank M. Archer, the Moxie Man, is too well known to need repeating here. But what Mr. Edgerly did not know was that for over a quarter of a century Mr. Archer had been searching for a quality ginger ale to offer as a companion drink to Moxie. He had his specialists experimenting for many years with various formulae. His representatives were in constant touch with developments in the beverage business, even visiting the Pureoxia plant four or five times a year. Mr. Archer finally decided he could never make a ginger ale that would be superior to Pureoxia, so he abandoned the search.

"Mr. Edgerly's offer to merge the company was a happy surprise. Mr. Archer's 25-year search was ended. He welcomed this opportunity to take over Pureoxia, the ginger ale for which a quarter of a century had been a standard of perfection, rated always in first place for the quality and purity of ingredients by pure food experts to whom Mr. Archer had submitted many samples.

"Unfortunately, a dark shadow marred this happy ending. Mr. Edgerly died before the final papers could be signed. But his last wishes were carried out. His son, Arnault B. Edgerly, continues with The Moxie Company as vice-president, and Pureoxia will hereafter be made at Moxieland in Boston..."

In the early years Pureoxia was known as the Pureoxia Distilled Water Company. A brochure issued circa 1905 noted:

"The Pureoxia Distilled Water Company was originally started in 1899 as an experiment in hygiene. Its product, however, received

Above: A Pureoxia advertisement from the 1930s features the Moxie Boy looking intently forward.

Right: Harry A. Edgerly, who founded the Pureoxia Company in 1899, was suffering from a terminal illness in 1930 when he contacted The Moxie Company, after which a merger was arranged. Edgerly passed away before the deal was completed, and his interests were represented by his son, Arnault Edgerly.

Below: A metal Pureoxia sign from the early 1930s. Similar format signs were made with Moxie inscriptions.

HARRY A. EDGERLY

such an acceptance by physicians and the general New England public it necessitated, before the completion of its first year's business, a building in the Back Bay, Boston, Massachusetts, constructed especially for its needs. This present plant has a capacity of 10,000 gallons of distilled water per day. Popular demand has also forced this company into other branches of business that had not at first been contemplated, such as the manufacture of high-class temperance drinks and artificial mineral waters. These are made in every case from the purest and best of ingredients and distilled water."

At the time the Pureoxia product line was dominated by distilled water. Other items included seltzer, lithia, Kissengen, Vichy, and carbonated water, all of which were put up in quart siphons. Pureoxia Club Soda was sold "in egg-shaped bottles that will stand upright without the use of a stand," Pureoxia Ginger Ale, made from distilled water, was offered in half-pints, pints, and quarts. Other products included sarsaparilla, birch beer, blood orange, champagne cider, Hop Bitters ("a popular English temperance drink"), and Iron-brew ("a non-alcoholic tonic, from the receipt of a celebrated Carlsbad physician—a combination of vegetable tonic and delicious aromatics which enriches and strengthens the blood, muscles, and brain; regulates the stomach and nervous system; relieves headache, nausea, dyspepsia, sleeplessness and general debility; and on account of its health-giving properties the most valuable tonic beverage on the market").

The *Boston Post*, January 1, 1931, ran this notice:

"MOXIE ABSORBS TWO COMPANIES, TO CONSOLIDATE ALL THREE PLANTS IN ROXBURY. After long negotiations between the directors of each of the three companies, the stockholders of The Moxie Company, the Pureoxia Company, and The Moxie Company of America at special meetings yesterday voted to merge into a single organization... According to the directors, a proposed plan of consolidation will prove a boon to Boston. All offices and plants of the three companies are to be consolidated at Moxieland at Roxbury. Plans have already been made, the director said, to move the New York plant, located at the Bush Terminal, to Roxbury; the plant of the Pureoxia Company, located on Norway Street, Boston, will also be moved... With this consolidation, the directors said they feel they will double the number of employees now at Moxieland. The three companies now do an aggregate business of about $4,500,000 a year. Over a period of years they have done more than $100 million dollars in business..."

Cover of a brochure issued circa 1905 by Pureoxia, then called the Pureoxia Distilled Water Company. At the time, emphasis was on health and sanitation. "In densely populated districts, the only sure safeguard against contamination lies in boiling all the water used for drinking purposes...," an inside page noted. Of course, Pureoxia Distilled Water would do the trick just as well!

On the next several pages are shown illustrations from the 1905 brochure.

Side View of Building showing Condensers.

Front View of Building.

Views of the Pureoxia building, circa 1905, located on Whipple Street, off 110 Norway Street, in the Back Bay district of Boston. This facility was maintained for many years.

Pureoxia was originally started in 1899 "as an experiment in hygiene," according to the brochure. The owner, Harry Edgerly, earlier operated a hotel in Florida. The plant shown above was said to have had a capacity of 10,000 gallons of distilled water per day.

Laboratory.

Bottling Room.

In an era in which newspapers and magazines were full of articles about purity and cleanliness, food and beverage firms, Pureoxia included, took pains to show the public their clean surroundings.

250 gallon Palatable Water Still.

Store Room

Additional views of the Pureoxia facility circa 1905.

DISTILLED WATER

AN Absolutely Pure and Palatable Water, free from all **salts** and **organic matter**, and put up in **sterilized** bottles and carboys. All packages are **sealed when bottled** at our establishment.

This water is particularly desirable for **drinking purposes** on account of its softness and its tendency to remove all surplus salts and acids from the system by reason of its great absorptive qualities which spring waters do not possess. It is thoroughly aerated and is **not flat.**

Prescribed by the best physicians as a **beverage.**

A **preventive** and a **cure** for **rheumatism** and kindred ills.

Peculiarly adapted to all **medicinal** and **chemical** work on account of its freedom from salts.

Desirable for the **Toilet** because of its **softness.**

5 gallon carboy	$ .35
6 two quart bottles in case	.35

A deposit of 65 cents required on all packages.

Tel. { 1147 / 1542 } Back Bay.   **Goods delivered at your residence.**

(As per page 16.)

Distilled water was the main Pureoxia product in 1905. Primarily a firm with local sales, Pureoxia offered free delivery to Boston suburbs on a rotating schedule basis. For example, on Thursday the communities of Brookline, Allston, Brighton, the Newtons, Auburndale, and Riverside were serviced, while Monday saw deliveries to Roxbury, Dorchester, Ashmont, Forest Hills, Hyde Park, and Milton.

WATER COOLERS

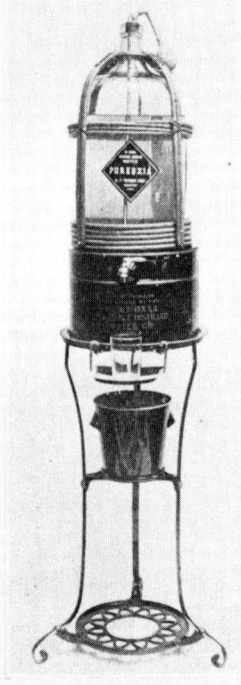

THESE coolers are specially designed to **keep ice** and **water sepe- rate**, and to **obviate** the necessity of **emptying the contents of the carboys by hand.**

In these coolers this operation is effected automatically by a siphon as each glass of water is drawn.

These coolers are made in two styles, **lacquered tin stand and ice box,** and **black Flemish oak stand,** with ice box of **Dutch earthenware.**

All parts with which water comes in contact are of pure block tin, and all ex- posed portions are handsomely nickel plated.

Office contracts a specialty. Coolers are **loaned** when a reasonable amount of water is used weekly.

Coolers also specially adapted to **house- hold needs.**

5 gallons distilled water in carboys (cooler loaned) . . . . . . $ .40
Coolers, including carboy, siphon and stand 8.50

For details inquire at office.

To aid the sale of distilled water, Pureoxia offered a siphon-type cooler on a loan basis to customers who used a reasonable amount of water each week.

In the 19th century, mineral waters from Kissengen (Germany), Vichy (France), and other locations were popular with those who could afford them. Others were apt to purchase imitations formulated with the same chemical compounds used in European waters. Examples are offered on the above catalogue page.

CLUB SODA

THIS club soda is of **particularly fine quality** as it is made of distilled water which is susceptible to **very high carbonation.**

Especially desirable for **club** and **family** use on account of its **great blending properties.**

Put up in **egg shaped bottles** that will **stand upright** without the use of a **stand.**

Patented **caps** used for stoppers **instead** of **corks.**

PRICE.

Per case 2 doz. bottles $2.45
Refund on empty box and bottles 95

(Making net price 75c. per dozen.)

Tel. { 1147 1542 } Back Bay.   Or Your Grocer.

Pureoxia Club Soda was a product that sold well in 1905 but was to sell even better in coming decades. It was put up in egg-shaped bottles, as noted.

DRY

G I N G E R   A L E

THIS ginger ale is in **every respect** the equal of any in the world, and possesses in addition the **unique advantage** of being **made from distilled water.** This permits of a **much more perfect blend,** than if spring waters were used in its manufacture, and consequently results in a much **finer flavor** and **greater brilliancy.**

Nothing but the purest ingredients are employed in its preparation, which makes it **especially desirable** for **children** and **invalids.**

A **special advantage** it possesses over the old style variety is that **corks** are replaced by **caps** as stoppers.

Bottles are white flint glass and hold 2 full glasses each.

They are packed 24 in an upright partitioned case, where they may remain until used. No covers or excelsior used in packing.

PRICE.

Per case of 2 doz. pint bottles $2.45
Rebate on empty bottles and box 95

(Making net price 75c. per dozen.)

Also put up in half-pints and quarts.

Tel. { 1147 / 1542 } **Back Bay.**   **Or Your Grocer.**

Pureoxia Ginger Ale was one of many products back in 1905. By the early 1930s, when the firm merged with Moxie, Pureoxia Ginger Ale was the dominant product.

The Pureoxia Company's early records, still in existence today, reveal, for example, that on January 15, 1904 the capital stock of the Pureoxia Company was valued at $51,770. The advertising agency for the firm was Wood, Putnam & Wood, whose talents were also employed by Moxie. In 1911 Pureoxia made $11,418.87 profit for the year. In 1912 the profit was a similar figure, $11,051.75, while other profits registered included 1913 $12,186.10, 1914 $14,318.01, 1915 $10,423.30, 1916 $27,642.19, 1917 $27,273.99, 1918 $21,100.82, and 1919 $84,018.82. In the latter year, total sales amounted to $400,862.14.

At the close of business on December 31, 1923, the assets of the Pureoxia Company, originally incorporated in the state of Maine (which had favorable laws involving corporate activities), were sold to the Pureoxia Company of Massachusetts. Assets at the time included $46,646 worth of land, $271,653 in buildings, $129,338 in machines and equipment, $58,120 in trucks, and $99,129 in inventories.

The first financial report issued by the merged firms appeared on September 30, 1931 and showed net income after taxes of $145,662. The merger seemed to be working, and all parties apparently were satisfied. Separate ledgers were kept for Moxie and Pureoxia in order to track each segment of the business. The two best customers of the time were the Great Atlantic & Pacific Tea Company, which from June 1 through October 1, 1931 bought 38,288 cases of Moxie and 4,187 cases of Pureoxia, and First National Stores, which during the same period bought 33,620 cases of Moxie and 5,985 cases of Pureoxia. A growing business in large carboys of soda water was developed, and shipments in this line increased steadily. Featured at this time was the Advertising Bottle Wagon, not horse drawn, but a motorized truck with a bottle in the back. One variety had two bottles mounted in the rear.

In November 1931, sketches were made up for new Pureoxia labels and caps, with Frank Archer directing. Color plans and sketches for Pureoxia *beer* labels were also made, perhaps indicating production was contemplated.

Pureoxia products were many. While ginger ale was the staple beverage, also bearing the Pureoxia label were sarsaparilla, birch beer, root beer, orange, lemon-lime, sparkling grape, mineral water, soda water, and distilled water.

Moxie continued to be sold in three sizes. The formula was derived from 23 different ingredients, according to an interview with A.W. Penney, superintendent of the plant at Moxieland. An Archer innovation was described in a 1931 announcement:

Above: Three electric delivery trucks used by the Pureoxia Company, Boston, circa 1910.

The Moxie Boy holds Moxie and Pureoxia in this advertisement of the early 1930s.

Following the merger of the Moxie and Pureoxia firms in 1931, the famous Moxie Horsemobile was used to advertise Pureoxia products as well. Actually, the above ad is a bit confusing, for at the top Moxie is indeed mentioned while at the bottom it is suggested that if "quality" is a question, Pureoxia might be a better choice!

"Frank Archer, Sr. has scored another bullseye in the presentation of Moxie Candy, another bright star in Moxieland's constellation. Moxie Candy is, to quote Mr. Archer:

" 'A pure delicious confection with the same distinctively different bittersweet flavor as Moxie, the beverage. It is made from genuine Moxie extract and is cut into pieces just the right size to pop into your mouth. Carefully wrapped in wax paper, about 15 of these pieces are packed in an airtight tin box, attractive in its red, yellow and black lettering, and you get the entire package complete for a nickel.

" 'The candy is a beautiful cherry-red, crystal clear and is as good for you as it is attractive in appearance and intriguing in flavor. It is candy in which even those in pursuit of the slender silhouette can indulge without qualms of conscience. And you will find it wonderfully popular with the little folks.' "

Reacting to competition, in 1931 Moxie dropped the price of the Kid Moxie size to 5c a bottle, calling it "the most drastic price reduction on one of the most popular and healthful beverages manufactured." This was to have a telling effect on Moxie's balance sheet, for nickel sales did not prove profitable, especially for bottles shipped great distances from Moxieland.

The senior Archer kept up his activity as a sponsor of marble tournaments, and in 1931 he reminisced for a Boston newspaper:

"My father, who was a country physician in the little town of Lincoln, Maine, where I was born, knew the value of good, healthy play in the open. He taught me to play a fair game of marbles, and in the years that followed I licked the whole countryside. Your tournament brings it all back to me."

According to Frank Archer, Jr., who stated his height as 6' 1" and his weight as 180, the senior Archer was 5'8" and weighed 138 pounds. "He was sensitive about posing for pictures even at family gatherings, and rarely did so."

Archer, approaching 70 years of age, maintained his show business friendships, but on a reduced scale. In May 1931, George M. Cohan, visiting Boston, had some words to say about him:

"I always get a kick out of show business. No matter whether I'm in it or out of it I get a kick just the same. That seems paradoxical, but it isn't... Also, too, there are the chances for renewals of old friendships. For instance, here in Boston I'm always glad to play just for the opportunity to meet up with Frank Archer..."

In an interview, Frank Archer stated that his first question to all job applicants is, "What newspaper do you read?" He then discusses recent events with them. "Those who haven't the time or the interest to read some newspaper regularly never get any further with him," according to an article appearing in the Boston *Evening Transcript.* "It doesn't make any difference to me which paper, nor where it is printed nor in what language. I want them to read some sort of newspaper every day and to be interested in what's going on in the general field of important news and along their own lines. After all, about all a college can do is train men and women so they are able to read their daily newspaper intelligently, and no one is so great a specialist or scholar or so fine a workman that he cannot further his real education by reading today's newspaper. The press is the greatest single educational medium in America today," he continued.

Another newspaper notice revealed that Frank Archer had requested radio engineers to survey Moxieland in order to install a large central receiving station capable of transmitting broadcast programs or phonograph records through loudspeakers in every department, an early version of piped-in music.

The work ethic of Archer, perhaps exaggerated, was discussed in a Boston *Traveler* article in August of the same year:

"Frank Archer, who makes Moxie and Pureoxia, recently took his first day off in 35 years. If you do not know Frank Archer, you may be amazed that a man should go that long without a day off. If you do know him, you will understand that he gets his fun in life out of making his fellow workers and friends happy. We say fellow workers, because Frank Archer detests the words 'employees' and 'help.'

"What did he do on his day off? Did he sleep late? Did he go in for a gay time? He arose shortly after dawn and went for a ride on a horse. Then he played golf. Later he had a swim.

"Here is a man with plenty of money. This is his idea of how to spend his only day off in 35 years. Don't get the idea that he does not know how to play. He plays all the time. He plays at the game of living happily and helping the other fellow do likewise. We like him. You may have guessed it."

Archer was the subject of a biographical profile by George C. MacKinnon in *The Daily Record,* September 21, 1931:

"He was born in Lincoln, Maine, August 12, 1862. He thinks that the date 'doesn't sound so good,' but with his patent hale and heartiness he should worry about dates!

This advertisement for Pureoxia Ginger Ale dates from the 1930s and features The Moxie Company.

Consistently Advertised for 50 Years
Retails at 10c per glass

Every fountain should display and push Moxie, the best profit-maker of all the syrups.

$4.00
Gallon

FREE—MOXIE DISPENSER
(same as cut) with initial
order of Moxie

Moxie Glasses
per doz., $1.00

In the early 1930s the price of Moxie syrup was raised to $4 per gallon, and glass dispensers were furnished to soda fountains, restaurants, and other outlets. The inverted gallon jug at the top of the bottle is covered with a cardboard advertisement.

The Boston Athletci Association-Feb.14,1931- $50.00
Program Forty Second Annual Games

QUALITY BEVERAGES

MANUFACTURED BY

THE MOXIE COMPANY

MOXIE
PUREOXIA PALE DRY GINGER ALE
PUREOXIA GOLDEN GINGER ALE
PUREOXIA SARSAPARILLA
PUREOXIA BIRCH BEER
PUREOXIA ROOT BEER
PUREOXIA ORANGE
PUREOXIA LEMON AND LIME
PUREOXIA SPARKLING GRAPE
PUREOXIA MINERAL WATER
PUREOXIA SIPHONS

This clipping from a scrapbook kept by The Moxie Company shows different products sold by the firm—as listed in an advertisement in the program for the Forty Second Annual Games of the Boston Athletic Association, February 14, 1931, such advertisement costing $50.

— 612 —

"His pet sport as a kid was strange. His dad was a doctor, and young Frank's delight was to go with him on long trips into the wild to visit patients in all kinds of weather. Often during these trips young Frank had to get out and shovel, the snow was that deep.

"His education? The little red school house—and that's about the extent of it. Leaving school, he drifted into the electrical business—manufacturing electric batteries and house lighting plants. He had no special training for the work, but the most startling thing about Frank is his ingenuity—as we shall see presently.

"Then one year he met Freeman N. Young, and a change came over the spirit of his dream, a change which ruled his whole life and brought a fascination equal to that experienced by the astronomer who sweeps the sky agog for new celestial discoveries—to that of the philosopher who feels himself hot on the trail of the ultimate causes of things.

"Freeman N. Young was one of Moxie's early promoters, and after meeting Frank he kept after him to join up with Moxie. In 1896 Frank finally decided to do so—and his decision made his life exactly the kind of adventure to suit him.

"Frank's first job at Moxie was that of 'reconstructionist'—and how he started reconstructing!

"First of the host of ideas which forever flow from his head concerning Moxie in a torrent out-tumbling Lodore's was to make sure that Moxie's ingredients were always uniform. Next he saw to it that the highest manufacturing standards were inaugurated. Anybody can go out to the Moxie plant on Heath Street and be taken through the same and see for himself that Frank Archer is the Ziegfeld—or at least one of them—of the American soft drink. He has glorified it.

"I went out to Moxieland because for years I had been entranced by Moxie advertising. It occurred to me that a very unusual person must sit in his sanctum and concoct methods for preventing you from forgetting Moxie's existence for very long at one time.

"I found the person, but he doesn't just sit in his sanctum and scheme advertising ideas. He thinks of them at meals, when walking or riding about, or when ensconced in Tom Lothian's office at the Colonial Theatre—one of his favorite relaxation spots.

"To get back to Frank's life and Moxie's—which amounts to almost the same thing—after standardizing Moxie's ingredients and installing the finest manufacturing equipment, Frank put on his fighting pants and started after imitators. The words were full of them at that time. Imitations were called such names as Proxie, Foxie, and such...

"Now we come to the reason why I went out and got this story: Archer is a fascinating genius and advertising man. Almost from his first day with Moxie he began doing something different. No need to describe the far-famed Horsemobile, which Frank properly proclaims is the most marvelous moving piece of publicity in the world. No need to describe—but interesting to tell how the idea of the Horsemobile popped into the Archerian mind.

"Moxie was one of the first users of autos, and in the autos of early days, if you could go around the block in an auto without trouble you were lucky. And when trouble smote with a lick, the street urchins would rasp, 'Get a horse!' One day, Archer, his ears ringing with this derisive injunction, was riding through Sudbury Street when he noticed a life-sized papier-mache horse in a harness shop window. Suddenly he exclaimed aloud, 'I'll show them the autos got a horse!' Horsemobile!

"More than half a million snapshots have been made of the Horsemobile. Thousands of celebrities have sat on its back. The late Gen. Edwards rode it on Boston Common during the war. The government used it with an officer atop it to stimulate recruiting. Other merchants complained. 'When you get something better,' said the federal lads, 'we'll use it.' 'But,' proudly states Frank Archer, 'that never happened.'

"To publicize Moxie, Frank has had wood carvings of Raymond Hitchcock, 10 feet high, paraded all over the country on trucks. He has had similar effigies made of Fred Stone, George M. Cohan, William Collier, and Jack Donahue. He has put out ads on which the name Moxie has hit you in the eye, puzzles of all kinds, balloons, coins, fans, suits of clothes (covered with newspaper ads praising Moxie), smoking sets of patent designs, ashtrays, Moxie toys (which boast a special trademark), wheelbarrows and carts, ponycycles (motorcycles with artificial ponies where the sidecar would be), bottle wagons, 110-piece dinner sets (so beautiful everyone wanted them) which were awarded to the handsomest cops, the list seems endless.

"Archer's been married 40 years and both he and his wife enjoy the best of health. His only offspring, Frank, Jr., has been trained from a kid to carry on the business.

"He claims a wider acquaintance with show folks that anybody else can boast. He is at Moxieland 7:30 every morning. He hasn't taken a vacation in 30 years. Moxieland is his business, his hobby and his recreation. He wears neither belt nor suspenders but his pants

During the 1920s and early 1930s the Moxie trademark within an oval was painted on the sides of many buildings, particularly in New England. Above is a West Barnstable, Massachusetts refreshment stand, to the right is one located at Wright's Hill Camps, Woolwich, Maine, while the one below, also in Maine, is part of Penobscot Bay Camps, Searsport Avenue, Belfast.

stay up okay. Actors visiting Boston for the first time are pretty sure to have been adjured by somebody to 'be sure to see Frank Archer.'

"He has never been ill. But once in an auto accident his shoulder was broken. The doctors, after conferring, told him that he would have to stay home for several weeks. 'But I was in Moxieland the next morning.'

"He doesn't attend society functions and hot dinners. He averages six hours sleep. He never gets sleepy during the day. He reads the *Boston Record*. He 'could talk 40 years about his business.' "

Beginning in the 1920s, Moxie became a generic word, moxie—a synonym for strength and courage, especially with regard to sports activities. An article in the *Boston Post*, August 12, 1931, took note of this:

"Frank Archer, the impresario of Moxieland, has achieved a fame which we think has not been surpassed by any advertising genius. He has made a trade name part of our language. Newspapers all over the country are using Moxie as a synonym for nerve and courage. When they say an athlete has plenty of moxie, they mean he has the nerve to stick to it when the going is rough. It is a high compliment, perhaps the highest that could be paid an athlete in competition."

Walter Winchell, a syndicated newspaper columnist, took a fancy to the word and noted that when someone says "He has plenty of moxie" he means he has "a mess of nerve." The same writer, discussing air travel, noted on August 30, 1931:

"Wish I could get up enough courage to ride in a plane... Nearly everyone I know rides in the air. Perhaps it isn't so terrible at that. Never thought I could get up enough moxie to step on an accelerator—and now wheee!"

Max Schmeling, the German heavyweight boxing champion, was popularly called "Moxie," a derivation of "Maxie," by many of his fans and the press around that time.

In the same year, Harry McLemore, United Press correspondent, wrote:

"Tremendous heart, or moxie, as the cauliflower boys would put it, not the year round practice in sound professional instruction they receive, is, in our opinion, the principal reason why California players dominate tennis today."

Amplifying this theme, Archer created several varieties of advertising signs which proclaimed "Moxie—The Drink that Made the

"Mr. Stohl, June 7, 1931," is the caption of this photograph from the Moxie archives showing the LaSalle Horsemobile.

Delivery truck of the Harbor Bottling Works, Ashtabula, Ohio, as photographed on June 7, 1931.

In Scranton, Pennsylvania, Mr. Spitzer stands in front of a Moxie delivery truck in 1931. At the time several dozen franchised bottlers handled Moxie.

Above: Moxie was a featured attraction of this filling station circa 1930. Gas was 21 cents a gallon, equally nostalgic! At the top of the Moxie sign is a popular slogan of the period "OK'd by Millions."

Below: Along the Mohawk Trail in western Massachusetts, Wing's White Birch Inn featured Moxie in this view, also circa 1930.

Name Famous." And, so, Moxie or moxie passed into the American language.

In 1962 William and Mary Morris, in their *Dictionary of Word and Phrase Origins*, wrote of Moxie, stating it was a New England drink popular since 1884. "Somewhat similar to root beer and cola drinks, it has a characteristic tartness which accounts for its popularity," they noted. "In sports parlance, *moxie* has come to mean courage of a rather high order. It has also the secondary slang meaning of 'nerve or gall.' Just how a respected trademark name came to acquire these slang connotations is a puzzle. One theory is that the original Moxie was so bitter that you had to have plenty of courage to drink the stuff."

In January 1985, an article by Kendall Holmes, distributed by the Gannett News Service, noted:

"As a politician, Ronald Reagan has plenty of pluck and perseverance. Now let it be known he also has moxie."

The article went on to relate that Sen. William S. Cohen (of Maine) presented the president with a Moxie T-shirt given to him by a constituent, Frank Anicetti, of Lisbon Falls, Maine, who "sells eight to 12 cases of Moxie a week at his corner store." Similar T-shirts and caps lettered with the double-entendre "I've Got Moxie" slogan were on sale at the Anicetti's store, according to the article.

In February 1985 an article by Gene G. Marchial in *Business Week* was titled: "All It Takes is a Track Record, Contacts—and Moxie." The story began: "You don't need millions of dollars to get into the business of [managing other people's money]. All that's needed is a creditable investment track record, a few contacts on Wall Street, $150 for the Securities & Exchange Commission registration fee, and a lot of moxie."

Archer's activities, including an advertising campaign to promote generic use of the Moxie-moxie word, were just the opposite of what later attorneys in the patent and trademark field would advise. Legal counsels for such products as Cellophane, Thermos bottles, Scotch Tape, Kleenex, Frigidaire, Victrola, and Xerox would expend enormous sums to keep the public from using the word in any context except for The Product.

Toward the end of 1931, stock was taken of old advertising matter on hand, and much of it was destroyed. An inventory showed the incredible quantity of 19,375 *Substitution Law* pamphlets in storage as well as 6,400 copies of Frank Archer's *Make Money With Moxie* brochure distributed in connection with his earlier Moxie

Company of America 1929 advertising campaign. Old things were scrapped in favor of new products. Pureoxia advertising materials were redesigned to feature the name of The Moxie Company. Another Archer innovation, a carrying case for a dozen bottles of Pureoxia, six per side, and a companion item for carrying six bottles, was hailed as a major breakthrough and was featured in advertisements and trade magazines. By using such a device one could tuck a supply of Pureoxia under one's arm, much like a book or umbrella.

Although Moxie's patent medicine days were but a memory, a small editorial notice in the *Boston American*, June 23, 1931, observed:

"MOXIE FOR THE NERVES. Nervous people will find that one glass of Moxie taken at bedtime will soothe the nerves and induce restful sleep. This health hint was a former prescription by a doctor and has been followed by good results."

Augustin Thompson could not have said it better himself!

The January 10, 1932 issue of the *Boston Herald* had a special section describing Moxie, giving a history of the firm and containing advertisements from various suppliers of goods and services. The Libbey Glass Manufacturing Company of Toledo furnished tumblers at the time, while the Owens-Illinois Glass Company of the same city, successor to the American Bottle Company, was the exclusive bottle supplier (although, apparently, some branch bottlers obtained their own bottles independently). Syrup dispensers were a product of Cordley & Hayes, New York City.

Syrup, promoted by Frank Archer in his short-lived Moxie Company of America venture, continued to be a staple article with the new enterprise. In June 1932 an article stated that 'Frank Archer says that owing to long and insistent public demand, Moxie syrup is now being distributed to soda fountains for those who prefer the Moxie beverage instantly served from the fountain." Counterfeiting and substitution problems had not ended, but they were sharply diminished from the seriousness of decades earlier.

Under Orville S. Purdy, Frank Archer's nephew and sales manager of the firm, results were excellent. The three month period ended June 30, 1932 saw a profit of $166,475. Sales of Moxie in new territories were gratifying, and "more syrup was shipped to franchised bottlers during the month of June this year than in the entire years of 1929 and 1930," according to Frank Archer, Jr., who at the time acted as financial spokesman for the company.

This Moxie exhibit of the 1930s featured Moxie and Pureoxia dispensed over a counter to patrons. The set up apparently was part of a show for restaurant and hotel operators.

Moxie and Pureoxia products on exhibit in the 1930s. The two enterprises merged in 1931.

"The Moxie Ambassadors," consisting of Arnault B. Edgerly, Edward L. Laurin (sales manager for Maine), and William Elliot, were scheduled to visit "every city, town, and hamlet in your state" and were set to give advice to Moxie agents, wholesalers, and jobbers.

Horsemobiles continued their popularity, and during the early 1930s they were seen throughout the East Coast. Arnault B. Edgerly, son of Pureoxia's founder, and Frank Archer, Jr. had plenty of time for fancy horses, fishing trips, and other recreational activities. Around this time, Edgerly occasionally appeared at Moxieland dressed in his riding outfit. In the meantime, the junior Archer's father was showing up every day at the office, including on August 12, 1932, when he was featured at a special 70th birthday party given by company employees. "At the age of 70, Mr. Archer is a conclusive refutation of the idea that at three score and ten a man's work is done. He is still in the prime of his life, as active as a man of 40," a newspaper account related. "His greatest pleasure is improving Moxieland and building up a greater volume of distribution and sales of the product which he has made known throughout the world." It was stated that the M in Frank M. Archer's name really meant "Moxie."

Archer's birthday party was held in the North Woods Log Cabin perched on the top of Moxieland, a place where visitors often gathered. Earlier in the year a newspaper article told of this feature, which cost $10,000 to create:

"A log cabin, like a penthouse in New York, where clubs and committees may hold their meetings, where ladies may play bridge or societies may gather for social or benevolent purposes, is the Moxieland latest innovation. In keeping with Frank M. Archer's unique ways of advertising his product, this log cabin is at the disposal of any social or business club for nothing more than the asking...

"The log cabin was opened last January, and ever since it has been the center of merry activity every afternoon. It accommodates 30 persons comfortably. Bridge tables gaily adorn the prevailing color scheme of the cabin, which is orange. Ready and waiting, Miss Rhoda Bates, the hostess, and her assistant, Miss Winnie McFarlane, are there to welcome the visitors. Frank M. Archer elects to play the role of the perfect host by having an ample supply of refreshing drink stored in the big electric refrigerator... Miss Mary Daly, President Archer's secretary, conducted me through the plant... The bookings now run into August, with several dates held out for emergencies. Several parties of the Moxie associates have already been given."

THE GLASS PACKER
and THE GLASS CONTAINER
Published at 45 East 17th Street, New York, N. Y., by Ogden-Watney Publishers, Inc.

C. O. WATNEY, *Manager*   JOHN T. OGDEN, *Editor*   WALLACE F. JANSSEN, *Assistant Editor*

Volume XI, No. 11   November, 1932

The Log Cabin, latest example of Moxie "showmanship," located in "Moxieland," the company's interesting and highly efficient plant. Boston women have this place booked months in advance for club meetings, bridge parties, etc. They see Moxieland, really one of the show places of Boston, and sample the company's various beverages, which are served free to all guests. The plan suggests the idea of carbonated beverages for parties and general home use. And, at the same time, it sells Moxie.

Showmanship Sells Moxie

Unique publicity methods employed to
promote products of famous beverage plant

Publicity for the Log Cabin located atop Moxieland, a lounge and gathering place for Moxie associates as well as the general public. The renovation cost slightly over $10,000.

*Boston Herald
Sunday - May 8, 1932.*

THE LOG CABIN at Moxieland, built in Roxbury of Maine logs and offered free to clubs and gatherings by Frank M. Archer, president and general-manager of the Moxie Co. (Boston Herald.)

Popular in 1932 were inexpensive stamped metal ash trays, which were made in several minor variations. During the 1930s, the Donaldson Art Sign Company of Covington, Kentucky, furnished large numbers of metal signs, a practice that was to continue for a number of years. Many of these featured the Moxie Horsemobile, which was enjoying a revival in fame and publicity, heralded by Rolls-Royce and LaSalle models.

There was trouble on the horizon, the country was in the Depression, and many local, regional, and national beverage bottlers closed their doors or terminated their affiliation with Moxie. Hundreds of thousands of franchise Moxie labels for the seven-ounce size intended for shipment to such agents as the Booth Bottling Co., Sweeney Brothers Bottling Co., Salt City Bottling Co., Jamestown Brewing Co., Maher Bottling Works, Polaski Bottling Works, Eagle Bottling Works, Egg Harbor Beverage Co., and others were destroyed. Some of these were still on hand at the firms which printed them, the Forbes Lithograph Manufacturing Co. and the American Lithographic Co., two companies which also produced much Pureoxia and Moxie advertising material.

Company records reveal, for example, that the Maher Bottling Works had its franchise canceled on July 11, 1930 and was sold under receivership on April 2, 1931, while the Princeton Bottling Co. was shipped a vast quantity of labels on June 16, 1930, but the bill was never paid because the company had gone bankrupt.

Many accounts were uncollectible in 1932, resulting in losses to the company. Columns of company ledgers were filled with such transactions. Still, sales to major clients remained encouraging, with the Great Atlantic & Pacific Tea Co. and First National Stores continuing to take large quantities of both Pureoxia and Moxie.

Sometimes great efforts were expended in attempts to collect amounts due. For example, the files of Drummond & Drummond, Portland, Maine attorneys, reveal extensive correspondence regarding a $842.76 debt of Louis Cohen, of Rumford, Maine, for merchandise delivered in July 1931. Mr. Cohen was followed for a number of years, during which time he went from one venture to another, including operating a gas station and distributing beer. He then returned to soft drinks via the Eagle Beverage Co., in which he acquired an interest, subsequently contacting Eugene Harrigan of The Moxie Company in May 1936. Harrigan wrote to Drummond & Drummond about the still-uncollected earlier debt:

"Mr. Cohen was in to see us the other day and wanted to purchase Moxie for his new company now operating in Rumford. We

Window display featuring Kid Moxie.

refused to sell him any except for cash and do not know whether he will buy again or not. He stated that his personal finances were in about the same condition as when we last talked to him."

Scrapbooks kept by The Moxie Company are sprinkled with interesting incidents of the period. A January 1933 account tells of the robbery of the Griswold Drug Store in Hartford, Connecticut: "Besides a half bottle of sherry, the thieves helped themselves to a drink or two of Moxie... When their party was over they replaced the empty bottles neatly beneath the counter."

"King and Queen of Moxieland" was the title of an article which appeared in August 1933. "Cute little Mrs. Frank M. Archer, Jr., in a snappy electric blue and white sports getup, flashed a gorgeous smile when a photographer snapped her, but her tall young husband seemed a bit embarrassed. Mr. Archer is a devoted horseman and has several beauties in his Newton stables and, need we tell you, is the junior Moxie tycoon," it was noted.

"It takes a lot of moxie for a football official to admit he was wrong," wrote sports columnist Eddie Hurley in 1933, while another observed that "with all of that moxie, it was simple to earn the pennant."

In 1932 and 1933 the Moxie Hall of Fame was featured in numerous advertisements, usually taking the form of a huge bottle enshrined in what seemed to be a marble temple, with numerous Moxie drinkers clustered on the steps. Representations of this were made in white-painted wood and featured in various fairs and exhibitions. The Pureoxia Hall of Fame was somewhat similar. Doing its duty, the Rolls-Royce Horsemobile racked up 100,000 miles of travel by the end of 1933. This and other activities were to little financial avail, for economic problems beyond the ken of Moxie resulted in a loss of $99,429 for the 1933 year. Happily, 1934 saw a turnaround, and at the end of fiscal year 1934, profits rebounded to $52,929.

The birthday of Frank M. Archer, then in his seventies, was celebrated with fanfare each year. On August 12, 1936, a special banner with the words "Our Boss and Our Friend—Happy Birthday" and a huge birthday cake decorated with roses and inscriptions greeted the septuagenarian.

Horsemobile activity continued intensely, and company records reveal that from five to seven units were in steady use. Gasoline pumps were maintained at Moxieland to fuel Horsemobiles, delivery trucks, and other vehicles. As a convenience, company employees were allowed to gas up, repaying the company each month. Taking advantage of this privilege in December 1935, for example, were

Appearing in "Bostonese" Magazine, the above picture was captioned: "KING AND QUEEN OF MOXIELAND. Cute little Mrs. Frank M. Archer, Jr., in a snappy electric blue and white sports get-up, flashed a gorgeous smile when our photographer snapped her, but her tall young husband seemed a bit embarrassed. Mr. Archer is a devoted horseman and has several beauties in his Newton stables and, need we tell you, is the junior Moxie tycoon."

This is his second wife, Louise (nee Fitzgerald). He divorced his first wife, by whom he had two daughters, in 1924.

Frank M. Archer, junior and senior, J. Cassidy, R. Cooper, M.E. Daly, E. Donovan, G. Ellis, R. Fitzpatrick, W.L. Freeman, L. Gibson, E.J. Harrigan, E.H. Hatch, W. Hill, F. Kenney, W.L. Lucas, T.J. MacKenzie, O.S. Purdy, H.G. Smith, L. Sutton, T.J. O'Reilley, F.L. Chase, R.S. Bissett, A. Corvellier, N. Zaffiro, and others. Antifreeze and other automotive items could be purchased at cost, and when company vehicles were disposed of, Moxie associates were given first chance to buy them.

Company journals reveal that employees at the factory were charged $1.25 for one shirt and $1.50 for one pair of pants, or $2.75 for a complete uniform. Those buying such in April 1937 included J. Bowman, William Clattenburg, A.J. Crockett, J.A. Cummings, George Ellis, R. Fitzpatrick, Arthur Ginnetty, Cornelius J. Ginnetty, D.J. Hennessey, Harry Jacobs, Henry Knight, Peter Lawless, J.B. McFarland, B. Moore, W.C. Newhook, J.J. O'Donnell, W.G. O'Donnell, J.P. O'Mera, L. Panarese, W.H. Poe, J. Portman, J.F. Reardon, Charles Spinale, J. Spinale, H. White, Nicholas Zaffiro, W. Colburn, R. Johnson, G.W. Morrill, F. Williams, W. Muldoon, J. Donnelly, J. Powers, H. Luhmann, and J.E. Caverly.

Delivery men were billed $3.40 for one pair of trousers, $2.10 for a cap or $5.50 for the outfit. A shirt with the "Drink Moxie" inscription, valued at $3.40, was contributed free of charge by the company. Delivery people wearing such outfits included W. Brennan, W.J. Byron, W. Callahan, R. Cooper, C. Dever, J.S. Driscoll, W. Flashner, T. Greeley, W.L. Freeman, H. Krim, E. Kuhns, A.J. Mathis, J. Mulreau, J.H. Murphy, T.J. O'Reilley, Sam Pimentel, A. Schlehuber, H.Shelnut, L.Sutton, R.Tucker, Carl H. Lermond, and D.C. Ryder.

The end of an era occurred in April 1937. Frank M. Archer, truly the Moxie Man for all ages, passed away. *The Chronicle*, April 8, 1937 reported:

"Frank M. Archer, Sr., nationally known as the Moxie Man and for many years one of Brookline's best known citizens, died suddenly from a heart attack in his home at 762 Washington Street this morning at the age of 75 years. He had been ill for several weeks. Mr. Archer was born in Maine and had been connected with The Moxie Company for more than 50 years, working his way up to the top by waging a successful war against imitators and counterfeiters of the beverage which he handled. He gained national fame some 10 years ago when he distributed Moxie Pushmobiles to poor children and newsboys. He had contributed generously to civic and welfare undertakings and thousands had benefited from his philanthropy. Surviving are a widow and one son, Frank M. Archer, Jr."

This window display from the 1930s features Pureoxia Golden Ginger Ale, Club Soda, Sarsaparilla, and Golden Orange. Formerly a beverage primarily distributed in Eastern Massachusetts, after the Moxie-Pureoxia merger, Pureoxia was distributed in many other parts of New England.

Roadside Moxie: From the
beginning years in the 1880s
billboards were a prominent
feature of every Moxie advertising campaign. Here are shown
some billboards from the 1930s
onward.

Another publication told of the funeral:

"With business associates and personal friends from all walks of life present to pay final tribute to his memory, the funeral of Frank M. Archer, Sr., head of The Moxie Company of Boston and one of Brookline's leading citizens, was held at All Saints Episcopal Church last Saturday morning [Archer had died on Thursday]. Out of respect to the deceased, Moxieland was closed all day, and a large delegation of workers attended the services.

"The services were conducted by the Rev. Allen W. Clark, and the church choir under the direction of Roland Halfpenny sang. Burial was in Walnut Hills Cemetery, where the committal services were read by Mr. Clark. The honorary pallbearers were John V. Mahoney (secretary to Governor Charles F. Hurley), Selectman Thomas J. Brady, Benjamin B. Avery, B. Devereux Barker, Dr. Robert Carmody, Arnault B. Edgerly, Robert G. Emerson, William S. Forbes, Dr. A. McKay Fraser, William F. Garcelon, Melvin F. Hill, Charles J. Innes, A.H. Marchant, Frederick A. Ordway, Edward W. Preston, Arthur J. Race, John Richardson, W.E. Stanwood, Henry Taylor, Francis E. Thompson, Harry A. Thompson, Joseph Toy and Guilbert Winchell."

An obituary in the *New York Times* carried a Boston dateline of April 8th and noted that Archer was chairman of the board of a beverage firm which had sold $140,000,000 worth of Moxie over a period of years.

The old order changed, Archer was gone, the quintessential spirit of Moxie faded, and things would never be the same...

Chapter 17

Later Years

Following the death of the senior Archer, Frank M. Archer, Jr. brought suit against Francis E. Thompson, stating that money was due to his father's estate. Disregarding historical facts, the action alleged that "around 1910 or 1913 Frank M. Archer, Sr. was employed by The Moxie Company, which was controlled by one Francis E. Thompson." It was further stated that the senior Archer stayed with the firm only because Francis E. Thompson stated that he would receive exactly the same amounts of money that Thompson's brother, Harry A. Thompson, received.

"Archer, Sr., continued to stay with The Moxie Company and, at some time prior to his death, asserted the claim against Thompson on the basis of the foregoing promise, claiming $300,000 was due to him from Thompson. No suit was brought in this claim, and it was under some negotiation when Archer, Sr. died."

Court papers reveal that the action was settled in the amount of $50,000, which was paid to the senior Archer's estate. The Internal Revenue Service claimed a share of this, but in a later action brought in 1948 by Frank M. Archer, Jr., a rebate of $11,000 was allowed, after lengthy litigation.

In the meantime, Frank M. Archer, Jr., the new chairman of the board of The Moxie Company, was named president of the Arlington National Bank. An April 1937 statement noted that he "has been a director of the bank for a number of years and is well known in the community, being the chairman of the board of directors of The Moxie Company, a director of the Cameo Corporation, a member of the board of governors of the Boston Athletic Association, vice-president of the Luncheon Club, and trustee of a number of estates." The junior Archer was widely liked and was considered to be one of the foremost assets in the town in which he lived. He had two daughters.

Moxie items from 1939. To the left is shown Frank Archer, Jr. president of the firm. The Horsemobile shown below has a refrigeration unit mounted on the back.

On September 24, 1939, the "Boston Herald" printed a rotogravure feature page on Moxieland. Illustrations are shown here and on the next several pages. Walter Ginnetty, who furnished the pictures to the present author, is shown slightly to the right center above, in front of a column. He joined Moxie in the 1930s and remained there, with an intermission for war service, until 1948.

Shown above is the labeling and packaging part of Moxie production.

"Part of the interior railroad of Moxieland conveying Moxie to the loading platforms and handling as many as 35,000 cases in eight hours," noted the original caption to this 1939 photograph.

Facing page: Top: Crowning machine, made by Liquid Carbonic Corporation, capping 230 bottles per minute, using Crown Cork & Seal Company caps; Middle: Test tanks where each bottle passes an inspection; Bottom: Syrup room under the direction of James Penney. About 18 ingredients were involved in the manufacturing process.

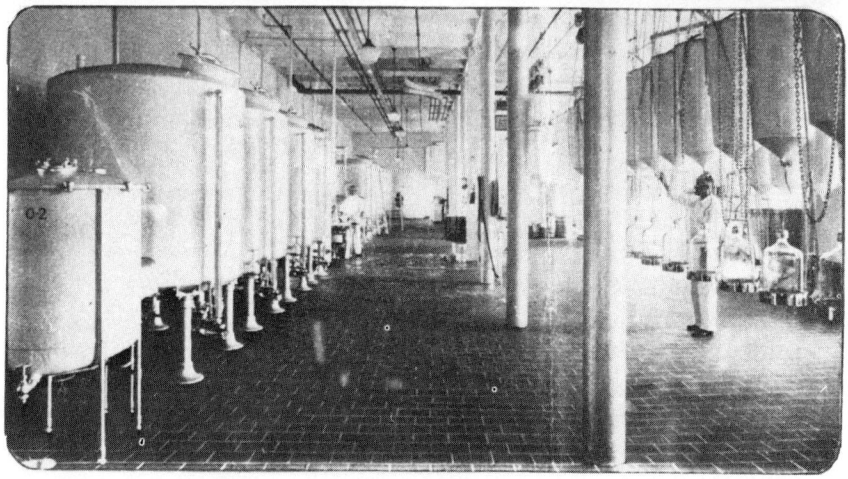

A legal skirmish took place in December 1937. An article was headlined: "MOXIE COMPANY LEGAL TANGLE—Company Sues Its President and Treasurer—Minority Stockholders Sue the Directors—Fraud and Excessive Salaries Alleged."

A group of current stockholders of the firm alleged that years earlier in 1903 Francis and Harry Thompson obtained 501 shares of the original Moxie Company from the widow of Dr. Augustin Thompson "by fraudulent use of the old corporation's money." An accounting was also demanded for allegedly exorbitant salaries voted in 1930 for a period of ten years to certain officers and employees, including $30,000 annually to the senior Archer, $20,500 to Francis E. Thompson, $20,000 to the junior Archer, and lesser sums to others. An explanation was demanded for dividends paid out from 1903 to 1932 to the Thompson brothers in the amount of $119,069 to Francis and $118,596 to Harry.

Attachments in the sum of $500,000 were levied against property of the Thompsons, the Archer estate, and Frank Archer, Jr. The suit, led by John Richardson, resulted in a $500,000 award to The Moxie Company, recalled Frank Archer, Jr.

Freeman N. Young, who had been inactive for many years, passed away. His car was regularly tended to by employees of the Moxie Company, and a small bill was submitted to the estate for a balance due. The use of the Moxie Horsemobiles was diminished, and of the fleet of seven vehicles, most were idle in storage. Profits for the fiscal year ended September 30, 1937 amounted to $54,474.12 before taxes.

On June 30, 1938, the board of directors voted a reorganization of stock and an adjustment of different stock classes. The fiscal year was revised to end on June 30th. Times were good, and the nine-month period ended June 30, 1938 yielded a profit of $84,314.05 before taxes.

In 1939 a number of changes took place. Several old-time employees, including Frank Archer's secretary (Mary Daly), were dismissed from the company service, following a cost-cutting suggestion made by the company's auditors, and were given several hundred dollars each as a settlement. Numerous items were written off the company records, including many cars. Old advertising items were reviewed, and 368 older-style "First for Thirst" cardboard display pieces, Moxie ice cream posters, Pureoxia displays, 556 wooden Moxie Maids, 25 cartons of *Substitution Law* booklets, 822 metal cigarette lighters, 149 Detroit Coolers, 55 Junior Coolers, 2,520 dozen Moxie glasses, 460,760 seven-ounce Moxie labels for various franchises, and other items were destroyed.

Among the Moxie products being sold in 1939 were Moxie in three sizes, syrup in three sizes (identified as jugs, kegs and barrels), large, medium, and small Pureoxia, Pureoxia club soda in the same three sizes, and soda water, distilled water, and vichy water in siphon, magnum, and carboy sizes. Walter Ginnetty, who worked there then, told the author that in 1939 80% of the production was devoted to Moxie and about 20% to Pureoxia products. About 50 cases of soda water siphons were shipped daily. Hotels were the prime user of distilled water and bought it in five-gallon carboys.

Horsemobiles were used sparingly, often with a sign, "Moxie Ship of Thirst," displayed on them.

Francis Edward Thompson, the elder son of Augustin, died in Arlington, Massachusetts on June 4, 1939. A subsequent (1941) notice in *The National Cyclopaedia of American Biography* noted in part:

"Francis Edward Thompson was born at Union, Maine, July 1, 1864, son of Augustin and Sarah (Stewart) Thompson, grandson of James and Harriet (Maxfield) Thompson and great-grandson of Story Thompson... He was educated in the Lowell public schools. When he was 20 years of age he went to Florida to manage an orange grove for his father. After a short time he returned to Lowell to engage in the preparation and sale of 'Moxie,' a beverage that had been originated by his father in 1884 as a nerve tonic...

"Some years prior to his father's death in 1903, young Thompson became president of the [Moxie] company. It was to his enterprising and vigorous advertising policy that the great growth of the business in subsequent years was chiefly due... By 1915 it had the largest sales of soft drinks in New England. Thompson continued as president...until his death, at which time the company's assets aggregated nearly $2,000,000, annual sales were in excess of $1,000,000, and the company was one of the five largest manufacturers of soft drinks in the world... The firm was noted for its liberality in the treatment of its employees, being one of the first manufacturing firms to grant a two-week vacation with pay and to establish a five-day week. Thompson was a member of the Boston Chamber of Commerce, the Masonic order (32d degree, Knight Templar) and the Rotary and Corinthian Yacht clubs. In religion he was a Unitarian and in politics a Republican. Personally he was a sympathetic, kindhearted, charitable man, loved his fellow men and was companionable to an unusual degree. His recreation was yachting. He was married at Brookline, Massachusetts, May 24, 1906, to Mrs. Mabel E. (Larock) Montgomery, daughter of Joseph Larock, a leather manufacturer of Bakersfield, Vermont, and widow of William Montgomery. He died, without issue, at Arlington, Mass., June 4, 1939."

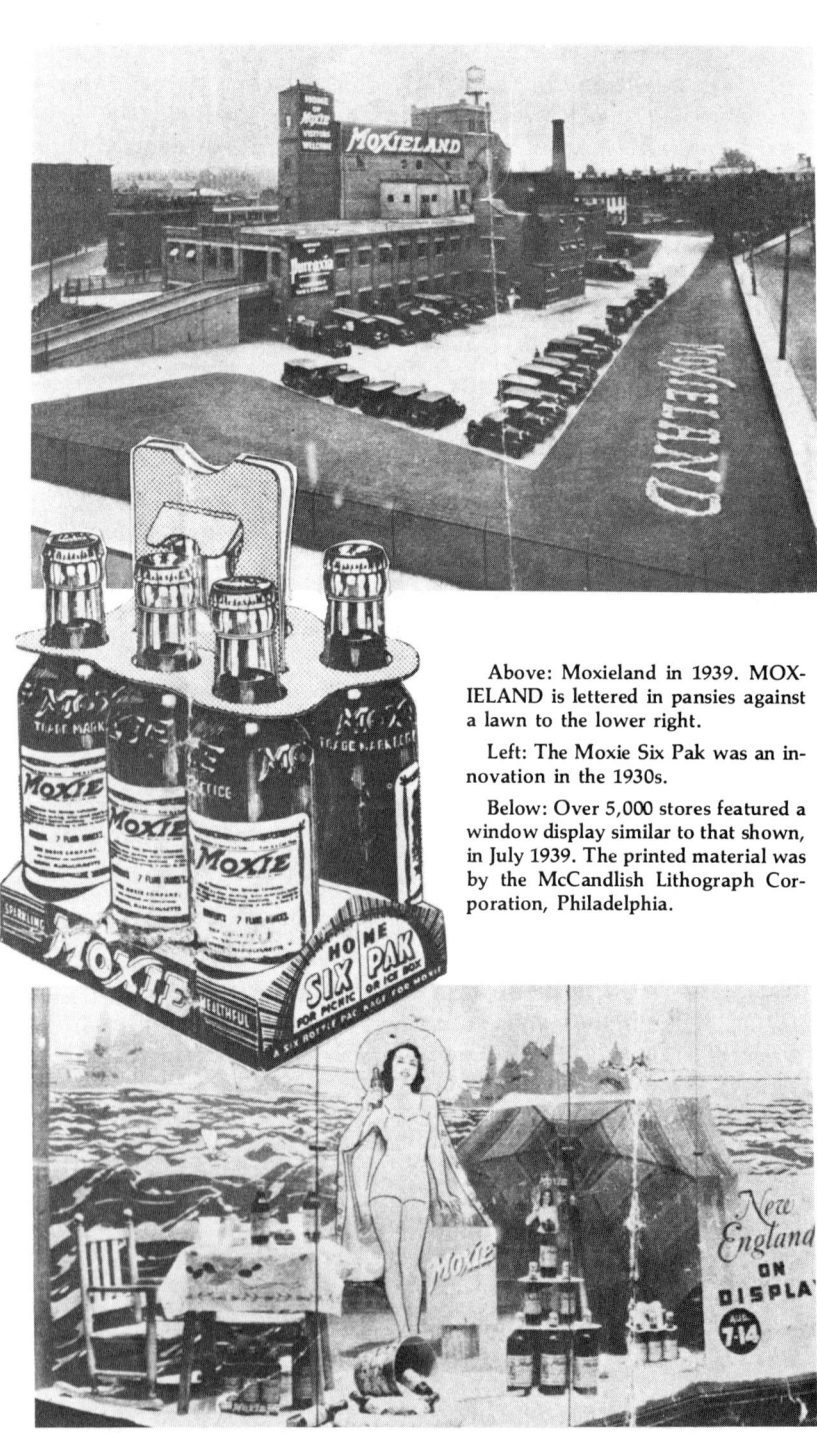

Above: Moxieland in 1939. MOX-IELAND is lettered in pansies against a lawn to the lower right.

Left: The Moxie Six Pak was an innovation in the 1930s.

Below: Over 5,000 stores featured a window display similar to that shown, in July 1939. The printed material was by the McCandlish Lithograph Corporation, Philadelphia.

Interestingly, this account of Moxie's success didn't mention Frank Archer!

Times were difficult, and most Moxie advertisements occupied relatively small space in newspapers. The "First for Thirst" campaign, in use for several years, was continued. One advertisement featured a bathing beauty holding a bottle of seven-ounce Moxie, with the caption "Invigorating as an ocean breeze—ice cold—sparkling Moxie is like a two-minute vacation," while another asked, "Are you just a little tired of all the ordinary drinks? Swing to Moxie... Call upon your Moxie Man today for Moxie in the big bottle, the single drink size, or take home the new six pak, the package to fit comfortably in your ice box." By the time the business year ended, a net loss of $156,487.98 was sustained.

In 1940 advertising was accelerated. Radio was used extensively, as were newspaper notices. Horsemobiles continued to be used on a reduced basis. The franchise bottler system, which was started in a big way by Frank M. Archer in late 1928 and 1929 under his Moxie Company of America venture, continued strong, and although various firms were added to or dropped from the list over the years, there remained a solid core of good customers. Company records reveal that on July 31, 1940 the following franchises participated in the year's cooperative advertising campaign: ABC Beverage Co., Aliquippa Bottling Co., Big Rock Water Co., A. Ciera Bottling Works, Chemung Spring Water Co., Crystal Beverage Co., Dietade Mineral Spring, Enterline Brothers, Green Mountain Soda Co., Hastings Bottling Works, Hersey Beverage Co., Kane Bottling Works, Keystone Bottling Works, Lambert Distributors, Moxie Company of Lehighton, Moxie Company of Saxton, A. Marinaro, MacAllister Bottling Works, George M. Moyle, Stoner Brothers, Welch Bottling Co., Whistle Bottling Co., Wilmerding Bottling Works, Yorkdale Beverage Co., U.J. Hedrich, Brassco Bottling Co., Hampden Bottling Co., Nutmeg Club Beverage Co., Pequot Spring Co., Star Bottling Co., Thompsonville Bottling Co., and Boyd & Gregg, among numerous others.

Such franchisees were furnished recordings of radio advertisements for use on their local stations, newspaper ads, and other sales aids.

The firm's accountants, Peat, Marwick & Mitchell, recommended the writing off of more unused advertising items from the past, including gray, black and green dispenser covers, three-bottle cartons of the puzzle style, 2,900 cartons in the shape of a house, Moxie Boy and Moxie Girl signs, 1,880 porcelain small Moxie buttons and 2,150 large buttons, old *TNT Cowboy* books, song sheets, carrying bags, and *What Is Moxie?* and *A Trip Through Moxieland* booklets. For the fiscal year, which ended September 30, 1940, a net loss of $68,321.42 was registered, an improvement from the preceding year but still a disappointment.

In 1941, store window advertising arrangements were made by the United Display Company. Orville S. Purdy reported that 1,665 were installed, of which 1,110 featured a 40-inch cardboard cut-out of a boy and 555 featured the Moxie Tennis Girl. Another type of display, of which 1,350 were set up, featured a bathing couple. At the end of the business year, September 30th, a profit of $40,028.08 was realized.

Frank Archer, Jr. related that in 1942 the outlook for Moxie's future was uncertain, and his personal financial situation was not good, for he had sustained large losses in the stock market. Representatives from American Distillers approached him about buying Moxie. A meeting with their lawyers lasted five hours, after which it took 10 weeks to complete a purchase agreement. Although Frank, Jr. agreed to stay with the firm for one more year, he later made an arrangement to leave in January 1943, although his name appeared on the September 30, 1943 annual report.

An indication of government procedures in World War II is evidenced by a ledger entry on July 28, 1942 noting that 72 empty carboys had been returned by the Navy supply officer, and a credit was due to the Navy of $23.04, "but because of red tape they cannot accept the balance due them." New cardboard cut-outs featured a soldier and workman and cost $1.10 each. "What this country needs is plenty of Moxie" pins were distributed, backed up by a radio campaign. At the end of the 1942 business year a profit of $132,190.42 was shown.

The next year was highlighted by a catchy slogan, "It's Moxie For Me in '43." The 1943 annual report, signed by Frank Archer (who by that time had dropped the Junior from his name), told of wartime restrictions and recorded a profit of $72,062.19. Stockholders were told: "During the past year your company has succeeded in maintaining the very satisfactory volume of business achieved in the preceding year, notwithstanding the difficulties imposed by the acute restrictions upon supplies of sugar, which left us inadequately provided to supply the greatly increased demand for our product.

"Despite the many prevailing operating difficulties and material shortages, the company is in the position of having a sufficient stock of all imported ingredients to cover normal requirements. The company continues to support fully all the government conservation pro-

The Moxie Tennis Girl.

"**SHE'S GOT MOXIE**"

TRADE MARK REG. US PAT. OFR.

The girl with Moxie is the girl who gets ahead. If you want to be popular, get the pep and sparkle that have made Moxie popular. Get ... day.

"**HE'S GOT PLENTY OF MOXIE**"

TRADE MARK REG. US PAT. OFR.

Winners go for Moxie. It's a wholesome, sparkling drink with a keen, refreshing taste. Not too sweet—but not bitter, either. Just between and just right. ....

5C EVERYWHERE

Moxie advertising of the early 1940s suggested that "plenty of Moxie" might refer not only to the drink but to a certain undefinable quality of energy and sparkle characteristic of achievers.

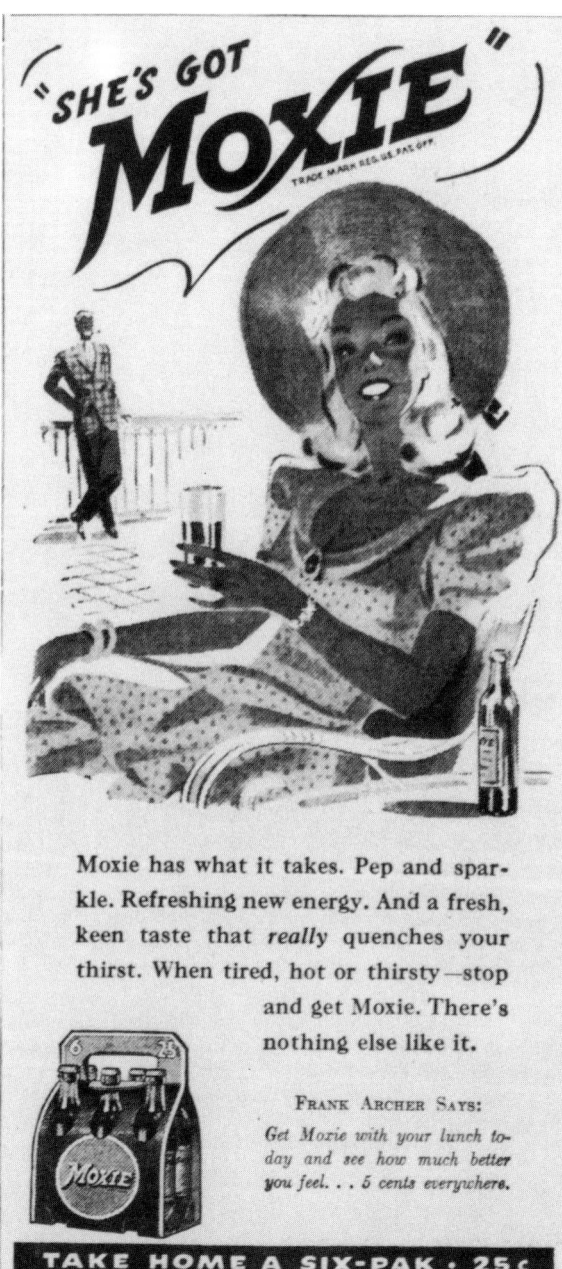

"SHE'S GOT MOXIE"

TRADE MARK REG. US. PAT. OFF.

Moxie has what it takes. Pep and sparkle. Refreshing new energy. And a fresh,
keen taste that *really* quenches your
thirst. When tired, hot or thirsty—stop
and get Moxie. There's
nothing else like it.

FRANK ARCHER SAYS:

*Get Moxie with your lunch to-
day and see how much better
you feel. . . 5 cents everywhere.*

TAKE HOME A SIX-PAK • 25¢

"She's Got Moxie" notes this advertisement from the early 1940s. The Frank Archer name refers to Frank M. Archer,
Jr., who took over the reins after his father's death in 1937.
The six-pak, an early Moxie innovation, later became a
beverage industry standard.

The Moxie Company was always ready to do its patriotic duty, and in World War II it sponsored a banner strung high across a Boston street: "No Loose Talk— Zip Your Lip—Save a Ship." Another wartime effort was a pin-back badge bearing the hat of Uncle Sam with the inscription: "What This Country Needs is Plenty of Moxie."

The World War II years were very profitable for The Moxie Company. In addition to domestic sales, quantities of Moxie were shipped to troops overseas, where soldiers from New England appreciated having a taste of home. A series of radio advertisements suggested that on the home front workers who drank Moxie would perform more energetically. After the war the fortunes of Moxie declined, so that by two decades later sales were only a tiny fraction of earlier figures.

grams. We enjoy the complete cooperation of our entire personnel, which is principally responsible for the results of last year. Our most pressing problem has been the equitable distribution of the limited quantities of our products to meet the greatly accelerated demands... It may be noted, by reference to the attached Statement of Income, that selling, delivery, advertising, and administrative expenses have been further reduced, reflecting increased efficiency which more than offset the steady rise in the cost of all materials and services..."

The report was then certified by the accountants at the time, Murray, Kearns & Co., New York. Members of the board of directors were Frank M. Archer, president; Arnault B. Edgerly, vice-president; Harry A. Thompson, treasurer; Eugene J. Harrigan; James A. Lowrey; and William E. Stanwood.

In 1945 Mabel E. Thompson, widow of Francis E. Thompson (who died in 1939), set up the Francis E. Thompson Scholarship Fund at the Arlington High School, endowing it with $50,000. Each year, candidates were to be nominated by the school principal. The scholarship was well received. By 1984 the endowment amounted to $37,000.

1944 and 1945 were very active years for Moxie. Walter E. Buck and his associates, affiliated with American Distillers, managed the firm. Frank Archer, Jr. was enjoying his retirement. Sugar was in short supply, and was under government regulation. Much of Moxie's sugar allotment was transferred to American Distillers. Around this time, corn syrup and molasses were substituted for sugar. During the first several years there was no problem with this. Around 1947, troubles began. John Gillespie, who signed on with Moxie as a salesman in 1947 (and remained there for the ensuing 30 years), related that Moxie with molasses tasted great when it was first made, but once the bottles were in storage or on store shelves they would ferment, forming an inch or so of a yeast-like substance on the bottom. Pressure would build up, and many bottles exploded. Sometimes a bottle would be uncapped, and the contents would spray 20 to 30 feet in the air, recalled another employee, Walter Ginnetty, who worked the production line at the time.

An account furnished to the author in 1984 by David A. Dion apparently reflects this:

"I used to live directly across the street from the Moxie factory when I was growing up as a kid in Boston. It was during the 1940s. We lived on Bickford Street. Moxie was situated on the corner section of Heath Street and Bickford Street and ran about one-third of the way up Bickford.

"On the other side of Moxie was the American Dry Bottling Company. Not too far up Heath Street was Canada Dry, and on Heath Street, across from Moxie, was the Croft brewery. If I remember right, the Ballantine brewery was in that area, too.

"An incident that stands out in my mind, and I think it hurt their sales quite a bit at the time, was when they had a bad batch. It seems like they had to destroy all their product on hand at the time. I remember seeing them pouring case after case of the stuff down the sewer. I can still picture in my mind the stacks of bottles and cases across the street from where I lived.

"Being kids, like most kids without a whole lot of sense, we would on occasion sneak onto the Moxie property grounds and drink some of the Moxie waiting to be thrown out. I never got sick from it! It has always been my favorite soft drink, and I'd sure like to have some now! Do they still make it? The last I heard, they were in the South somewhere.

"I lived in the old Heath Street Housing Project during World War II and until the early 1950s. When they built the Bromley Street Housing Project, the old Moxie factory, American Dry, and all the old tenement and town houses, plus all the corner stores and bars in that multi-block area, were torn down."

Another old-timer, Walter Ginnetty, said the 1947 fermentation problem was traced to bacteria in the production line. At that time the attention paid earlier to cleanliness had been lost in efforts to maximize profits. Arthur Penney, the production manager, sent employees to buy Clorox and other disinfectants to remedy the mess.

In the late 1940s the fortunes of Moxie declined. The company's assets became eroded. In 1949 arrangements were made with the American Dry Ginger Ale Company to take over part of Moxie's business. American Dry purchased delivery trucks and other properties from Moxie and commenced to engage in Moxie and Pureoxia sales. In August 1949, real estate owned by American Dry Ginger Ale Company on Edgewood Street was acquired for $60,000 in the form of $30,000 cash and a $30,000 note. Many assets were sold, and others were moved to Edgewood Street or Brighton. The number of Moxie franchises had diminished, but a loyal group still bottled and sold the product, primarily in New England.

The composition of the board of directors had changed, and in 1949 it consisted of John R. Barry (New York City), Thomas S. Brown (Bronxville, New York), Walter E. Buck (San Francisco), and William H. Damour (Peoria, Illinois), gentlemen who were affiliated with American Distillers. Buck served as president and Damour occupied the treasurer's office. Orville S. Purdy, who had been with the firm since the early 1920s, was the vice-president and clerk of the corporation, while Alta Brown was treasurer.

In the meantime, Frank Archer, Jr. and his second wife, who had moved from 401 Beacon Street, Newton Centre, were enjoying their retirement. They vacationed in Europe and went on an African safari, among other activities. After living for 20 years in Wellesley Hills, they relocated to Wayland, where they remained for 17 years, later relocating to their present (1985) address.

A report submitted on February 1, 1951 reviewed the results for the 1950 business year and stated in part:

"The operations of The Moxie Company for the fiscal year ended September 30, 1950 resulted in a net loss of $105,173.75 before depreciation of $15,186.71. A relatively large portion of this loss arose from a substantial write-off in the bottle and case account due to breakage, obsolescence, and like causes... Your company's franchisees in many areas have suffered from the apparent necessity during the last fiscal year of maintaining a 5c price for Moxie in small bottles. As long as competitive conditions necessitate the maintenance of this price in the face of rising costs in many distribution areas, any startling improvement in the distribution of case goods cannot reasonably be expected.

"The stockholders have heretofore been informed that your company's management would devote its primary efforts to the manufacture and distribution of extracts, syrups, and concentrates and would promote all Moxie and Pureoxia products through franchises. Progress has been made along these lines, and it is believed that during [the next year] definitely favorable results will be obtained from the development of this policy. During [last year] arrangements were made with the American Dry Ginger Ale Company for the bottling and distribution of Moxie within the metropolitan Boston area..."

By the early 1950s, just three Moxie Horsemobiles, all LaSalles, survived. One of these was used, but only on an occasional basis. John Gillespie recalled that when he first joined Moxie a few years earlier, his first job was to drive the Horsemobile to downtown Boston for some publicity photographs. The other two Horsemobiles were derelict. The horses were removed from these two, and the chassis were scrapped. One horse went to Sam Weinstein, a Boston used car dealer on Tremont Street, who mounted it on top of his building, where it remained as a prominent landmark for years afterward. The other went to the Gay Nineties Restaurant in Yarmouth

An updated version of The Moxie Boy highlights this window display of
"The Boston Post" in the 1940s. "Brace Up With Moxie," "Moxie for Pep!,"
and "Braces First, Chases Thirst" were slogans at the time.

on Cape Cod. Later, this horse came into the possession of collector Eddie Clark. The remaining Horsemobile saw service through the early 1950s. At one time John Gillespie took the unit to Portland, Maine and displayed it on Congress St., the busiest thoroughfare. The driver was dressed in a cowboy outfit and carried a dummy guitar which he seemed to play. The attraction was considerable, throngs gathered, the police were notified, and the Horsemobile had to move to less crowded areas. Shades of 1916!

Around the same time the Horsemobile was exhibited in Ogunquit, Saco, and other Maine coastal towns. One day the Horsemobile and its driver disappeared into thin air. An all-points bulletin was put out through the state police. Finally, the Horsemobile was located in Pennsylvania, where it had been driven. A Moxie employee was dispatched to retrieve it.

After Moxieland was closed down in Roxbury, bottles were moved to three warehouses for storage. One in Brighton sustained a fire, causing the bottles to become smoke blackened and stained. No amount of rinsing would make them usable, so in accordance with the settlement of the insurance claim, tons of bottles were smashed into pieces and were used as fill under the football field of Boston College. So, presumably, the gridiron squad of that institution has plenty of moxie!

John Gillespie recalled that many of the bottles stored in other locations, and which had escaped damage, were sold for five cents each to Moxie franchisees.

In the 1950s The Moxie Company granted a license to a New York bottler, who subsequently produced a drink called Foxy Moxie, put up in green bottles with a fox on the label. The beverage was not a success and it was soon discontinued. A Massachusetts firm produced Moxileine, which was unauthorized and was quickly stopped by Moxie's lawyers.

In 1953 a new product, Sugar-Free Moxie, described as non-fattening and dietetic, reached the market. Separately, a new slogan was copyrighted, "Since 1884, Moxie. Enjoy a lift the healthful way." In the same year Golden Ginger Ale achieved a small measure of popularity and was billed as "old fashion, mellow, full flavor."

The formula of basic Moxie was changed from time to time and, increasingly, old timers complained that Moxie "doesn't taste like it used to." In the meantime dietetic Moxie and other ideas failed to capture a significant share of the market.

In the same year, 1953, the company relocated to a smaller premises at 290 Reservoir Street, Needham Heights, Massachusetts.

As Moxie sales dwindled, new ideas were tried. "New Moxie" featured an unfamiliar sweet taste unlike the "Original Moxie." It was not a success in the marketplace.

The 1954 annual report is reflective of the diminutive size of the Moxie enterprise at that point. Total income amounted to just $93,961.42, of which $19,323.70 was profit on the condemnation of the old Moxie plant. However, selling, advertising and administrative expenses amounted to $109,580.76, and after various charges, a net loss of $17,925.12 resulted. The annual message of Walter E. Buck, president, noted in part:

"The year's operations resulted in a net loss of $17,925.12... Sales were approximately the same as for the preceding year, despite an exceptionally unfavorable summer season in New England which resulted in substantial decreases in retail beverage sales generally. Our maintenance of sales volume may be ascribed to an increased acceptance of Sugar-Free Moxie and to an expanded radio and television advertising program throughout New England in which our franchised bottlers actively participated. During the year we appointed three new franchise bottlers for the state of Pennsylvania and have been engaged in a program of development of a Moxie flavor especially designed to the requirements of the territory outside of New England. Tests of this product have been made for the past three months in Pennsylvania, and the results have been very encouraging to your management..."

At the annual meeting of stockholders, held on December 21, 1954, Orville Purdy, the manager of operations, was asked why the company was losing money. He replied that the beverage industry in New England was very hard hit and had its worst season in 21 years. He noted that not only Moxie but other beverages took a loss during the same time. "The beverage industry is very sick, as prices are too low," he informed his small audience, noting that although bread cost twice as much as it used to, people still expected to buy two quart bottles of tonic for just 25c. On a favorable note, he related that although the soft drink industry as a whole in New England was down about 25 percent in sales volume, the total sales of Moxie had about held their own.

Orville Purdy kept minutes of the meeting which related:

"Mr. [Samuel A.] Bearse asked if the company was going to continue to operate at a loss until everything was gone. He said that he knew that Mr. Purdy was as conscientious and honest a person as he had ever met but that figures were figures. Mr. Damour remarked that the industry is plagued by the five-cent drink of Coca-Cola. He said that when that gets out of the way—if ever—the soft drink companies might make some money. The chairman said that he agreed 100 percent with Mr. Bearse's statement regarding Mr. Purdy. He said that he thought that Mr. Purdy had planned carefully and had done everything possible for the good of the company. He said that he, like all the rest of them, was disappointed with the volume.

"Mr. Bearse stated that he did not think the company should continue to operate at a loss until the last dollar was gone—that it would be better to close up. The chairman asked Mr. Purdy to comment on this, and Mr. Purdy replied that Moxie had never sold very well outside of New England, but that the company needed business outside in order to get sufficient volume to enable it to operate at a profit. He said that to promote the regular Moxie outside of New England would cost a fortune in advertising. He said that modified Moxie flavor was being tried in Pennsylvania and that if it is accepted there it would be promoted in other places. Mr. Bearse did not think that this was a solution...

"Mr. Bearse inquired about Pureoxia and was informed by Mr. Purdy that it was not being sold at all." (Pureoxia products were last produced several years earlier.)

Examination of the reports furnished by Orville S. Purdy to the stockholders and officers of Moxie during the next few years reveals a loyal and dedicated group of employees trying their best to market Moxie amidst vagaries of the marketplace, changing preferences, rising costs, and strong pressure from directors to diversify into areas other than soft drinks.

In 1955 The Moxie Company reported a net profit of $4,278.53, a cheery prospect compared to the loss of the preceding year. Orville Purdy told shareholders that Moxie sales in 1955 had increased 28 percent over the preceding year, which was greater than the average for the industry. He noted that a new Moxie flavor, somewhat like cola, was being sold with some success in Pennsylvania and hoped that outside of New England it would be accepted more regularly than the regular Moxie flavor. However, he noted that it would take a lot of time and money to build up sales volume.

At the annual meeting of stockholders, held that year on December 20, Dr. Paul Davis, who served on the audit committee many times in preceding years, introduced a resolution concerning Walter E. Buck, president of the firm, who lived in San Francisco:

"That since the president of the corporation has not deemed it fit to attend the annual stockholders' meeting for several years, that he resign from the company as president."

There was no second to the motion, and the chair ruled that the resolution was lost.

The advertising agency at the time was the Ingalls-Miniter Company. In 1955 the primary thrust consisted of advertising messages on the radio, in newspapers, and on billboards. The budget for advertising for 12 months beginning May 1, 1955 was set at $34,977.37, of which the franchise bottlers were to reimburse Moxie $12,651.75, at the rate of $3 per gallon of regular concentrate syrup purchased and $1.20 per gallon on the sugar-free concentrate shipments made after May 15, 1955.

Toward the end of 1955 a metal highway sign campaign was proposed. On December 2nd of the year, Orville Purdy presented bids from two companies and was authorized to purchase 1,000 such signs, each measuring approximately 3 by 4 feet. The Moxie Horsemobile was wearing out, and Orville Purdy advised the company officers that unless restoration was done, it would no longer be useful.

A proposal was made that Ted Williams be enlisted to sell Moxie. A lively discussion ensued, but no action was taken. At the time Ted Williams was the premier star of the Boston Red Sox and was a nationally known figure.

For the business year ending September 30, 1956, a profit of $2,716.86 was earned. "A factor in the reduced income was a loss incidental to disposing to our bottlers of all of the used bottles and cases at our Hanover warehouse, resulting in a loss of $11,000," Walter E. Buck noted in his annual message. "During the past year we franchised four new bottlers, three in Pennsylvania and one in Halifax, Nova Scotia—and canceled one Pennsylvania franchise. In addition to our usual radio, newspaper and outdoor billboard advertising we erected 700 highway signs and 850 floor display stands during the year... We also intend to allot a greater part of our advertising budget to the Sugar-Free Moxie which has had a good acceptance."

Actions described as "nuisance suits" were brought by Natalie M. Gold, Bella S. Gavin, and Mary E. Gavin, while certain other investors formed the Stockholders' Protective Committee, but by the end of 1956 no further suits had been brought against The Moxie Company.

In 1956 a Moxie sales convention was held in March in Boston, and bottlers were invited to attend, with The Moxie Company picking up the tab for an overnight hotel stay and for food the following day. It was successful, and another was scheduled for early 1957.

Early in 1957, a proposal by Ted Williams to endorse Moxie was again brought before the board of directors and was again turned down. Orville Purdy was authorized to spend a sum not to exceed $41,000 for advertising for 12 months beginning May 15th. Among the expenditures were authorizations to rent space for 50 24-sheet posters in the greater Boston area for June, July, and August and an appropriation for a 60-second radio spot.

On August 7, 1957, Walter E. Buck resigned as president, William H. Damour resigned as treasurer, and Thomas S. Brown resigned as vice-president. Each also resigned his directorship. Maurice H. Kamm, Mrs. Mildred Kamm, Joseph Borenstein, and Mrs. Alta B. Lunan were elected directors, with Maurice H. Kamm becoming president, Borenstein serving as treasurer and Mildred Kamm as assistant clerk. Maurice Kamm was from Illinois and represented another instance of absentee management, at least so far as day to day operations were concerned. As before, Orville S. Purdy superintended the plant and most operations. Throughout this era, Orville Purdy was the individual who did more than any other to hold the organization together. Described as a kind person, he was well liked by his associates.

The records of the directors' meeting held on September 19, 1957 note:

"Mr. Purdy stated that he had given some thought to working out an agreement with Ted Williams of the Boston Red Sox relative to publicity for Moxie and he indicated that Mr. Williams would be willing to participate in a program of publicity if given an option to acquire Moxie stock for $2 per share."

After some discussion it was resolved that Mr. Purdy should negotiate with Ted Williams and report to the directors. It was also urged that a merger be made between The Moxie Company and the South Bend Toy Manufacturing Company, an Indiana corporation. Mr. Benjamin F. Forhman, representative of the South Bend firm, then made a report which was recorded by Orville Purdy.

"The South Bend Toy Manufacturing Company has been doing a dollar volume of $3,000,000 annually and realizing a net profit before taxes in excess of $350,000. Mr. Forhman and his associates, as owners of all the stock of the toy company, would accept $550,000 in debentures executed by Moxie and $200,000 in shares of common stock of Moxie. These assets, apart from the good will of the South Bend Toy Manufacturing Company are worth far in excess of the value of the debentures and the stock, even if Moxie stock were valued at $2 per share. The earnings from the combined corpora-

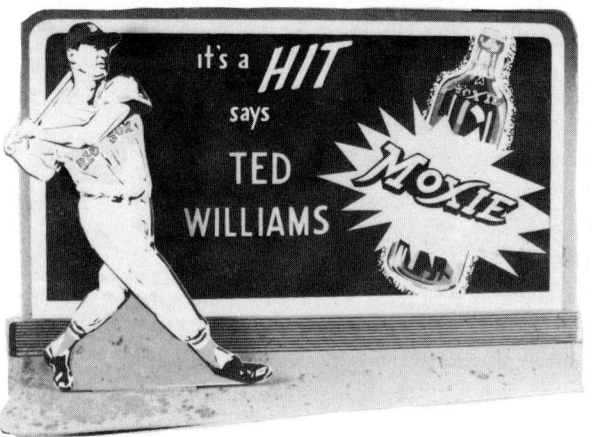

Beginning in 1957, Ted Williams endorsed Moxie for a period of several years, in return for $1,000 per year plus a stock option. Shown here are two cardboard point of purchase display items from the era.

tions would be sufficient to pay a dividend of 50c per share on all the outstanding stock of Moxie after consolidation. A formal offer and the balance sheet of the South Bend Toy Manufacturing Company would be presented to the directors after Mr. Forhman conferred with Mr. Kamm."

It was further stated that after the merger Moxie stock could be listed on the American Stock Exchange and there would be other advantages. Maurice H. Kamm was then authorized to proceed with merger negotiations.

The record books of The Moxie Company reveal significant happenings at the meeting held on November 8, 1957, at which Maurice H. Kamm, Orville S. Purdy and Alta B. Lunan were present:

"Mr. Purdy read an agreement dated November 1, 1957 between the corporation and Theodore S. Williams, Miami, Florida, which agreement was executed on behalf of the corporation by its vice-president, Orville S. Purdy, subject to the approval of the board of directors of the corporation, and pertains to the employment by the corporation of Mr. Williams as assistant advertising manager for a period of five years from November 1, 1957 at a salary of $1,000 per annum; and it also gave an option to Mr. Williams for five years to purchase 50,000 shares of the corporation's no-par common stock at $1.50 per share..."

The directors ratified Purdy's actions and made the agreement effective. At the time the shares were trading for about $1 each. It was further agreed that for a period of five years, beginning with the year ending September 30, 1958, that Orville S. Purdy, in recognition of his services, be paid an annual bonus equal to 10 percent of the net profit of the company, before taxes, calculated on any amount in excess of $5,000. He was also given an option to purchase 20,000 shares of no-par common stock at $1 per share. John Gillespie, Sam Pimentel, and Frank D. Orvitt, salesmen, were each given a $10 per week salary increase.

Moxie shareholders met at their annual meeting on December 17, 1957. Maurice H. Kamm, president, reported a net profit of $9,172.27 for the year, an increase more than tripling the nominal profit made the preceding year. Enthusiasm concerning the Ted Williams contract was expressed, and the minutes of the meeting noted:

"Mr. Purdy explained that under the contract Mr. Williams' picture would be used in newspaper advertising, on outdoor posters, labels, cartons, and all point of purchase material and that this year his voice would be used for a series of radio skits on the theme of 'High Points in the Career of Ted Williams.' Mr. Purdy stated that

Mr. Kamm's suggestion of a product for the younger people has been followed and that the company is working on a root beer styled for them and that the drink would be marketed under the name of 'Ted's Root Beer.' He said that about $5,000 would be spent this year to promote and market-test it in a single area and that the bottlers would buy the glass. Mr. Kamm said that he was afraid if junior didn't like Moxie, he wouldn't drink it even if Ted Williams did endorse it, and that the company would lose much of Ted Williams' publicity."

Stockholders were advised that the possibility of merging with the South Bend Toy Manufacturing Company was under consideration and that Uptown Eastern Sales, Incorporated had made a proposal whereby The Moxie Company would sell Uptown, a lemon drink, noting that Uptown was second in popularity only to 7-Up in the lemon field. Both proposals eventually came to naught.

Although Ted Williams was featured prominently in advertising in 1958, the annual report for the year ended September 30th revealed a negligible profit of just $176.29. "The failure of our accelerated advertising program to produce a much greater sales volume was largely due to the exceptionally poor summer weather experienced by New England, our franchise bottlers reporting a 20 percent to 30 percent decrease in the season's soft drink business," it was reported. "Moxie franchises were awarded to one New York and two New Jersey bottlers."

Ted Williams, who had appeared at various exhibitions on behalf of Moxie and who had autographed countless "Moxie baseballs," held discussions with Orville Purdy and stated that since he, Williams (born in 1918), would probably be playing ball for only a few more years, that Frank Malzone (born in 1930), who in his opinion would soon be one of the outstanding players on the Red Sox team, should be employed by Moxie to endorse the product. It was reported that Malzone would act in this capacity for a total compensation of $1,000 for a period of three years. Orville Purdy stated his enthusiasm for the proposal, and the board of directors approved.

Ted's Root Beer, which had been test marketed in Fitchburg (Massachusetts), received an enthusiastic reception, according to reports. By early December 1958, 11 bottlers were franchised for Ted's Root Beer, $16,000 had been spent in advertising it, and 49,300 cases had been sold.

Orville Purdy reported that a very good bottler in California signed up for a Moxie franchise and had already purchased 80 gallons of concentrate. He noted that for the first time in 30 years the company had exhibited at the National Bottler's Convention. Purdy reported on Kamm's address to the assembled shareholders at the annual meeting:

"Mr. Kamm said that the present tendency for many firms is for diversification, and if the right business were found, he would favor something like that for The Moxie Company. He said that the sale of Moxie and Ted's Root Beer should be pushed and that he was very advertising-minded. It was stated that nothing was done in the area of the lemon drink as the terms presented were expensive and of dubious value to The Moxie Company. It was noted that free publicity was given to Moxie by Arthur Godfrey last fall in his advertising program. It was suggested that the health angle should be stressed in Moxie advertising by use of a statement such as 'Aid to digestion' and also mentioning the low calories of Sugar-Free Moxie. The situation that Ted's Root Beer was priced at 5c higher than the Hires Root Beer in the Boston area was mentioned, with Hires selling for 39c per large bottle and Ted's at 44c. Outside of the Boston area they both normally sold for 44c."

Maurice Kamm continued his search for merger partners, and in the autumn of 1959 an exchange agreement was proposed between Earl Smalley, Jr. and The Moxie Company. It was provided that two corporations controlled by Mr. Smalley, one called Landlogics Corporation and the other named Smalleylogics Corporation, both primarily involved in Florida land investments, be acquired for 548,674 shares of common stock of The Moxie Company. Appraisals indicated that the Florida real estate had a value of approximately $850,000, of which $301,000 was mortgaged. Company records reveal the outcome:

"Mr. Purdy expressed his opinion that the whole thing was a speculation at best and was not a proper investment for The Moxie Company. Mr. Bearse stated that the directors are responsible to over 1,000 stockholders and stated that he was absolutely against the entire deal. He stated that the purchase price of the equity controlled by Mr. Smalley was much too high, the tracts of land were encumbered by several mortgages, and the basis of exchange of $1 per share for Moxie stock was not fair, and that the income from the Florida properties was far less than the interest and amortization required to be paid on the mortgage of the properties.

"Mr. Gibbons stated that he was in favor of the exchange. He thought Mr. Smalley was a good man and that the investment firm of Hayden & Stone endorsed the deal. Harold Kamm stated that he did not like the valuation put on the Florida properties nor the value given for the Moxie stock. He said he was afraid that the directors would be sued if it were consummated. After, Maurice and Gibbons voted in favor of the motion, Purdy and Bearse voted against it, and Harold Kamm refrained from voting, thus the motion was lost."

In 1959 the company showed a profit of $16,637.40. Diversification was still on the minds of the directors, and the annual report noted that the directors had "investigated several possibilities during the year with this in mind. While none of these has materialized, it is their intention to continue their efforts in this direction."

In 1960, Maurice Kamm was instrumental in arranging a merger between The Moxie Company and the United Manufacturing & Engineering Company, a firm with factory facilities in Independence, Missouri, under the direction of Wayne J. Wills of Topeka, Kansas. At a special meeting, the directors voted to go ahead with the exchange, with Samuel A. Bearse voting against it and Orville S. Purdy abstaining.

In subsequent meetings, the number of directors was increased from five to seven, and Charles E. Ince of Kansas City, Missouri, and Carl W. Anderson of Topeka, Kansas, were added to the board to represent Wills' interest. The directors were told that United expected a net profit in 1960 of $200,000. Meanwhile, back at The Moxie Company's main activities, the business year ended September 30, 1960 showed a net income of $4,238.56 on sales that were six percent higher than the preceding year. Advertising expense amounting to about $70,000 was spent on four television stations, on radio, for billboards, for limited newspaper advertising, and on point of purchase material, displays, and demonstrations. Particularly effective were in-store demonstrations in which an attendant, amidst dozens of cases of Moxie, would dispense sample drinks to passersby.

At the annual meeting, held December 7, 1960, Maurice H. Kamm proposed acquiring King Juices, Inc., Cicero, Illinois, which motion was passed. With great expansion in mind, it was decided to form a corporation in the state of Delaware so that authorized capital could be increased to 1,500,000 common shares and 12,000 preferred shares, with suitable exchanges arranged with existing stock. This never materialized.

Although rosy predictions were given for United Manufacturing & Engineering, problems were on the horizon, and before long The Moxie Company was involved in what can be charitably described as a big mess. Legal actions were considered as was the company's responsibility for certain loans they had guaranteed on behalf of

United. The King Juices firm proved to be a loser, and an agreement was made whereby Maurice Kamm turned his Moxie stock into The Moxie Company for cash compensation plus Moxie's interest in King Juices. Maurice Kamm's career came to an abrupt end when, while waiting in a Chicago courtroom, he shot himself.

Control passed to still other individuals, and in 1963 Morris J. Reef became president and director, Orville S. Purdy vice-president, William J. Sharrio treasurer and director, Neil Zais assistant clerk and director, Richard Kates director, and Lewis L. Chandler clerk and director. As before, Orville S. Purdy was the guiding light of The Moxie Company and managed its day to day operations.

Morris J. Reef had his finger in many pies and was president and director of the Great Northern Insurance Company and director of Raymo Discount, Inc., a finance company, vice-president and director of Hudson Associates, also a finance company, a director of R.C.S. Investment Company, a federal licensee under the Small Business Investment Act of 1958, and was very active in the Massachusetts insurance industry and accounting profession.

William J. Sharrio, of Cambridge, Massachusetts, was senior partner in the accounting firm of Sharrio & Reef and was involved in various accounting and banking activities. By late 1963, financial figures for the preceding year, 1962, were not ready yet, but an estimate of gross sales of approximately $189,000 and pre-tax profits of $14,000 was given, with a notation that 1963 might see a pre-tax profit in the $20,000 range.

Morris J. Reef noted in 1963 that non-returnable bottles had been released and had been well accepted, replacing the earlier deposit type. To provide local talent, on October 15, 1963 an "advisory committee" consisting of 10 people was appointed, with the statement that "formerly, The Moxie Company was controlled by absentee management; the new board of directors as well as the advisory committee is made up of persons living in the immediate area."

Various avenues for increasing sales were explored. Two years earlier, 1962, the Ted Williams contract had been terminated when it became evident that sales of Moxie had not benefited as much as had been hoped from the endorsement and, more important, Williams wanted to be released from his contract so that he could endorse the products of Sears, Roebuck & Company.

Morris Reef and William Sharrio studied the feasibility of having a marketing and advertising research report for The Moxie Company done by the graduate school of the Babson Institute of

Wellesley, Massachusetts, they investigated using vending machines to sell Moxie, and they conducted research in other directions.

On June 30, 1964, a special meeting of stockholders was called. Subsequently approved was the acquisition of the Winslow Chip Company, Inc. for $50,000 in cash and 74,000 Moxie shares. "It is the unanimous opinion of your directors that the proposal to purchase the Winslow Chip Company, Inc. will benefit The Moxie Company by providing diversification into an allied food line, as well as adding a profitable old-line company with its substantial annual dollar volume of sales as a wholly-owned subsidiary. In addition, the management of the Winslow Chip Company, Inc. headed by John N. Barbas, as president, has demonstrated an ability to operate profitably and efficiently which should be maintained after the acquisition, since Mr. Barbas has agreed, as part of his proposal, to remain with the Winslow Chip Company, Inc., in his present capacity as president and general manager..."

Again there were clouds on the horizon, and in 1966 the Winslow Chip Company became bankrupt. $30,000 was borrowed from three directors of the company, Reef, Sharrio, and Barbas, to loan to the Winslow Chip Company "in order to fund the plan of reorganization presented by that company to the creditors." An agreement was subsequently made to sell the firm to Roy Winslow, its founder, on a deferred payment plan.

Chapter 18

The Modern Era

Things looked up toward the end of 1966, when new investors became interested and enthusiasm was revived. An article by Donald White in the *Boston Globe*, March 31, 1967, titled "New Management Bets on Old Name—MOXIE," noted that the traditional soft drink was once bigger than Coke and that from the standpoint of tradition, only Hires was older. "Now [Moxie] is barely two-tenths of 1% of the New England soft drink market. Something went wrong somewhere. The name is Moxie, and if you are over 50 it may strike a responsive taste bud."

"That's the trouble," Moxie's new president, Macgregor Kilpatrick was quoted, "the average age of our customers is, like me, around 60." This spelled trouble in an age of hippies and swingers. White continued his narrative:

"But Kilpatrick, an attorney, has faith in the name and he and his two associates, 'tired of practicing law in a small town [Branford, Connecticut],' are trying to bring the drowning Needham Heights company up for the third, fourth, fifth, maybe even the sixth time.

"The way Kilpatrick tells it, he and his colleagues were sitting around the law office one day looking for an unexploited business with a good trade name. Kilpatrick had experience in business. He was a vice-president and general manager of Marketing, Inc., a company with Silly Putty as its claim to fame. He said it taught him how to make something intrinsically worthless and give it market value.

"They came up with the Moxie name. 'Even if you arrive from Mars the Moxie name would be on your list of top trade names— along with Kodak, Escalator, Cellophane, [and others],' Kilpatrick said.

"So Moxie's would-be rescuers contacted incumbent management and started talks. They took over at the annual meeting of stockholders in January 1967.

"Former president Morris J. Reef remains a director. Other directors are Kilpatrick, his colleagues Richard W. Kahl and Stanley D. Josephson (treasurer), and John Barbas, a substantial stockholder.

"In effect, Kilpatrick says, his group took over nothing but a name. Every asset could be offset. He also, of course, gained possession of the secret Moxie formula. 'It's an extract of gentian root combined with about 12 essential oils,' he grinned. 'It is still roughly the same combination that started life as Moxie Nerve Food, although much of the characteristic bitterness has been removed.'

"Kilpatrick says it was first made in Salem [sic] in 1884 by a Dr. Thompson. Bottling began in Lowell. The business passed to the late Frank Archer, a man who never took off his hat in the office and who had a great knack for getting himself and his product in the news.

"It was during Archer's era, the 20s, that the Moxiemobile made its bow. Remember? Rolls-Royce and, later, LaSalle cars with a large white horse in the cockpit and a red-coated huntsman who would drive the car from the horse's saddle.

" 'Great on a sunny day, but no place to be when it rains,' recalls Orville Purdy, company vice-president and a nephew of Archer. Purdy, who joined Moxie in 1924, remembers when Moxie's plant in Jamaica Plain [Roxbury district] employed nearly 100. 'There are nine of us here now.' The big drop in personnel can be partly explained by the fact that Moxie has since gone [to franchise bottling]."

The article went on to relate that about 37 bottlers around New England produced more than 600,000 cases of Moxie, not too much less than during the peak years of World War II when the figure was stated to be about one million cases per year. According to Kilpatrick, Moxie had " 'withdrawn about as much as it could. Last year's financial report lists $132,168 as gross profit on sales. There was a net loss, however, of $30,821.' Nowhere in the report is there a mention of gross sales. Kilpatrick, who dismissed the report with a rueful look, said that sales were about $200,000. Next year's report will be different he said. By that time he hopes to report a 39 percent sales increase and a break-even situation. 'Quite modest,' he says. 'We are going to learn the business for a year.'

"He has not been idle in the two months of his management, however. Already he has attracted new capital, disposed of a losing potato chip operation, embarked on a new corporate labeling and imaging program, and decided to plug his product largely on radio. Moxie needs the acceptance by the under-sixty swingers, he admits. Oh, he has just about decided to exhume the Moxiemobile and its white aluminum horse that is gathering dust in a local garage. Looks like the White Knight is in for competition. It was Damon Runyon, apparently, who wrote the word Moxie into the dictionary by reporting about a fighter who had moxie or courage."

The report further stated that The Moxie Company had about 1,600 stockholders.

On February 5, 1985, Stanley D. Josephson, one of the "rescuers" of The Moxie Company, had an interview with the author. In his own words, here is the story:

"On November 15, 1964, Macgregor Kilpatrick and I were sitting around. It was a Friday afternoon after work, and we were discussing our ambitions. We desired to do for ourselves the same kind of work in building companies as we had done as attorneys for other people.

"Macgregor and an associate named Peter Hodgson had started a thing called Silly Putty, which was quite successful, and Macgregor acquired much experience in marketing, advertising and promotion. I had spent some time doing public relations for the university I had been to and also while in the Navy. We sat down and decided that what we wanted was something like Silly Putty, something which intrinsically has very little value. It had to be something with a good name, a valid trademark, and something bought by men, women, and children all seasons of the year and every day of the year. We tried to think of what such a thing would be!

"The next day, November 16, 1964, I saw a story in *The New York Times* in which the question 'What ever happened to the old Moxie Company?' was posed. That got me thinking. The following Monday, I telephoned Moxie in Massachusetts, after I had met with Macgregor in the morning and had said, 'Hey, let's do something with Moxie!'

"What we eventually decided to do was to sell chewing gum. Literally, *chewing gum*. But we couldn't find a proper name for it. We hit on the idea that Moxie would be ideal. To make a long story short, I telephoned, and Orville Purdy answered. I told Orville who I was and what I wanted to do. I wanted to get a license to use the Moxie trademark for chewing gum.

"We met with Orville, Bill Sharrio, and Morris Reef, the people who ran Moxie, a month later—this was in December 1964. In

January or February of 1965 we obtained a license agreement with them to make Moxie chewing gum. I thought that the next thing was going to be easy—finding someone to make chewing gum for us. But, it wasn't.

"Clark's, which was part of Philip Morris at the time, agreed to make the chewing gum for us, then they came back and said they couldn't do it, for their capacity was too low. Then we thought we had someone else in Long Island agree to do it. Finally, I personally telephoned Bill Wrigley, of the gum company that bears his name, and asked him to do it. By then—and this was a couple months later, we realized that there had to be a change in the pricing structure and a change in the packaging. Wrigley at that time was operating a seven-stick packaging machine in Canada. He was going to let us use that capacity in Canada to make a seven-stick package which we were going to sell for a dime. Everyone else was selling fewer sticks in a package for a nickel at the time. Now [in 1985] gum costs 50 or 60 cents a pack.

"Wrigley considered the proposal and then called us back to say that their capacity was overtaxed and that they couldn't make the gum for us. We dropped the idea of doing anything with Moxie. About a year later the thought occurred that we should take a shot at trying to buy the company from Reef and Sharrio, or at least their stock interest. I think at this point they owned something like 30% of the company. We then went back to Massachusetts in 1966, and finally, in January 1967, Dick Kahl, our third law partner, Macgregor Kilpatrick, and I made a purchase of 30,000 shares.

"Reef and Sharrio owned 203,000 shares totally out of around 700,000 shares outstanding. They gave us the option to buy an additional 120,000 shares. All of their stock and all of our stock was put into a voting trust agreement. Macgregor, Richard [Kahl] and I were given the right to vote those shares. Macgregor and I went to work on a full-time, part-time basis running the company. We would spend Tuesday, Wednesday, and Thursday of every week up in Needham. Macgregor took care of the relationship between the company and the bottlers, and I took charge of manufacturing and salesmen on the road. Literally, we worked the road. I remember cleaning shelves in East Boston on a snowy January or February. It was snowing and bitter cold, and I was traipsing around with one of the salesmen dusting bottles and cases!

"Macgregor and I worked that way for about three months, January, February, and March. We realized afterward that we had a very significant opportunity to take this small franchise business and combine it with a whole bunch of other franchise businesses,

THERE ARE TIMES WHEN YOU HAVE TO REACH FOR SOMETHING SPECIAL

It may be the extra effort necessary to win the big game, or a really special soft drink that can quench a major league thirst. That's why I reach for Moxie when I want a soft drink that is better than the rest. Moxie isn't like everyday colas or root beer. It has a unique, refreshing taste all its own that New Englanders have been enjoying since 1884. Take it from me, Moxie is the soft drink that is something special.

Ted Williams

Boston Red Sox outfielder Ted Williams hits dramatic ninth inning homerun that wins the 1941 All-Star game for the American League.

There's just no substitute for

MOXIE

Ted Williams, Boston Red Sox baseball star, was featured extensively in Moxie advertising in later years. The newspaper advertisement shown here dates from the 1970s, although most advertising featuring Williams was used a decade or so earlier.

for we saw that the soft drink business had changed dramatically from where it had been 10 or 20 years earlier. At one time there were thousands of bottlers and, at that point, I guess the bottlers had dropped to something like 1,800. There were dozens, literally dozens, of brands available from parent franchise companies. They were getting smaller, and our thought was the only way these small brands are going to survive is by being combined under one parent organization. Macgregor and I realized that we were not going to be able to do it ourselves, because we didn't have the money or the time or the manpower.

"We met with a lawyer in New York named Barry Cohen, whom I had known through other engagements. I told Barry what we were looking for. We were seeking people who had management talent, money, and marketing experience. Barry put us together with two men he represented at the time, Frank Armstrong and Jim Wickersham.

"Frank Armstrong at that time was chairman of the executive committee and executive vice-president of McCann-Erickson, one of the world's largest advertising agencies and had extensive experience with the Coca-Cola account. Wickersham worked with another branch of the parent company of McCann-Erickson. Anyway, they were interested in working with us on an advisory basis—just a friendly thing to do in view of their relationship with Barry Cohen. Perhaps they would make an investment and perhaps they wouldn't. They visited Moxie to see what it was like.

"They became intrigued with the concept of expanding the Moxie business, and Wickersham quit his job with McCann. It is my recollection that he and Frank Armstrong invested about $500,000. Macgregor, Dick and I gave them half of our options free. Wickersham then came to work full-time for the company. Wickersham and Armstrong also enlisted Salomon Brothers in New York to make an investment. With sufficient capital, when we found that the Nu-Grape Company was available we bought it. Moxie was moved down to Atlanta, after which other acquisitions were made...

"Monarch Citrus Products became available and we bought it. There was a candy company in Boston, Gum Products, and we acquired that as well. Then we started a whole series of acquisitions during which we purchased six or seven other franchise houses over as many years.

"The soft drink business was changing dramatically as a result of innovations and packaging, manufacturing, and marketing. Today the soft drink business is divided into two parts: the cola business,

Frank Armstrong, chief executive officer of Moxie Industries, as shown in a 1974 photograph. In 1985, Armstrong purchased The Monarch Company from Moxie Industries and began operating it as an independent entity. Among the Monarch products is the Moxie beverage.

dominated by Coca-Cola and Pepsi-Cola—and everything else. The Coke and Pepsi people control probably 60 to 70% of the entire soft drink market. They have huge automated bottling plants that produce literally hundreds of bottles or cans of finished drink a minute. When Macgregor and I started, back almost 20 years ago, there would be 22, 28, 30, or 45 bottles per minute—that was as modern as there was. The bigger companies have changed the market, and the mom and pop bottlers and the small community bottlers have mostly gone out of business. There are many left, but nothing like it used to be. When Macgregor and I took over, there were something like 54 independent bottlers with the Moxie franchise. Now, I don't know how many there are, but I venture that there aren't more than 10.

"Frank Armstrong then replaced Jim Wickersham as president, with Wickersham going into a financial business in New York. As president and chief executive officer, Frank gets the credit for all of the company's growth. He was the draftsman of the projects along the way. We became involved in many other products including such areas as food emulsifiers and stabilizers in Atlanta, a food processing factory in Baltimore, vitamin companies in California, and others. This was done as a hedge, or perhaps for diversification, because we felt that the soft drink business was going to change dramatically, and we had to have another market to operate in.

"Early in the project, after we first acquired it, Ted Williams had departed, although Ted's Root Beer remained one of our products. We intended to use the Moxie name for a whole range of soft drink flavors and other food products. We intended to keep the original Moxie, but in addition we hoped to make Moxie cola, root beer, orange, lemon and lime, strawberry, and other flavors. Inspired by Frank Archer's innovative advertising and give-aways of decades earlier and his various programs, we hoped to intensively promote these new flavors and support stores with local advertising. However, we never had the chance to do it.

"Although Moxie sales are not mentioned separately in company financial reports, the basic gallonage has remained about the same for the past 10 years and has been more or less a break-even situation. When Macgregor and I took over, concentrate sales were something like $180,000 per year. Last year the sales were far in excess of that, due to rising costs, but, as mentioned, the quantity of the product has not increased that much..."

Still another view of the beginnings of the new Moxie enterprise was given by *Boston Globe* writer Donald White in an October 30, 1967 article, "Moxie Betting on New Blend." He related:

"It has been five months since The Moxie Company of Needham found itself a sugar daddy. James C. Wickersham, New York advertising executive, became Moxie's chief executive and put $260,000 of new money into the struggling soft drink company. He vowed he would crack the $2 billion a year United States market for soft drinks.

"Stirring stuff, but how is he doing now that the fanfare has died down? 'The results have been heartening—more heartening than I expected,' he says.

"He reported these developments—a flavor that 'still appeals to the old Moxie drinker' but also designed to switch on the swingers. The ingredients, principally gentian, are the same, but a different blend has lightened the color. A successful month-long test in a Minneapolis department store was encouraging enough for Wickersham to sign up the first franchise bottler outside New England. Another has since been signed in New York, and both are due to begin producing within a few days.

"Packages and labels have been redesigned incorporating the slogan 'Mad About Moxie.' A 52-week radio advertising campaign begins in New England today. 'Financially,' Wickersham said, 'the position is much more positive than when I took over.' But he declined to talk figures until he has notified stockholders.

"When Wickersham took over, annual sales of Moxie were around $200,000. His aim is to snag two percent of the soft drink market. He claims to have been traveling almost continually in the past five months, the emphasis at first being on the 45 franchise bottlers in New England. Now he is beginning to think beyond New England and plans to give his company and product national exposure at the upcoming National Soft Drink Association show in Houston.

"Also on tap is a revamping of the small headquarters building off Route 128 in Needham where the Moxie extract is prepared and which should insure adequate production capacity for at least another 18 months, according to Wickersham.

"He gives the impression of a man breathing a little easier. As he says, everything depended upon whether the drink flavor could be changed to heighten appeal without losing the hardcore Moxie tosspots. Wickersham took the gamble, and he claims that the result 'gave me the heart I needed.' "

Another article noted that Moxie had been invented in 1876 (*sic*) by Augustin Thompson, and that the name was boosted by Damon Runyon who used the word to describe people with "courage, guts, nerve and savvy." Actually, Runyon was just one of a host of writers, Walter Winchell and Robert Considine among them, who took fancy to the word. Later, John Ciardi, the wordsmith and poet, was to write a mini-essay on its meaning, which appeared in *A Browser's Dictionary* in 1980:

"Moxie. *Slang.* Pluck (includes the whole range from raw courage to brazen effrontery). *The Kid took a beating but fought back on pure moxie; You have a lot of moxie to tell me I don't know my own business. Business.* Moxie, registered trade name. A bitter herbal carbonated soft drink popular in New England. Origin unknown. Some refer *moxie* to Yiddish, but none, to the best of my knowledge, suggest a Yiddish word that could be the base. Capitalized trade name *Moxie* also of unknown origin. Could it be from the herb mugwort, *Artemisia moxa?* This suggestion is pure speculation: I do not know that mugwort is used in the soft drink. Yet whatever its origins, moxie has had a language effect.

"It was once a standard New England custom to come out of the winter long johns in early April to take a 'spring drench' of sulphur and molasses at the time of the change. That drench was a tonic, a body toner. New Englanders seem to have developed a taste for their dreadful dosage and that depraved taste is perpetuated not only in *Moxie*, but in the fact that in New England all carbonated soft drinks are called *tonics*, as *lemon tonic, orange tonic, cherry tonic.*

"As a further speculation: to take one's spring tonic was believed to make one fit for the labors of plowing and planting, hence, ready to face anything. It is so, I conjecture, that *to have one's moxie,* originally 'to be toned and fit,' came to mean 'ready for anything.' But this is conjecture only and, therefore???"

In his book, *Manner of Speaking*, the same writer told of his acquaintance with Moxie:

"It must be 30 years since I used to drink Moxie without thinking anything about it. My uncle used to like it and kept a supply on ice. He was given to aperitifs made of sweet and dry vermouth with a shot of Ferro-China bitters, and Moxie, he said, gave him a related taste. I can myself testify that the two tastes are close enough to be pleasant when one concentrates on the moment of the taste, and irrelevant as soon as the moment has passed. I do at times recall mixing a little Moxie with other soft drinks to kill their oversweetness and give them a little zing. I suppose a person given to a taste for medicinal bitters might even do something with Moxie and vodka, and I mean to try it the next time I'm in Boston, although I make myself no promises in advance.

Moxie advertising of the 1970s and early 1980s repeated familiar themes. The LaSalle Horsemobile, by then restored and used for exhibition purposes, appeared frequently. The Moxie logotype with the distinctive X, a fixture since 1907, likewise remained in use.

"In any case, I was in Boston not long since and, being offered a bottle of chilled Moxie, I accepted and poured it into a glass. 'Can you get it in New York?' my host said. I told him I had never seen the stuff out of Boston. Then, for nostalgia's sake, I took a sip. Not bad, really not bad at all...

"Whatever its merits, Moxie is a Boston norm and aptly called a tonic, suggesting compounds of bitterroot, quinine, and Indian snake oil, though I don't know that it actually contains any of those substances. It is my private guess that Moxie is descended from the days of medicine men, folk medicine, and the spring drench to which husbands and children were subjected while ladies took something equivalent out of the pharmacopoeia of Lydia Pinkham. I suspect, moreover, that Moxie must have something to do with the survival of 'tonic' as the standard name for a Bostonian's soft drink."

On May 6, 1968, the legal mailing address of record for the Moxie Company was changed to 600 Pleasant Street, Norwood. By that time an interesting acquisition had occurred, as later told in a story by Laurence Collins of the *Boston Globe:*

"A couple of years ago a New England tradition of sorts slipped out of town with nary a word of farewell. The Moxie Company, producer of the venerable soft drink of the same name, left its Needham Heights plant and moved down to Atlanta, Georgia, the home of—you should pardon the expression—Coke.

"There it linked up with the National NuGrape Company, which Moxie had acquired for $3 million in cash and stock in January 1968. Since Moxie's sales in 1967 amounted to a mere $198,582 against $2.5 million for NuGrape, it was a classic tail-wagging-the-dog transaction...

"Since the Moxie-NuGrape nuptials, still another bride has joined the harem, so that what used to be the just plain Moxie Company is now (deep breath here) Moxie-Monarch-NuGrape Company, not terribly imaginative, company president Frank A. Armstrong concedes, 'but descriptive as hell.'

"The Monarch portion of the handle comes from the Monarch Citrus Products Company ($1.7 million in sales) acquired in December 1969. The acquisition of Monarch also meant another move for the growing firm—to Monarch's plant in Doraville, Georgia. Armstrong describes the latter merger as 'ideal,' a case where sales are added but total expenses are reduced. The company estimates it cut costs by more than $500,000 in the transaction."

A new relationship with the Cumberland Packing Corporation of Brooklyn, New York was described, whereby Moxie-Monarch-

In the 1970s the Moxie Monarch Nugrape Company, located in Georgia, took the only remaining Moxie Horsemobile, a LaSalle, and restored it to like new. Pictures on this page were taken shortly after the restoration was completed. An attractive "Moxie Girl" is shown above, while company officials are shown below.

Following the restoration, the Moxie LaSalle Horsemobile, with the name changed to the "Moxiemobile" in company literature, was a frequent sight along the Eastern Seaboard, particularly in the New England states where it made appearances in fairs, shopping centers, and tourist attractions.

NuGrape would market diet drinks. When queried about new additions and the possibility of tacking other segments onto the already-long name, President Armstrong noted: "We'll probably go back to the old Moxie Company."

The *Boston Globe* article suggested that going back to the "old" Moxie name might not be all that bad, for it had a precedent in the drink itself. "About three years ago the company launched a razzle-dazzle campaign for a 'new formula' Moxie, a brew that was supposed to be geared toward the young swingers. It bombed. Today the company produces two Moxies," the article contined. "One is the 'old fashion' brand favored by New Englanders, and the other is a new formula favored by, well, out of 1.7 million cases of Moxie sold last year, 1.5 million were sold in New England."

Armstrong went on to note that the various products of the expanded firm had 900 distributors in the United States and 35 foreign countries. He intended to introduce Moxie to some of these outlets. "In 1970 the company reported a ten-fold increase in profits over 1969 results—$425,000, or 19c a share, on sales of $4.8 million. This compares with net earnings of $41,000, or 2c a share, on sales of $3.3 million in 1969." Just a tiny portion of those figures pertained to the Moxie beverage, however.

From 1967 through the early 1970s numerous interviews with company officials were reported in the press. Another *Boston Globe* article related that "Moxie the drink as well as Moxie the company has changed. The flavor has been altered to get rid of a medicinal aftertaste, the package has been restyled, advertising has been stepped up with emphasis on the young swingers, new bottlers have been added and old ones re-enthused. It appears as though life is beginning at 84 for the company that has the endorsement of a United States president. Wickersham related yesterday that Theodore Roosevelt once spoke of Moxie as 'a necessary adjunct to the strenuous life.' "

In its November 10, 1969 issue, *Newsweek* ran an article stating that Moxie had been given new life by two former McCann-Erickson advertising executives, noting that "The Moxie revival was really started by *Mad* magazine, whose campaign to 'make Moxie a household word once more' was seized by Frank A. Armstrong, Moxie president, and James C. Wickersham, board chairman... They moved the firm [to Georgia], modernized its formula, and are now aiming for an expansion into a national market."

Earlier, *Mad* magazine, the forum of Alfred E. Neuman and the "What—Me Worry?" slogan, inserted tiny Moxie signs into many of its cartoon strips. Thus, a new generation of readers not familiar with the soft drink came to know the name.

The Moxie-Monarch-NuGrape Company name became effective on April 28, 1970. On May 19, 1972, the title of the firm was changed to Moxie Industries, Inc., a name that remained in use from that time forward.

The *New Hampshire Sunday News*, November 11, 1973, carried an article on the Cocheco Bottling Works, Rochester (New Hampshire), which was stated to produce 300,000 cases of Moxie per year. The firm was started by Alfred Legasse in 1917. In the early years, Cocheco simply distributed the product under contract. When franchising became a reality, Cocheco started bottling Moxie. By 1973 the firm was the only Moxie bottler in New Hampshire.

The article noted: "The label carefully emphasizes 'Old Fashion' Moxie, and there is a reason. Moxie hasn't always stayed the same."

Herve Lagasse, son of the founder, was quoted as saying, "The home company went through a period in the 1960s when they wanted to sell more Moxie. They took the advice of an advertising outfit that if they sweetened it up it would sell. They advocated cashing in on the sticky-sweet mania. But the fact was that when people bought Moxie, they expected the stuff inside to taste like Moxie, and there was a lot of complaining. People hated the new stuff, and even the old label was gone. I began getting a lot of returns. In fact, in one month I actually had zero sales.

"The company soon reversed direction and resorted bottling the same old Moxie," the article continued. "The Moxie Boy, removed from the label for a time, went back. Sales returned to normal. 'I guess the lesson was that Moxie isn't a drink for everybody,' said Herve Lagasse. 'It appeals to a certain kind of person who is looking for a certain kind of taste.' "

The Moxie-Monarch-NuGrape Company issued a six-panel foldout brochure titled *History of Moxie*. It noted, in part:

"In 1967 the world's oldest soft drink company was revived, and the name of MOXIE has once again taken a prominent position in the soft drink industry. Today, Moxie is growing at a rapid pace. Our new solid corporate structure within the company can put MOXIE wherever people want it.

"Our famous Moxiemobile is in its final stages of restoration and will soon be seen not only on every street of Atlanta but everywhere OLD FASHION MOXIE is sold. MOXIE is in a class all by itself. There is none made to match its truly distinctive taste. So, ask for MOXIE. It's the drink for those who are at all particular."

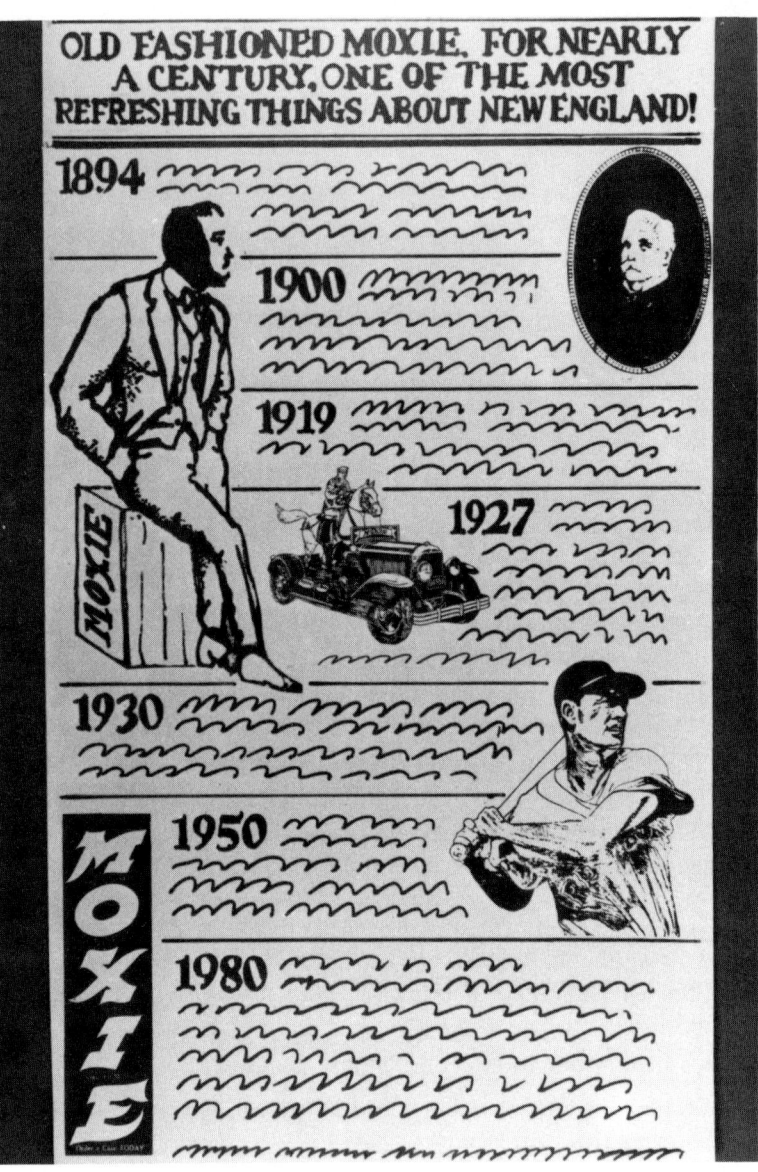

An artist's rendering, 1980, for a proposed Moxie advertisement. Undoubtedly the top "1894" date should read 1884. Illustrated are Augustin Thompson, the "discoverer" of Moxie, George M. Cohan sitting on a Moxie crate, a Horsemobile, and Ted Williams.

The same brochure touched upon Moxie history, the gentian ingredient, and taste:

"MOXIE, in its original form, was not a soft drink but a concentrated liquid, taken by the spoonful immediately before meals. It was an aid to digestion. It guaranteed to make you eat better, sleep better, feel better. The main ingredient of the product was derived from extracts of the gentian root, a flower-herb named after Gentius, an Illyrian king, living from 180-167 B.C...

"The doctor, impressed by the progress of carbonated beverages, developed the current soft drink, MOXIE, by placing its medicinal extract in carbonated beverage form. Not a cola or a root beer, the MOXIE taste is distinctively its own—a delicious blend of the bitter and the sweet, a drink to satisfy everyone's taste. This cannot be hurried. It takes exactly 10 days to extract the flavor from the gentian root..."

The 1974 annual report of Moxie Industries, Inc., signed by President Frank A. Armstrong, revealed the changing nature of the business and the relative unimportance of Moxie in the corporate scheme of things. Sales that year amounted to $21,311,000, yielding a net income of $178,000 after certain reductions and adjustments.

The soft drink division of the enterprise operated four plants in Orlando (Florida), Cayce (South Carolina), Church Point (Louisiana), and Ridgely (Maryland), which turned out flavor and chocolate drink concentrates. Illustrated in the annual report were such drinks as Brownie, Chocolate Soldier, SunCrest, NuGrape, Kist root beer—and Moxie. An insert furnished with the report noted:

"May 1, 1975. Moxie Industries, Inc., of Atlanta, Ga., and The Clorox Company of Oakland, California, today announced that Moxie has acquired the Nesbitt's Franchise Bottling Division for soft drinks from Nesbitt Food Products, Inc., a wholly-owned Clorox subsidiary. Clorox received 150,000 shares of Moxie common stock as part of the consideration... Moxie management indicated that this acquisition would greatly strengthen the bottlers system of the company by adding over 200 franchised bottlers..."

The same report told of other products, including RichLife Vitamins, Isle of Aloe skin care products, Dari-Tech ingredients for the dairy industry (including stabilizers, emulsifiers, skim milk boosters, and flavors), bubble gum and candy, institutional and wholesale bulk food products, and other activities.

The board of directors at the time consisted of Frank A. Armstrong (president), Ignazio F. Caruso, Barry Lee Cohen, George R.

Simpson

THE SIMPSON SPRING CO.
SIMPSON SPRING
S
SPRING
ESTABLISHED IN 1878

Spring™

On this and the facing page are photographs taken in February 1985 of liter-size Moxie being bottled at the Simpson Spring Co., South Easton, Massachusetts. The firm has distributed Moxie since 1912 and in recent decades has bottled the product. The Simpson Spring Co., founded in 1878, bottles several dozen different beverages. A museum of Simpson Spring memorabilia is maintained on the premises.

Dixon, Sam H. Dixon, Robert L. Harrison, Stanley D. Josephson, Macgregor Kilpatrick, Arthur Lisker (treasurer), and Lionel H. Stutz.

The 1983 annual report showed net sales in excess of $59 million resulting in a profit of $208,000. In the several previous years, Moxie Industries had turbulent times, with substantial losses registered on several occasions. Moxie, the beverage, merited only brief mention in the 1983 report:

"The company's soft drink operations are conducted primarily through a division, The Monarch Company, which represents a combination of four long-established companies in the soft drink industry: The Moxie Company, National NuGrape Company, Monarch Citrus Products, and Frostie Enterprises." By that time a West German firm, Peter Eckes, had acquired a majority ownership of the firm's stock and had installed several directors on the board: Peter Friedrich, Reinold M. Fries, and Alfred Wiesenberger. Other directors at the time included Frank A. Armstrong (president), Barry Lee Cohen, Stanley D. Josephson, Macgregor Kilpatrick, and J.T. Moore.

An April 3, 1984 notice to stockholders of Moxie Industries, Inc. noted that majority shareholders at the time were Peter Eckes, a West German partnership with an interest of 3,181,990 shares (61.07 percent of the outstanding common stock), and Frank A. Armstrong with 336,300 shares.

Moxie history continues to evolve. In February 1985, Frank Armstrong furnished recollections to the author, covering a span of time from his first involvement until the current era.

"In 1969 Macgregor Kilpatrick and Stanley Josephson made the decision to bring full-time marketing management into The Moxie Company. It was their feeling at that time that if the company was going to grow into a significant enterprise, it would require people who had in-depth experience in marketing in the soft drink industry.

"After a search, Kilpatrick and Josephson met James Wickersham and myself. Both of us had the experience they were looking for. We were top management executives in McCann-Erickson. At that time I had moved out of the promotion agency I had formed for McCann five years earlier and had moved up to chairman of the Executive Board of the McCann-Erickson agency on a worldwide basis. I also was the senior management executive on the primary account of the agency, the Coca-Cola Company, which had billings of over $100 million. I had joined McCann-Erickson in 1958 and had started all of the affiliated companies of McCann-Erickson, with Sales

Communication, Inc., as the first entry. Subsequently, a research company and a public relations company were added.

"Wickersham was president of Sales Communication, Inc. a company that specialized in sales promotion work for major corporations that were clients of McCann, including the Coca-Cola Company. Wickersham and I had worked closely together in the agency. We decided to invest in Moxie. As a result, we joined Moxie and, in the process, gained what became a controlling interest in Moxie stock. At that time, Moxie was a small company with annual sales of approximately $200,000. There were about 25 small franchise bottlers in the New England area handling the product.

"At the time of our investment, Wickersham and I made the decision based upon the appeal of the Moxie brand name. We felt that if the name Moxie could be promoted into a major soft drink brand, as it was once during the 1920s and 1930s, it would do well. The name also had great appeal within the financial community and, as a result, it was possible to attract additional equity financing to support a program of growth that began with the National NuGrape Company. This firm was acquired by Moxie in 1969, and headquarters of the company were moved from the Moxie offices near Boston, to Atlanta, Georgia. This acquisition was in large part funded by Salomon Brothers, the New York investment company.

"National NuGrape had two famous brands that were very popular in the Southeast. The primary one was the NuGrape brand, which was and still is the number one grape drink in America. In addition, there was a flavor line, SunCrest Flavors, which offered orange, grape, strawberry, cream soda, lemon-lime, punch, and other flavors.

"The partnership between myself and Wickersham that had been so productive in McCann-Erickson did not continue in the same form after we joined forces to run and build Moxie. Within a year, the informal partnership began to splinter, and Wickersham left the company to pursue other interests.

"In 1971, I put a major program into place to expand the base of the company from soft drinks into other areas. The objective was to build revenues and profits to the point at which the company could begin to grow significantly. Three acquisitions were made in 1971. The first was Gum Products, Inc. of Boston, which was the second largest bubble gum company in the industry. Next was the Dairy-Tech Co. of Atlanta, which manufactured a variety of stabilizers and emulsifiers used in ice cream and frozen desserts in the dairy industry. And finally, the most important, I arranged the acquisi-

A Moxie Boy look-alike: Walter Ginnetty, who worked for The Moxie Company during the 1930s and 1940s (punctuated by an intermission as Sgt. Ginnetty with the 90th Fighter Squadron in Burma during World War II, for which he received a commendation), is a dead-ringer for the "new" Moxie Boy—as shown at the top of the facing page. It is believed that the revised Moxie Boy is an artist's composite, but Ginnetty may have had a strong influence!

Modern versions of the Moxie Boy are illustrated by a cardboard cut-out at the top of the page and, below, a 1984 advertisement. Somehow, the 1984 version lacks the piercing gaze of his predecessors.

Moxie Newspaper

NEWS AD
MONC 84014

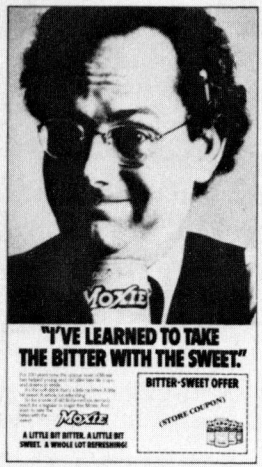

NEWS AD
MONC 84013

NEWS AD
MONC 84015

NEWS AD
MONC 84012

Moxie advertising up-to-date: 1985 newspaper ads distributed to franchised bottlers by The Monarch Company.

tion of the RichLife Company of Los Angeles, producer of natural vitamins and food supplements.

"With these acquisitions, the company established a larger base from which to grow. In a year and a half, sales grew from $200,000 to over $10,000,000! Over the years, additional acquisitions were made.

"After the acquisition of the National NuGrape Company in 1969, the effort was continued to build a soft drink business. In 1975, Nesbitt's line of flavored drinks was acquired from the Clorox Company, and this provided a base of business in the midwestern and western states that the company needed. Then, in 1980, one of the leading root beer brands was acquired, Frostie Root Beer. In addition to acquiring these leading brands, the company also acquired a number of smaller soft drink brands, including Dr. Wells, Kickapoo Joy Juice, and Mason's Root Beer.

"A key factor in the development of the soft drink business was the economy achieved through consolidation. All concentrates were and are produced in one plant. There is one management group and one sales organization for all brands.

"The Monarch Company, as the soft drink business was called, provided the cash flow during the period 1970 to 1978 for the expansion of Moxie Industries into its additional businesses: vitamins, dairy ingredients, and bubble gum. (The gum business was sold in 1979.) By 1984, sales of Moxie Industries, Inc. had climbed to $60,000,000 from the original $200,0000 back in 1969.

"Monarch soft drink brands are sold and distributed by 20% of all United States bottling plants. The company has 684 franchises in 471 bottling plants. Some bottlers have more than one Monarch brand. This broad base of business gives The Monarch Company strength for added expansion and avoids the risk factor of having large blocks of business concentrated in a limited number of large customers. One or more Monarch brands are sold in all but five of the 50 states. Franchises are broadly spread over the different bottling plants that also bottle primary brands such as Coca-Cola, Pepsi-Cola, 7-Up etc...

"In 1971 a program was initiated for Moxie to expand the brand name beyond its New England territory. Bottlers were signed up in Atlantic City, Gadsden (Alabama), Orlando, and Augusta (Georgia). All of these bottlers were attracted to the Moxie tradition. The brand was and is well known within the soft drink industry. Almost every bottler is familiar with the name.

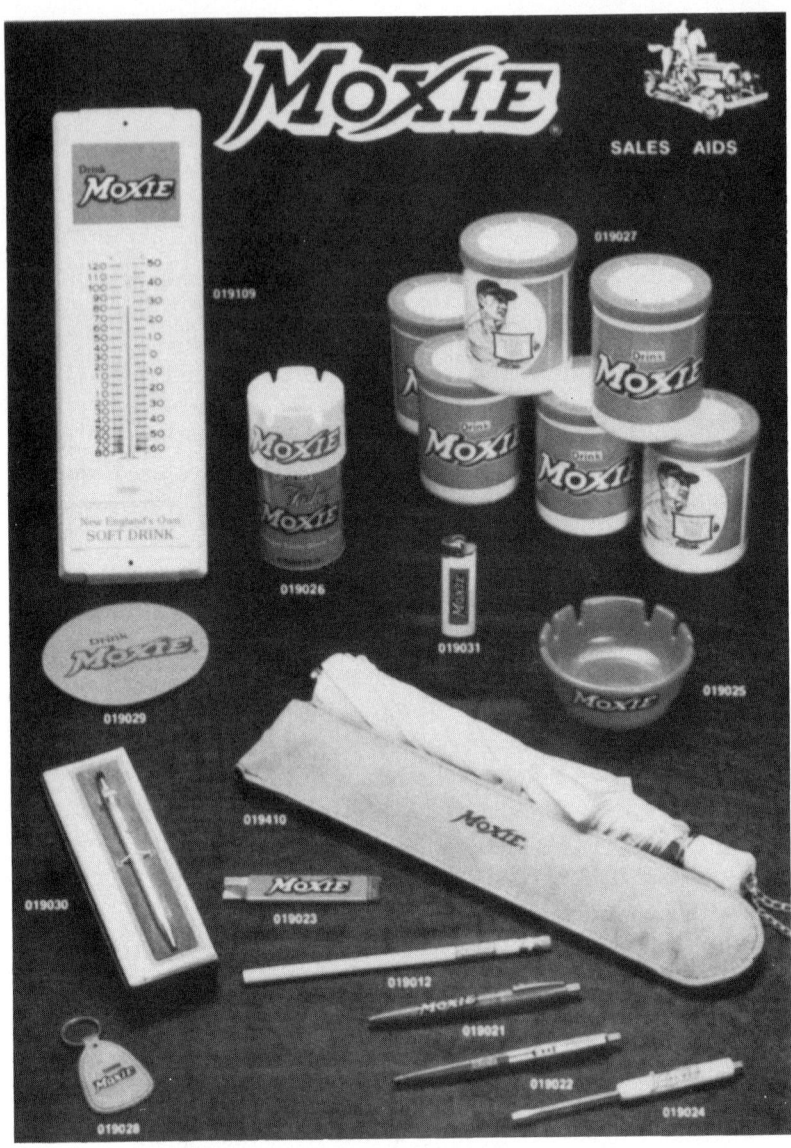

Moxie advertising items and give-aways of the modern era—items from a 1985 catalogue sent to franchised bottlers and agents by The Monarch Company. Some of the items feature the image of Ted Williams, who was an active Moxie promoter in the late 1950s and early 1960s.

"The Moxiemobile, long famous in New England, was restored and put in working order and, once again, was used as a special event, particularly at fairs and special holiday parades. The Moxie drink was reformulated into a caramel-colored version of cola which stood a series of exhausting taste tests. However, in each New England market the results were negative. Also it became evident that to introduce 'another cola' in a market where Coca-Cola and Pepsi-Cola were long established and dominant was an all but impossible task. Even with millions of dollars of advertising support, it is doubtful if Moxie could have been expanded into an important brand in the soft drink industry. An investment in this type of activity would, in fact, be one of high risk and one that could not be recommended to investors.

"On January 18, 1985, I resigned as chairman of the board of Moxie Industries and acquired The Monarch Company. After 16 years of building Moxie to the point at which the diversified corporation achieved a sales level of $60,000,000 in sales, I made the decision to return to the base on which Moxie Industries had been built.

"The Moxie brand is still popular in New England and is bottled by the following companies. Polar Corporation (Worcester, Massachusetts), Simpson Spring (South Easton, Massachusetts), Coca-Cola (Presque Isle, Maine), Cocheco Bottling (Rochester, New Hampshire), Manhattan Bottling (New Bedford, Massachusetts), X-tra Bottling (Springfield, Massachusetts), Briggs (Bangor, Maine), Coca-Cola (Farmington, Maine), and Salem Coca-Cola (Salem, New Hampshire).

"You may be interested in the tradition of the different brands. Moxie is said to have been started in 1884, while NuGrape uses a 1920 starting date, SunCrest was established in 1930, Nesbitt's in 1935, and Frostie Root Beer in 1938."

Thus, coming years will undoubtedly see new chapters in the evolution of Moxie. Will its glory days ever return? This, of course, is the question of questions! Moxie enthusiasts, whose numbers are legion, of course hope it will again rise to greatness.

In the 1970s and early 1980s, a new element of interest appeared, that of collectors. Moxie history became the topic of photographs and articles in such varied publications as the *This Fabulous Century* series of volumes by Time-Life books, *Yankee*, *Western Collector*, *The Antique Trader*, and a host of other publications. A book, *The Moxie Mystique*, by Frank Potter, attracted favorable notice. Newspapers picked up the interest, and many columnists reported on Moxie history or the current state of affairs. Information was apt to vary. Readers might learn that Moxie was first formulated in 1876, in 1884 (the date that the firm prominently featured in its advertising), in 1873, or even 1892! The Moxie Horsemobile for some reason became the "Moxiemobile." This change was somewhat official, for modern company literature spelled it that way.

Drawing upon the 1884 date celebrated in Moxie advertising since the 1920s (by which time the 1885 trademark date had been forgotten), plans were set in 1984 for the "centennial" of Moxie at the fairgrounds in Union, Maine. Scheduled for July 15th, the event was to feature exhibits by collectors of Moxie memorabilia, a band playing the *Moxie Song*, an automobile parade featuring the Moxie LaSalle Horsemobile, and other attractions. The day before, July 14th, a related celebration was scheduled for Lisbon Falls, Maine.

July 15th arrived, and on hand at the Union Fairgrounds were several hundred visitors who sipped samples of Moxie, fraternized with collectors and enthusiasts, listened to music, and had a really great time. The Matthews Museum, located on the Fairgrounds, was open, and numerous Moxie memorabilia items, many obtained from Union residents Robert and Muriel Heath, were shown, as was an oil portrait of Augustin Thompson. Visitors came from far and near. Collectors mounted exhibits in a building set aside for that purpose. Celebrants wearing bright orange Moxie caps and T-shirts sipped Moxie and nibbled a new version of Moxie candy. Augustin Thompson would have been proud!

Modern Moxie: An aluminum can for Sugar-free Moxie, 1985.
The Moxie Boy still beckons with his pointing finger.

Appendices

On the Trail
of
The Moxie Girls

While many girls were featured in Moxie advertisements over the years, best remembered and identified were the Moxie girls who appeared on fans of the 1915-1925 decade. Lillian MacKenzie, Muriel Ostriche, Ann Pennington, Eileen Percy, Frances Pritchard, and Laura Walker each achieved fleeting fame with Moxie drinkers, with that of Ann Pennington being more fleeting than the others, for the author was able to locate only press clippings mentioning that fans were *scheduled* to be made with the Pennington portrait (no captioned examples of such fans have been seen).

Of the Moxie Girls, Muriel Ostriche seems to have been the most captivating, the most worthy of gossip columns, the most interesting, while Eileen Percy seems to have achieved the greatest success on the silver screen.

Lillian MacKenzie

The author was able to locate little in the way of information involving the relationship between The Moxie Company and Lillian MacKenzie. A scrapbook kept by Frank Archer placed Miss MacKenzie's address circa 1919 at 20 South Eliot Place, Brooklyn, New York.

Empire THEATRE
Continuous 10.30 to 10.30

TODAY AND TUESDAY
Remarkable Double Feature Program

The Famous **MURIEL OSTRICHE**
Moxie Girl
With Carlyle Blackwell, in the Five
Act Drama of Love and Intrigue

"SALLY IN OUR ALLEY"

Can a girl, born of intemperate parents in the slums of a big city, rise to a state of womanhood where she will be claimed by society? This is the big question asked and answered in this photo play.

—— ADDED FEATURE ——
Sure, It's Ireland Itself! The Five Act Triangle Production
"THE MARRIAGE OF MOLLY-O"
An Artistic Love Romance With Talented Mae Marsh and Robert Harron in the Leading Roles.

ANOTHER SPLENDID TWO ACT COMEDY FULL OF LAUGHS.

COMING WEDNESDAY AND THURSDAY
The Most Beautiful **LINA CAVALIERI**
Woman in the World
ported by Lucien Muratore, in the Five Act Drama
"THE SHADOW OF HER PAST"
Just Out of College"—Adapted From
Famous Comedy.

DON'T FAIL TO SEE THE
MOXIE GIRL

MURIEL OSTRICHE
—IN—
SALLIE IN OUR ALLEY
AT THE PARK THEATRE

You Know Her Well
You Have Seen Her On the
Moxie Signs for Years

NOW GO AND SEE HER IN HER
GREAT PHOTO-PLAY

DON'T FORGET THAT
MURIEL OSTRICHE
The Celebrated Photo-Play Actress
at the Park Theatre, is the
MOXIE GIRL

Muriel Ostriche, the Moxie Girl, was widely featured by the firm during the 1915-1920 years. Miss Ostriche, who was a teenager when she first posed for Moxie, appeared on several varieties of fans, on cardboard cut-outs, and as part of advertisements in many other places. In the process she became synonomous with the Moxie product. The 1916 advertisements shown here feature one of her many films, "Sally In Our Alley."

— 698 —

Muriel Ostriche

Muriel Ostriche, born in New York in 1897, was just 17 years old when she appeared on Moxie fans in 1915. Her face, with different hair styles and poses, was featured for several years thereafter on fans and as the Moxie Girl on cardboard cut-outs, the latter with Ostriche pixieishly peering from behind a Moxie sign or a crate of Moxie bottles. She first posed for Moxie at the age of 15, when she was the winner of a "Moxie Girl" contest which saw 1,500 entries compete for the honor.

Educated in the New York City public schools, she appeared on the screen at an early age. In 1915 *Motion Picture Magazine* reported:

MURIEL OSTRICHE. Only seventeen, looks fifteen, and can make up to fool you into believing her half that age—this is Muriel Ostriche. And she is a leading woman—a photoplay star—for the Princess department of the Thanhouser Company.

Muriel Ostriche was born in New York and danced her way through school. She has been dancing ever since with great success when she has not been embodied in film. The smart hotels and winter gardens in New York say that she is a clever tangoist and has captured prizes galore.

She started in at 15, playing as an extra at the Biograph studio after high-school hours. After that she played through a whole Pathe picture, and then joined the Eclair Company as a stock member. But when Princess wanted an ingenue lead, a pirouetting one with russet-brown hair, they captured Muriel Ostriche.

The Daily Press, Portland, Maine, noted in an article dated August 21, 1916:

EMPIRE THEATRE: Two remarkable photoplay productions will be presented on the double feature program at the Empire Theatre Monday and Tuesday as Muriel Ostriche and Carlyle Blackwell will be seen in the wonderful five-act picturization of "Sally in our Alley," while Robert Harron plays the leading role in the five-act Triangle drama, "The Marriage of Molly-O." Besides these two big five-act productions the program will include another dandy two-act comedy. Muriel Ostriche, star of the picturization of "Sally in our Alley," is one of the most famous beauties appearing in the silent drama and also has won international fame as the Moxie Girl. "Sally in our Alley" is an appealing production replete with high-strung situations which make the heart jump, the nerves quiver, the hand tremble, a fascinating document of society and lower East Side life, contrasted as never before on the screen, blending in a most pleasant concoction, a touch of comedy and tragedy, a bit of life and strife, love and hatred, dissolving into a most absorbing melodrama of the times.

The story deals with the struggle of a girl born in the slums and her rise to a state of womanhood where she is eventually claimed by society...

The movie *Sally in our Alley,* also spelled *Sallie* in certain advertisements, appeared at the Park Theatre for an extended engagement in Boston. The Moxie Company helped promote the film, running advertisements which noted, in part: "Don't Fail to See the Moxie Girl, Muriel Ostriche, in *Sallie in our Alley* at the Park Theatre. You Know Her Well—You Have Seen Her on the Moxie Signs for Years...Don't Forget That Muriel Ostriche is THE MOXIE GIRL."

On October 20, 1916 the *Boston Journal* featured the following notice concerning Muriel Ostriche under "Theatre Gossip," by E.F. Harkins:

Though Muriel Ostriche is but nineteen years old, she has already been starred by three film companies. She made her debut on the screen when she was attending high school in New York, her native city. At first she took only extra parts, of course, having had no experience as an actress, then she became an "ingenue in stock." This was with a modest enterprise known as the Eclair Film Company. Adventures were heaped upon her. She had to play roles where she was compelled to be in a lion's cage; she had to venture into water three times as deep as she is tall, while she could not swim; and soon she was christened "The Daredevil of the Movies."

The movies are crowded with these daredevils, as a matter of fact, but it was strange work for a little girl who was the very personification of sweet sixteen.

The Thanhouser Company evidently took note of this fact, for it captured cute little Muriel and starred her for two years in the "Princess" plays which numbered 100 before they were done. Then the Vitagraph Company engaged her to be leading woman with Robert Edeson and after this quite serious work—you may remember her winning ways in "Mortmain," for example—she resumed her career as a daredevil. Her work all around was so popular that the Equitable Company last year offered her a salary of $300 a week to play leading ingenue roles, and this is what she has been doing ever since. The Equitable is now part of the World Company and Miss Ostriche appears with Carlyle Blackwell. The salary in question is a good one for either stage or screen productions. Fancy salaries are paid only to a few, which is the universal rule.

Like other starlets of the day, Ostriche became a favorite with columnists. *Photoplay Magazine* gave her horoscope and predicted her marriage:

NATIVITY OF MURIEL OSTRICHE, BORN MARCH 24th. This native came to this world to be a mother of a very high order. I have never seen such a strong tendency in any nativity to be always mothering somebody, but strange as it may seem, she should not have the care of children; she would be too good to them and they in return would be unruly under her guidance. In the drama, she will do well in parts where she has to suffer from her children's cruelty and neglect, from the loss of fortune and from the injustice of her parents who may drive her away from home. She is musical, poetical, mystically inclined and very quick-witted. This nativity does not indicate how much money earned or even saved from the earnings, but it does point out a number of legacies left her from father, mother and husband, or someone who holds a public position. Marriage should be very pleasant. The husband will have much worldly goods and be a leader. In 1918 and 1919 she will have several offers of marriage, two from men of over fifty, which are good matches, but the real man whom she will marry for love will be about her own age.

Frederick James Smith, a contributor to *Motion Picture Classic* magazine, reported a breathless interview on the run with Muriel, who at that time was dividing her attention between high school and acting, noting that no less a personage as David Wark Griffith considered her "too young to be made love to and too old not to." At the time she may have been living at 141 West 73rd Street, New York City, her address away from home for several years:

"WHAT TIME IS IT?" asked Muriel. We have accomplished interviews under all sorts of trying circumstances. We have "helped" stars pick out gowns. We have motored into Westchester with them. We have dined, tea-d, Ziegfeld roofed, suppered, lunched and—whisper—even breakfasted with them. Many times they have been in a hurry, but to the best of our present disturbed recollection, nobody was ever quite in so much of a hurry as Muriel Ostriche.

The task of interviewing a cute ingenue—film ingenues are becoming more extinct every day—rather intrigued us and we were exactly on time at Miss Ostriche's uptown hotel.

Two minutes later—3:32 p.m. to be exact—Miss Ostriche appeared in the hotel reception room. She had a tiny package in her hand.

"I'm awfully sorry," she began. "You see, I'd been planning to take a 4:10 train to the beach for the weekend and I thought our interview was to be earlier and—but I'll take a later train."

Of course, we knew that she really didn't want to take a later train. Also, we could not conscientiously upset the schedule of an ingenue. So we asked a porter to summon a taxi. "We'll interview you enroute," we confided.

"That'll be wonderful," sighed Miss Ostriche, with something we suspected sounded like relief. "Better start now before the taxi comes. Want a—er—pencil?"

"We never use 'em," said we, trying to maintain our editorial poise in the face of the Ostriche optics. "What about your traveling bag?"

"Don't need it," giggled Miss Ostriche. "I have everything here (indicating the tiny bundle). Bet you can't guess the contents."

Our poise was slipping. Where on earth was the taxi?

"Guess," insisted Miss Ostriche.

We mopped our brow. "It's a hot day," we said, deftly changing the subject.

"A toothbrush and a nightie," continued Miss Ostriche remorselessly. "What do you think about that?"

But the taxi arrived before we were forced to commit ourselves. (The scene changes to the interior of an open taxi.)

"Tell me the time and ask some questions!"

"3:51—and how did you get into pictures?"

"We'll make it— I'm a New York girl— Did you guess it?— Nobody ever does— Of course, I had the movie bug— Every girl has, sometime or other— A boy who knew me at school, Christy Cabanne, was in pictures at the old Biograph studio and he asked me to come up for a try-out— My people objected—furiously— What time is it?"

"3:56—and go on."

"We'll make it— I didn't know a thing about pictures, naturally— They asked me to do a scene— You know, for a screen-try out— I was scared something awful— Do you know what one of the camera-men said?— What time is it?"

"3:59—what did he say?"

" 'Some lamps!'— Funny, wasn't it— Of course, I didn't know what that sort of slang meant then— He was talking of my eyes, you know— What—"

"4:02—and we guessed it—and we don't blame him."

"We'll make it— Well, after the test Griffith came around and said, 'I don't know what we can do with her, she's too young to be made love to and too old not to. Tell her to come around tomorrow.'— But I told them I was going to school and could only work Saturdays and Sundays— I guess he was angry— What—"

"4:04—you'll make it!"

"I did a few extra parts at Biograph and then I applied at the old Eclair studio— A French director there gave me my first chance— I didn't know until the production was half over that I was playing the leading role— Of course, I had to keep working every day and I had to give up school— My folks were—"

"Furious," we interrupted. "It's 4:06. Two more blocks and you'll be at the Pennsylvania Station."

"After that I worked at Thanhouser, World Film, and now I am making a series of pictures for Arrow— You must see them?— I'm going to California to do several— Promise me you'll see them?"

"Yes," we said rashly. "It's 4:08 and there's your station."

(Business of exiting rapidly from taxi and settling with driver who, naturally, has no change.) At the train gate Miss Ostriche remarked to our gasping self, "Thanks awfully— Hope you've got enough material."

We struggled for self-possession. "Don't lose that package, whatever you do," we begged. The gate closed upon our interviewee. We turned and staggered into the station drugstore. "One chocolate soda," said we hoarsely. From sheer force of habit we looked at our watch. It was 4:10.

"You'll make it," we mumbled to the soda clerk.

"I am," said he, laconic-like.

By 1914, Ostriche had left Eclair and was featured by the Thanhouser studio. By 1916 she had moved to Vitagraph and had a leading role in *Kennedy Square*, with Charles Kent and Antonio Moreno. For the same studio she acted in *Mortmain*, after which she moved to Equitable for parts in *A Daughter of the Sea*, *A Circus Romance*, and *By Whose Hand?* For World she filmed *The Man She Married* and *A Square Deal*, while for Peerless-World she did *Moral Courage*, *The Dormant Power*, *Leap to Fame*, *Tinsel*, *What Love Forgives*, *The Bluffer*, *The Moral Deadline*, and *The Hand Invisible*. For Schomer-Ross she starred in *The Sacred Flame*. The latter was released on November 8, 1919.

The February 1, 1917 issue of *Amusement Record*, a periodical devoted to motion picture exhibitors in the northwestern part of the United States, carried two items concerning Muriel Ostriche, noting that on February 19, 1917 the movie *A Square Deal*, starring Carlyle Blackwell, June Elvidge, Henry Hull and Muriel Ostriche, a five-reeler, was scheduled for release.

Another item noted unusual movie names: "Just a few names of screen stars: Louise Lovely, Arline Pretty, Blanche Sweet, Bessie Love, Lillian Peacock, Muriel Ostriche, Eleanor Crowe, Mona Darkfeather, Fritzi Brunette, Betty Schade, Irene Howley, Ethel Tearle, Louise Glaum, Lillian Gish and Doris Pawn. Such is life in the studio."

Offstage and off-screen, Muriel Ostriche apparently was "having fun" with William J. Lewis, who happened to be married to someone else at the time, as an article which appeared on August 2, 1918 noted:

BROKER SUES WIFE: MUST PAY ALIMONY. MISS OSTRICHE, MOVIE ACTRESS, FIGURES IN LEWIS FAMILY TROUBLES. In the suit of William J. Lewis, who is connected with a large piano house, against Hattie Lewis, for divorce on the grounds of her alleged fondness for her cousin, Henry J. Butler, the wealthy lumber merchant, Justice McAvoy today ordered the husband to pay his wife suitable alimony pending the determination of the action in which she brought a counterclaim asking for a separation. Mrs. Lewis is to have custody of her child pending a decision.

Several of Mrs. Lewis' brothers are in the stock brokerage business. Her father left her considerable money. In her counterclaim she alleges that in their ten years of married life she has frequently been required to draw on her own resources for household expenses, while her husband expended both time and money with others. She alleged that his latest diversion was a "Miss Ostriche," a moving picture actress. From what Mrs. Lewis says about her husband's associations with Miss Ostriche, it is likely that if the wife and Miss Ostriche should meet, some Ostriche feathers would fly...

During the year 1919 Muriel Ostriche was a prominent figure in New England, during which travels she spent some time with Frank M. Archer, who had a penchant for red-haired girls (Miss Ostriche's hair was described as "russet-brown") and who staged several "prettiest red-head contests" in New England. Her travels around New England were chronicled by various newspapers. Samples follow:

From the *Boston Post*, March 1919:

Muriel Ostriche, who is not only beautiful in the face and figure and an accomplished actress, but is known all over the world as "The Moxie Girl," will assume a dual capacity this week at the Park and Franklin Park Theatres. She will be seen in a photoplay and will also appear in person, giving a brief talk to the audiences on timely topics. In her honor The Moxie Company will put at her disposal a golden car driven by Brig Young, and in this gorgeous vehicle Miss Ostriche will be conveyed from one theatre to the other.

The Lowell *Courier Citizen*, March 11, 1919, carried the following notice:

MURIEL OSTRICHE PAYS VISIT TO LOWELL. Muriel Ostriche, the famous Moxie Girl and noted screen star, appeared in person at the Strand yesterday afternoon and last night. Capacity audiences were on hand to greet her and she was given a most enthusiastic reception at both performances.

The star came to Lowell accompanied by General Manager Sorerio, and between the afternoon and evening performances made a run up to Nashua, New Hampshire, where they were entertained as guests of the Nashua Country Club at a dinner party.

Miss Ostriche came to town in the Moxie "gold car" and after a short sightseeing trip around the city—the real home of Moxie—reached the Strand for the first performance of the afternoon. She was introduced to the audience by manager Sorerio and her presentation was marked by a genuine welcome from all. She spoke of the motion picture business—its trials and tribulations, as well as its pleasures and comforts—and told a few amusing stories about herself and some of the other stars of filmdom. Later she held a reception in the lobby of the theater and met personally a majority of the patrons. The same schedule is carried out at the night performance. In connection with her presence on the stage, a short film in which she appeared was shown on the screen. It gave the audiences an opportunity of seeing Miss Ostriche as a "reel star" and in "real life." The comparison was interesting indeed.

In New Hampshire, the *Nashua Telegraph* took notice of Miss Ostriche's visit:

LITTLE MOXIE GIRL GREETED BY THOUSANDS. Muriel Ostriche, the winsome little Moxie Girl, famed as a World movie star, came to Nashua, liked the city, appeared at two performances at the Park Theatre, dined at Nashua's famous Country Club, and departed having made many new friends among her myriads of screen admirers.

When you say that Muriel is a winsome little miss she is just that. As movie queen she is certainly a stellar attraction, and Manager Thomas of the Park is to be congratulated at adding this attraction to the many excellent features he is introducing to Nashua audiences.

Muriel has been touring New England in a gold car—a Moxie car. Of course it isn't all gold, that is the wheels are just ordinary auto wheels and the tires are of rubber and the windshield is glass and iron, the top is leather, and so on, but the body panels are finished in gold leaf as are the tire supports, the wheel hubs, mud guards, hood cover, and various and anon features converting a big Cadillac roadster into an automobile attraction that makes everyone who sees it sit up and take notice.

And Muriel can certainly drive that car. She has driven it over a part of New England already and she's going to run up a few more miles before she gets back to business at the New Jersey studio.

Tuesday Muriel came from Lowell to Nashua. In the Spindle City [Lowell] she was met by a Nashua reception committee who saw her perform at the Strand theatre. Then Muriel got into one of Howard Hartman's Franklin sedans and taking hold of the wheel headed for Nashua. It certainly was some ride. Muriel thought the road from Nashua to Lowell was a dandy, particularly the stretch from the state line to the city. Every few moments on the auto ride to this city she would exclaim about this and that feature of the Franklin car. She says it's a great car to ride in, but a perfectly wonderful one to drive. And these were not idle words as Muriel is to have a fine new closed model Franklin of her own, all finished in the nattiest of colors and upholstery. She says that when she is behind a Franklin wheel she has no fear of traffic cops or anything. The car simply has to glide along, and Muriel certainly knows how to make it glide.

On her arrival in Nashua, Muriel went at once to the Park Theatre, where she was greeted by Manager Thomas, Treasurer Erb and others.

Her appearance in film and on the stage brought forth rounds of applause from a crowded house, while the clerks in the stores and operatives in the factories could hardly wait until evening to get a real view of a real live screen favorite.

The evening performance was greeted by a house that tested the seating capacity to the limit. Muriel's entrance upon the stage was greeted by storms of applause. She was presented with a large bouquet of sweet peas.

Today Manager Thomas is receiving congratulations on every side on bringing a popular screen artist to the city.

On the same day, March 11, the Boston *Herald* carried an article which mentioned Moxie fans:

MOXIE GIRL AT THE PARK. While crowds in the lobby of the Park Theatre today were waiting to get a glimpse of Muriel Ostriche, the World film star, before her appearance there, a Traveler representative was greeted at her suite in the Hotel Lennox by the diminutive Muriel herself.

"Oh, yes, I've been in Boston before," Miss Ostriche replied to the first question. "I made an appearance at the Park Theatre over a year ago. It was the first personal appearance I had ever made, and I was frightened to death. My knees just shook!

"Today I will tell some of my experiences in the movies," she continued. "I wanted to sing a little song, but the only man who can play it is not in Boston. I expect to make other appearances in New England. In between times I am going to see Boston. I think Boston is the loveliest place."

Miss Ostriche's representative told how, when the film star was but fifteen years old, she posed for the famous Moxie advertisements, selected from 1,500 applicants. Every time you smile back at the Moxie Girl, sitting on a big box or peeking at you from a cardboard fan, you are smiling at Muriel Ostriche.

On the same day the *Boston Post* told of her appearances at two Boston theaters:

FRANKLIN PARK THEATRE. Muriel Ostriche, "The Moxie Girl," made a personal appearance at the Franklin Park Theatre at both performances yesterday and was greeted by her many admirers. Ethel Barrymore in her latest photoplay, "The Divorcee," adapted from "Lady Frederick," offered the star ample opportunity to display her versatile talents. The vaudeville show was exceptionally good. The Vitagraph comedy produced many laughs. There will be an entire change of bill the last half of the week.

PARK THEATRE. Muriel Ostriche, "The Moxie Girl," greeted hundreds of her admirers at the Park Theatre yesterday when she appeared in person and was given a remarkable reception by the audience. Heading the pictures was "Wilson or the Kaiser." It is not a war picture, but depicts the lives of the two most talked of men in the world. Kitty Gordon was seen in "The Unveiling Hand," a striking story of a man's cowardice and a woman's faith. An all-star cast includes Irving Cummins and George McWuarrie. Maciste in "The Liberator," the second episode of the serial, proved most popular, and Madame Clavert, the soprano, and Madeline Childs, violinist, completed the bill.

The *Daily Free Press-Tribune*, published in Waltham, a town close to Boston, noted in its issue of Wednesday, March 12, 1919:

Muriel Ostriche will appear in person at the Waldorf Theatre in the near future. Miss Ostriche is known everywhere as "The Moxie Girl" and the people of Waltham will be glad to see and meet the popular photoplay star. After the performance she will have a reception for the public. Tea will be served and every lady present will receive a souvenir.

On March 13, 1919 large advertisements noted that Muriel Ostriche was scheduled to appear at the Strand Theatre, Chelsea (Massachusetts), stating in part: "First Time in the History of Chelsea—Will Appear in Person MURIEL OSTRICHE, World Film Star," by special arrangement with our Park and Strand Circuit, MURIEL OSTRICHE has agreed to make her appearance... Be sure to see this famous movie star. She will arrive here in a gold limousine, through the courtesy of The Moxie Company. A well-known girl, sometimes called the Moxie Girl. 2,000 FANS GIVEN AWAY FREE, OF MURIEL OSTRICHE."

Muriel Ostriche made the news in Rhode Island in April and the *Providence Bulletin* carried this story on April 19, 1919:

MURIEL OSTRICHE AND HER $25,000 GOWN TO APPEAR. Muriel Ostriche with her $25,000 gown, and Olive Thomas, movie star, whom Harrison Fisher, the artist, has pronounced the most beautiful girl in America, are among the latest photoplay notables who have sent word to the movie ball committee that they will come to this city for the benefit to be given in the state armory, April 24, for the Fatherless Children of France Fund... One of the side features will be the taking of moving pictures of the stars as they arrive in this city and while they are at the armory.

In an article appearing in the summer of 1919, Frank Archer discussed some of the firm's promotions, including his favorite movie star:

"One of the chief summer amusements," declares Frank Archer, the vice-president of The Moxie Company, "is drinking Moxie." But if that isn't enough, Moxie fur-

STRAND THEATRE
BROADWAY
CHELSEA

~ THURSDAY ~

MURIEL OSTRICHE

(WORLD FILM STAR)

THE FIRST	FOLLOW THE
APPEARANCE	CROWD
OF A	
Movie Star	TO SEE
in CHELSEA	HER

WILL APPEAR IN PERSON

Your opportunity to see the World Star
at our Theatre, THURSDAY EVE.

2000 Fans Given Away with Her Photograph

ALWAYS KNOWN AS THE "MOXIE GIRL"

Will Arrive In A Gold Limousine

The most famous of the early Moxie Girls was Muriel Ostriche, here featured in an advertisement for the Strand Theatre, Chelsea, Massachusetts. "2000 Fans Given Away with Her Photograph" notes the caption, which also states that Muriel is "Always Known as the Moxie Girl."

nishes all sorts of free amusements to the public through its features. There is Fred Wilson, for example. He is the champion stilt walker for the world, bar none. He is a nonpareil attraction. Wilson is in demand everywhere there is a desire to catch the eye of the crowd. The Moxie Company has on file a list of country fairs which have applied for him. All Wilson has to do is walk down any street anbd business and traffic is suspended.

Wilson is about twelve feet tall or thereabouts. He is preternaturally solemn, pensive as it were. Looking down on the public from a height like the gods from Olympus enables him to see many things that the rest of us miss. Perhaps that is why he is melancholy.

Then there is the Moxie Horsemobile. This weird vehicle doesn't carry a line of advertisement upon it. A white horse riding in an automobile. Perhaps a red-headed girl is riding the horse and guiding the machine through a steering wheel in the animal's neck. Perhaps the girl wears one of those Moxie costumes of white duck dotted with tiny cuts, and other advertising devices, but the Horsemobile is innocent of any advertising.

Muriel Ostriche is certainly entertaining. Muriel is one of the most brilliant of the photoplay actresses. In the last two or three years she has forged to the front of the World Film Company. She is now the charming little creature who may be seen in any drugstore in the land perched upon a case of Moxie. Miss Muriel appears on all sorts of advertising from fans to complete dinner sets.

Mr. Archer, however, intends to get into the amusement business even stronger. He has a big card up his sleeve which he will spring very soon. When it is displayed old P.T. Barnum will have nothing on Moxie as a promoter...

On July 14, 1919 it was announced that Miss Ostriche would appear in Boston again:

PARK THEATRE PATRONS TO SEE MISS OSTRICHE. The patrons of the Park Theatre this week will have a chance to see Miss Muriel Ostriche herself, who will appear in person on Monday afternoon and evening at the Park Theatre. This has been done by special arrangement with William A. Brady, World Film Corporation, who has Miss Ostriche under contract, and in whose pictures she appears. She will be remembered by the many patrons of the Park who saw her in "Sally in our Alley," featured with Carlyle Blackwell. Miss Ostriche is well known all over the country as The Moxie Girl and is one of the most beautiful stars on the screen today. Manager Thomas D. Sorerio of the Park Theatre is giving away on Monday 1,000 fancy china ice cream dishes with Miss Ostriche's picture painted on each one.

For Bonnie-B, an imported hair net, Muriel Ostriche appeared in a July 1919 advertisement in *The Motion Picture Magazine*. Muriel was shown seated at her dressing table, mirror in hand, and, in another pose, lounging on a sofa. The caption noted:

HOW I KEEP MY HAIR SMOOTH AND LOVELY—By Muriel Ostriche, Famous Film Star:

You'd think that after a strenuous day in the studio, my hair would be in a wildly flying state—but it isn't! I've discovered the way to keep my hair beautifully arranged all day long—I wear a Bonnie-B Imported Human Hair Net.

The Bonnie-B Human Hair Net is so delicate, it matches my hair so perfectly, that its absolutely invisible. My hair always looks as though I'd just arranged it. The Bonnie-B is as strong as it's dainty—it lasts three times longer than ordinary hair nets.

The little booklet—"Artistic French Coiffures," by Cluzelle—which comes with every Bonnie-B Hair Net, tells you how to arrange your hair in the newest, most fascinating styles.

Muriel Ostriche poses for a Bonnie-B Human Hair Net advertisement. Muriel was the best known of the Moxie Girls.

You can get the Bonnie-B at the Veiling and Notion counters of the better shops—they're 15c two for 25c—white or gray, 25c each—or write to the Bonnie-B Company, 216 Fourth Avenue, New York.

Do try the Bonnie-B—I'm sure you'll like it. And Bonnie-B Veils—they're irresistibly French! —MURIEL OSTRICHE

P.S. If you will write me at the above address and send me the stamps for your Hair Net, I shall be very glad indeed to tell you how I arranged my hair.

In October 1919 *Billboard* ran an article datelined New York, October 5:

MURIEL OSTRICHE TO STAR IN MUSICAL COMEDY. WILL MAKE DEBUT IN "DREAM GIRL," BRAND NEW PLAY, SPONSORED BY POPULAR PRODUCTIONS, INC. Everything is in complete readiness for the debut of Muriel Ostriche as a musical comedy star in a brand new musical play titled "Dream Girl," which is the joint work of Walter Irving and Arthur C. King, the initial performance taking place in the Lyceum Theatre, Paterson, New Jersey, October 13.

The Popular Productions, Inc. is sponsoring the Ostriche show which will have an attractive feminine chorus of sixty voices, with everything new, including the scenery, wardrobe and equipment. The Popular Productions, Inc. has routed "Dream Girl," through one-night stands adjacent to New York, preparatory to whipping the show into perfect shape for its forthcoming New York premiere.

Miss Ostriche has long been a motion picture star, her work with World and Thanhouser subjects being well remembered by the movie fans. Large, capable, and competent cast surrounds her with such "names" from the big musical revues and legitimate realm as Paul E. Burns, late of "Fiddlers Three"; George Leonard, from "A Royal Vagabond,"; Edward S. Forbes, recently of "Oh Boy"; Ely Dawson, late of George White's "Scandals of 1919"; Fay Tunis of Lew Fields' show, "A Lonely Romeo"; Gene Leoni, Bobbi Lorens, Barry Melton, Matty Scanlon, etc...

James Gorman has put on the dances, and among some of the big numbers Miss Ostriche will be given a chance to display her singing and dancing ability... The Popular Productions, Inc. plans to make a picture production of "Dream Girl," with Miss Ostriche as the picture star, the photoplay proposition to feature the New York opening of the show.

Muriel Ostriche, by then married, was having problems with her parents, observed an article in the New York *World*, December 17, 1919:

SUES PARENTS FOR $32,400 SHE SAYS SHE EARNED. Mrs. Muriel Ostriche Brady, former popular moving picture star and now the wife of Frank A. Brady, architect and builder, appeared in Justice Giegerich's part of the Supreme Court yesterday with her husband and her attorney, Edward W. Drucker, to press her suit against her parents for an accounting of $32,400 which she alleges she deposited with them before she became of age. She claims they have refused to turn over her money to her. She is now 23 years old, her attorney said.

Mrs. Brady left high school and began acting in the movies when she was fifteen. She alleges that she turned over $32,400 of her earnings to her parents, Mr. and Mrs. Abraham Ostriche, of the Hotel San Remo, 74th Street and Central Park West, with the understanding that they were to hold it in trust for her and give her the principal and the accrued income when she became of age. She married Mr. Brady almost two years ago.

Her parents contend, according to her attorney, that parents have the right to collect a minor child's earnings and that the money belongs to them because she was not legally of age when she gave it to them. Mrs. Brady's lawyer stated yesterday that he would produce bank books showing deposits of many thousands of dollars made by "Miriam Ostriche in trust for Muriel Ostriche."

During the film production year from September 1, 1920 to August 31, 1921, Muriel Ostriche was listed under just one feature, *The Shadow*, directed by J. Charles Davis for Schomer-Ross, which by that time had moved from its temporary offices at 1440 Broadway, New York City, to 126 West 46th Street. Unfortunately, reviewers paid little heed to the star of the film or to the film itself, and *The Shadow* was soon forgotten.

One of Muriel Ostriche's final recognitions in the trade appeared in the *Motion Picture Studio Directory Trade Annual*, 1921 edition, published by Motion Picture News, Inc.:

OSTRICHE, MURIEL; Born New York, 1897. Educated public schools, New York; Screen career, Eclair, Thanhouser, Vitagraph ("Kennedy Square," "Mortmain"), Equitable ("A Daughter of the Sea," "A Circus Romance," "By Whose Hand?"), World ("The Man She Married," "A Square Deal"), Peerless-World ("Moral Courage," "The Dormant Power," "Leap to Fame," "Tinsel," "What Love Forgives," "The Bluffer," "The Moral Deadline," "The Hand Invisible"), Schomer-Ross ("The Sacred Flame"), Arrow ("Betty Sets the Pace," "Betty's Green Eyed Monster"), Address: 141 West 73rd St., New York.

There was trouble in paradise, and in a large feature article published in *The American Weekly* in 1925, "Mrs. Brady's New Idea of Married Life," readers learned:

Six years ago the Frank A. Bradys, who live down in the smart Great Neck, Long Island colony of artists, stagefolk, writers and thinkers, were married. Mr. Brady is a very clever and successful young architect. Mrs. Brady was Muriel Ostriche, the youngest grown-up motion picture actress in the world, and successful star of "Kennedy Square," "Mortmain," "Daughter of the Sea," and a dozen more first-rate pictures. Now she is going back again to the screen.

For six years the Bradys played the game of married life according to the best accepted standards. They teed off in perfect harmony, and in due course the little twosome became first a threesome and then a foursome.

Mrs. Brady put her career in a closet and locked the door on it. During those four years she looked after the house and the babies, and her husband, in the old-fashioned way. When they went away, they always went together. So just a few days ago the neighbors were much surprised to see young Mr. Brady standing on his doorstep, with two heavy suitcases in his hands, while young Mrs. Brady, holding the baby, Margot, 19 months old in her arms, and three-year old Gloria at her skirts was plainly bidding him good-bye.

But they would have been more surprised if they had heard the conversation between the two, just before the parting.

"Well, goodbye my dear," said Mr. Brady, in effect. "I will always cherish the memory of those days when you and I lived together in old-fashioned matrimony, and took turns walking up and down at midnight with our mutual children. Ah, well—I suppose those days are over. You will keep your house and I will keep mine, but nothing dearest, nothing will ever change my feeling for you."

"Now be a good boy," she had also said to him, in effect. "Remember art is long, but anybody can get married almost any day in the week. I will be glad to see you, always, and glad to be invited to your house—when you can spare the time. Dearest, my heart is yours forever more, even though you and I are not going to keep house together any longer."

What had happened was that after those six years of old-fashioned wedlock, Mrs. Brady had an entirely new idea of what married life ought to be, and she and her husband were putting the theory into practice.

But what was wrong with the idea that made Mrs. Brady take up anew? She explains:

"In the first place," she says, "I don't think that this has anything to do with divorce. Nothing could be further from my heart and mind than that. Mr. Brady is leaving or I am simply putting him out of the house, because we have agreed to divorce our artistic and working selves. We are separating for ourselves our work in life, our art. But as for hearts, our sympathies, our love, our harmony, and our mutual children, all of these are more united than they ever have been since we were first married.

"We are living in separate establishments from this time forth to preserve the bloom on the butterfly wings of romance. We do not want to rust our love with untidy glimpses of each other the first thing in the morning or with grumpy breakfast faces or plunges for the same bathtub at the same time, or difference of opinion on how to cut the grass or harboring the neighbor's cat. We are clearing the matrimonial index of all the litter and bothersome detail of marriage, keeping the paint clean and the sails white for the voyage of our love.

"In short, we have decided we can manage to preserve both our careers and our romance if we don't see each other so much every day. For the first years of our marriage it was right we should live together, because the children were coming to us, and I was devoting myself entirely to being a wife and a mother, and in such cases a wife needs her husband and she doesn't worry over her career. I gladly put mine aside for four years. But now I am going back to the pictures. I have done my duty to the race, and I know how I have got to live to be a success on the screen. I have got to nourish my ego. I have got to encourage my ambition. I have got to think about getting on all day long. I haven't time to worry over the daily details of a husband.

"But Mr. Brady must also think of his career, and it is quite impossible for us to do our best together under one roof.

"Naturally, we are each absorbed in our art, as we should be to succeed, we each want to talk about our own plans, ambitions, success, etc. What happens when you try to park two artistic temperaments and two matrimonially inclined hearts together? Well, consider a typical breakfast scene which might have taken place after my re-entry into the pictures.

"Still full of things of the day before, I might have begun—'Well, I had a great day, I tell you. So and So said that he had never seen finer acting—'

" 'Those plans I made for So and So are far ahead of anything I've ever done. That's what old Mr. So and So told me today—' my husband might have interrupted, paying no attention to me at all.

" 'Yes,' I might have gone, heeding him just a little, 'there are darned few women who can wear clothes like I do, if I do say it—'

"And then he might have suddenly realized my inattention and have come back with something like this: 'Oh you make me tired with your conceit and your chatter...you talk as if your career was the only one in the world. Listen to me while I tell you some plans I made today—'

"And then the day would have been utterly spoiled for both of us.

"There I would have probably interrupted, and no husband likes his wife not to hear him through to the end. Mr. Brady, gentle though he is, might even have been pushed to the point of hurling the bacon and eggs at me and then, of course, no wife with any spirit in her could forbear to retaliate with the rolls and the marmalade. And what a scene for the children! No, we decided we would never drift that way. We have too much respect for each other's ambitions, our children and our love. So we are divorcing to keep the hearts united.

"That doesn't mean that we won't often be together and I won't often be just crazy to have him come out to see me at my house, and hopeful that he will invite me to his house."

But how about the children under the new idea? Won't they miss Papa if they stay with Mama—or Mama if they stay with Papa? And won't Papa miss them? Also, what about the training of them by the father?

"Under our plan," answers Mrs. Brady, "Mr. Brady has a standing invitation to spend his weekends with his wife and children. He will have from Friday night till Sunday night with us. They may miss him at first though [they will get used to it]. When he comes out for the weekends I am strictly my husband's wife until Sunday night. But not so when he comes out other times to see the children. Then he may see me or he may not.

"If, on the other hand, Mr. Brady should get lonely for me during the week, he will telephone and ask me if he may come out that night. There probably will be some conversation as this over the phone:

"Mr. Brady—'Hello, Darling, I want to come out and see you.'

"Mrs. Brady—'For dinner or the evening? Or to spend the night?'

"It will depend upon his answer is what mine is.

"If I should feel the same urge, I shall expect to follow the same formula. We will each have our own friends as well as our mutual friends; we will each go where we please and see whom we please and do as we please—within limits, of course. These limits will be our own sense of right and wrong. As for the financial arrangements, I will keep my house and he will keep his. Certain expenses of the children we will share. I am fortunate in being able to do this, because I, too, am a money-maker. When we went into this arrangement we settled the details beforehand. He left upstairs two closets full of clothes. He will, moreover, always send his laundry home. There must ever be a tender bond between a man and a woman when he has the confidence to trust his washing to her. And I shall always want to keep a wifely eye on his socks and shirts, the old darling. He shall be mended up. So Mr. Brady and I are very pleased with our foresight, we feel that we have really wisely crossed our bridges before we came to them. The last advantage of all is the surprise of courtship to which we have gone back. I watch the mails for his letter. Each time the telephone rings I think it might be him..."

Thus little Miss Brady explains her new idea of how to be happy though married. Just how her experiment will turn out, and when if ever, Mr. Brady will insist upon coming home again to live, nobody can say. To be sure, one other well known couple have already tried the same plan and made it succeed. The brilliant novelist, Fanny Hurst and her husband, who only meet for breakfast once or twice a week, recently celebrated their tenth anniversary with a two week's honeymoon, taken together. The new kind of marriage has succeeded with them. This difference, though, Mrs. Brady had six years of matrimony before she tried her idea and Miss Hurst had none.

However this latest experiment of the young Bradys may turn out, there is no question but what they have entered it sincerely, and they believe it will cement their very great affection. In the meantime, the children are getting older and perhaps, in a year or two, little Miss Gloria and little Miss Margot may take the reins into their own hands, like good American children, put down their little feet and go bring Papa home to Great Neck and Mama.

Ann Pennington

Ann Pennington, born in Camden, New Jersey, on December 23, 1892, attracted notice as an amateur dancer in Philadelphia at an early age. In November 1911 she first appeared professionally at Aston, New York, in *The Red Widow*, after which she went on tour across the nation.

In Chicago, September 1912, she played Hansel in *A Polish Wedding*, but widespread attention did not come until she appeared on the stage of the New Amsterdam Theatre, New York, on June 16, 1913, in the Ziegfeld Follies of that year. She became a favorite of Florenz Ziegfeld and stayed with the Follies until 1918.

Her film debut occurred in early summer 1916 in *Susie Snowflakes*, a Famous Players-Paramount production. *The Antics of Ann*, produced in 1917 by the same studio, and *Sunshine Nan*, a Zukor-Paramount production of early 1918, furthered her screen career. During the 1920s she appeared in many movie roles, including *Madame Behave* (with Stanhope Wheatcroft and Julian Eltinge; Producers Distributing Corporation).

Unlike most other movie personalities of the era, Ann Pennington maintained a heavy stage acting schedule. In November 1917 she appeared in *Miss 1917* at the Century Theatre, at the Liberty Theatre in June 1919 she was part of the *Scandals of 1919*, which went to Boston toward the end of the year, at which time she was interviewed by Frank Archer, who suggested that she might do the role of Betty (from Archer's *TNT Cowboy*) on the stage. She continued her "scandals" appearances intermittently through the 1920s and also starred in several Ziegfeld Follies revues.

Ann Pennington remained an active figure throughout the 1930s and 1940s, appearing in many stage productions, nightclub acts, and other activities. In later life her address was the Hotel Lincoln, 44th and 45th Streets at Eighth Avenue, New York City.

After appearing in *Susie Snowflakes*, the dancer captured the attention of gossip columnists and was featured from time to time in movie magazines. Randolph Bartlett penned an early feature, "Only Bad Pennies Return," noting that Ann was a "very good Penny" and for this reason "hasn't been back to Camden since she left it to become a star." The same writer noted that she was "small, but, gee whiz, how bright!" Her diminutive height was mentioned in another review of the period: "Ann Pennington is the famous small sample of Mr. Ziegfeld's instructive entertainment, the Follies. She was born in Camden and began to dance as soon as her mother began bringing willow switches into the house. In the last two years the tiny Pennington has twinkled quaintly for the Famous Players."

In 1918 a reviewer observed that "Ann's Oriental dance in the current or 1918 Follies is one good reason why the line at the box office never dwindles. You have to be a personal friend of Mr. Ziegfeld or somebody to get in." The review continued:

> This is Ann Pennington—"Penny" to her good many friends. She's dancing with the latest edition of Mr. Ziegfeld's well-known national institution, now on tour. They say Penny is one of the best little reasons why Mr. Ziegfeld's show answers to the call of the ne plus ultra of entertainment which combines, to the satisfaction of all concerned, girls and music—which means a little music and some girls.
>
> When is she coming back to pictures? She left the Famous Players studio one day and it begins to look as though she left like the heroine in the melodrama, never to return. In the movies they want her to act soulful and sedate and Penny can't do it, she simply can't. "I'd like to do some more pictures if they would give me suitable stories," she said. Perhaps if Miss Pennington were coaxed—anyway, it should mean a pretty penny for the producers.

Eileen Percy

In 1921 a directory of the motion picture industry named Eileen Percy as a "star" and listed productions in which recently she had a leading role, including *Beware of the Bride, Big Town Ideas, Blushing Bride, The Husband Hunter, The Land of Jazz, Why Trust Your Husband, The Tomboy, Maid of the West, Hicksville to Broadway,* and *Little Miss Hawkshaw.* A year earlier, another directory noted that highlights of her screen career included *Some Liar, Where the West Begins, Brass Buttons, The Gray Horizon, The Beloved Cheater, Told in the Hills, In Missoura,* and *Desert Gold,* noting that "at present she is on world tour."

With Douglas Fairbanks, Eileen Percy starred in *Down to Earth* in 1917. She appeared in several other pictures with him during the same period, leading one columnist to designate her as "Fairbanks' *leading* leading lady." A picture caption of the time noted: "Douglas Fairbanks has the reputation of having had more leading women than any other picture star. Eileen Percy is his latest, and this little showgirl from the stage has taken to pictures like a duck to water," while another review note observed: "Upon Eileen's completion of *Her Honor the Mayor* comes the announcement that she will shine under the Fox banner with this as her first starring vehicle. Too we are informed that stories especially adapted to her type have been purchased for her use, and Eileen herself is overjoyed at her rise to a star's estate."

A movie magazine article by Marguerite Sheridan noted that Eileen had come from Broadway's Cocoanut Grove to the enviable position of being Douglas Fairbanks' leading lady, "and now she's a confirmed screenite." The story went on to say:

Not so many months ago, there lived in Manhattan a pretty little girl of seventeen, who was trying her best to demonstrate the theory that an energetic person can do a number of things at once and do them well. In addition to being a very fetching ingenue in support of the jovial Frank Tinney at the Ziegfeld-Dillingham "Century Girl" production at the Century Theatre, she was one of the most attractive reasons why the Cocoanut Grove became so famous, and even found time to sit for an occasional magazine cover by Harrison Fisher, Clarence Underwood, or Howard Chandler Christy.

She danced divinely, her voice was charming, her personality at once demure and bewitching—certainly, Eileen Percy's life was far from being monotonous, and from a theatrical and artistic viewpoint she was speeding along the starry way close behind Ann Pennington, Frances White, Emma Haig, and all the other fascinating "show girls" of New York's midnight playgrounds.

It remained for Elsie Janis to pick this particularly shining example of feminine charm for the celluloid profession. Miss Janis has done a lot for pictures—even lending her own lovely presence to several Bosworth productions a couple of seasons ago—but she was the photoplay's good fairy when, through her influence, little Eileen Percy was made a screen personage. It all happened at an informal little tea-party at the Plaza. Douglas Fairbanks, on the eve of his departure for California to film that cyclonic uproar which has since shaken the whole world into gales of laughter, "Wild and Wooly," mentioned the fact that he couldn't find just the right kind of girl to play Our Little Nell in the production. Miss Janis, ever on the alert to do someone a good turn, remembered the little Irish Eileen who had played in her "My Lady's Slipper" company. Presto! Miss Percy was "discovered," persuaded to give up New York and its attractions for a while at least, and a couple of weeks later found herself at the Artcraft studio, in Hollywood, ready to face the camera.

"And to think," said Miss Percy, "I had never given a motion picture even a moment's thought. Of course, I like the movies immensely and never miss a bill at the Rialto; but I just couldn't see myself as a second Mary Pickford and concluded that the stage was a pretty good place for Eileen Percy."

With the same vigor that characterizes all of her efforts, she went into the picture game, and when "Wild and Wooly" was released and a new leading lady was introduced to play opposite the optimistic gentleman who rejoices in the sobriquet "America's Greatest Exponent of the Smile," Miss Janis' prophecy was more than fulfilled.

Miss Percy has a reputation around broadway of being one of the best-dressed girls on the New York stage. The first Fairbanks picture in which she played limited her wardrobe to a western costume of the khaki species, "chaps and spurs" and a broad-brimmed Stetson; but when she played the blase debutante in "Down to Earth," she was allowed to give full rein to her fancies, and the array of gowns, from the most exquisite evening frocks to the laciest of negligees, caused a general wave of envy among the feminine population from Alaska to Panama.

It's a howling shame that the camera refuses to disclose such actualities as Irish blue eyes with curling dark lashes, wonderful swirl of ash-blonde hair and a complexion of the "peaches-and-cream" variety; but it does show Miss Percy as the owner of a winning smile, a vivacious disposition and unusual acting ability.

"I suppose I am what you would call 'a sidewalk child,'" laughed this charming little lady—"I've lived in New York hotels for so many years that a real home was something I never hoped to possess. Now, here in California I have a bungalow all my own, and I love it. There is the duckiest kind of a little garage in the rear, just

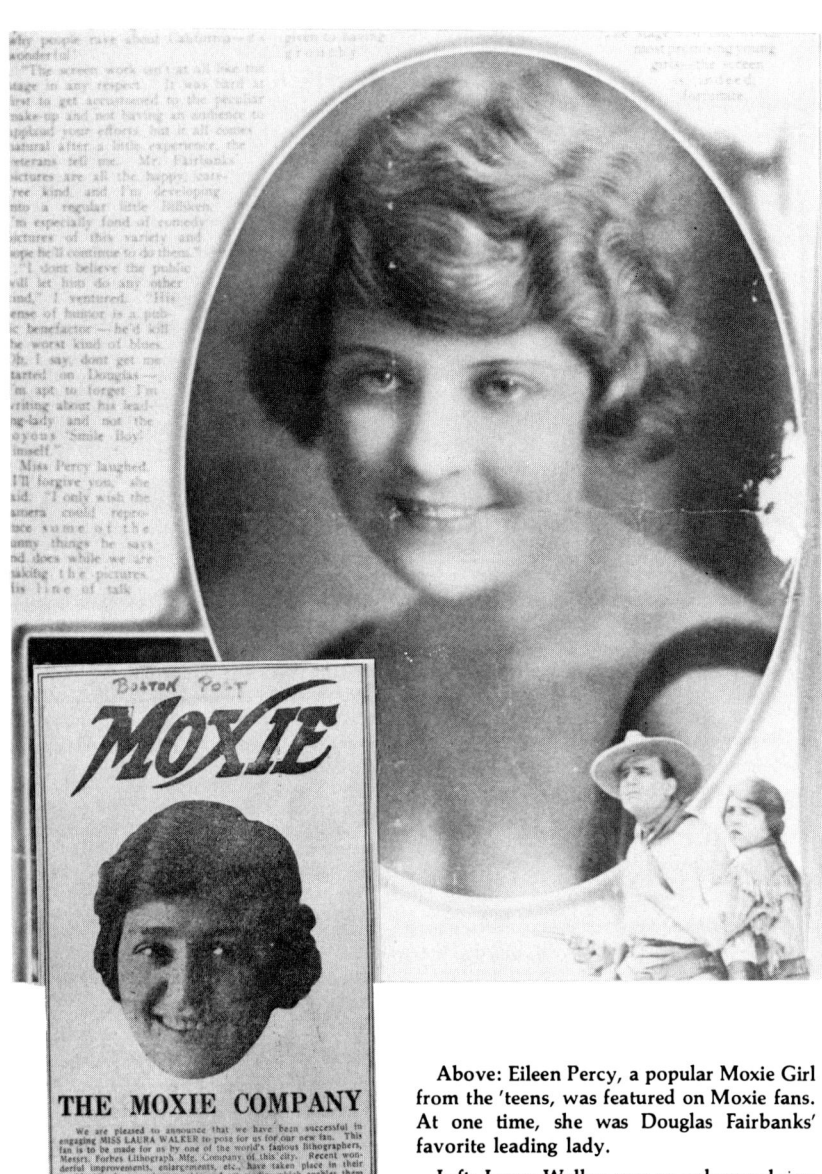

Above: Eileen Percy, a popular Moxie Girl from the 'teens, was featured on Moxie fans. At one time, she was Douglas Fairbanks' favorite leading lady.

Left: Laura Walker was an ephemeral personality in show business. The advertisement shown here notes that "we have been successful in engaging Miss Laura Walker to pose for us for our new fan."

yearning to be occupied by a stunning roadster I saw the other day. My sister is with me, and we're having a glorious time pretending to keep house.

"But don't you think I'm going back on New York," continued Miss Percy, "because I'm not! There's no place in the world like it, and I'll confess that I get really homesick for Broadway about three times a day. I wouldn't stay away from there permanently, but the West is splendid for a change. I can readily see why people rave about California—it's wonderful!

"The screen work isn't at all like the stage in any respect. It was hard at first to get accustomed to the peculiar make-up and not having an audience to applaud your efforts, but it all comes natural after a little experience, the veterans tell me. Mr. Fairbanks' pictures are all the happy, carefree kind, and I'm developing into a regular little Billiken. I'm especially fond of comedy pictures of this variety and hope they'll continue to do them."

"I don't believe the public will let him do any other kind," I [the interviewer] ventured. "His sense of humor is a public benefactor—he'd kill the worse kind of blues. Oh, I say, don't get me started on Douglas—I'm apt to forget I'm writing about his leading lady and not the joyous 'Smile Boy' himself."

Miss Percy laughed. "I'll forgive you," she said. "I only wish the camera could reproduce some of the funny things he says and does while we are making the pictures. His line of talk keeps us all in good humor, from the ferocious 'Bull' Montana down to the most serious camera-man. I don't believe I have had a grouch since I've started in pictures, unless it was when I first beheld myself all made up in yellow paint—I can't get used to the picture make-up; it's ghastly."

"I don't believe you're given to having grouchy moments anyway," I remarked. The celebrated Percy smile flashed; the Percy dimples appeared.

"Um-well, maybe not," she said. "I'm Irish, you know, and we're supposed to be rather light-hearted.

"Yes, I'm going to stay in pictures," she said, in answer to my inquiry—that is, just as long as I show an inclination to go up the ladder."

When Miss Percy was nine years old she made her first stage appearance in the New York production of "The Bluebird." For the next few years she played numerous child parts in New York plays and, when she grew up, was given a part in "The Man Who Came Back." The stage lost one of its most promising young girls—the screen is, indeed, fortunate.

Who's Who on the Screen, edited by Charles Donald Fox and Milton L. Silver, 1920, devoted a page to Eileen Percy, noting:

Eileen Percy was born in Ireland and educated there and at a convent in Brooklyn, New York. She became an artist's model at 11, a musical comedy actress at 14, and a motion picture star at 18. As a child she posed for Fisher, Stanlaws, Flagg and other well-known artists. Her first stage appearance was with "The Bluebird," in which she played every principal role at one time or another during its run. She entered motion pictures three years ago and was Douglas Fairbanks' leading lady in six productions as well as leading lady with many other well-known male stars. Miss Percy is a perfect blonde with gray eyes. Her chief charm is her unspoiled manner. She has had neither time nor inclination to become spoiled by success. She is five feet high and weighs 126 pounds.

In August 1919 the press carried notices of the marriage of Eileen Percy to Ulrich Busch, millionaire grandson of the late Adolphus Busch, St. Louis Brewer. On July 31, 1919 it was noted that the couple was "today on their honeymoon somewhere in Southern California." A newspaper article told the story:

EILEEN PERCY MARRIED. Eileen Percy, who plays the role of the Shower of Gold in Benjamin B. Hampton and Eltinge F. Warner's picturization of Zane Grey's "Desert Gold," distributed by W.W. Hodkinson, being showered with congratulations and well wishes following the announcement of her marriage in Los Angeles to Ulrich Busch, grandson of the late Adolphus Busch, founder of the world-known St. Louis brewing organization.

The wedding is a culmination of a romance that had its inception last November shortly after Miss Percy arrived on the coast to begin work as one of the featured players in the Zane Grey production. The bride, who is not yet out of her teens, has long been noted in the theatrical world for her beauty. She began her stage career three years ago as a chorus girl at the Cocoanut Grove. The following season William A. Brady engaged her for a part in "The Man Who Came Back." During the run of the Jules Eckerd Goodman success on Broadway Miss Percy devoted her mornings and afternoons, unbroken by matinees, to laying the foundation for a career on the screen, playing small roles in a number of worthwhile productions.

Her picture training completed, Miss Percy was selected by Douglas Fairbanks as an ideal type for his productions and became his leading woman, appearing with him in four of his most popular pictures.

Following the wedding ceremony the couple announced that they will shortly start on a tour of the world. Los Angeles newspapermen, who interviewed the bride regarding her plans for the future, are still in the dark as to whether Miss Percy's beauty and talents have been lost to the screen and stage.

Eileen Percy apparently did not stay away from the movie studios for long, for soon another article appeared:

After hearing that Eileen Percy went and got herself married to a Los Angeles millionaire, we now hear Miss Percy is coming back to the screen in "Making Good," Bert Lytell's next picture, and incidentally, his own brain child. Eileen Percy, you will remember, is the pretty blonde child whom Douglas Fairbanks selected for leading woman in some of his most successful screen plays. Miss Percy had not had any picture experience, but under the auspices of the Fairbanks training she became well known and created a following for herself.

The *Film Encyclopedia*, by Ephraim Katz (Thomas Crowell, 1979), gave Eileen Percy's birth date as August 1, 1899 in Belfast, Ireland. The author noted that after making an auspicious beginning in 1917 as Douglas Fairbanks' leading lady in four hit productions, she settled into the routine of a minor actress in unimportant films, retiring from the screen in the early 1930s, after which she was a society reporter for the Los Angeles *Examiner*. Songwriter Harold Ruby, whom she took as her second husband in 1936, was the subject of a film biography, *Three Little Words* (1950), in which Eileen Percy was portrayed by Arlene Dahl. She died in 1973.

The same compiler, Ephraim Katz, noted her films included: *Wild and Woolly, Down to Earth, The Man from Painted Post, Reaching for the Moon* (1917), *The Empty Cab* (1918), *Brass Buttons, In Mizzoura, Where the West Begins, Beloved Cheater* (1919), *The Third Eye* (serial), *Her Honor the Mayor, Beware of the Bride, The Man Who Dared* (1920), *Why Trust Your Husband?, The Blushing Bride, Hicksville to Broadway, Little Miss Hawkshaw, Maid of the West, The Tom Boy* (1921), *Elope if you Must, Western Speed, The Fast*

Mail, The Flirt (1922), *The Prisoner, Within the Law, Children of Jazz, East Side, West Side, The Fourth Musketeer, Let's Go* (1923), *Missing Daughters, Sons of Flame* (1924), *Under the Rouge, Souls for Sables, Fine Clothes, The Unchastened Woman, The Shadow on the Wall, Cobra* (1925), *The Phantom Bullet, Race Wild, Lovey Mary, That Model from Paris* (1926), *Backstage, Burnt Fingers, Twelve Miles Out, Spring Fever* (1927), *Telling the World* (1928), *The Broadway Hoofer* (1929), *Wicked* (1931), and *The Cohens and Kellys in Hollywood* (1932).

Frances Pritchard

Although a brief biography of Frances Pritchard, a Boston girl who "loved Moxie," is given on one of her fans (the description to which refer in Volume II of the present work), little about her was saved for the historical archives of The Moxie Company.

A January 1920 advertisement noted that she was scheduled to appear at B.F. Keith's Colonial Theatre for a week which her "Initial New York Presentation" would be featured. The vehicle was the play *You'd Be Surprised* directed by Arthur Klein with scenery by the Robert Law Studios. Assisting Miss Pritchard were Nelson Snow and Charles Columbus.

Laura Walker

On the top of the back of the last page of the *Boston Post* issue of March 30, 1918, The Moxie Company ran a large display ad featuring a portrait of Miss Walker and the following announcement:

THE MOXIE COMPANY

We are pleased to announce that we have been successful in engaging MISS LAURA WALKER to pose for our new fan. This fan is to be made for us by one of the world's famous lithographers, Messrs. Forbes Lithograph Manufacturing Company of this city [Boston]. Recent wonderful improvements, enlargements, etc. have taken place in their world-wide, famous photographic and art studio, which enables them to do this subject in a befitting manner.

LAURA WALKER

I am very proud of having been selected out of many thousands as the leading and chief exponent of the subject to be portrayed on the MOXIE Fan, for which I am to pose. I wish I might be able to tell you the nature of the subject that you might, perhaps, be better able to judge whether I have attempted a task beyond me. Those who selected me feel that my 740 performances in THE MAN WHO CAME BACK have particularly fitted me for this task. I do so hope that all interested will be able to obtain one of them, and that it proves I bear up the judgment of the critical commission who passed on my selection.

MISS WALKER IS NOW PLAYING IN THE MAN WHO CAME BACK.

Appendix II

Moxie Horsemobile Press Notices

Early in 1916 Frank M. Archer conceived the idea of mounting a horse made of wood, plaster, and metal to a car chassis. Named the "Horsemobile," the contraption made its debut in the summer of the same year. "Moxie Joe" (Joseph P. King), who was billed as a jockey and vaudeville performer, straddled the device as it delighted citizens in Massachusetts and other New England states, later traveling to New York. By the end of October 1916 the Horsemobile odometer registered nearly 10,000 miles. In the process many press notices were garnered. Those reproduced below are from a brochure issued by The Moxie Company in 1917.

Realizing the novelty and advertising value of the Horsemobile, Frank M. Archer applied for a design patent for an "ornamental design for an automobile" on November 21, 1916 and was granted registration on February 27th of the following year.

BROOKLINE TOWNSMAN, July 1, 1916

Space will not permit reproducing all the newspapers have said of this unique and original publicity feature. It has proven such a wonderful publicity feature that The Moxie Company is arranging to put out a fleet of them.

This wonderful publicity feature has been reproduced by one of America's greatest lithographers, size about fifty-four by forty. You see from the measurements that this is largely life-size and when displayed in the dealers window causes the most favorable criticism.

This differs from other publicity features in that it interests everybody, regardless of age, occupation or environment. Admittedly the one best publicity feature.

"HORSEMOBILE" to be shown here July 4. New vehicle will probably be one of the features of auto parade. The "Horsemobile" is the latest thing in motor vehicles, and it will be seen for the first time by residents of Brookline on the Fourth. The Horsemobile consists of a wood and iron horse bolted to a runabout. Mr. King, who is to operate the "Horsemobile," states that it is a little "balky" at present, but that he hopes to have it "broken in" by the Fourth.

* * *

BOSTON AMERICAN, July 4, 1916

Dick Sears said in the Boston American, "It really looked alive." "It looked like a horse taking a ride in an automobile." "I was sure I had seen the horse before." Ever hear of a HORSEMOBILE? Dick Sears has. He saw one, he rubbed his eyes and took another look and there it was just the same; so Dick "shot" it for the movies.

* * *

BOSTON JOURNAL, August 1, 1916

A publicity feature that stops everybody but a blind man. A few weeks ago, when the "HORSEMOBILE" was completed, it was taken out in the country to give the jockey an opportunity to become used to it. And it was out there that a motion picture man discovered it and immediately reeled off 1200 feet of film on the unique feature.

* * *

BOSTON HERALD, August 2, 1916

The MOXIE HORSEMOBILE taking so well that policemen everywhere give it the right of way, knowing that if it halted long traffic would be stopped for blocks by the crowd. A minister in New Jersey who saw its picture in the Herald has written asking that it come to his town, so the children can see it.

* * *

BOSTON POST, August 13, 1916

In bringing out this strange combination of horse and automobile the designers managed to slip one over on the ever-present small boy of the early automobile days, who always called out "Get a horse" whenever he found an enthusiastic motorist stranded on the wayside. It appears as if a runaway horse had accidentally jumped on top of the chassis and got stuck there.

* * *

NEW YORK WORLD, August 13, 1916

Of all the "uniques and freaks" that have been born into the motor world of late years, perhaps the most startling and revolutionary is the MOXIE HORSEMOBILE, which recently created such a sensation in Boston and now is about to break into New York. At a little distance the contrivance looks like a large white horse, ridden by a jockey in his colors, pushing a new 1917 model automobile.

* * *

LOWELL SUN, August 18, 1916

HORSEMOBILE the cleverest "ad" yet. When it comes to a unique form of advertising the HORSEMOBILE has got them all going. The imitation horse is so real to life that many persons until they get a very close look at the invention are of the opinion that the horse is riding in the automobile.

* * *

LYNN DAILY EVENING ITEM, August 19, 1916

Lynn got its first view of the much heralded MOXIE HORSEMOBILE today, and was in no way disappointed. The only visible connection with the summer refreshment is shown on the jockey's coat and cap, yet everybody is aware of its origin and use. The bridle, a beautiful piece of harness, was made in Mexico of plaited and colored horse hair. The jockey today stated that the HORSEMOBILE was kind and gentle, suitable for a lady to drive, but had an enormous appetite for high-priced gasoline.

* * *

SALEM EVENING NEWS, August 19, 1916

Salem gets view of HORSEMOBILE. The MOXIE HORSEMOBILE stopped in Salem yesterday afternoon. It's the newest and queerest thing on the road. A white horse of iron, built by an artist at a cost of $1000, is mounted on the running gear of an automobile. The machine will make 40 miles an hour. But that would break Salem's new speed laws. Anyway, the operator prefers 15 miles an hour, for "safety first" is his rule when riding a HORSEMOBILE. Besides, the HORSEMOBILE is to be seen by the crowd, not rushed away.

* * *

LYNN EVENING NEWS, August 21, 1916

The combination of a horse and automobile startled many people who had to brush their eyes before they realized the horse was not a living animal. This interest-riveting machine was "stalled" for the night at the Liberty Garage. It was taken out early Saturday morning, its appearance being a signal for the gathering of crowds everywhere.

* * *

BROCKTON DAILY ENTERPRISE, August 22, 1916

The HORSEMOBILE OWNED BY THE MOXIE COMPANY toured Brockton Monday, attracting wide attention from the crowds on Main Street. The HORSEMOBILE is the first of its kind.

* * *

BOSTON POST, August 25, 1916

HORSEMOBILE makes record. A new world's record was established at the Marshfield Fair race track yesterday by the MOXIE HORSEMOBILE . To the cheers of thousands, the HORSEMOBILE tore around the mile track in two minutes flat. Even though the world's record for HORSEMOBILE racing was shattered, the HORSEMOBILE was held in check during the entire race. "It's a wonder," has been the general comment and "Have you seen the MOXIE HORSEMOBILE?" have been bywords among the visitors.

* * *

FALL RIVER HERALD, August 25, 1916

The HORSEMOBILE HITS FALL RIVER. Moxie equine is some steed. MOXIE, gr. g, 13.4, the fastest horse alive, galloped into town this morning with the speedometer registering 50. Moxie is some horse. He eats gasoline and motor oils and runs on four wheels. He is only one horse but he has thirty horse power, and when it comes to being a smooth advertising proposition the aforesaid H.P. rises to about 2000. The "guy" who stood talking with the traffic cop at Bedford and Main streets mopped his brow when the outfit whizzed past him; felt his pulse to make sure he was awake, and then signed a mental pledge. "Believe me, Joe,' he said, "I'm not joking, I saw a horse and an automobile go racing right by here, and I think the horse was either ahead, or else inside of the automobile."

* * *

OLD COLONY MEMORIAL, PLYMOUTH, MASS., August 25, 1916

HORSEMOBILE coming. The "HORSEMOBILE" of The Moxie Company, which has attracted so much attention all over the country wherever it has been exhibited, will make a visit to Plymouth soon, and will doubtless prove as much of a novelty here as it has elsewhere.

* * *

FALL RIVER EVENING NEWS, August 26, 1916

Is a unique get-up and attracts general attention. The MOXIE HORSEMOBILE came into town today and since its arrival has been the center of attraction. It is one of the most novel and successful advertisements ever originated.

* * *

FALL RIVER GLOBE, August 26, 1916

Moxie man makes a big hit with "HORSEMOBILE." Everywhere the HORSEMOBILE stopped crowds gathered to admire the handsome white steed astride an automobile, with its brilliantly attired jockey in attendance. The HORSEMOBILE first made its appearance last June and since that time has covered 7,822 miles. A strange prize was won by this new wonder at Marshfield last week when it was awarded the blue ribbon for being the best and prettiest horse on the grounds.

* * *

NEW BEDFORD SUNDAY STANDARD, August 27, 1916

The MOXIE HORSEMOBILE, which has attracted attention in different cities throughout New England, arrived in this city yesterday, and as it went up and down the streets it was inspected by hundreds of persons. At the Marshfield Fair, from which it came to New Bedford, it went a mile in two minutes flat.

* * *

NEW BEDFORD TIMES, August 27, 1916

Moxie Horsemobile is big attraction. The MOXIE HORSEMOBILE arrived in the city yesterday and aroused widespread interest as it toured the principal streets. As an advertising novelty it is one of the most effective that has been seen here in a long time. So intense was the interest in the contrivance that traffic was blocked at many points by the stopping of vehicles and pedestrians to get a view of the "feature that cornered curiosity."

* * *

BARNSTABLE PATRIOT, August 28, 1916

Greet McCall at Barnstable Fair; and Moxie too. The famous MOXIE HORSEMOBILE and numerous prizes and souvenirs given by The Moxie Company helped to gladden the thousands of visitors.

* * *

POPULAR MECHANICS, September, 1916

Should the time ever dawn when the horse is extinct, it may be that those who crave for brisk early morning canters across the hills or along bridle paths will resort to some such device as recently astonished hundreds of spectators during a Massachusetts parade. It was a rare vehicle and consisted of the combination of a life sized wooden horse and a light motor car.

* * *

POPULAR SCIENCE MONTHLY, September 1916

When the horse tops it over the automobile. Lives there a man with soul so dead who never to himself hath said, "What a hero I look on horseback." A Boston man, however, has evolved an idea for mounting a wooden horse on an automobile and getting the picturesque effect and the little tickling of his vanity without sacrificing the speed of his getting about.

* * *

WORCESTER POST, September 6, 1916

HORSEMOBILE has patrons staring. An attraction that was not billed had patrons of the New England Fair staring wide eyed and open mouthed and is evidence that the age of wonders is at its height. The freak is a HORSEMOBILE. The freak horse rides on the chassis of an automobile. Although the horse is on wheels the speed at which it travels round the race track has fooled many of the patrons and at a passing glance it might easily be mistaken for a regular race horse.

* * *

THE LANDMARK, WHITE RIVER JCT., September 7, 1916

Watch out for the MOXIE HORSEMOBILE at the Vermont State Fair. It is the event that cornered curiosity.

* * *

ORANGE ENTERPRISE & JOURNAL, September 8, 1916

The MOXIE HORSEMOBILE, one of the most unique advertising stunts of the day, appeared in Orange yesterday.

* * *

CLAREMONT EAGLE, September 9, 1916

The famous MOXIE HORSEMOBILE arrived in town this morning and stood on the square for several hours, where it created much comment. The wooden horse, standing on an automobile, is ridden by the driver of the machine. The driver, a former jockey, is known everywhere as "Moxie Joe."

* * *

FITCHBURG DAILY NEWS, September 9, 1916

Horse on automobile keeps crowds guessing. Deciding that it surely is "horse" on an automobile many Fitchburg people have been following the suit of thousands of other fellow-beings in various cities and closely inspected the famous MOXIE "HORSEMOBILE" during its brief stay here. Riding the horse is a celebrated "stunt" actor who in the days of yore was wont to be made up as a rube. He operates the machine with perfect ease and safety, clad in full regalia of a jockey.

* * *

PAWTUCKET EVENING TIMES, September 9, 1916

Strange vehicle advertises Moxie. One of the oddest vehicles in history passed through Pawtucket's business streets a few days ago. Astride a handsome gray horse in a four wheeled motor vehicle sat a man in the rig of a jockey. At first glance he appeared to be driving a charger drawing an automobile.

* * *

GARDNER NEWS, September 12, 1916

HORSEMOBILE. Moxie man makes his way about town by his neck. The famous MOXIE HORSEMOBILE passed through Gardner the other day and attracted a whole lot of attention. The rider, dressed as a jockey, sat in the "saddle" and operated the machine by means of a steering apparatus through the neck of the "horse."

* * *

BOSTON HERALD, September 13, 1916

Vermont to honor MOXIE HORSEMOBILE. It has just been learned on excellent authority that the state of Vermont will singly honor the MOXIE HORSEMOBILE at the White River Fair this week. With appropriate ceremonies, the key of the state will be presented to the champion of the world. Never before has such signal honor been shown to man or beast. But the state authorities felt that every man, woman and child in Vermont should have an opportunity to see this marvelous creation.

* * *

LYNN EVENING NEWS, September 13, 1916

Moxie Joe, the chauffeur jockey of the famous Moxie Horsemobile, on his way to the fair to be held at White River Junction, Vermont, this week, when coming into one of the large places, saw the chief of police in the center of the street with his hand up, indicating "stop."

This was a surprise to Moxie Joe, as heretofore the police had bowed to him and beckoned to him to come on, afraid he would block traffic. The chief, however, stood stolid, with his hand up. Moxie Joe stopped. The chief said, "get down." More surprise to Moxie Joe, but he obeyed. When he got out of the saddle the chief got in, took hold of the wheel, picked up the reins, snapped the whip; and in doing so the sleeve of his coat caught in the throttle and turned on the gas and the Horsemobile shot through the streets at a terrific pace.

The chief was too dazed to throw out the clutch, put on the brake and throw off the throttle; and something serious might have happened, except that they ran over a water bar, which partially closed the throttle and allowed the Horsemobile to slow down, at which time one of the traffic cops mounted on a magnificent Kentucky thoroughbred, had caught up with the chief, although considerably winded, reached over and turned off the gas, hollered in the chief's ear to put on the brake and throw out the clutch, which the chief had presence of mind enough to do.

By that time, however, the boys from emergency hook and ladder truck No. 93, together with the assistant chief, had arrived. There was no need of their services, however.

By this time Moxie Joe, who had hailed a passing autoist, who had a speedster, caught up and the talk between he and the chief perhaps had better not be recorded. It is only fair to the chief and Moxie Joe, however, to say that they both took it good naturedly, and parted the best of friends.

As they were parting and Moxie Joe was riding away, one old lady looked up at him and said: "My, son, but that steed can go some."

* * *

MANCHESTER DAILY MIRROR, September 13, 1916

Moxie Joe and HORSEMOBILE are here. So ingenious and unique a publicity feature is the MOXIE HORSEMOBILE that thousands of people have made suggestions relative to the thousands of different ways that the word MOXIE could be attached to it. The combining of the horse and automobile is done in such an ingenious manner as to bring forth the most favorable comments.

* * *

BELLOWS FALLS TIMES, September 14, 1916

The famous HORSEMOBILE advertising Moxie reached Bellows Falls Friday and caused a lot of attention and comment wherever it was seen. The horse on the HORSEMOBILE was a beast of noble mien, but might have been made of the same materials as the famous horse the Greeks presented to the Trojans. It was mounted on the four wheels of an auto and driven by a trappy looking fellow dressed as a jockey.

* * *

ATHOL CHRONICLE, September 15, 1916

The Moxie Co., which for years has been foremost in the advertising field, sent a new novelty to Athol Thursday, in the way of a HORSEMOBILE, a combination of horse and auto. Hundreds of people were attracted by this advertising novelty. It consisted of a life-like wooden horse, mounted on an automobile chassis. It evidently got the attention of the people.

* * *

CONCORD DAILY PATRIOT, September 15, 1916

The MOXIE HORSEMOBILE, which is coming to Concord, is one of the wonders of the age. The horse represents a famous Kentucky thoroughbred and is combined with the automobile in a most ingenious manner. Moxie Joe, the rider on this famous steed, is a most versatile individual, being an actor who has appeared in many varied roles. He is a jockey as well as a horse mechanician.

* * *

GRANITE STATE FREE PRESS, LEBANON, N.H., September 15, 1916

Free Press receives distinguished caller. The MOXIE HORSEMOBILE cantered into town yesterday and the driver, Moxie Joe, brought his steed to a "whoa" at our office door. This is the famous white horse on "wheels" that has been so much talked about the past few weeks. The horse was presented with a mammoth key—the key to the state of Vermont—and was awarded "blue ribbons" at the fair.

* * *

MANCHESTER UNION-LEADER, September 19, 1916

Considerable attention was attracted upon the streets of Manchester this morning by the appearance of a "horse motor car" the like of which has never been seen here before. It is called the MOXIE HORSEMOBILE. The steed is of milky whiteness and seated upon his back is jockey "Moxie Joe." The steering gear comes up through the neck of the horse and the car is so guided by its rider.

* * *

LAWRENCE TELEGRAM, September 20, 1916

"Moxie Joe" in Lawrence. Drives famous HORSEMOBILE through city on way north. "Moxie Joe," driving his far famed HORSEMOBILE, passed through Lawrence yesterday and attracted considerable attention along Essex Street. The novelty of a wooden horse fitted into the body of an auto and traveling along the street, caused considerable attention.

* * *

NASHUA TELEGRAPH, September 20, 1916

Moxie horse is admired as he is ridden through Nashua going to Fair. Moxie Joe and his thoroughbred Moxie horse, in white enamel, and mounted on an automobile chassis, arrived in Nashua before noon yesterday, halted at the Rexall store for a brief spell, during which he was admired by quite a throng, and then continued his way through the principal streets of the city, to Lowell.

* * *

LOWELL COURIER CITIZEN, September 22, 1916

Most original and unique ceremony used at the union of the horse and the auto.

The officiating Peace Justice delivered a well prepared discourse on the novelty and originality of the same. The horse and the auto were represented by MOXIE JOE.

The Peace Justice asked the horse, "When your jockey hollers 'whoa' will you stop?" Moxie Joe answered for the horse, "Yes, if you will throw out your clutch, turn off the gas and put up your brake at the same time." The Justice asked the auto, "Will you run true and smooth at all times?" Moxie Joe answered for the auto, "Yes, if you will keep me in good repair and give me plenty of gas." The Justice asked the horse, "Will you always try to keep yourself as neat and clean as you are now, and your mane and tail braided?" Moxie Joe answered for the horse, "Yes, if you will cause me to be painted regularly and washed frequently, and my mane and foretop frequently braided, then you can depend on my looking better than any horse you know." The Justice asked the horse, "Do you adopt this life and union as your life and union?" Moxie Joe answered for the horse, "You bet your life I do." The Justice asked the auto, "Do you take this horse to be your body both in sunshine and rain?" Moxie Joe replied for the auto by saying, "I do." The horse was asked, "Will you always be to the front. Will you always in the future as in the past continue to be the trophy winner?" Moxie Joe answered for the horse, "Yes, with the proviso that the auto will take me over the country, through the show rings, and around the tracks, with the same speed and grace that it has in the past."

The Justice then suspended between the auto and the horse a horseshoe, which was to cement for all time the union.

The world famous jockey chauffeur, MOXIE JOE, was then by willing hands seated in the saddle of the famous Moxie HORSEMOBILE, and proceeded to drive through the streets lined with cheering people, preceded by such members of the old Swanzey Band, of which Moxie Joe was a member, as now survive. They alternated the music between the HORSEMOBILE TROT and the MOXIE JOE LAME DUCK STEP, until they arrived at the triumphal arch, which was made from bales of hay and parts of automobiles. As they went through this arch, The Justice proclaimed, "I hereby pronounce you horse and auto, and give you, and all offspring resembling the combination, the name by which you shall be known throughout all generations, the Moxie HORSEMOBILE."

At the completion of the ceremony, Moxie Joe gathered up the reins, raised his whip, turned on the gas, and by the operation of the wheel, drove gaily through the streets to the tune of "JUST MAKE IT MOXIE FOR MINE." This is said to have been the most unique and pretentious union of any ever held.

At the close of the ceremony, Mr. Peace Justice thereupon presented to Moxie Joe, as representing the Horse and Auto, the following certificate:

This is to certify that this day Mr. Horse and Mrs. Auto were by me legally and mechanically united.

Given under my hand and seal, this day.

                                                        PEACE JUSTICE.

(Seal)
  Witnesses:
    Mr. Steam Engine
    Mr. Lawn Mower
    Mr. Trotting Horse
    Mr. Trolley Car.

It is also proper to note that at the close of the ceremony the customary kissing of the bride was omitted.

The best men were Mr. Bill Auto Truck and Mr. Bert Williams Auto.

The bridesmaids were Miss Alice Racehorse, Miss Lillian Carriagehorse.

The ushers were Mr. Shetland Pony, Mr. Welch Pony, Miss Bronco, and Miss Mexican Pony.

The ceremony was managed by Clydesdale Horse and Pacing Horse.

The flowers were distributed by Mr. and Mrs. Bicycle, Miss Tricycle and Mr. Motorcycle.

All of the U.S.A.

* * *

ROCHESTER N.H. COURIER, September 22, 1916

The MOXIE HORSE AUTOMOBILE was one of the sights that attracted much attention. A white horse, life-like in the extreme, and mounted by a rider in white livery, was fastened to an automobile base and paraded the streets. It was a combination of the old and new, that was most appropriate.

* * *

CAMBRIDGE CHRONICLE, September 23, 1916

The most unique thing of all the achievements in the advertising line undertaken by the Moxie Company was the creation of the now famous and wonderful MOXIE HORSEMOBILE, the joining of the horse and the automobile in a motor contraption that is ornamental, ingenious and wonderful. It certainly is a magnet that allures and people can hardly keep their eyes off from it.

* * *

PORTLAND EVENING EXPRESS September 23, 1916

One of the most unique sights ever seen in this city appeared on the streets today in the shape of the famous MOXIE HORSEMOBILE, the only HORSEMOBILE in the world. The rider of the horse is known as "Moxie Joe," and he has ridden his white steed something over 7000 miles. The famous horse and its no less famous rider attracted large crowds as they made a brief visit to the office of the Express-Advertiser this morning.

* * *

TAUNTON GAZETTE, September 25, 1916

MOXIE HORSEMOBILE a great novelty. A novelty as means for attracting attention is being used by the Moxie people. It is a wooden horse, saddled and bridled and of the hunter type. It is mounted on a low chassis, propelled by a gasoline motor, and the gears and control appliances are at hand for the jockey. During its stop it was surrounded by a throng.

* * *

PORTLAND ARGUS, September 26, 1916

Ad advertising conceit which has attracted great and universal attention is now making a visit to Portland. It is the famous MOXIE HORSEMOBILE. It is the only vehicle of the kind in the world. "Moxie Joe," who has won quite widespread repute as has his steed, is still the man behind the equine-auto wonder, and the rare combination is worth going without sleep to see.

* * *

PORTSMOUTH TIMES, September 26, 1916

If you see a strange mixture of horse and automobile proceeding down the street don't get frightened. It isn't a runaway nor there hasn't been an accident. It is simply Moxie Joe and the MOXIE HORSEMOBILE. "Simply" perhaps is not a good word to use in connection with the HORSEMOBILE, as it is the most unique publicity feature ever invented, and has attracted more attention throughout the United States than any advertising scheme yet placed before the public. The MOXIE HORSEMOBILE will go down in history as a remarkable achievement in the advertising world.

* * *

KENNEBEC JOURNAL, AUGUSTA, MAINE, September 27, 1916

We really thought the land of lost toys had come into its own right in the city of Augusta late Tuesday afternoon, when there suddenly appeared on the street before the Journal office the queerest sight, and still a pleasing one, in the form of a horse on an automobile, or an automobile on a horse, whichever. A pure white horse, standing 20 hands high, as one farmer in the crowd calculated, affixed to an automobile so that the appearance was most deceptive, for at first glance it would be hard to tell which was the motive power. The MOXIE "HORSEMOBILE" is labeled as a "Unique Moxie publicity feature," and we sincerely believe it is all that.

* * *

NEWBURYPORT DAILY NEWS, September 30, 1916

The MOXIE HORSEMOBILE made its appearance in this city yesterday noon, and it was quickly the cynosure of all eyes. "The horse has never balked once," said Mr. Hodgman in describing the slick working of the HORSEMOBILE. The name given the horse is "Gets-um" and its driver states that the steed gets-um in all parts of the country, meaning the attention of the people.

* * *

LOWELL COURIER-CITIZEN, October 8, 1916

The HORSEMOBILE A DOCILE BEAST. He's fat but he never eats. His face bespeaks intelligence, but never cracks a smile nor carries a tear. He's the only one of his kind in captivity. He has the goods to advertise, hence the horse that never gallops, that never walks, but moves serenely along the cynosure of all eyes.

* * *

SCIENTIFIC AMERICAN, October 17, 1916

Motoring on horseback is what this man is doing, not as a sport, but as a new idea in publicity. The HORSEMOBILE as the new vehicle is named, consists of a light pleasure car, stripped and slightly altered, upon which is mounted a wooden model of a thoroughbred Kentucky racer.

* * *

SPRINGFIELD NEWS, October 18, 1916

The average person who thinks it a difficult stunt to cling to the back of a real live horse, going at the rate of approximately 10 miles an hour, should change places for a few moments with "Moxie Joe," rider of the famous MOXIE HORSEMOBILE. After a brief session on the back of "Moxie Joe's steel steed," bucking broncos would have no further terrors for him. Despite the fact the HORSEMOBILE is equipped with the steering gear of an automobile, it has a handsome bridle, and incidentally it is of interest to know that this bridle was woven of horsehair by a convict who is serving a life sentence.

* * *

SPRINGFIELD UNION, October 18, 1916

"Moxie Joe," riding in the famous MOXIE HORSEMOBILE, appeared in Springfield this morning and attracted a crowd in front of the Union office, where he waited a few minutes to see what was going on in town. The bridle is said to have been made by the wizard of the cowboy tribe, the blue ribbon winner at every round-up. The saddle was obtained from one of the most prominent horsemen in New England, who in turn obtained it from one of the greatest trainers and horse traders in existence.

* * *

WESTFIELD JOURNAL, October 10, 1916

Ninth wonder of the world in Westfield. Pedestrians gaped at the wonder with wide open mouths. Traffic cops in Park Square let it pass and then consulted their rule books in vain. Horses shied and cattishly remarked, "It may be one of us, but oh my." Autos whizzed by and stopped. Carburetors developed bad cases of emphysema and throttled respiration. But the HORSEMOBILE ambled on, even refusing to have a drink of water at the PARK fountain. Hairless, hideless and hobbleless, it made its way up the street. The HORSEMOBILE is a clever combination of a horse and automobile, conceived with the advantages of each, and forgotten with the disadvantages of both. Everyone says, "My, why didn't someone think of it before."

* * *

BERKSHIRE GAZETTE, NORTHAMPTON, October 20, 1916

The MOXIE HORSEMOBILE, ridden by Moxie Joe, visited this city today and attracted a great deal of attention. Many of the fairs in New England have been visited and Moxie Joe will soon return to New York, where the HORSEMOBILE and Moxie Joe have been engaged by the movies.

* * *

NORTH ADAMS TRANSCRIPT, October 24, 1916

"Moxie Joe" and funny Horsemobile visit city. Moxie Joe and his HORSEMOBILE, attended by two runabouts decorated in a striking manner, paid his first visit to North Adams today. Astride his plaster of paris steed, "Moxie Joe" swung down the Mohawk Trail and into the streets, the wonder of the children and an object of curiosity for the grown-ups. Moxie Joe said he had traveled 8,000 miles on his white charger.

* * *

HARTFORD COURANT, October 27, 1916

HORSEMOBILE attracts much attention here. The famous MOXIE HORSE-MOBILE, which has traveled more than 9,000 miles through the East, arrived in Hartford yesterday and attracted considerable attention in the center of the city. Moxie Joe was in the saddle with a fine coat of tan and enthusiastic over the stamina of the steed.

* * *

NEW BRITAIN DAILY HERALD, October 31, 1916

Moxie "Horse" here. Famous animal makes his appearance on the city streets and acts like any Kentucky thoroughbred. At last the famous horse of Church street has a rival in the shape of the Moxie "Horse," which was a visitor in town today. The only advertising matter on either animal or rider is a red sash worn by the rider and containing the word MOXIE.

* * *

MERIDEN DAILY JOURNAL, October 31, 1916

Moxie Joe and hs wonderful HORSEMOBILE came to Meriden today on its way home from the New England fairs. The big white horse which prefers gasoline to hay drew up in front of the Journal building soon after noon. Moxie Joe's steed is as near to a horse as an automobile can be and as near an automobile as a horse can be.

* * *

BRIDGEPORT POST, November 1, 1916

One of the fastest horses, if not the fastest, came to Bridgeport early this morning. This equine thoroughbred is making a tour of the New England states at the present time, taking on all comers and bears the enviable reputation of never having suffered a defeat. Moxie, as the horse is called, is credited by his managers with doing a mile in 1.20 flat on a circular track. The grass bridle on the speed king was woven by one of the "lifers" in Sing Sing Academy, New York.

* * *

MERIDEN MORNING RECORD, November 1, 1916

Much attention attracted by the contraption accompanied by the two other famous autos. Leaving the city as mysteriously as he came in, "Moxie Joe" drove about the streets of Meriden Tuesday on his famous HORSEMOBILE. One of the features of the animal is the bridle, which cost $75. It is made entirely of horsehair, and is said to have been woven by an outlaw while serving his prison term.

* * *

SOUTH NORWALK EVENING SENTINEL, November 2, 1916

The first mechanical horse that has ever passed through this town was seen here today when the MOXIE HORSEMOBILE drove through here. The pose of the horse is so natural you have to look twice before you are sure it is not alive.

*　*　*

NEW ROCHELLE EVENING STANDARD, November 4, 1916

New Rochelle was surprised Thursday to see a horse car, but not of the ancient variety. This was a brand-new idea, consisting of a large horse, perfect in every detail, of sheet metal, papier mache and canvas, and mounted on a chassis. Moxie Joe operates the HORSEMOBILE in his blue soldier's uniform and red sash bearing the Moxie trademark. Moxie Joe is an old-time jockey and seems to enjoy riding the HORSEMOBILE as much as he did the ponies of by-gone days.

*　*　*

THE COMMERCIAL CAR JOURNAL, PA, December 15, 1916

A life size model of a horse mounted on the chassis of a light automobile is the latest device for attracting the attention of the man on the street. The post of the steering wheel is extended through the neck of the horse, so that while the driver appears to be manipulating the bridle, he is directing the car. The vehicle was driven through the streets of Boston recently and resulted in blocking traffic until the crowds got used to the sight of a "Horsemobile."

*　*　*

PORTLAND EVENING EXPRESS, January 3, 1917

MOXIE AUTO PLACARDS. The Moxie Horsemobile will be remembered by Portland people last summer as attracting considerable attention while traveling through Maine. The placards are exact reproductions of the machine, which shows a combination of a horse and an automobile, and stands almost three feet high. They first used the horse, then the automobile, and now have combined the two into the horsemobile. We wonder what is next.

*　*　*

LEWISTON DAILY SUN, January 5, 1917

MOXIE HORSEMOBILE. Large pictures of the famous Moxie Horsemobile were placed in the prominent stores yesterday. They stand about three feet high. This novelty will be sure to draw crowds at the places it visits next summer especially when the people have seen the placards of it.

*　*　*

A MOXIE HORSEMOBILE "NEWS" ITEM

While The Moxie Company reproduced extracts from numerous press notices concerning the Horsemobile, some of these news items were a result of their own advertising efforts. So great was public interest in the Horsemobile that it is possible that some of these "news" articles may have been run free of charge as a so-called public service, but the present author suspects that others were simply paid advertisements.

The *Rochester* (New Hampshire) *Courier*, September 22, 1916, carried a three-column feature titled: "COMING—MOXIE HORSEMOBILE—A UNIQUE MOXIE PUBLICITY FEATURE." The rambling text, containing numerous sentence fragments and stray thoughts, was intended to generate public interest in "Moxie Joe" (Joseph P. King, the first of numerous Horsemobile drivers; later drivers, no matter what their first names might have been, were referred to in publicity notices as "Moxie Joe" as well!), the Horsemobile, and, of course, the Moxie beverage itself.

Illustrated with a picture of Mr. King astride his white horse on the Horsemobile, the notice reads as follows:

A horse and automobile made into one. For horseback riders that are timid this is a shyless horse. The louder and the more noise there is, the less he hears of it. The first hairless horse ever ridden through the streets. The only practical marriage of the horse and the automobile.

The familiar by-word, "whenever an auto goes wrong get a horse," we have got it. The oft used expression, "get an auto when the horse goes wrong," we have got it.

The first combination of the horse and automobile to be a blue ribbon winner. The Moxie HORSEMOBILE has been a blue ribbon winner in every event.

The Moxie HORSEMOBILE is so natural that horses and colts whinny as it goes by.

So life-like and wonderful is this combination that it is the first national advertisement that required no inscription.

It thoroughly cornered curiosity, to an extent that the observer bided his time for an opportunity to ascertain its origin, what it stood for, and the product it advertised.

Hundreds and thousands have paid tribute to it.

Evidence of its superiority over everything else has been indicated by the awards made it, those awards having been made and attached to it by some of the biggest men of our country.

So ingenious and unique a publicity feature is the Moxie HORSEMOBILE that thousands of people have made suggestions relative to the thousands of different ways that the word MOXIE could be attached to it.

The horse is representative of a famous Kentucky thoroughbred.

All horsemen beg to get on his back. They examine his eyes, his head, his ears, his nostrils, his legs, his mane, his tail and his body. The confirmation is so perfect that it brings forth enthusiastic favorable comment of its make-up.

The combining of the horse and automobile is done in such an ingenious manner as to bring forth the most favorable comments.

In every city, fair ground, village, four corners, etc., it has gone through, the eyes of everyone that could see were riveted on it until it passed from view and the oft heard comment was, "will wonders never cease?"

The first state licensed HORSEMOBILE of any state in the union. Imagine riding horseback on a horse which was licensed under the vehicle laws.

The license number of the Moxie HORSEMOBILE is 82877.

The most talked about horse and automobile in the world.

An advertisement that brings good cheer and causes laughter and merriment from everyone. Never an unfavorable comment or criticism.

The first publicity feature to corner the entire good will of every man, woman and child, regardless of age, occupation or standing.

As good a carriage horse as a saddle horse. Attachments to make it as operative that way are under the saddle conceived at the birth of the automobile and the horse.

The policemen bow to it.

Has had greater publicity in the same period of time than any other publicity feature ever used.

The thousands of lines that have been written of the HORSEMOBILE by the smartest and wittiest and far-seeing of all professions, the newspaper boys, would fill a book. Their sayings are witty and pertinent.

The rider of this famous steed is MOXIE JOE.

Moxie Joe is the first rider of a HORSEMOBILE in the world. He is the first to ride, drive, or lead, a hairless horse through the streets. He is the first to enter contests or show rings with a combination of horse and automobile.

Moxie Joe was selected for the guiding of this equine star performer because of his cheerfulness, his admiration for the kiddies, and his wonderful experience covering more than a quarter of a century.

Moxie Joe was doing rube turns long before many of the so called run, jump and lame duck movie artists were heard of. The operation of this combination becomes natural to Moxie Joe, and if you will take it up with "papa," and "mamma," or even "grandpa," they will say, "Oh yes, I remember him on Tremont street, that is the man with the India rubber toes that used to walk on a bicycle wheel as readily as most people walk on sidewalks." The stunts he did then were a wonderment to everyone. He is a physical exercise expert. He has lectured before the police departments of our large cities and has assisted in arranging their physical apparatus. He was one of the first to make "down-homers" think of home, when he went through the streets with his carpet bag and straw hat. So skilful was he in the art of falling that the mere egress from the top of a large building to the ground was accomplished without the breaking of bones.

Look at Moxie Joe's eyes. They follow you everywhere you go. Judge for yourself whether there is expression or not.

Moxie Joe comes from a family tree of which has as many prominent branches as the family tree of most anyone. Who has not heard of "General Doucette?" Talk with Moxie Joe and see how lovingly he speaks of him. No doubt when Mother and Father were on their wedding trip, either at Revere Beach, Coney Island, Atlantic City or Washington, D.C., Moxie Joe was smiling at them from the Moxie bottle wagon.

We have told you that Moxie Joe was one of the famous Swanzey band. Moxie Joe led the choir in the Reuben Ryder quartet, which must be well remembered by those of mature years at any of the great food fairs or agricultural fairs throughout the country. Moxie Joe has played the nephew to Reuben Ryder to attract attention to the Moxie stand. Moxie Joe, with his straw hat, short coat, long legged boots, and always the carpet bag, with the lame duck walk; would start down the hall or across the fair grounds, as the case might be, and by and by Uncle Reuben would get after him with an ox goad; and you can imagine the scenes and by-plays as Uncle Reuben chased him around the grounds and finally came leading Moxie Joe back...

Feeling that he had had a wonderful experience, which stood him in the way of a lecturer, etc., he went about the country to the police departments and other places, instructing them in physical exercise. He also played an important part in the human moveless window display. He comes of a family that has studied the art of standing still for a period of time without apparently breathing or moving. In this venture he was a great success. He finally met his Waterloo in one of the stores of Greater New York. They were exhibiting a preparation that would keep flies and mosquitoes away from you. If you used the preparation when going hunting, fishing, etc., you would never be bit. To show how it worked, they had one corner of the window arranged to show that preparation, and Moxie Joe in the other corner. One of the pests got unruly, however, and stung Moxie Joe, and he refused to be the moveless man in the window any longer.

Moxie Joe is the first jockey to be a horse mechanician. Moxie Joe has such steady nerves that he easily could be used as a dummy in demonstrating the ability of the life saving fenders on street cars, to pick up a person without injuring him.

Years ago, to get an audience, he used to drop down in front of an onrushing street car, causing a congestion of traffic. When the crowd got thick enough, he would open up his carpet bag and pass around Moxie circulars. He was the first one to tame and train the "Dodo bird." His publicity feature for Moxie in the King Dodo days caused Raymond Hitchcock to make one of his famous curtain speeches...

The Moxie HORSEMOBILE has engagements covering 1916 and 1917, a greater booking than any other combination in history.

THE MOXIE HORSEMOBILE is the first publicity feature to be sought after as an attraction for fairs, theatricals, food shows, etc., so natural that it is frequent for people to jump one side, into doorways, or behind trees for fear there is a runaway.

So simple that everyone remarks, "Why didn't somebody do it before?"

The design, material and workmanship in the construction of this combination are such as to excite wonder, and it is so simple that it is easy to see what put the S in SIMPLE.

The bridle of this famous steed has a history that is a book in itself. It is said to have been made by a famous bandit now serving a life term in a western prison. Jesse James was a marble player as compared with this bandit.

The saddle worn by this famous horse comes from the stable of one of the most famous horsemen in the world. We have begged his permission to tell the true history of this wonderful saddle.

The most wonderful game in the world, played as solitaire or by many.

A puzzle to the curious.

It has been shown in most all the scientific books through the world.

This famous Moxie HORSEMOBILE has been moved times without number.

The number of men, women and children that have taken snap shots of the HORSEMOBILE would be interesting. The many pictures of the HORSEMOBILE that have been taken could they be shown in composite form, would make a wonderful composite picture.

It is due us to show our appreciation of the most wonderful patronage we have enjoyed from the great Moxie public for more than a quarter of a century. We have tried to be amusing, clean and forceful, in our publicity features. I think it is admitted that we have been original. It is said that Moxie and its publicity features have enjoyed more imitations than all other combined. We sincerely wish there were enough that could stand on their own bottom and be original. We think it would be better for them, as no one likes an imitator.

The public has been of great aid in helping us run down these sharks, hyenas, etc., of commerce, and we thank them for their aid. Our corps of men throughout the country at the fairs and other places, have been continuously inviting everyone they could possibly reach to visit our laboratories that we might show them what we believe to be the best plant of its kind in the world. You are always welcome. No appointment necessary.

As an evidence of your most hearty support, we would say that this year, over a corresponding period of last year, we have shipped more than one hundred and forty-seven carloads more, or one million and sixty-two thousand, one hundred and fifty-six bottles. This is the gain over last year. The above figures represent only increase or gain. If we were to give you the figures of the entire shipments, we believe they would be too stupendous to be easily comprehended.

Our Mr. A.W. Hodgman with the famous Moxie Gold Car, and our Mr. L.A. Hagar with the famous Moxie White Car, are included in the state wide campaign we are making in your state. We are sure these are features that cannot be outdone.

Index

Index

Bowers, Q. David, 8, 9, 19
Bowman, J. (Moxie employee), 628
Boyd & Gregg, 641
Bradford Fair (Vt.), 340
Brady, Frank A., 709-711
Brady, Gloria, 710
Brady, Margot, 710
Brady, Mrs., 710-712
Brady, Thomas J. (selectman), 631
Brady, William A., 707, 718
Braine Fude (product), 331
Branette, Fritzi, 702
Brass Buttons (play), 714, 718
Brasso Bottling Co., 641
Bremen (ship), 412
Brennan, Joseph T., 213-215, 265, 277
Brennan, W. (Moxie employee), 628
Bridgewater Bottling Works, 264, 265
Bridgeport Post (newspaper), 733
Briggs, 691
Brigham, George W., 74
Brightly, Capt. Keele (character in play), 55
Brightly, Zina (character in play), 51, 55
Brinton & Brosious, 144
Broadway After Dark (play), 310
Broadway Hoofer, The (play), 719
Broadway Theatre, 478, 496, 500, 511, 512
Brockton Fair (Mass.), 168
Brockton Public Market (Mass.), 544
Brown University, 386
Brown, Alta, 649
Brown, Thomas S., 648, 656
Brownie Soda, 248, 681
Brownies, 247-249, 251, 343, 380
Brownies: Their Book, The, 247, 251
Brown's Store (Bridgewater, Vt.), 220
Browser's Dictionary, A., 674
Bryan, William Jennings, 126
Buck, Walter E., 647, 648, 652-654, 656
Buffum, J.B. & Company, 143
Buick (automobile), 359, 425
Bullen, Major G.D., 47
Bunker Hill Monument, 312
Bunte Brothers, 370
Bunte Marshmallows, 370
Burke, C.A., 509
Burke, S.M., 112
Burns, Paul E. 709
Burnt Fingers (play), 719
Burroughs, 370
Burton, W.A. (pharmacist), 205
Busch, Adolphus, 717, 718
Busch, Ulrich, 717
Bush Terminal, 555, 596
Business Week, 619
Busy Bee, The (store), 382
Butler, Henry, 703
Butterfly Farm, 386
Buttnar's Store (Vt.), 211
"Buy a Bale of Cotton Campaign", 389

Byam, George A., 26, 61, 85, 87, 165
B.Y.G. Champion (poster), 492
Byron, W.J. (Moxie employee), 628
Bywater, Elizabeth, 439
By Whose Hand? (play), 702-710

C

Cabanne, Christy, 701
Cadillac (auto), 704
Cafe-Cola (softdrink), 356
Cahoon, Captain George C., 520
Calder (illustrator of *TNT Cowboy*), 461
California Fruit Beverage Co., 273
Callahan, D.J., 442, 445
Callahan, W. (Moxie employee), 628
Cameo Corporation, 633
Campbell Kids, 18
Cana-dry Cola, 296
Canada Dry, 648
Canary & Lederer, 456
Canobie Lake (amusement park, N.H.), 508, 509
Cape Cod Magazine, 237, 518, 520, 521
Carbonated Water (by Pureoxia), 596, 603
Carbonator and Bottler, The (publication), 549
Carlson, Charles (Moxie Society member), 184
Carmody, Dr. Robert, 631
Carr Cola, 356
Carter, C.E., 24
Carter, Ella B. (W.C.T.U. worker), 191
Caruso, Ignazio F., 681
Cary, Eleanor (actress), 97
Casino Theatre, 456
Cassidy, H.P., 342, 389
Castallian, 113
"Cataract" (carbonator), 156
Cate, Edward C., 118
Cavalieri, Lynn (actress), 698
Caverly, J.E. (Moxie employee), 628
Celery Cola, 356
Cellophane, 619, 665
Centennial Grove (Essex, Mass.), 343
Central Maine Fairgrounds, 408
Century Company, 247
Century Theatre, 713, 715
Chandler, G.W., 115
Chandler, Lewis L., 662
Chaplin, Charlie, 431
Charles L. Bastian Manufacturing Company, 213
Chase, F.L. (Moxie employee), 628
Chase, R.C., 26, 72
Chelmsford Spring, 201
Chelsea Day Nursery, 502
Chelsea Record (newspaper), 478
Chemung Spring Water Co., 641
Cheri Cola, 296
Chesapeake & Ohio Railroad, 18

White, Donald, 665, 672
White, Frances, 715
White, George, 709
White, H. (Moxie employee), 628
White House (Washington, D.C.), 518
White Knight, 667
White River Fair (Vt.), 726
White Slave Girls, 465
White Steamer (auto), 359, 516
Whitehead, Joseph P., 74
White's Scandals of 1919 (play), 487
Whitney, G.J. & Company (N.H.), 197
Who's Who on the Screen, 717
Why Mollie Takes Such An Early Car (book), 465
Why Trust Your Husband (play), 714, 718
Wicked (play), 719
Wickersham, James, 670, 672, 673, 684, 685
Wier, W. (Moxie Society member), 184
Wilbur Theatre, 432
Wilcox, George, 438
Wild and Wooly (play), 715, 718
Wild Mike (horse), 471, 472
Wildes, E.E. (Moxie sales rep.), 175, 184
Willard, Elizabeth (Moxie office girl), 352
Williams, F. (Moxie employee), 628
Williams, Theodore S. (baseball player), 655-659, 662, 669, 672, 680, 690
Willow Dale (Lowell, Mass.), 119, 328, 329
Wills, Wayne J., 661
Wilmerding Bottling Works, 641
Wilson, Fred H., 412-417, 707
Wilson or the Kaiser (play), 705
Wilson, Woodrow, 415
Winchell, Walter (columnist), 616, 674
Winchester, F.A., 63
Winchester's (candy mfr.), 512
Wing's White Birch Inn (Mass.), 618
Winn, H.F. (Moxie sales rep.), 170
Winslow Chip Company, Inc., 663
Winslow, Roy, 663
Wisenberger, Alfred, 684
Witch City Appetizer, 201, 265-267, 269
Witch City Bottling Works, 265, 267
Within the Law, (play), 719
Witschi, Mr. (Moxie agent), 440
Wittemann Brothers, 156
Wolcott, Roger, 129, 152
Wolfeboro Historical Society (N.H.), 194
Wolffe, W.H. (Moxie sales rep.), 170, 174, 184
Women's Christian Temperance Union, 191, 192
Wonderland Park (Revere Beach), 183, 208
Wood, Putnam & Wood (Moxie adv. agent), 189, 606
Woodman, Col. 45

Woolworth Stores, 372
Worcester Post (newspaper), 725
Worcester Tea, 386
World (newspaper, N.Y.), 310, 425, 709, 722
World Film Company, 412, 702, 703, 706, 707, 709
World War I, 405, 465
World War II, 642, 646
World's Columbian Exposition, 141
Worth, Jacob, 74
Wright's Hill camps (Maine), 615
Wrigley, Bill, 668
Wynn, Ed (stage personality), 493, 496

X

Xerox, 619
X-tra Bottling, 691

Y

Yale (university), 386
Yankee Corporate (play), 51
Yankee Magazine, 134, 691
YMCA, 471, 475
Yorkdale Beverage Co., 641
You'd Be Surprised (play), 719
Young, Brig (sheriff), 475, 511
Young, Fanny L. (Miss), 407
Young, Freeman N., 41, 51, 64, 65, 69, 71, 73, 118, 144, 151, 153, 157-159, 161, 162, 165, 175, 180, 184, 198, 213-215, 334, 335, 347, 353, 386, 485, 509, 510, 511, 516, 526, 548, 549, 613, 638
Young's Champagne Cider, 144, 153
"Yousay" (tradename), 184, 353, 509
Youth's Companion (publication), 237

Z

Zaffiro, Nicholas (Moxie employee), 628
Zais, Neil, 662
Za-Zar, 286
Zender, Marguerite (actress), 456
Ziegfeld, Florenz, 492, 507, 713, 714
Ziegfeld Follies, 416, 713
Zina: The Slave Girl (play), 51
Zukor-Paramount, 713